# A Sad Fiasco

## War and Genocide

**General Editors:** Omer Bartov, Brown University; A. Dirk Moses, University of Sydney

In recent years there has been a growing interest in the study of war and genocide, not from a traditional military history perspective, but within the framework of social and cultural history. This series offers a forum for scholarly works that reflect these new approaches.

*The Berghahn series* Studies on War and Genocide *has immeasurably enriched the English-language scholarship available to scholars and students of genocide and, in particular, the Holocaust.* —**Totalitarian Movements and Political Religions**

*Recent volumes:*

**Volume 29**
A Sad Fiasco: Colonial Concentration Camps in Southern Africa, 1900–1908
Jonas Kreienbaum

**Volume 28**
The Holocaust in Bohemia and Moravia: Czech Initiatives, German Policies, Jewish Responses
Wolf Gruner

**Volume 27**
Probing the Limits of Categorization: The Bystander in Holocaust History
Edited by Christina Morina and Krijn Thijs

**Volume 26**
Let Them Not Return: Sayfo—The Genocide Against the Assyrian, Syriac, and Chaldean Christians in the Ottoman Empire
Edited by David Gaunt, Naures Atto, and Soner O. Barthoma

**Volume 25**
Daily Life in the Abyss: Genocide Diaries, 1915–1918
Vahé Tachjian

**Volume 24**
Microhistories of the Holocaust
Edited by Claire Zalc and Tal Bruttmann

**Volume 23**
The Making of the Greek Genocide: Contested Memories of the Ottoman Greek Catastrophe
Erik Sjöberg

**Volume 22**
Genocide on Settler Frontiers: When Hunter-Gatherers and Commercial Stock Farmers Clash
Edited by Mohamed Adhikari

**Volume 21**
The Spirit of the Laws: The Plunder of Wealth in the Armenian Genocide
Taner Akçam and Ümit Kurt

*For a full volume listing, please see the series page on our website:*
*http://berghahnbooks.com/series/war-and-genocide*

# A SAD FIASCO

*Colonial Concentration Camps in Southern Africa, 1900–1908*

**Jonas Kreienbaum**

Translated from the German by Elizabeth Janik

berghahn
NEW YORK • OXFORD
www.berghahnbooks.com

Published in 2019 by
Berghahn Books
www.berghahnbooks.com

English-language edition
© 2019 Berghahn Books

German-language edition
© 2015 Hamburger Edition HIS Verlagsges. mbH, Hamburg, Germany. This translation from German is published by arrangement with Hamburger Edition.

Originally published in German as
*"Ein trauriges Fiasko": Koloniale Konzentrationslager im südlichen Afrika 1900–1908*

The translation of this work was funded by Geisteswissenschaften International—Translation Funding for Work in the Humanities and Social Sciences from Germany, a joint initiative of the Fritz Thyssen Foundation, the German Federal Foreign Office, the collecting society VG WORT, and the Börsenverein des Deutschen Buchhandels (German Publishers & Booksellers Association).

All rights reserved. Except for the quotation of short passages for the purposes of criticism and review, no part of this book may be reproduced in any form or by any means, electronic or mechanical, including photocopying, recording, or any information storage and retrieval system now known or to be invented, without written permission of the publisher.

**Library of Congress Cataloging-in-Publication Data**

Names: Kreienbaum, Jonas, 1982– author. | Janik, Elizabeth, translator.
Title: A Sad Fiasco: Colonial Concentration Camps in Southern Africa, 1900–1908 / Jonas Kreienbaum; translated from the German by Elizabeth Janik.
Other titles: Trauriges Fiasko. English
Description: New York: Berghahn Books, 2019. | Series: War and genocide; volume 29 | Originally published in German as "Ein trauriges Fiasko": Koloniale Konzentrationslager im südlichen Afrika 1900–1908. | Includes bibliographical references and index.
Identifiers: LCCN 2019019141 (print) | LCCN 2019020083 (ebook) | ISBN 9781789203271 (ebook) | ISBN 9781789203264 (hardback: alk. paper)
Subjects: LCSH: Concentration camps—Africa, Southern—History. | Concentration camps—History—20th century. | Germany—Colonies—Africa. | Great Britain—Colonies—Africa.
Classification: LCC DT34.5 (ebook) | LCC DT34.5 .K7413 2019 (print) | DDC 968.049—dc23
LC record available at https://lccn.loc.gov/2019019141

**British Library Cataloguing in Publication Data**

A catalogue record for this book is available from the British Library.

ISBN 978–1–78920–326–4 hardback
ISBN 978–1–78920–327–1 ebook

# Contents

List of Illustrations — vi

Acknowledgments — vii

Introduction — 1

Chapter 1
The Context: Colonial Wars in South Africa and South-West Africa — 27

Chapter 2
The Purpose of the Camps — 64

Chapter 3
How the Camps Functioned — 115

Chapter 4
Deadly Learning? Observation and Knowledge Transfer — 212

Chapter 5
Comparative Reflections on Colonial and National Socialist Camps — 227

Final Observations. "A Sad Fiasco" — 241

Bibliography — 249

Index — 272

# Illustrations

## Figures

**3.1** The Norvals Pont camp, outfitted with bell tents and marquees (War Museum of the Boer Republics).   120

**3.2** Huts in the Aliwal North camp (War Museum of the Boer Republics).   121

**3.3** The concentration camp near the old fortress in Windhuk (National Archives of Namibia, no. 1843).   162

**3.4** Postcard of the reordered concentration camp near the old fortress in Windhuk (National Archives of Namibia, no. 11495).   163

**3.5** The concentration camp on Shark Island near Lüderitzbucht (National Archives of Namibia, no. 9780).   163

## Maps

**2.1** Concentration camps in the South African War.   66

**2.2** Concentration camps in German South-West Africa.   88

## Tables

**3.1** Internee numbers in the Transvaal and Orange River Colony (ORC) camps between March and December 1901.   124

**3.2** Selected official rations for adults in the concentration camps of South Africa and South-West Africa.   168

# Acknowledgments

I began my work on colonial concentration camps eleven years ago, and I am grateful for the support of many persons and institutions over the course of this project. I would first like to thank my advisor Andreas Eckert, who accepted me as his doctoral student in 2008 and has actively supported me ever since. The same is true of my second advisor, Ulrike von Hirschhausen, who assumed this role in the final phase of my dissertation project and has consistently provided valuable advice and suggestions.

Conversations with different scholars during the conception and development of this project have helped me tremendously. I thank Dieter Gosewinkel, Birthe Kundrus, Stephan Malinowski, Michael Wildt, and especially Iain Smith for engaging with my ideas and offering critical feedback. I likewise thank the organizers of the numerous colloquia, workshops, and conferences who allowed me to present parts of my research, as well as the participants who helped me hone my arguments with their comments and criticism.

My research would not have been possible without the financial support of an Elsa Neumann Scholarship from the city of Berlin, which allowed me to visit archives in Berlin, Koblenz, Freiburg, Wuppertal, London, Birmingham, Oxford, Windhoek, Pretoria, and Bloemfontein. In all of these places I relied on the knowledgeable assistance of numerous archivists and librarians, to whom I extend my sincere thanks.

I have also received help and profited immensely from my conversations with friends and colleagues—especially Andreas Eckl, Moritz Feichtinger, Aidan Forth, Dörte Lerp, Claudia Siebrecht, and Andreas Stucki. I owe a particular debt of gratitude to Christoph Kamissek, who accepted the surely irksome assignment of proofreading the entire manuscript.

There would not be an English version of this text without the commitment of several persons. I want to thank Hamburger Edition, my German publisher, and especially Paula Bradish, who submitted my book for the Geisteswissenschaften International prize that secured funding for the translation. I am grateful to Elizabeth Janik, who proved a most able translator, to Dirk Moses and Omer Bartov for including my book in their *War and Genocide* series, and to the editors at Berghahn Books, Chris Chappell and Soyolmaa Lkhagvadorj, for their professional and friendly support.

Finally, I extend my heartfelt gratitude to my family; they have been not only my most dedicated proofreaders but also a steadfast source of support. I am particularly grateful to my wife and two sons, who accepted my frequent absences on research trips.

# Introduction

"The whole thing has been a sad fiasco," Sir Alfred Milner admitted to the Liberal politician Richard Haldane, in a confidential letter dated 8 December 1901. Milner was the British high commissioner, the most powerful civilian in South Africa. In recent weeks, he had devoted nearly all of his time and energy to a single goal—halting the masses of deaths in the concentration camps.[1] But he had just received the latest numbers from the second half of November, which indicated that the worst was not yet over.[2] With resignation, he wrote to his superior in England, colonial secretary Joseph Chamberlain:

> It was not till six weeks or two months ago that it dawned on me personally, (I cannot speak for others), that the enormous mortality was not merely incidental to the first formation of the camps and the sudden rush of thousands of people already sick and starving, but was going to continue. The fact that it continues, is no doubt a condemnation of the Camp system. The whole thing, I think now, has been a mistake.[3]

Milner's acknowledgment that the camps were a mistake should not distract from the responsibility he shared for them. He had, after all, been among the proponents for interning civilians in mid-1900.[4] The camps had seemed like an effective means for ending the war in South Africa, which had dragged on far longer than anyone had foreseen, and was in the meantime being conducted as a guerrilla war by the Boers. But by the end of 1901, the internment of much of the population of the Boer republics—including Africans—in concentration camps had not yet ended the conflict, although the policy had cost tens of thousands of civilian lives. It was a mistake, a fiasco even, but Milner reasoned that "it is easy to be wise after the event. The state of affairs that led to the formation of the camps was wholly novel and of unusual difficulty, and I believe no General in the world would not have felt compelled to deal with it in some drastic manner."[5]

In fact, the situation was not quite as new as Milner suggested. Just five years before, the Spanish general Valeriano Weyler y Nicolau had found himself in a comparable situation. In Cuba, the Spanish military was confronted with an independence movement that adopted similar guerrilla tactics; the movement was difficult to conquer because of its broad support among the civilian population. Like the supreme commander in South Africa, Weyler responded "in drastic manner." Beginning in February 1896, he drove nearly the entire rural population of the Caribbean island into guarded communities—"reconcentrating" the population, as the policy was called at the time. The conditions endured by the so-called *reconcentrados* in the towns and villages were catastrophic, and the masses of deaths earned Weyler the derisive title of "butcher" in the international press.

Cuba and South Africa were not the only sites around the turn of century where generals confronted stubborn resistance movements in a colonial war, finding themselves—in Milner's words—"compelled" to respond with the drastic action of concentrating the civilian population in guarded camps or localities. In the Philippines, the American military introduced "concentration zones" in 1901, having failed to "pacify" the archipelago for the previous two years. And in German South-West Africa, a German "protection force" (*Schutztruppe*)[6] established concentration camps in the war against the Herero and Nama in 1904–05.

These cases of concentrating the population in a colonial territory around 1900 were associated with one another in the minds of contemporaries, and they shared several common characteristics. The concentration efforts were introduced as a means of ending stubborn resistance movements during colonial wars. The concentrated populations were malnourished for long periods of time, and epidemics broke out at the internment sites. Briefly put, in each of these cases concentration led to mass death. In all, well over 200,000 people lost their lives in the concentration camps and zones around the turn of the century.[7]

This fact alone makes the colonial concentration of populations in Cuba, the Philippines, South Africa, and South-West Africa a significant topic of study. In addition, the camps suggest answers to some of the central questions that have been raised by recent research on colonialism.[8] However, the phenomenon of colonial concentration camps and concentration zones has been relatively neglected to this point.[9] This is the gap that the following study seeks to fill.

## Framing the Question

The central question of this study is: What characterized the colonial concentration camps and concentration zones? It makes sense to sharpen this question by linking it to different scholarly approaches and debates that have shaped colonial historiography in the past several years. Four sets of issues are especially relevant to the investigation of colonial concentration policies.

### *Motives of Colonial Expansion: From Civilization to Annihilation*

Scholars have repeatedly grappled with the fundamental character of colonial expansion. As Horst Gründer asks, was colonization mainly about "genocide, or forced modernization?"[10] Was European colonialism defined by mass violence? Can it be understood as a gigantic modernization project or "civilizing mission,"[11]—or was it primarily about economic exploitation?[12]

The aforementioned cases of concentrating civilians in camps raise similar questions. Were the camps sites of punishment and intentional murder? A natural consideration, given the tremendous mortality of the internees. Could the camps even be considered instruments of genocide, as has been argued in all four cases?[13] Were these paternalistic projects that sought to "uplift the savages"? Did the concentration camps function as sites of "education" for black African workers?[14] Were they experiments of social engineering that sought to turn internees into "useful" elements of colonial society? Or were they primarily a means of exploiting internee labor?

### *Continuities between the Colonial and National Socialist Camps?*

Questions about the extermination function of the colonial project in general, and the camps in particular, are closely intertwined with the discussion of potential continuities with National Socialism. An intensive debate over the colonial roots of National Socialist crimes—spurred on by Jürgen Zimmerer, in particular—has percolated in the past several years, using Hannah Arendt's *Origins of Totalitarianism* as a point of departure.[15] This debate has particularly influenced interpretations of the concentration camps in German South-West Africa, which numerous authors have identified as a forerunner of the later National Socialist camps.[16] But the Nazi camps have also provided a scholarly reference point for the South African and Cuban examples.[17] Can the origins of the Nazi camps really be traced back to practices of colonial concentration at the turn of the century? Or are these different phenomena, merely bearing the same name?

## Colonial Policy between National Paths and Universal Imperial Practice

Discussion about the connection between colonial violence and National Socialist crimes necessarily raises the question of special national paths (*Sonderwege*).[18] Because of specific characteristics of German colonialism, should we consider only the continuities "from Windhuk to Auschwitz"?[19] Or should we instead proceed from a common European, or universal, historical imperial experience, in which national differences play only a secondary role?[20] The question about specific national paths of colonization is relevant even beyond the continuity debate.[21] The extent of the differences between the camps of different colonial powers should certainly be discussed. Did the camps of each power embody a specific military culture?[22] Were the German camps in South-West Africa characterized by a tendency toward excessive violence (as Isabel Hull proposes) because—in contrast to the British system—there were no effective civilian or democratic controls that might have exerted a restraining influence on the military?[23] Should a line of distinction be drawn between the liberal democratic and authoritarian colonial powers?

## Colonial Concentration Camps as Flashpoints of Transnational History

In response to scholars who emphasize national particularities of the (colonial) past, there is a growing trend toward transnational perspectives.[24] Transnational histories tease out not only common approaches among the various colonial nations but also mutual entanglements.[25] They focus on processes of exchange and the transfer of knowledge and culture. Numerous studies of the concentration camps in South Africa and South-West Africa presume that such a transfer of knowledge occurred. Great Britain is said to have learned from the Cuban example, and Germany, from the British. But this thesis has hardly been proven.[26] This study, therefore, seeks to investigate whether, and to what extent, the colonial powers observed and borrowed concentration practices from one another. Transimperial learning would, in any case, explain the noteworthy fact that within one decade "concentration camps" were constructed in four different regions of the world, and in different imperial spheres of influence. A final consideration is whether the camps can be understood as prime examples of transimperial interrelationships in the colonial world, as flashpoints of transnational history.

These four sets of issues in colonial historiography inform the central question of this study (about the particular characteristics of the colonial concentration camps) and lead to the following sub-questions: From the perspective of the colonial powers, what was the purpose of the camps? How did the camps function day to day? And, closely related to the first two questions: How should the masses of deaths in the concentration camps be explained? How were the colonial concentration systems related to one another and to other camp systems—especially to those of the National Socialists? The primary goal of this study is to answer these questions on the basis of empirical research. At the same time, these empirical investigations can provide a point of departure for further investigations within the four areas outlined above.

## Case Selection and Methodology

In order to do justice to this catalog of questions, the intensive study of different sources for each case is essential. Because this would be impracticable for all four cases, my focus is on the British camps in South Africa and the German camps in former South-West Africa. This selection is informed by several factors. First, narrowing the scope of study to two settlement colonies in southern Africa avoids a transnational comparison and helps to minimize problems of contextualization.[27] Second, because the South African War was an international media event, the conflict is especially well suited to explore how other powers may have "copied" the institution of the concentration camp. Third, the war in German South-West Africa—which Zimmerer has called a "portent" for Auschwitz[28]—is a logical point of departure for a comparison with the National Socialist camps. Moreover, the South African War has frequently been interpreted as the first modern war and a harbinger of the world wars that followed. In their own propaganda, National Socialists construed the British concentration camps as setting a precedent for their own.[29] Fourth, compared with the United States or Spain around 1900, Great Britain and Germany were more influential colonial powers, beginning with the expanse of their colonial territory. Thus, I reference the Spanish-Cuban and American-Philippine cases only occasionally in my discussion of the two main examples.

Because the camps can be understood only within the specific situation of their respective colonial wars, I begin by exploring the context of the wars in South Africa and South-West Africa. A comparison of the camp systems follows.[30] From a functional perspective, I ask what end the colonial powers pursued with the concentration camps. Were the camps primarily instruments of punishment, murder, protection, exploitation, or education? Can they even be reduced to just one of these functions? From a phenomenological perspective, I investigate the characteristics of the different camps. Insofar as the sources allow, this includes a close description of the camps and their methods of operation. Following Wolfgang Sofsky, I examine the geography of the camps; the phenomena of work, violence, and death; as well as the social structures of the camps.[31] In contrast to Sofsky, my investigation of social relations is not limited to interactions between and among the camp personnel and internees, but it also includes "third parties" who played an important role in the colonial camps, such as missionaries and other clerics, diplomats, and the internees' masters or employers. In order to understand the complex functions of the colonial camps, my focus is not on the isolation of a prototype but on specific characteristics and changes within the individual camps and camp systems. These changes have often been neglected in the study of colonial camps to this point. Finally, I seek to highlight discrepancies between the motives of the colonial powers, with respect to the camps, and how they actually functioned.

After these comparative observations, I discuss the possibility of transfer. Was the establishment of camps in the two colonies in southern Africa inspired by the example of other powers? Could the camps in German South-West Africa have been conceived without the precedent in the neighboring British colony? Did the colonial powers also draw upon the experiences of their own dominions? Or did similar structural challenges drive the formation of camps in the different colonial wars?

Considering the potential of transfer involves identifying the channels and stations through which the idea of concentration camps spread across state borders. Information about the South African camps sometimes came, for example, from the German civilian and military press, which especially drew from British media reports. German diplomats, military observers, and volunteers gathered information on site that did not necessarily make its way back to the mother country but instead crossed the border directly into the German colony. It is important to keep in mind that processes of adaptation often take on a life of their own. Pieces of a "foreign" import can be reworked and reassembled with domestic components, resulting in the creation of something new.[32] A camp that was "copied" need not resemble the original in every respect.

Finally, by comparing the colonial and National Socialist camps, I seek to contribute to the aforementioned discussion about the possible colonial roots of National Socialist crimes.

## Sources

The following study is based on a broad spectrum of primary and secondary sources. Comparative camp research has tended to neglect the colonial concentration zones and camps around 1900, so its relevance here is limited. Andrzej Kaminski (who wrote the first general history of concentration camps) and the authors of more recent publications on the subject dedicate only a few pages, or even sentences, to the colonial camps.[33] These works tend to consider the early colonial camps only insofar as they can be understood as the "origin" of later, especially National Socialist and Stalinist, camps.[34] The most thorough studies have been written by Joël Kotek and Pierre Rigoulot, and also Andrea Pitzer. The former devote more than forty pages to the colonial camps but still fail to draw a convincing portrait of the phenomenon. It completely ignores the camps for blacks in South Africa and concentration policies in the Philippines. The authors' discussion of Cuba also fails to mention that not only the Spanish troops but also the Cuban Liberation Army played a role in the reconcentration of the civilian population.[35] Pitzer considers all of these examples of concentration, but she bases her remarks on a rather narrow sample of literature and includes a number of inaccuracies and factual errors.[36] Only recently has the scholarly deficit begun to be corrected with the first published articles that focus directly on the phenomenon of the colonial camps around 1900.[37] These comparatively framed investigations are the first attempts at establishing a transnational history of colonial concentration. To this point, however, no monograph on the topic has been written.[38]

This is the gap that my study seeks to fill. My work draws upon relevant scholarly literature on the camps in South Africa and South-West Africa, as well as both archival and published primary sources. The comparison with the National Socialist camps, and occasional references to Cuba and the Philippines, are based upon existing secondary literature.

A vast amount of scholarship has been published on the history of the Boer War—or better, the South African War.[39] Fred R. van Hartesveldt's bibliography from the year 2000 lists more than 1,300 titles, and dozens more have appeared since.[40] These publications include a number of studies of the concentration camps, many of which were written in the immediate aftermath of the war or on the occasion of the conflict's centennial. To generalize broadly, a divide is evident between English- and Afrikaans-speaking authors.[41] If the latter have tended to emphasize the suffering of internees in "hell camps" and their miserable treatment by the British,[42] the former have often served as apologists for British policy.[43] Johannes Cornelius Otto's *Konsentrasiekampe*, written in the 1950s, can be included among these largely one-sided publications; it was long the only general history of the camps for Boer civilians.[44] There was no other comprehensive, scholarly portrait of the South African concentration camps until the publication of Elizabeth van Heyningen's *Concentration Camps of the Anglo-Boer War* in 2013.[45] Other academic works have focused on more specialized areas. The most important of these remains Stephanus Burridge Spies's analysis of British measures against the Boer civilian population, including the camps.[46] There have also been studies of individual camps[47] and investigations of specialized topics like the camp schools,[48] mortality,[49] and medical care.[50] For years, the parallel existence of camps for "blacks" and "coloreds"[51] was completely overlooked, having no place in the historiography of a conflict that was long perceived as a "white man's war." Only in the 1970s and 1980s, as Spies and Peter Warwick published the first findings of their research, did the black camps begin to receive greater attention.[52] In 2012, the Anglo-Boer War Museum in Bloemfontein posthumously released Stowell Kessler's long unpublished dissertation.[53] Nevertheless, the black camps remain insufficiently studied. Historical overviews of the South African War[54] help to contextualize these studies, which are complemented by specialized works on the role of the black population in the war,[55] on Boer participation on both sides of the conflict,[56] and on British postwar policy.[57]

An array of firsthand accounts from the camps for whites—by Boer internees[58] as well as camp personnel—provide another helpful resource. The latter encompass a wide variety of perspectives and include accounts by the head of the Transvaal camp administration, Samuel John Thomson; by the Boer volunteer nurse Johanna van Warmelo-Brandt; and by a Dutch Reformed chaplain in the Bethulie camp.[59] Firsthand accounts provide insight into the perspective of camp inmates, beyond what can be gleaned from the official British reports. The writings of British philanthropist Emily Hobhouse played a particularly important role. After visiting different camps at the beginning of 1901, she opened the eyes of the British public to the camps' catastrophic conditions.[60] My study also draws upon the voluminous official publications of the British government known as "blue books." These include the report of the Fawcett commission, which, in response to Hobhouse's revelations, was tasked by the War Office with visiting all of the Boer camps to gather information about their conditions.[61]

Archival material, finally, is essential to this study. The most important official document collections are in the National Archives in London, the South African National Archives in Pretoria, and the Free State Archives Repository in Bloemfontein. Among other documents, these collections contain thorough monthly reports by the individual camp superintendents, detailed inspection reports, and nearly complete statistics and camp registers. Some of these communications were reprinted in the blue books, but wherever possible, I cite directly from the archival holdings. Documentation is comparatively sparse only for the early phase of the camps for whites, before the military commanders atop the camp hierarchy were replaced by civilian superintendents in February/March 1901. These official documents are supplemented by the private papers of a few key figures: Commander-in-Chief Kitchener, High Commissioner Milner, and Colonial Secretary Chamberlain.

The wealth of source material allows much more detailed conclusions to be drawn about the South African Boer camps than about the other cases, especially the black camps in South Africa. No firsthand accounts of these camps exist, and official documentation is also sparse. All that remains are a few inspection reports, rudimentary statistics for the period between June 1901 and the end of 1902, and other scattered snippets of information. There are hardly any missionary sources, so important for South-West Africa, because the supervisors of the black camps actively sought to keep clerics away.

For many years, the war in German South-West Africa, like German colonialism overall, received only marginal scholarly attention. The first important monographs by Horst Drechsler and Helmut Bley were published in the 1960s, and they remain relevant today. The East German historian Drechsler was the first to argue that the battle against the Herero was conducted with "methods of genocide."[62] This thesis provided the point of departure for an intensive scholarly debate that unfolded around the one-hundredth anniversary of the war in 2004. The discussion was influenced particularly by Jürgen Zimmerer, who declared the mass murder of the Herero a forerunner of National Socialist crimes, tracing a line of genocidal violence from "Windhuk to Auschwitz."[63]

Several essays on the concentration camps in German South-West Africa were published within the context of this discussion about historical continuity. The role of extermination is central to this discussion, which has focused primarily on the camps on Shark Island and in Swakopmund, where the most people died.[64] Different authors have emphasized these camps' resemblance to National Socialist concentration camps,[65] which seems to impede their impartial analysis of the camps in the German colony. Thus, Benjamin Madley identifies the camp on Shark Island as a "rough model for later Nazi *Vernichtungslager* . . . like Treblinka and Auschwitz";[66] while David Olusoga and Casper W. Erichsen suggest that they have traced the invention of the "death camp" to southern Africa: "a military innovation that went on to become an emblem of the century and take more lives than the atom bomb."[67] Other aspects of the camps—insofar as they are considered at all—are subsumed within the paradigm of extermination and their anticipation of the Nazi camps. The important issue of forced labor has been discussed primarily within the context of "annihilation through labor" (*Vernichtung durch Arbeit*), which does not do justice to the phenomenon.[68] Although there are some persuasive texts,[69] a general history of the camps in South-West Africa has yet to be written. A goal of this book is to draw a more complex portrait of these camps.

The aforementioned essays on the camps, and general historical depictions of the war in South-West Africa, provide a foundation for my analysis of the camps in colonial Namibia. I also draw upon the work of Gesine Krüger and Jan-Bart Gewald, who have investigated the effects of the war and the camps on the Herero,[70] as well as the books of Andreas Heinrich Bühler and Walter Nuhn on the Nama war.[71]

In addition, I consult various primary sources, most of which have already been utilized by other scholars, although not with a systematic focus on the concentration camps. In the course of my research, however, some important documents came to my attention that had not yet been considered in the scholarly discussion.

Official records of the German institutions provide the most important source base for the chapter sections on South-West Africa. There are many relevant documents in the files of the Imperial Colonial Office (*Reichskolonialamt*) in the Federal Archive in Berlin, as well as in the records of the colonial government and district (*Bezirk*) and division (*Distrikt*) offices in the National Archives of Namibia in Windhoek. But there are no regular reports, as there are about the white camps in South Africa. If such reports ever existed, they were destroyed with the rest of the colonial forces' records during World War II. Only tiny leftovers of this collection remain in the Military Archive in Freiburg and the National Archives in Namibia. Thus, the files of the Rhenish Missionary Society, which was active in the former colony, assume special importance. Its missionaries repeatedly advocated for improving conditions in the camps. Their reports on the camps are now held in the Archives and Museum Foundation of the United Evangelical Mission in Wuppertal and in the Archives of the Evangelical Lutheran Church in the Republic of Namibia (ELCRN). The missionary reports not only provide a broader perspective on the camps but also convey—unlike official texts—an impression of everyday experience. The personal papers and, in some cases, published memoirs of military and government officials stationed in South-West Africa round out the aforementioned holdings.

Unfortunately, sources written by the interned Herero and Nama hardly exist. It is, therefore, difficult to reconstruct their perspective. A few letters from internees can be found in the archive of the ELCRN. During World War I, South African occupation troops conducted some interviews with former camp inmates and other eyewitnesses, which were published in a blue book.[72] But the historical value of this collection, which was produced for propaganda purposes, is disputed.[73] Recent oral history projects have attempted to compensate for the lack of African sources. But interviews conducted today, multiple generations later, can hardly help to reconstruct the events of 1904 to 1908. They can only tell us something about how the war and the camps are remembered today.[74] Thus, the source base resembles that of the black camps in South Africa; references to operations and daily life in the camps must be pieced together from information scattered across many different holdings.

To address the question of potential models for the establishment of the concentration camps, I consult—in addition to the aforementioned sources—the military and daily press,[75] as well as the reports of German diplomats who were in South Africa during the Boer War.[76]

## Important Terms and Concepts

Some terms in this study require clarification, as they come freighted with various associations and connotations. This is especially true of "concentration camp." Isabel Hull observes that the term today is immediately associated with the National Socialist camps, rendering it unusable for the colonial camps. As an alternative, she proposes "collection camp."[77] The counterargument, however, is that the term "concentration camp" (or *Konzentrationslager*) arose from the colonial context. It was used to identify camps in both South Africa and South-West Africa, even as it coexisted with other local terms.[78] It was likewise adopted for the Philippine and Cuban cases, although in these instances the sites of concentration were not actually camps.

In German, *Lager* are generally understood to be sites of "temporary, improvised shelter for many people."[79] The English "camp" has military origins and explicitly refers to shelter away from an urban environment.[80] Because the Cuban and Philippine civilians were interned in villages and towns, in these cases it makes more sense to speak of concentration "centers" or "villages," rather than "camps," although the notion of concentration remains apt. The military motive was concentrating an otherwise scattered group in one location, in order to keep it under control as closely as possible. With this background in mind, I use the terms "concentration camp" and "concentration center" in the following chapters—but the words are not explicitly intended to suggest proximity to the National Socialist camps.

The concept of genocide, which plays a role in the cases presented in this book, is also highly charged. The "closely interwoven ethical, political, scholarly, and legal dimensions" of the term are especially problematic, freighting the term with too many demands that cannot be fulfilled all at once, thereby complicating an analytically useful definition.[81] The most influential definition comes from the UN Genocide Convention of 1948: "acts committed with intent to destroy, in whole or in part, a national, ethnical, racial or religious group."[82] The convention is often criticized, and rightfully so. On one hand, its definition of genocide is too narrow because it excludes some important victims, such as political and social groups. On the other hand, it is also too broad, incorporating cases that fall short of mass murder.[83] Other authors have recently invoked the "father" of the convention, Raphael Lemkin, to plead for a broader understanding of the term that could also include the destruction of a group's cultural identity, even without mass murder.[84] A final criticism is that the perpetrators' intent is a problematic criterion.[85] The result of these debates has been a flood of definitions and proposals, which has not exactly solved the problem. Thus, the heuristic value of the term for historical scholarship remains a subject of debate.[86]

For these reasons, I do not use genocide as an analytic concept in this study. The term appears here only if it is part of the secondary literature on the cases being discussed. There is, however, one point closely related to the genocide concept that cannot be ignored—the question of intentionality, with respect to the mass mortality in the colonial wars, and particularly in the camps. The criterion of intentionality in the Genocide Convention is controversial, but even critics concede the importance of the question of intent. Birthe Kundrus and Henning Strotbek argue that the genocide concept is no longer useful for scholars today. Even so, they suggest that although the outcome may be the same "if millions are systematically killed, or if these lives are treated as expendable—this does make a difference for scholarship that is concerned about reasons and underlying causes."[87] Thus, this study does consider the extent to which the mass mortality in and around the camps was intentional, and which parts might be attributed to logistical problems, disinterest, ignorance, etc. A differentiated view of how the camps' functions evolved over time must not be neglected in this context.

A few words about the concept of labor are also in order. Particularly for the camps in South-West Africa, the involuntary nature of work must be emphasized. Scholars have frequently referred to both "forced" and "slave" labor.[88] Because the internees were not the property of the people for whom they had to work, I favor the term "forced labor."[89] There was, however, a certain connection to slave labor. The colonial powers had legitimized the seizure of African land in the late nineteenth century "as a humanitarian crusade against slavery and the slave trade," thereby officially excluding slave labor as a legitimate component of the colonial economy.[90] Nevertheless, there remained a great need for (cheap) labor. Because Africans were only rarely willing to work voluntarily as wage earners in the colonial economy, the colonial powers experimented with different forms of forced and migrant labor—which, from the perspective of those involved, hardly differed from older forms of slavery.[91]

Moreover, it is difficult to draw a clear line of division between free and unfree labor. Michael Mann has noted that "a person in dependent labor relations may have more room to negotiate the output, scope, and hours of his labor than a free industrial worker," raising questions about the analytical usefulness of a binary opposition between free and unfree labor.[92] It is, therefore, important to identify the specific elements of compulsion and free will that distinguished the labor of the concentrated populations.

## Historical Precedents and the "Invention" of the Concentration Camp in Cuba

Spanish general Valeriano Weyler y Nicolau is usually identified as the "inventor" of the concentration camp in the relevant historical literature.[93] He was appointed captain general of Cuba on 18 January 1896, so that he could stop the war of independence that had broken out there one year earlier. His mission was to keep the island, a Spanish colony since the early sixteenth century, in the hands of the motherland. Only days after his arrival on the large Antilles island, Weyler gave his first "concentration order" on 16 February 1896. The rural population was to resettle in the closest town or the closest village occupied by Spanish troops, within eight days. By the end of May 1897, he had successively expanded the policy of reconcentration across the entire island.

These measures primarily pursued a military goal. They sought to deprive Cuban guerrilla fighters of their basis for waging war, the support of the civilian population. The same motive was decisive for British concentration policy in South Africa and for American strategy in the Philippines, as we will see in the pages ahead. As Weyler himself explained:

> The orders I dictated regarding the concentration of peasants ... were imposed ... by the necessities of war. They were designed to deprive the enemy of all kinds of services provided by peasants, sometimes voluntarily[,] other times by threats and violence. These services were extremely important to the insurgents. They included cultivating crops and caring for livestock to feed [the insurgents]; acting as local guides; supplying intelligence to direct their operations; and serving as spies to reveal [our plans].[94]

Without this support, Weyler hoped, the Cuban troops would not be able to keep up their resistance. Once the land was cleared of civilians, and all shelter and food resources eliminated according to the dictates of "scorched earth" policy, hunger and disease would grind down the opponent. The Cuban freedom fighters would have to give in or fight openly[95]—exactly what they had successfully avoided to this point. Knowing that they would be unable to conquer the better armed and numerically superior Spanish forces, Máximo Gómez, chief commander of the revolutionary troops, had turned to guerrilla warfare: "Cuban forces would avoid the Spanish except under very controlled circumstances and attack instead the economic resources of the island: crops, structures, and civilians."[96] According to this calculus, if the Cuban economy—particularly the lucrative sugar industry in the west—were destroyed, Spain would lose interest in the "Pearl of the Antilles," and the path to independence would be clear.[97]

Because of Weyler's reconcentration orders, but also because many civilians fled the wake of devastation left by the Cuban guerrillas,[98] the number of people in the cities multiplied in 1896–97. In the end, more than 400,000 *reconcentrados* lived in more than eighty reconcentration centers.[99] For their sustenance, Weyler encouraged the creation of *zonas de cultivo*—small, supervised zones for agricultural cultivation close to towns and cities, where internees would work the land in order to feed themselves. "The assumption was that Cuba's fertile soil would allow for a first harvest within two months," Andreas Stucki summarizes.[100] Then provisions for the *reconcentrados* would no longer be drawn from military supplies, which, in any case, were intended only for families with no relation to the rebels.[101]

It soon became evident that the cultivation zones were insufficient for feeding the internees. The local administrations responsible for sustaining the *reconcentrados* lacked resources. And Weyler himself was not interested in solving these problems.[102] There was not enough food or shelter in the overcrowded internment centers. Hygiene was catastrophic, and disease spread quickly.[103] The inevitable consequence was mass mortality, the dimensions of which are still debated by scholars today. John Lawrence Tone, who has written the most detailed empirical study to date, places the number of deaths at 155,000 to 170,000. This corresponds to about one-third of the more than 400,000 internees, and just under one-tenth of the entire Cuban population, which was estimated at 1.7 million before the war.[104]

The success of the reconcentration policy is likewise debated. There is strong evidence that controlling the civilians paid off militarily, contributing decisively to Weyler's success in pushing back the Cuban guerrilla fighters to the eastern side of the island in 1897. But the concentration policies simultaneously incited international outrage and bolstered the US administration's arguments for one of the first "humanitarian interventions" in history.[105] The new liberal government in Madrid called Weyler back to Spain in October 1897, responding in part to American pressure. After the explosion of a US warship in the harbor of Havana, the United States declared war on Spain in April 1898 and occupied Cuba within a few weeks. In this respect, reconcentration paradoxically assumed a key role in the Spanish loss of Cuba.[106]

After the end of the Spanish-American War, the United States took control of the Philippines and other Spanish possessions, thereby "inheriting" the conflict with the Philippine independence movement that soon developed into guerrilla war.[107] In this war, the American military adopted the same concentration measures—at least in some of the most contested provinces of the archipelago[108]—that it had supposedly fought to end in Cuba. US commanders, too, sought primarily to separate guerrilla fighters and civilians, in order to cut off the former from their support network and to prevent them from posing as peaceful peasants when American troops approached. The parallel destruction of all food reserves in the contested territories was supposed to render any further operations by the "rebels" impossible. Concentration zones were also supposed to protect those Filipinos who did not want to help the guerrilla fighters, or who were prepared to support the Americans.[109] As we will see, this aspect of concentration also played a role in the British Boer camps. The zones soon figured prominently in the American civilizing mission, too. Michael Adas has depicted plans to "Americanize" the Filipinos by introducing "the colonizers' institutions, material culture, and ways of life."[110] Sites of concentration were also to serve as "camps of instruction and sanitation," as formulated by Senator Foraker of Ohio.[111] The British Boer camps had an assimilating function as well.

Even so, the situation for those who were concentrated in designated zones within wholly overcrowded towns and localities was as precarious as in Cuba. The number of residents in Batangas City climbed from 3,000 to 33,000. Food shortages were widespread, and sanitary conditions were dire. Sicknesses like malaria, measles, dysentery, and finally, cholera spread through the concentration zones. Internee mortality climbed rapidly, even if—presumably because of the short duration of the concentration measures—the deaths did not reach Cuban proportions.[112]

Despite the American press's fierce criticism of Weyler's reconcentration measures in Cuba,[113] the US military repeatedly oriented itself toward the Spanish example. After implementing "reconcentration policy" on the island of Cebu at the end of 1901, one officer proudly reported that he was known as the "Weyler" of his district.[114] Journalists, too, frequently drew a connection to the concentration policies in Cuba and British South Africa:

> With what astonishment do we read that a general of our army in the far-off Philippines has actually aped Weyler and Kitchener? Here in this country where we have held our heads so high and so prized the encomiums showered upon us for our ministrations to a suffering humanity, we have actually come to do a thing we went to war to banish.[115]

These quotations seem to underscore the familiar depiction of Weyler as the "inventor" of the concentration camp. But this label is problematic for two reasons. For one, the Cuban (and Philippine) reconcentration centers were existing villages and towns, not actual camps. And the term *campos de reconcentración*, which is frequently used by scholars today, does not seem to appear in Spanish communications of that time. But one cannot deny the semantic coincidence of US Senators using the terms "reconcentration camps" and "reconcentrado camps" to speak of concentration zones in the Philippines in 1902.[116] The Senators' language likely reflected a mixture of "concentration camp," which was associated with South Africa and received worldwide attention through the press in 1901, and the Spanish labels *reconcentración* and *reconcentrado*.

A second problem is that "invention" does not correspond to the situation in Cuba, since efforts to combat guerrillas by instituting controls over the population were not new. The Spanish military had already used the concentration of local rural populations as a counter-guerrilla measure in previous wars of independence in Cuba, the Ten Years' War

(1868–1878) and the Guerra Chiquita (1879–1880), and it had also experimented with similar methods in the Philippines. Beginning in the late 1860s, there was even discussion about the use of reconcentration among military theorists, so it is not surprising that Weyler adopted this tactic in 1896.[117]

Comparable attempts to foil the operations of guerrilla fighters, by deporting the civilian population and thereby removing their base of support, can also be found in other regimes and in earlier eras. During the American Civil War, General Thomas Ewing evacuated nearly all of the residents of four Missouri counties and then laid waste to the land. After a bloody attack on Lawrence, Kansas, Confederate guerrillas had retreated into neighboring Missouri. Ewing saw the resettlement of around 20,000 civilians as the only way to "neutralize" the guerrilla fighters known as bushwhackers.[118] Reservation policy in the wars against Native Americans is another example of military control over a population, and it was explicitly cited by American officers in the Philippines as a precedent for concentration policy.[119] And in the 1840s, Russia separated Murid guerrillas from the civilian population of the Caucasus with a *cordon sanitaire* of military outposts.[120]

Alongside the military control of civilians in guerrilla warfare, additional precedents for the concentration camps can be found before 1900. Andreas Gestrich points to three different traditions that can be traced from the premodern era to the camps of the late nineteenth and early twentieth centuries. The revolutionary wars around the turn of the nineteenth century introduced "a strategy of isolating prisoners of war in camps away from the towns, under strict supervision." Camp construction was increasingly oriented toward the model of prisons, and architectural elements of these camps eventually found their way into the design of the later concentration camps. Gestrich points to the segregation of immigrants, which began during the plague epidemics of the fourteenth century, as a second contributing tradition. During epidemics, migrants were placed under quarantine in special lazarettos to protect the native population from infection. One example of this was an unguarded and unfenced tent camp for the "poor Palatines" (emigrants from the Palatinate region, in present-day Germany) that was erected near London in 1710. A third tradition is the institution of the workhouse, where since the eighteenth century "beggars, vagrants, and gypsies" were put to work in order to be molded into useful members of society.[121]

The following pages explore how these precedents developed into the first concentration camps, and especially what distinguished these camps, at the beginning of the twentieth century.

## Notes

1. Alfred Milner to Richard Haldane (8 December 1901), Bodleian Library Oxford (BLO), Milner Papers (MP), D.2.1, 185, pp. 287–92.
2. Alfred Milner to Hamilton Goold-Adams (4 December 1901), BLO, MP, D.1.3, 173, pp. 245–48.
3. Alfred Milner to Joseph Chamberlain (7 December 1901), BLO, MP, D.1.2, 171, pp. 48–54.
4. See Stephanus Burridge Spies, *Methods of Barbarism? Roberts and Kitchener and Civilians in the Boer Republics, January 1900–May 1902* (Johannesburg, 2001), 159–60.
5. Milner to Chamberlain (7 December 1901), BLO, MP, D.1.2, 171, pp. 48–54.
6. A number of terms in this book appear in quotation marks even when they are not a direct quotation. The quotation marks highlight euphemisms such as "pacify" or "protection force," or the description of a territory that is "cleansed" of people. They also identify terms—like "rebellion"—that clearly reflect the colonizers' perspective, or terms such as "native," which have pejorative, often racist, connotations.
7. The numbers of deaths in the different cases will be examined more closely in the chapters to come.
8. See the next section in this chapter, "Framing the Question."
9. See the section in this chapter on "Sources."
10. Horst Gründer, "Genozid oder Zwangsmodernisierung?—Der moderne Kolonialismus in universalgeschichtlicher Perspektive," in *Genozid und Moderne*, ed. Mihran Dabag and Kristin Platt (Opladen, 1998), vol. 1, 135–51. See also Boris Barth, *Genozid: Völkermord im 20. Jahrhundert: Geschichte—Theorien—Kontroversen* (Munich, 2006), 134–35; and Mihran Dabag, Horst Gründer, and Uwe-K. Ketelsen, "Einleitung," in *Kolonialismus: Kolonialdiskurs und Genozid*, ed. Mihran Dabag, Horst Gründer, and Uwe-K. Ketelsen (Munich, 2004), 7–18.
11. See Jürgen Osterhammel, "'The Great Work of Uplifting Mankind': Zivilisierungsmission und Moderne," in *Zivilisierungsmissionen: Imperiale Weltverbesserung seit dem 18. Jahrhundert*, ed. Boris Barth and Jürgen Osterhammel (Konstanz, 2005), 363–425; and Alice L. Conklin, *A Mission to Civilize: The Republican Idea of Empire in France and West Africa, 1895–1930* (Stanford, 1997).
12. For the German colonial empire, see Harmut Pogge von Strandmann, "The Purpose of German Colonialism, or the Long Shadow of Bismarck's Colonial Policy," in *German Colonialism: Race, the Holocaust, and Postwar Germany*, ed. Volker Langbehn and Mohammad Salama (New York, 2011), 193–214. Theodor Leutwein himself asserted that the "main purpose of all colonization is ... a business. The colonizing race ... looks after its own advantage." See Theodor Leutwein, *Elf Jahre Gouverneur in Deutsch-Südwestafrika* (Windhoek, 1997), 451.
13. See, for example, Nick Deocampo, "Imperialist Fictions: The Filipino in the Imperialist Imaginary," in *Vestiges of War: The Philippine-American War and the Aftermath of an Imperial Dream 1899–1999*, ed. Angel Velasco Shaw and Luis H. Francia (New York, 2002), 225–36; and Jürgen Zimmerer, "Krieg, KZ und Völkermord in Südwestafrika: Der erste deutsche Genozid," in *Völkermord in Deutsch-Südwestafrika: Der Kolonialkrieg (1904–1908) in Namibia und seine Folgen*, ed. Jürgen Zimmerer and Joachim Zeller (Berlin, 2003), 45–63. The latter essay collection has been translated into English as *Genocide in German South-West Africa: The Colonial War (1904–1908) in Namibia and its Aftermath* (Monmouth, 2008). See also Andreas Stucki, "Streitpunkt Lager: Zwangsumsiedlung an der imperialen Peripherie," in *Welt der Lager: Zur "Erfolgsgeschichte" einer Institution*, ed. Bettina Greiner and

Alan Kramer (Hamburg, 2013), 71; and Elizabeth van Heyningen, *The Concentration Camps of the Anglo-Boer War: A Social History* (Johannesburg, 2013), 3–4.
14. Sebastian Conrad, "'Eingeborenenpolitik' in Kolonie und Metropole: 'Erziehung zur Arbeit' in Ostafrika und Ostwestfalen," in *Das Kaiserreich transnational: Deutschland und die Welt 1871–1914*, ed. Sebastian Conrad and Jürgen Osterhammel (Göttingen, 2004), 107.
15. Hannah Arendt, *The Origins of Totalitarianism* (New York, 1951). Jürgen Zimmerer's contributions to the discussion are collected in *Von Windhuk nach Auschwitz? Beiträge zum Verhältnis von Kolonialismus und Holocaust* (Berlin, 2011). See also A. Dirk Moses, "Empire, Colony, Genocide: Keywords and the Philosophy of History," in *Empire, Colony, Genocide: Conquest, Occupation, and Subaltern Resistance in World History*, ed. A. Dirk Moses (New York, 2008), 3–54. For a critique of the continuity thesis, see Birthe Kundrus, "Grenzen der Gleichsetzung: Kolonialverbrechen und Vernichtungspolitik," *iz3w* 275 (2004): 30–33; Birthe Kundrus, "Von den Herero zum Holocaust? Einige Bemerkungen zur aktuellen Debatte," *Mittelweg 36*, 14, no. 4 (2005): 82–92; and Robert Gerwarth and Stephan Malinowski, "Hannah Arendt's Ghosts: Reflections on the Disputable Path from Windhoek to Auschwitz," *Central European History* 42, no. 2 (2009): 279–300.
16. See, for example, Joachim Zeller, "'Wie Vieh wurden hunderte zu Tode getrieben und wie Vieh begraben.' Fotodokumente aus dem deutschen Konzentrationslager in Swakopmund/Namibia 1904–1908," *Zeitschrift für Geschichtswissenschaft* 49, no. 3 (2001): 242. This view has recently been espoused with particular vehemence in David Olusoga and Casper W. Erichsen, *The Kaiser's Holocaust: Germany's Forgotten Genocide and the Colonial Roots of Nazism* (London, 2010), especially 360–61.
17. For Cuba, see Andreas Stucki, *Aufstand und Zwangsumsiedlung: Die kubanischen Unabhängigkeitskriege 1868–1898* (Hamburg, 2012), 4. For South Africa, see Liz Stanley, *Mourning Becomes. . .: Post/Memory and Commemoration of the Concentration Camps of the South African War 1899–1902* (Manchester, 2006), 87; and Fransjohan Pretorius, "The White Concentration Camps of the Anglo-Boer War: A Debate Without End," *Historia* 55, no. 2 (2010): 41. Moreover, Aidan Forth has recently associated the different camp systems in the British Empire—especially in South Africa—with the Soviet Gulag. See "Britain's Archipelago of Camps: Labor and Detention in a Liberal Empire, 1871–1903," *Kritika*, 16, no. 3 (2015).
18. See, for example, Henning Melber, "Ein deutscher Sonderweg? Einleitende Bemerkungen zum Umgang mit dem Völkermord in Deutsch-Südwestafrika," in *Genozid und Gedenken: Namibisch-deutsche Geschichte und Gegenwart*, ed. Henning Melber (Frankfurt, 2005), 13–21. and Andreas Eckert, "Namibia—ein deutscher Sonderweg in Afrika? Anmerkungen zur internationalen Diskussion," in Zimmerer and Zeller, *Völkermord in Deutsch-Südwestafrika*, 226–36.
19. Zimmerer, *Von Windhuk nach Auschwitz*.
20. See, for example, Gerwarth and Malinowski, "Hannah Arendt's Ghosts"; and George Steinmetz, *The Devil's Handwriting: Precoloniality and the German Colonial State in Qingdao, Samoa, and Southwest Africa* (Chicago, 2007), 19 and 69–70.
21. Hartmut Pogge von Strandmann, for example, has recently described the goal of German colonial efforts as exploitation, in contrast to France's civilizing mission. See Strandmann, "The Purpose of German Colonialism."
22. Isabel V. Hull, *Absolute Destruction: Military Culture and the Practices of War in Imperial Germany* (Ithaca, 2005), 91–196.
23. Ibid., 182–96.
24. For transnational, or global, approaches to historical scholarship, see Sebastian Conrad and Andreas Eckert, "Globalgeschichte, Globalisierung, multiple Modernen: Zur

Geschichtsschreibung der modernen Welt," in *Globalgeschichte: Theorien, Ansätze, Themen*, ed. Sebastian Conrad, Andreas Eckert, and Ulrike Freitag (Frankfurt, 2007), 7–49; Sebastian Conrad, *What Is Global History?* (Princeton, 2016); Albert Wirz, "Für eine transnationale Geschichte," *Geschichte und Gesellschaft* 27, no. 3 (2001): 489–98; and Kiran Klaus Patel, "Transnationale Geschichte: Ein neues Paradigma?," *Connections*, 2 February 2005.

25. See, for example, Ulrike Lindner, "German Colonialism and the British Neighbor in Africa Before 1914: Self-Definitions, Lines of Demarcation, and Cooperation," in Langbehn and Salama, *German Colonialism*, 254–72; and the proposal for a new research agenda in colonial studies in Ann Laura Stoler and Frederick Cooper, "Between Metropole and Colony: Rethinking a Research Agenda," in *Tensions of Empire: Colonial Cultures in a Bourgeois World*, ed. Ann Laura Stoler and Frederick Cooper (Berkeley, 1997), 1–56.

26. For South Africa, see Andrzej J. Kaminski, *Konzentrationslager 1896 bis heute: Geschichte, Funktion, Typologie* (Munich, 1990), 35; and Joël Kotek and Pierre Rigoulot, *Das Jahrhundert der Lager: Gefangenschaft, Zwangsarbeit, Vernichtung* (Berlin, 2001), 61 and 80. For South-West Africa, see Casper W. Erichsen, *"The Angel of Death Has Descended Violently Among Them": Concentration Camps and Prisoners-of-War in Namibia, 1904–1908* (Leiden, 2005), 1; Benjamin Madley, "From Africa to Auschwitz: How German South West Africa Incubated Ideas and Methods Adopted and Developed by Nazis in Eastern Europe," *European History Quarterly* 35, no. 3 (2005): 446; and Dominik J. Schaller, "Kolonialkrieg, Völkermord und Zwangsarbeit in 'Deutsch-Südwestafrika,'" in *Enteignet—Vertrieben—Ermordet: Beiträge zur Genozidforschung*, ed. Dominik J. Schaller et al. (Zurich, 2004), 175. A positive exception in this regard is the recent collection *Welt der Lager*, which focuses solidly on the "transnational learning and transfer processes" that contributed to the spread of the institution of the camp. See Alan Kramer, "Einleitung," in Greiner and Kramer, *Welt der Lager*, 11.

27. On problems of comparison and contextualization, see Ludolf Herbst, *Komplexität und Chaos: Grundrisse einer Theorie der Geschichte* (Munich, 2004), 76–99.

28. Zimmerer, "Krieg, KZ und Völkermord," 63.

29. See Paul Moore, "'And What Concentration Camps Those Were!': Foreign Concentration Camps in Nazi Propaganda, 1933–9," *Journal of Contemporary History* 45, no. 3 (2010): 649–74.

30. On comparative theory, see Hartmut Kaelble, *Der historische Vergleich: Eine Einführung zum 19. und 20. Jahrhundert* (Frankfurt, 1999), 76–99.

31. Wolfgang Sofsky, *Die Ordnung des Terrors: Das Konzentrationslager* (Frankfurt, 2004).

32. See Christiane Eisenberg, "Kulturtransfer als historischer Prozess: Ein Beitrag zur Komparatistik," in *Vergleich und Transfer: Komparatistik in den Sozial-, Geschichts- und Kulturwissenschaften*, ed. Hartmut Kaelble and Jürgen Schriewer (Frankfurt, 2003), 399–417. For a more critical position on the concept of transfer, see also Michael Werner and Bénédicte Zimmermann, "Vergleich, Transfer, Verflechtung: Der Ansatz der Histoire croisée und die Herausforderung des Transnationalen," *Geschichte und Gesellschaft* 28, no. 4 (2002): 607–36.

33. Kaminski, *Konzentrationslager*, 34–39; Wolfgang Wippermann, *Konzentrationslager: Geschichte, Nachgeschichte, Gedenken* (Berlin, 1999), 23–24; Hermann Scharnagl, *Kurze Geschichte der Konzentrationslager* (Wiesbaden, 2004), 23–41; and Dan Stone, *Concentration Camps: A Short History* (Oxford, 2017), 11–22.

34. See, for example, Stucki, *Aufstand und Zwangsumsiedlung*, 378.

35. In addition, there are a number of factual errors. Kotek and Rigoulot, *Das Jahrhundert der Lager*, 45–86.

36. Andrea Pitzer, *One Long Night: A Global History of Concentration Camps* (New York, 2017).
37. Iain Smith and Andreas Stucki, "The Colonial Development of Concentration Camps (1868–1902)," *The Journal of Imperial and Commonwealth History* 39, no. 3 (2011): 417–37; Jonathan Hyslop, "The Invention of the Concentration Camp: Cuba, Southern Africa and the Philippines, 1896–1907," *South African Historical Journal* 63, no. 2 (2011): 251–76; and Sybille Scheipers, "The Use of Camps in Colonial Warfare," *The Journal of Imperial and Commonwealth History* 43, no. 4 (2015): 678–98.
38. Marouf Hasian, a professor of communications, has recently published a comparative monograph that examines contemporary discourses on colonial camps. However, his work lacks a thorough base in archival sources and specialized literature, and his depiction of events in the colonies is often inaccurate. Marouf Hasian, Jr., *Restorative Justice: Humanitarian Rhetorics, and Public Memories of Colonial Camp Cultures* (Basingstoke, 2014).
39. The names "Boer War" and "Anglo-Boer War," which are common in older scholarship, imply that the war involved only the English and Boer segments of the South African population, thereby reinforcing the myth of the "white man's war." Because this was not the case—the war was just as consequential for the black population—newer histories increasingly favor the more inclusive label "South African War." See Peter Warwick, *Black People in the South African War 1899–1902* (Cambridge, 1983), 4.
40. Fred R. van Hartesveldt, *The Boer War: Historiography and Annotated Bibliography* (Westport, 2000).
41. See Fransjohan Pretorius, "The White Concentration Camps of the Anglo-Boer War," 34–49.
42. Ewald Steenkamp, *Helkampe* (Johannesburg, 1941). Johannes C. Otto, *Die Konsentrasiekampe* (Pretoria, 2005) is also part of this group.
43. Napier Devitt, *The Concentration Camps in South Africa* (Pietermaritzburg, 1941); and Arthur C. Martin, *The Concentration Camps, 1900–1902: Facts, Figures and Fables* (Cape Town, 1957).
44. Otto, *Die Konsentrasiekampe*. See also Elizabeth van Heyningen, "Costly Mythologies: The Concentration Camps of the South African War in Afrikaner Historiography," *Journal of Southern African Studies* 34, no. 2 (2008): 510–11.
45. Elizabeth van Heyningen, *The Concentration Camps of the Anglo-Boer War*. Most recently, see Aidan Forth, *Barbed-Wire Imperialism: Britain's Empire of Camps, 1876–1903* (Berkeley, 2017).
46. Spies, *Methods of Barbarism*.
47. These include Elizabeth van Heyningen, "Pietermaritzburg Concentration Camp," *Natalia* 40 (2010): 62–76; and Johan M. Wassermann, *The Eshowe Concentration and Surrendered Burghers Camp during the Anglo-Boer War* (Congella, 1999).
48. Eliza Riedi, "Teaching Empire: British and Dominions Women Teachers in the South African War Concentration Camps," *English Historical Review* 120, no. 489 (2005): 1316–47; and Paul Zietsman, "The Concentration Camp Schools—Beacons of Light in the Darkness," in *Scorched Earth*, ed. Fransjohan Pretorius (Cape Town, 2001), 86–109.
49. Daniel Low-Beer, Matthew Smallman-Raynor, and Andrew Cliff, "Disease and Death in the South African War: Changing Disease Patterns from Soldiers to Refugees," *Social History of Medicine* 17, no. 2 (2004): 223–45; and Elizabeth van Heyningen, "A Tool for Modernisation? The Boer Concentration Camps of the South African War, 1900–1902," *South African Journal of Science* 106, no. 5/6 (2010): 58–67.
50. Elizabeth van Heyningen, "Women and Disease: The Clash of Medical Cultures in the Concentration Camps of the South African War," in *Writing a Wider War: Re-*

*thinking Gender, Race, and Identity in the South African War, 1899–1902*, ed. Greg Cuthbertson, Albert Grundlingh, and Mary-Lynn Suttie (Athens, 2002), 186–212; and Bruce Fetter and Stowell Kessler, "Scars From a Childhood Disease: Measles in the Concentration Camps During the Boer War," *Social Science History* 20, no. 4 (1996): 593–611.

51. The labels "black" and "colored" reflect the common practice in scholarly literature to distinguish the Bantu-speaking "blacks" from the "coloreds," who often spoke Afrikaans or English, and whose ancestors came not only from Africa but also Europe or Asia. These population groups still use the historically-freighted terms to identify themselves today. In this study, I use the terms as a neutral descriptive. See Christoph Marx, *Südafrika: Geschichte und Gegenwart* (Stuttgart, 2012), 9; and Christopher C. Saunders, *Historical Dictionary of South Africa* (London, 2000), 43–44.
52. Spies, *Methods of Barbarism*, especially 247–52 and 288–91; Warwick, *Black People*, 145–62.
53. Stowell V. Kessler, *The Black Concentration Camps of the Anglo-Boer War 1899–1902* (Bloemfontein, 2012). Kessler completed the dissertation, "The Black Concentration Camps of the South African War," at the University of Cape Town in 2003.
54. Rayne Kruger, *Goodbye Dolly Gray: The Story of the Boer War* (Alberton, 2008); Thomas Pakenham, *The Boer War* (London, 1982); Bill Nasson, *The South African War 1899–1902* (London, 1999) and the significantly expanded new edition, *The War for South Africa: The Anglo-Boer War 1899–1902* (Cape Town, 2010); and Martin Bossenbroek, *The Boer War* (New York, 2018).
55. Warwick, *Black People*; and Bill Nasson, *Abraham Esau's War: A Black South African War in the Cape, 1899–1902* (Cambridge, 1991).
56. Albert Grundlingh, *The Dynamics of Treason: Boer Collaboration in the South African War of 1899–1902* (Pretoria, 2006).
57. Donald Denoon, *A Grand Illusion: The Failure of Imperial Policy in the Transvaal Colony during the Period of Reconstruction 1900–1905* (London, 1973).
58. Emily Hobhouse, *War without Glamour: or, Women's War Experiences Written by Themselves 1899–1902* (Hill Cliffe, 2007) is one collection of such accounts.
59. Samuel John Thomson, *The Transvaal Burgher Camps* (Allahabad, 1904); Johanna Brandt, *The War Diary of Johanna Brandt* (Pretoria, 2007); and August Daniel Lückhoff, *Woman's Endurance* (Cape Town, 1904).
60. Especially Emily Hobhouse, *Report of a Visit to the Camps of Women and Children in the Cape and Orange River Colonies* (London, 1901) and also *The Brunt of the War and Where it Fell* (London, 1902).
61. Cd. 893, *Report on the Concentration Camps in South Africa by the Committee of Ladies Appointed by the Secretary of State for War* (London, 1902).
62. Horst Drechsler, *Südwestafrika unter deutscher Kolonialherrschaft: Der Kampf der Herero und Nama gegen den deutschen Imperialismus (1884–1915)* (Berlin, 1984), 20; Helmut Bley, *Kolonialherrschaft und Sozialstruktur in Deutsch-Südwestafrika 1894–1914* (Hamburg, 1968). Both works have been translated into English. See Horst Drechsler, *Let Us Die Fighting: The Struggle of the Herero and Nama against German Imperialism, 1884–1915* (London, 1980); and Helmut Bley, *South-West Africa under German Rule, 1894–1914* (Evanston, 1971).
63. Zimmerer, *Von Windhuk nach Auschwitz*. On the continuity debate, see note 15.
64. Casper W. Erichsen, "Zwangsarbeit im Konzentrationslager auf der Haifischinsel," in Zimmerer and Zeller, *Völkermord in Deutsch-Südwestafrika*, 80–85; Joachim Zeller, "'Ombepera i koza—Die Kälte tötet mich': Zur Geschichte des Konzentrationslagers in Swakopmund (1904–1908)," in Zimmerer and Zeller, *Völkermord in Deutsch-Südwestafrika*, 64–79; and Zeller, "'Wie Vieh.'" The role of extermination in the camps is also discussed in Hull, *Absolute Destruction*, 70–90; Olusoga and Erichsen, *The Kai-*

ser's Holocaust, 162–71 and 207–30; and Jonas Kreienbaum, "'Vernichtungslager' in Deutsch-Südwestafrika? Zur Funktion der Konzentrationslager im Herero- und Namakrieg (1904–1908)," Zeitschrift für Geschichtswissenschaft 58, no. 12 (2010): 1014–26. Recent additions to the discussion include Matthias Häußler, "Zwischen Vernichtung und Pardon: Die Konzentrationslager in 'Deutsch-Südwestafrika' (1904–1908)," Zeitschrift für Geschichtswissenschaft 61, no. 7/8 (2013): 601–20; and Jürgen Zimmerer, "Lager und Genozid: Die Konzentrationslager in Südwestafrika zwischen Windhuk und Auschwitz," in Lager vor Auschwitz: Gewalt und Integration im 20. Jahrhundert, ed. Christoph Jahr and Jens Thiel (Berlin, 2013), 54–67.

65. For example: Zeller, "'Wie Vieh,'" 242; Olusoga and Erichsen, The Kaiser's Holocaust, 10 and 360–61.
66. Madley, "From Africa to Auschwitz," 446.
67. Olusoga and Erichsen, The Kaiser's Holocaust, 10. I discuss the problematic nature of such statements thoroughly in Chapter 5, "Comparative Reflections on Colonial and National Socialist Camps."
68. See, for example, Kotek and Rigoulot, Das Jahrhundert der Lager, 80; Scharnagl, Kurze Geschichte der Konzentrationslager, 39–40; and Olusoga and Erichsen, The Kaiser's Holocaust, 215 and 361.
69. Especially Hull, Absolute Destruction, 70–90.
70. Jan-Bart Gewald, Herero Heroes: A Socio-Political History of the Herero of Namibia 1890–1923 (Oxford, 1999); and Gesine Krüger, Kriegsbewältigung und Geschichtsbewusstsein: Realität, Deutung und Verarbeitung des deutschen Kolonialkriegs in Namibia 1904 bis 1907 (Göttingen, 1999).
71. Andreas Heinrich Bühler, Der Namaaufstand gegen die deutsche Kolonialherrschaft in Namibia von 1904–1913 (Frankfurt, 2003); and Walter Nuhn, Feind überall: Der Große Nama-Aufstand (Hottentottenaufstand) 1904–1908 in Deutsch-Südwestafrika (Namibia): Der erste Partisanenkrieg in der Geschichte der deutschen Armee (Bonn, 2000). Nuhn's study is linguistically problematic because it adopts the terms of the colonizers without reflection, but empirically it holds up well.
72. Union of South Africa, Report on the Natives of South-West Africa and Their Treatment by Germany (London, 1918). The book was reprinted in an annotated edition. Jeremy Silvester and Jan-Bart Gewald, eds., Words Cannot be Found: German Colonial Rule in Namibia: An Annotated Reprint of the 1918 Blue Book (Leiden, 2003).
73. For a critical view of the blue book, see Andreas Eckl, "S'ist ein übles Land hier": Zur Historiographie eines umstrittenen Kolonialkrieges: Tagebuchaufzeichnungen aus dem Herero-Krieg in Deutsch-Südwestafrika 1904 von Georg Hillebrecht und Franz Ritter von Epp (Cologne, 2005), 17–23. For a positive assessment of its value as a source, see Erichsen, "The Angel of Death," 94–101.
74. Casper W. Erichsen, ed., "What the Elders Used to Say": Namibian Perspectives on the Last Decade of German Colonial Rule (Windhoek, 2008). It is striking that the interviewees confuse Trotha and Hitler on multiple occasions. There are no insights about the camps in Annemarie Heywood, Brigitte Lau, and Raimund Ohly, eds., Warriors, Leaders, Sages, and Outcasts in the Namibian Past: Narratives Collected from Herero Sources for the Michael Scott Oral Records Project (MSORP) 1985–6 (Windhoek, 1992), or in Andreas Kukuri, Herero-Texte (Berlin, 1983).
75. Steffen Bender's dissertation, which examines perceptions in the German press of the "white" camps in the South African War, is a valuable resource in this respect. See Steffen Bender, Der Burenkrieg und die deutschsprachige Presse: Wahrnehmungen und Deutungen zwischen Bureneuphorie und Anglophobie 1899–1902 (Paderborn, 2009), 101–20.
76. The latter can be found in the Political Archive of the Foreign Office in Berlin.
77. Hull, Absolute Destruction, 73.

78. Such as "refugee camp" and "burgher camp" in South Africa, and *Gefangenenkraal* in South-West Africa.
79. "Lager," in *Brockhaus Wahrig*, vol. 4 (Wiesbaden, 1982), 381. On the definition and evolution of the term *"Lager"* in German encyclopedias, see Christoph Jahr, "'Diese Concentrationen sollten die Pflanzstätten für den militärischen Geist des Heeres bilden...': Fragmente einer Begriffsgeschichte des Lagers," in Jahr and Thiel, *Lager vor Auschwitz*, 20–37.
80. See the entry for "camp" in *Encyclopædia Britannica*, vol. 5 (London, 1926), 120–21.
81. Birthe Kundrus and Henning Strotbek, "'Genozid': Grenzen und Möglichkeiten eines Forschungsbegriffs—ein Literaturbericht," *Neue Politische Literatur* 51, no. 2/3 (2006): 400.
82. United Nations, "Convention on the Prevention and Punishment of the Crime of Genocide," 9 December 1948. See also Alfred Grosser, *Ermordung der Menschheit: Der Genozid im Gedächtnis der Völker* (Munich, 1990), 52–53.
83. Barth, *Genozid*, 12–28; and Eric D. Weitz, *A Century of Genocide: Utopias of Race and Nation* (Princeton, 2003), 9.
84. Adam Jones has called this a "return to Lemkin." See Adam Jones, "Editor's Preface: The Present and Future of Genocide Studies," in *New Directions in Genocide Research*, ed. Adam Jones (London, 2012), xix–xxvii, especially xx; and Moses, "Empire, Colony, Genocide."
85. Barth, *Genozid*, 19–20; Kundrus and Strotbek, "'Genozid,'" 406–7; Dominik J. Schaller, "Genozidforschung: Begriffe und Debatten: Einleitung," in Schaller et al., *Enteignet—Vertrieben—Ermordet*, 14.
86. For some of the most important, new definitions see: Helen Fein, "Definition and Discontent: Labelling, Detecting, and Explaining Genocide in the Twentieth Century," in *Genozid in der modernen Geschichte*, ed. Stig Förster and Gerhard Hirschfeld (Münster, 1999), 11–21; and Frank Chalk and Kurt Jonassohn, "Genozid—ein historischer Überblick," in Dabag and Platt, *Genozid und Moderne*, 294–308.
87. Kundrus and Strotbek, "'Genozid,'" 421.
88. On slaves and slave labor, see Brigitte Lau, "Uncertain Certainties," in *History and Historiography: 4 Essays in Reprint*, ed. Annemarie Heywood (Windhoek, 1995), 39–52; and Kotek and Rigoulot, *Das Jahrhundert der Lager*, 79. On forced labor, see Hull, *Absolute Destruction*, 70–90; and Erichsen, "Zwangsarbeit im Konzentrationslager auf der Haifischinsel."
89. This distinction can also be found in the files of the German administration in South-West Africa. See Etappenkommando to the District Office Windhuk (9 April 1906), National Archives of Namibia (NAN), Bezirksamt Windhuk (BWI) 407 E.V.8. spec. vol. 4. On the terminology of forced and slave labor in the National Socialist camps, see Marc Buggeln, *Arbeit und Gewalt: Das Außenlagersystem des KZ Neuengamme* (Göttingen, 2009), 218–25; and Kaminski, *Konzentrationslager*, 70–72. For an abbreviated English translation of Buggeln's work, see *Slave Labor in Nazi Concentration Camps* (Oxford, 2014).
90. Andreas Eckert, "Der langsame Tod der Sklaverei: Unfreie Arbeit und Kolonialismus in Afrika im späten 19. und im 20. Jahrhundert," in *Sklaverei und Zwangsarbeit zwischen Akzeptanz und Widerstand*, ed. Elisabeth Hermann-Otto (Hildesheim, 2011), 311. Although the Europeans officially rejected slavery, they took no decisive action against it. In practice, the colonizers tolerated many forms of slavery because they feared that economic production would otherwise collapse.
91. Ibid.; Andreas Eckert, "Europa, Sklavenhandel und koloniale Zwangsarbeit: Einleitende Bemerkungen," *Journal of Modern European History* 7, no. 1 (2009): 26–35; Kevin Grant, *A Civilised Savagery: Britain and the New Slaveries in Africa, 1884–1926* (New York, 2005); and Frederick Cooper, *From Slaves to Squatters: Planta-*

*tion Labor and Agriculture in Zanzibar and Coastal Kenya, 1890–1925* (New Haven, 1980).
92. Michael Mann, "Die Mär von der freien Lohnarbeit: Menschenhandel und erzwungene Arbeit in der Neuzeit: Ein einleitender Essay," *Comparativ* 13, no. 4 (2003): 17–22.
93. Kaminski, *Konzentrationslager*, 34. Wippermann speaks of "Weyler's 'invention,'" while Scharnagl refers to the "Spanish original" and the first organized concentration that took place in Cuba in 1896. See Wippermann, *Konzentrationslager*, 23; and Scharnagl, *Kurze Geschichte der Konzentrationslager*, 24 and 29.
94. Quoted in John Lawrence Tone, *War and Genocide in Cuba, 1895–1898* (Chapel Hill, 2006), 203–4.
95. Stucki, *Aufstand und Zwangsumsiedlung*, 202–3.
96. Tone, *War and Genocide*, 57.
97. Ibid., 58.
98. Ibid., 60–61.
99. Stucki, *Aufstand und Zwangsumsiedlung*, 7.
100. Ibid., 158.
101. Ibid., 156. Because *reconcentrados* with family ties to insurgents were also excluded from the cultivation zones, Tone describes the Spanish policy as a "death sentence for a portion of refugees." See Tone, *War and Genocide*, 207.
102. Stucki, *Aufstand und Zwangsumsiedlung*, 153–55 and 206–12.
103. Ibid., 271–345.
104. Tone, *War and Genocide*, 209–24.
105. Davide Rodogno has recently published a history of an even earlier case—European interventions in the Ottoman Empire after 1815. See Davide Rodogno, *Against Massacre: Humanitarian Interventions in the Ottoman Empire, 1815–1914* (Princeton, 2012).
106. Tone, *War and Genocide*, 209; and Stucki, *Aufstand und Zwangsumsiedlung*, 240–50. On the reasons for the outbreak of the Spanish-American War, see Sebastian Balfour, *The End of the Spanish Empire: 1898–1923* (Oxford, 1997), 21–33.
107. On the Philippine-American War, see Brian M. Linn, *The Philippine War, 1899–1902* (Lawrence, 2000); Stuart Creighton Miller, *"Benevolent Assimilation": The American Conquest of the Philippines, 1899–1903* (New Haven, 1984); and Schumacher, "'Niederbrennen, plündern und töten sollt ihr': Der Kolonialkrieg der USA auf den Philippinen (1899–1913)," in *Kolonialkriege: Militärische Gewalt im Zeichen des Imperialismus*, ed. Thoraf Klein and Frank Schumacher (Hamburg, 2006), 109–44.
108. The islands of Marinduque, Cebu, and Samar, as well as different regions on the main island of Luzon, including the provinces of Batangas and Laguna.
109. On the military aims of concentration, see Andrew J. Birtle, *US Army Counterinsurgency and Contingency Operations Doctrine, 1860–1941* (Washington DC, 1998), 119–35; Brian M. Linn, *The US Army and Counterinsurgency in the Philippine War, 1899–1902* (Chapel Hill, 1989); John M. Gates, *Schoolbooks and Krags: The United States Army in the Philippines, 1898–1902* (Westport, 1973); and Reynaldo C. Ileto, "The Philippine-American War: Friendship and Forgetting," in Shaw and Francia, *Vestiges of War*, 3–21.
110. Michael Adas, *Dominance by Design: Technological Imperatives and America's Civilizing Mission* (Cambridge, 2006), 165–66. On American plans for social engineering in the Philippines, see also Glenn A. May, *Social Engineering in the Philippines: The Aims, Execution and Impact of American Colonial Policy, 1900–1913* (Westport, 1980).
111. "Bacon and Hoar," *Boston Daily Globe*, 21 May 1902. See also Gates, *Schoolbooks and Krags*, especially 260 and 263.

112. Conditions and mortality in the concentration zones have hardly been studied. The first works in this field examine the province of Batangas, where Brigadier General J. Franklin Bell led the largest concentration effort between January and April 1902. In the four months of concentration, around 9,000 of the 300,000 internees perished. On Batangas, see Glenn A. May, "The 'Zones' of Batangas," *Philippine Studies* 29, no. 1 (1981): 89–103; *The Battle for Batangas: A Philippine Province at War* (New Haven, 1991); and "Was the Philippine-American War a 'Total War'?," in *Anticipating Total War: The German and American Experiences, 1871–1914*, ed. Manfred F. Boemeke, Roger Chickering, and Stig Förster (Cambridge, 1999), 437–57.

113. See Joseph E. Wisan, *The Cuban Crisis as Reflected in the New York Press (1895–1898)* (New York, 1934).

114. "'Butcher' Weyler is being Outdone by the Americans," *Atlanta Constitution*, 26 December 1901.

115. *Literary Digest* 24 (1902): 4, quoted in Miller, *"Benevolent Assimilation,"* 209. On American efforts to learn from the more experienced colonial powers, see Frank Schumacher, "Lessons of Empire: The United States, the Quest for Colonial Expertise and the British Example, 1898–1917," in *From Enmity to Friendship: Anglo-American Relations in the 19th and 20th Century*, ed. Ursula Lehmkuhl and Gustav Schmidt (Augsburg, 2005), 71–98; and Frank Schumacher, "Kulturtransfer und *Empire*: Britisches Vorbild und US-amerikanische Kolonialherrschaft auf den Philippinen im frühen 20. Jahrhundert," in *Kolonialgeschichten: Regionale Perspektiven auf ein globales Phänomen*, ed. Claudia Kraft, Alf Lüdtke, and Jürgen Martschukat (Frankfurt, 2010), 306–27.

116. See Stucki, *Aufstand und Zwangsumsiedlung*, 13–15, and "Aufbruch ins Zeitalter der Lager? Zwangsumsiedlung und Deportation in der spanischen Antiguerilla auf Kuba, 1868–98," *Mittelweg 36* 20, no. 4 (2011): 28–31.

117. Stucki, "Aufbruch," *Mittelweg 36*, 22–25; "Die spanische Antiguerilla-Kriegführung auf Kuba 1868–1898: Radikalisierung—Entgrenzung—Genozid?" *Zeitschrift für Geschichtswissenschaft* 56, no. 2 (2008): 123–38; and *Aufstand und Zwangsumsiedlung*, 117–26. See also Tone, *War and Genocide*, 195–96.

118. Charles R. Mink, "General Orders, No. 11: The Forced Evacuation of Civilians during the Civil War," *Military Affairs* 34, no. 4 (1970): 132–37.

119. Tone, *War and Genocide*, 195. See also Andrew J. Birtle, "The US Army's Pacification of Marinduque, Philippine Islands, April 1900–April 1901," *The Journal of Military History* 61, no. 2 (1997): 271.

120. Ian F. W. Beckett, *Modern Insurgencies and Counter-Insurgencies: Guerrillas and Their Opponents since 1750* (London, 2001), 36.

121. Andreas Gestrich, "Konzentrationslager: Voraussetzungen und Vorläufer vor der Moderne," in Greiner and Kramer, *Welt der Lager*, 43–61. On the nexus between workhouses and the National Socialist concentration camps, see Jane Caplan, "Political Detention and the Origin of the Concentration Camps in Nazi Germany, 1933–1935/6," in *Nazism, War and Genocide: Essays in Honour of Jeremy Noakes*, ed. Neil Gregor (Exeter, 2005), 22–41.

## Chapter 1

## The Context
### Colonial Wars in South Africa and South-West Africa

The concentration policies in South Africa and South-West Africa can be understood only within the context of the colonial wars in which they emerged. What distinguished the South African War and the conflicts with the Herero and Nama in the neighboring German colony?

**The South African War: Guerrilla War and Scorched Earth Policy**

Only months after reconcentration measures in Cuba had effectively ended, the South African War began, on 11 October 1899, as troops of the allied Boer states, the South African Republic (Transvaal), and the Orange Free State, attacked the British possessions of Natal and the Cape Colony. Over the course of this war, the British came to introduce "concentration camps" as part of their military strategy.

The roots of the South African War can be traced back to the early years of the nineteenth century. Great Britain had taken the Cape from the Dutch during the course of the Napoleonic Wars. Dissatisfied with the new administration, and particularly with the beginnings of emancipation for the black population, around six thousand Afrikaners embarked on the "Great Trek" between 1834 and 1844, seeking to leave British-controlled territory. The Afrikaners were descendants of Dutch, German, and French immigrants who had first come to the Cape in the mid-seventeenth century, establishing themselves primarily as farmers (Boers). The "Voortrekkers" first moved to Natal, which was subsequently annexed by the British in 1843. After bloody battles with the displaced African population, they ultimately settled in the South African interior, where they founded the South African Republic and the Orange Free State. These two states were recognized by the British in the early 1850s.

In 1877, Great Britain annexed the South African Republic (at this point, the least developed of the four settler states), with the goal of creating a South African federation on the Canadian model. In the following years, the British succeeded where the Boers had failed; by conquering the Zulu and then the Pedi, they secured the Transvaal against its most powerful African opponents. This marked the end of an effective African resistance, which had been a factor in South Africa throughout the previous century. Freed from African opposition, the Boer population of the Transvaal now pushed to regain independence. They succeeded over the course of the Transvaal War (1880/81), dealing the British troops two humiliating defeats at Laing's Nek and Majuba Hill. Eager to bring the conflict to an end, the newly elected Liberal government in London offered far-reaching concessions and allowed the Transvaal to regain independence.[1]

In the coming years, the distribution of power changed rapidly in South Africa, providing further potential for conflict in the region. In 1884, Imperial Germany's acquisition of land in neighboring South-West Africa posed a potential threat to Britain's as yet unchallenged claim to regional supremacy. And only two years later, the discovery of the world's largest gold deposits in the Transvaal ushered in a dramatic change of fortune for the South African Republic, which went from the most destitute area of South Africa to its economic center within just a few years. With the vast expansion of its own territory in the South African interior, Great Britain did succeed in cutting off Germany geographically from the Transvaal, thereby keeping Germany out of South Africa. But in London, fears arose that the rise of the South African Republic might result in a South African union under Boer leadership.[2]

The first attempt to stave off this possibility by attacking the South African Republic, the Jameson Raid of 1895, was a spectacular failure. The ringleader of this coup was the diamond and gold magnate Cecil

Rhodes, who was first elected prime minister of the Cape Colony in 1890. An uprising of *Uitlanders* (foreign workers) near the Transvaal gold mines was supposed to provide the pretext for an armed invasion from Bechuanaland under the leadership of Leander Starr Jameson. The undertaking failed. The uprising never happened, and Jameson's men—who nevertheless advanced into Boer territory—were routed by Boer commandos and disarmed after a short battle. This episode, which was interpreted by some contemporaries as a British declaration of war against the Transvaal, ushered in the final phase of the conflict that led to the South African War in 1899.[3]

The *Uitlanders*, who had poured into the South African Republic during the gold boom but were barred from voting, again played a decisive role. Sir Alfred Milner, who arrived in Cape Town as the new high commissioner for South Africa in 1897, was particularly determined that the foreigners (who were mostly British) should receive equal political rights. His vision was to claim victory for Great Britain in the "great game for mastery in South Africa,"[4] and he hoped for a pro-British regime change in the Transvaal.[5] The high commissioner speculated that he might then be able to reshape South Africa as Lord Cromer had done in Egypt, where Milner had served as undersecretary for finance between 1889 and 1892. The Transvaal government under President Paul Kruger, who had himself participated in the Great Trek as a child, regarded England warily. Under no circumstances did Kruger want to permit the *Uitlanders'* political integration. He not only feared a loss of power for Boer elites, but also the erosion of the traditional Boer way of life.[6] Supported by the colonial secretary Joseph Chamberlain in London, Milner had been working since February 1898 toward the "great day of reckoning,"[7] when the Transvaal would either have to give in to British demands or else go to war. After Great Britain mobilized its troops in South Africa and called for reinforcements from England in the fall of 1899, the two Boer republics issued a joint ultimatum, demanding that all British forces pull back from the borders of the Boer republics. Although the Orange Free State had not been a direct participant in the previous disputes, it now unambiguously took the side of its ally. And when Great Britain allowed the deadline to pass without removing its troops, the Boer commandos launched a joint attack on 11 October 1899.[8]

The origins of the South African War have been debated intensely throughout the past century. While John A. Hobson argued that the war was primarily waged to serve the interests of the gold industry, Leo Amery emphasized the political, rather than economic, character of the conflict between Great Britain and the Transvaal.[9] Building upon these two interpretations, which had already been formulated by the year 1900, scholars have since drawn a much more differentiated picture of the war's origins, taking into consideration economic, political, as well as strategic interests.[10] A dominant assessment is that Great Britain bore the chief responsibility for the war,[11] with particular emphasis on the individual roles of Chamberlain and (especially) Milner.[12]

Contemporaries quickly realized that the South African War was in no way the short "tea time war" that the British had expected would end before Christmas. Quite to the contrary—the conflict developed into the largest and most expensive war that Great Britain waged between the Napoleonic Wars and World War I. Instead of three to four months, the war lasted more than two and a half years. It cost £230 million—twenty-three times more than expected. Four hundred and fifty thousand soldiers from the British Isles and other parts of the empire were deployed, twenty-two thousand of whom lost their lives. In addition, there were around thirty-four thousand Boer casualties, combatants and civilians, and more than twenty thousand Africans killed.[13]

A speedy end to the war had been predicted on the Boer side as well. A decisive opening offensive was supposed to take advantage of the Boers' temporary superiority. At the beginning of the war, the Boer republics boasted more than thirty-five thousand armed fighters, while there were only twenty-two thousand British soldiers in all of South Africa in October 1899. Immediately after the ultimatum expired, Boer commandos pushed into the territory of the Cape Colony and Natal and besieged the towns of Mafeking, Kimberley, and Ladysmith. The hope was to deal the British several decisive defeats and thereby incite rebellion in the Cape Colony, which had a white population that was two-thirds Boer. Great Britain would be brought swiftly to the negotiating table, as had occurred in the Transvaal War of 1880–81.[14]

But it was not only the uprising at the Cape that did not go as planned. The Conservative government in London had no interest in following the example that had been set by the Liberals in 1880. Instead, British Prime Minister Lord Salisbury asserted that "the real point to be made good to South Africa is that we, not the Dutch are Boss."[15] And so the British launched a counteroffensive in December 1899, bolstered by a twelve-thousand-man expedition corps under Sir Redvers Buller, who assumed the position of South African commander-in-chief.

The second phase of the war began with a series of bitter setbacks for the British.[16] During a single "Black Week," British troops were soundly defeated at Stormberg, Magersfontein, and Colenso. General Buller faced a torrent of criticism, and Lord Roberts of Kandahar was sent with reinforcements to South Africa as the region's new commander-in-chief.[17]

Frederick Sleigh Roberts was already sixty-seven years old when he accepted the post. During his forty-one years in India, he had earned his reputation as a "Victorian military hero,"[18] especially in his role as commander-in-chief during the Second Anglo-Afghan War (1878–1880), which he had ended through harsh action. Despite his age and scant experience in South Africa—he had spent no more than twenty-four hours in Cape Town—he was the logical choice to succeed Buller after the string of defeats.

In January 1900, Roberts launched the second British offensive from Cape Town, with the goal of liberating Kimberley. This succeeded on 15 February, and a few days later Roberts's army surrounded the slow-moving Boer troops near Paardeberg. General Cronjé surrendered, along with four thousand men. About the same time, Buller successfully broke through the Boer lines in Natal and freed Ladysmith from Boer siege. The tables had turned, and the war shifted to the territory of the Boer states. By mid-March, Roberts's army occupied Bloemfontein, capital of the Orange Free State. A typhoid epidemic and logistical difficulties halted the British advance for several weeks, but by June the war seemed to be drawing to a close. Roberts's forces not only liberated Mafeking, the last of the besieged cities, but also took Johannesburg—and with it, the gold mines—as well as Pretoria, capital of the South African Republic. At the end of May, Roberts announced the annexation of the Orange Free State (now the Orange River Colony), and on 1 September, the acquisition of the South African Republic (as the Transvaal Colony). In the meantime, the Boer forces retreated toward Mozambique, where Paul Kruger boarded a ship bound for Europe on 19 October.[19]

Roberts, who had been proclaiming an imminent end to the war since the capture of Pretoria, asked Lord Lansdowne, the secretary for war, for permission to leave South Africa. His request was informed not only by the belief that "the big military task was over,"[20] but also by his desire to succeed his rival, Lord Garnet Wolseley, as commander-in-chief of the forces in London after Wolseley's term ended on 31 October 1900. At the end of September, Roberts heard the good news that he would receive the top post at the War Office, and on 29 November he handed off the command in South Africa to his successor, Horatio Herbert Kitchener.[21]

The fifty-year-old Kitchener, who had come to South Africa as Roberts's chief of staff, was considered a rising star in the British military. He had made a name for himself above all in Sudan, where he had successfully crushed the "Mahdi uprising" in the Battle of Omdurman in 1898, and then demonstrated remarkable diplomatic finesse in his meeting with the French at Fashoda.[22] From North Africa, Lord Kitchener of Khartoum brought along a reputation as a brilliant organizer, which he could in no way live up to. In South Africa, he became known as "K of Chaos" instead. There he was distinguished more by his inexhaustible energy and gift for leadership, which he used to rally his men toward a single goal: attaining clear military victory.[23] Having set his sights on the post of commander-in-chief in India, Kitchener sought to put his mission in South Africa behind him as quickly as possible.[24] But even before he had accepted the command from Lord Roberts, a growing number of signs indicated that the war was in no way over, but merely entering a new phase.

After the annexation of the Orange Free State, numerous burghers[25] had surrendered in response to the proclamations of Lord Roberts, which guaranteed that they could return to their farms as long as they swore an oath of neutrality. But already in April, as Roberts's army forcibly set up camp in Bloemfontein, numerous Boers—some voluntarily, some less so—had rejoined the commandos, giving rise to circumstances that would figure prominently in the establishment of the first concentration camps. Now the commandos increasingly targeted British lines of communication.[26]

The summer of 1900 was a period of transition for Boer leadership. The old commanders, who had been chosen for top military positions largely on account of their social status, lost the conventional war when the British captured their capital cities. They were replaced by a new generation of young military talents. Louis Botha, Jan Smuts, Koos De la Rey, and Christian De Wet were all part of this new group, and they promptly pursued a different strategy: guerrilla war.[27]

This final phase of the war, and especially British actions to combat the guerrilla fighters, provide the immediate context for the establishment of the concentration camps. Without this context, the function of the camps cannot be understood. Since March 1900, Boer commandos had increasingly targeted the supply lines of the advancing British army. De Wet, in particular, repeatedly attacked and destroyed the railway lines behind Roberts's forces.[28] Once the Boers were pushed to the border of Mozambique and the last open-field battles were fought in September, the conventional phase of the war drew to a close. Boer commandos in eastern Transvaal symbolically burned their oxcarts and most of their remaining artillery; these were no longer useful in guerrilla warfare, which depended upon maneuverability and catching one's opponent by surprise.[29] Beginning in the second half of October, small groups of Boer commandos launched numerous assaults in order to demonstrate their unflagging resistance. They raided various localities in the south of the Orange River Colony, including an ambush of Kitchener's bodyguard at Kromspruit on 4 January 1901. Commandos led by Piet Kritzinger and

J. B. M. Hertzog had already succeeded in attacking the Cape Colony in December. There were numerous raids in the Transvaal as well. On 13 December, British forces conceded one of the most humiliating defeats in the entire war, as guerrilla units led by De la Rey and Christiaan Beyers overran Richard Clement's camp at Nooitgedacht.[30]

Lord Roberts responded harshly to the guerrilla tactics of the Boers. To protect the railways from attack, he forced influential Boer civilians to ride as hostages on trains.[31] Above all, he ordered retaliatory measures against the local civilian population in response to attacks on communication lines. He issued this proclamation on 16 June:

> Whereas small parties of raiders have recently been doing wanton damage to public property in the Orange River Colony and the South African Republic by destroying railway bridges and culverts and cutting telegraph wires; and whereas such damage cannot be done without the knowledge and connivance of the neighbouring inhabitants and principal civil residents in the districts concerned: Now therefore I . . . warn the said inhabitants and the principal residents that, whenever public property is destroyed or injured in the manner specified above, they will be held responsible for aiding and abetting the offenders. The houses in the vicinity of the place where the damage is done will be burnt and the principal civil residents will be made prisoners of war.[32]

Farm burning, which had begun in March 1900 following the British invasion of the Orange Free State, now became a centerpiece of British counter-guerrilla measures.[33] Not all instances were targeted retaliatory measures, as had been ordered by Roberts, and later Kitchener. Despite the commanders' repeated attempts to limit the practice, burning down all farms whose owners were away on commando became standard procedure. One reason for this was certainly that Roberts failed to take disciplinary action against non-approved burnings, even welcoming them in some cases.[34] Thus, as Spies asserts, commanding officers must have gained the impression "that farm-burning as a punishment had received their chief's stamp of approval."[35] After the war, Milner estimated that around thirty thousand houses in all were destroyed or heavily damaged, including entire villages.[36] Already in December 1901, he wrote to London that "the country surrounded by blockhouses except in the immediate proximity of railway lines is a desert."[37] Few farms anywhere in the former Boer republics survived the war unscathed. Most were presumably burned under Roberts's command in the period between September and November 1900.[38]

Beyond retaliation for attacks on British lines of communication, the destruction of farms fulfilled another strategic aim. The land was to be stripped of all means of subsistence, to prevent the Boer commandos from returning to now devastated districts. In August, Lord Roberts directed his chief of staff Kitchener to give the commanding officers the following instructions: "Whilst giving protection to loyal inhabitants in his district, the General Officer Commanding will see that the country is so denuded of forage and supplies that no means of subsistence is left for any commando attempting to make incursions."[39] This would restrict the commandos' freedom of movement, concentrating them in certain areas so they remained within the grasp of British troops.[40]

This scorched earth policy had consequences not only for Boer combatants, but especially for the civilian population, as a communication from Lieutenant-General Kelly-Kenny to Lord Roberts makes clear:

> General MacDonald refers to me for definition of the expression lay waste ... I suggest following answer ... Gather all food, wagons, Cape carts, sheep, oxen, goats, cows, calves, horses, mares, foals, forage, poultry. Destroy what you cannot eat or remove ... burn all houses and explain reason is that they have harboured enemy and not reported to British authorities as required ... The questions of how to treat women and children and what amount of food and transport to leave them will arise. As regards the first part they have forfeited all right to consideration and must now suffer for their persistently ignoring warnings against harbouring and assisting our enemy.[41]

Roberts agreed with Kelly-Kenny's directions without reservation, commenting only days later: "The more difficulty the people experience about food the sooner will the war be ended."[42] He had apparently counted on the suffering of Boer civilians as a means of exerting pressure on the commandos. If they did not surrender soon, the well-being of their families would be at risk. Or, in the more radical formulation of Major-General Hunter: "I gather Lord Roberts decides ... to use consequent starvation as a lever to bring the recalcitrant fanatics to their senses ... There now remains to the inhabitants only two alternatives, either to see their families starve and their homes laid waste or to submit."[43]

Kitchener was an even stronger advocate for clearing the land than his predecessor. In a memorandum from 7 December 1900, he explained:

> He [the Commander-in-Chief, J. K.] urges on officers commanding columns that they should fully recognize the necessity of denuding the country of supplies and livestock, in order to secure the two-fold advantage of depriving the enemy of means of subsistence and of being able to feed their own columns to the fullest extent from the country.
>
> These and not the destruction of farms and property should be the objects of all columns second only to actual defeat of the enemy in the field.[44]

In order to clear the land more thoroughly, in January 1901 Kitchener began his "drives," or "sweeps," systematically combing through individual districts to "cleanse" them of resources and people—guerrilla fighters and non-combatants alike.[45] Civilians who were removed from their farms in this way were placed in a growing number of concentration camps, which will be discussed more thoroughly in the pages to come.

Boers were not the only affected civilians. Black Africans also experienced the consequences of Roberts's and Kitchener's measures. The goal was "the removal of all men, women and children and natives from the district which the enemy's bands persistently occupy," and Kitchener added: "With regard to natives it is not intended to clear Kaffir locations, but only such kaffirs and their stock as are on Boer farms."[46] At no time was the conflict purely a "white man's war," as was often asserted by contemporary authors.[47] The African population was involved in the war in many ways: as civilians affected by British counter-guerrilla tactics, as auxiliary laborers for British and Boer troops, as armed scouts, as guards in subsequently constructed blockhouses, and in battles with Boer commandos, particularly on the borders of Swaziland, Basutoland, and "native" districts in the Cape Colony.[48]

The possibility of bringing the war to a speedy end materialized suddenly in February 1901. Kitchener—like Roberts before him—had attempted to send influential Boers into the commandos' territory to persuade them to surrender. Although this strategy yielded no immediate success (emissaries were more likely to be viewed as traitors and sentenced to death), it did lead to peace talks between the leading commanders, Kitchener and Louis Botha.[49] Thanks to the mediating efforts of Botha's wife, peace talks were held in Middelburg on 28 February. Kitchener was prepared to offer generous terms of peace, insisting only upon the annexation of the two republics as non-negotiable. High Commissioner Milner, by contrast, believed that a premature peace settlement could endanger the future of South Africa under British rule, and he fundamentally rejected any such "Kaffir bargain."[50] He particularly objected to Kitchener's plan to grant immunity to all Boers, including British subjects of the Cape Colony and Natal, who had sided with the commandos and were considered rebels by the British. The Cabinet in London agreed with Milner on this point, calling also for a guarantee of greater rights for the black African population. Negotiations finally fell apart on 16 March, largely over the question of amnesty.[51] Kitchener was beside himself and blamed Milner for the failure, accusing him of representing that "small section in both Colonies who are opposed to any conciliatory measures being taken to end the war, and I fear their influence is paramount; they want extermination, and I suppose will get it."[52] It is, however, highly questionable whether the Boer leadership would have been prepared at this point to agree to a peace that included the annexation of their republics.[53]

Kitchener was clearly frustrated by the collapse of negotiations, not least because remaining in South Africa meant that he could not accept the position he most desired, commander-in-chief in India. Facing this situation, he made several radical proposals for ending Boer resistance, including deporting all Boers who had fought in the war, along with their families, to Madagascar, Fiji, or Java.[54] Such "flashes of extremism"[55] were blocked by London, and Chamberlain remarked: "I do not blame him for these absurd proposals but they show that he was too much occupied with military matters to be able to give his mind to other things and we poor civilians have therefore to think for him."[56]

There was a warmer reception in London for a more moderate suggestion from Kitchener—the threat of deporting the republican leadership and confiscating their property. On 7 August 1901, the commander-in-chief was granted permission to issue a proclamation that ordered the surrender of all Boer commandos by 15 September. All officers and members of the government who disregarded this summons were to be permanently deported, their property confiscated and used to sustain their families in the concentration camps. The summons, which in any case did not go far enough for Kitchener, did not meet with success. Its threats were never implemented, and few Boer combatants actually surrendered.[57]

Kitchener's military measures met with greater success. Even as the Middelburg peace negotiations hung in the balance, Kitchener continued to refine his counter-guerrilla measures. The drives that had taken place since January had proven ineffective. Although Kitchener's flying columns had successfully corralled masses of civilians and their resources, the number of guerrilla fighters who were captured or killed was still too small. Boer commandos repeatedly evaded the British troops because the land was so vast.[58] Kitchener proposed to address this problem by introducing a new element into his strategy: blockhouses. Since January, these cheap structures made from earth and corrugated iron—costing just £16 each—had been built along railway lines to protect them from enemy attack. The system now underwent massive expansion. By the war's end, Kitchener had ordered the construction of more than eight thousand blockhouses, each within sight and shooting distance of the next, and connected to one another by barbed wire. These lines of blockhouses became a "guerrilla-catching net."[59] Drives were now coordinated so that the enemy commandos were pushed up against one of the blockhouse lines. Without artillery, the Boers could not destroy these defensive structures. And although De Wet did succeed in breaking through many of the lines, Kitchener's system played a key role in gradually breaking Boer resistance.[60]

Other factors also began to take effect. The widespread use of "native" troops led to enormous improvements in reconnaissance, decisively enhancing British forces' effectiveness.[61] In addition, a growing number of Boers joined the British army as scouts. By the war's end, close to 5,500 Afrikaners were fighting as "joiners" on the side of the British, whereas just 17,000 of the initial 35,000 *bittereinders*[62] continued to push for the independence of the annexed Boer republics. This had a palpable effect on the Boer commandos' morale. In a conflict that increasingly resembled a civil war, the commandos feared they would soon be "outnumbered by 'their own people.'"[63] Moreover, Kitchener changed his policy toward women and children in mid-December 1901. Now women and children were no longer brought to concentration camps but were instead left behind on lands that had been "cleansed" by British forces. They had to rely on the guerrilla fighters for survival, considerably hindering operations. For Pakenham, this was "perhaps the most effective of all anti-guerrilla weapons."[64]

Another wartime measure had consequences for morale. Kitchener also used blockhouses to secure "protected areas," spaces where civilian life might thrive again. Extending outward from Bloemfontein, Pretoria, and the Rand (the gold mining region around Johannesburg), these protected areas—which were actually Milner's idea—grew larger over time. By the end of October 1901, more than fourteen-thousand square miles had been secured. The first gold mines resumed operations in May 1901, and by April 1902 gold production was up to one-third of its prewar volume. This development was particularly significant for African internees in the black camps, because the reopening of the mines heightened demand for their labor. The protected areas also gave them an opportunity to cultivate large stretches of land. These events decisively altered the black camps.[65]

Although recurring setbacks in the form of Boer victories visibly frustrated the commander-in-chief through October 1901, British efforts had clearly borne fruit by the year's end. In November, Ian Hamilton was sent to South Africa as Kitchener's chief of staff, not only to support the commander-in-chief but also to report back confidentially to London on his emotional state. On 13 December, however, Kitchener declared that the Boer resistance would likely be broken by April 1902.[66] And his assertion would prove correct. In March 1902, the warring parties renewed their peace negotiations.

The deliberations of the Boer delegation quickly demonstrated that British measures had taken their toll. Although De Wet believed that continuing the guerrilla war in the former Orange Free State was still a possibility, the Transvaal commandos announced they were near defeat. Smuts, too, saw few prospects for victory. He had been on the move in the Cape Colony since October 1901, and now had around 3,300 men in the west and northwest of the colony. The uprising of Cape Boers that he had hoped for had not come to pass, and there was little hope for intervention by another European power or a change of course in London.[67] A full military victory was within reach for Great Britain, and so the Transvaal generals prevailed in their push for an immediate peace. The underlying idea, as Pakenham concisely states, was "winning the peace while they could still fight for peace."[68]

On the British side, Milner continued to hold that a negotiated peace was a mistake, particularly since an unconditional Boer surrender now seemed within reach. He wanted a clear victory, which would provide the basis for realizing his vision of a united South Africa under British leadership, and he saw the negotiations in Vereeniging as a threat to this goal.[69] Kitchener, on the other hand, feared that an unconditional surrender would effectively prolong the guerrilla war at the basest level, since not all commandos would lay down their arms. In his opinion, this could only happen with a negotiated peace.[70]

Kitchener ultimately prevailed, in part because the British public was war-weary and ready for peace, but Milner's fears were well-founded. With the signing of the Treaty of Vereeniging on 31 March 1902, the Boers lost the war but came close to their goal of winning the peace. There were three key differences with the conditions from Middelburg one year earlier—all of which favored the Boers. The annexation of the Boer republics remained, but the amnesty clause was extended to the Cape rebels, with the exception of their leaders. Financial assistance for the former republics was expanded, and the question of voting rights for "natives" was postponed until the colonies governed themselves.[71] The last of these differences meant that the British had dropped their demand for improving the status of the African population because no Boer government—as soon as it was in power—would approve voting rights for blacks and coloreds. Thus, the peace treaty not only enabled the establishment of autonomous governments for the new colonies in 1906 and the unification of South Africa in 1910; it also allowed the Boer-led union to successively reduce the rights of the black and colored populations in the Cape. The unjust system of apartheid, which was institutionalized by the Nationalists after 1948, was grounded upon developments that were set into motion by the peace treaty of 1902.[72]

The Peace of Vereeniging ended the South African War, which was fought in a colony but does not necessarily fit the label of a "colonial war." In contrast to the "savage wars of peace"[73] that Great Britain had waged to "pacify" its colonies in previous decades, the opponent in South Africa was white. Even so, parts of British society and the British military were inclined to view the Boers as racially inferior.[74] The best known expression of this sentiment came from Kitchener, who called the Boers "uncivilized Africander [sic] savages with only a thin white veneer."[75] But even Kitchener understood that when the war was over the Boers would become subjects of the British crown, part of the white population that would continue to dominate South Africa in the future.[76] The Boers were of European descent and not "natives." The two warring parties oriented themselves toward the laws and customs for war from the Hague Convention of 1899, even though in this case the agreement was not legally binding because the Boer republics were not signatories.[77] In "normal" colonial wars, by contrast, the consensus of the colonial powers was that the "customs of civilized warfare" did not apply.[78] It is possible, therefore, to view the South African War as a European war on colonial soil.[79]

Nevertheless, the conflict from 1899 to 1902 was not the "gentleman's war" that British officers, in particular, later recalled.[80] The phrase may hold a certain validity for the first months of the war, but during its guerrilla phase the two warring parties underwent rapid radicalization.[81] Pakenham writes:

> Among Kitchener's scattered mounted columns, the isolation intensified the sense of bitterness against an enemy who would not fight, or broke the rules when he did. The sight of the bodies of British scouts—mainly black or Coloured but occasionally white men—taken prisoner and then shot by the Boers, started a spiral of reprisals.[82]

Some of the irregular British colonial troops no longer took prisoners as a rule, but shot them instead.[83] On both sides, there were numerous reports about the use of dum-dum bullets. This type of munition was known for causing terrible wounds and had been banned by the Hague Convention on land warfare.[84] But above all, as Spies convincingly depicts, it was British scorched earth policy that clearly violated several points of the Hague Convention and did not fit within the scheme of a "gentleman's war."[85] The longer the South African War lasted, the more it began to take on the features of a "normal" colonial war, with a growing number of violations against the "customs of civilized warfare." It remained, however, a war between whites[86]—a key distinction with the war in German South-West Africa, which erupted less than two years later in the neighboring colony.

## The War in German South-West Africa: From Annihilation to Concentration

The war in German South-West Africa consisted of two successive conflicts that were only loosely connected with one another. I will discuss each one in turn.

### *The War with the Herero*

On 12 January 1904, the war in German South-West Africa began when the Herero rose up against German rule. The Herero were a seminomadic people, numbering around eighty thousand, who occupied the region's central high plain. The German "protectorate" (*Schutzgebiet*) in South-West Africa had been officially established in 1884. Around the turn of the century, its legitimacy rested on "treaties of protection" (*Schutzverträge*) that the long-serving governor Theodor Leutwein had signed with different indigenous peoples in the 1890s. In the early phase of colonization, the effects of German rule were minimal. The colonial "protection force" (*Schutztruppe*) consisted of twenty-one white soldiers in 1889. In 1891, there were still just 310 Germans living in the colony, who could not even begin to assert effective control over an area that was one-and-a-half times as large as their home country. The situation gradually changed with the arrival of more Europeans—settlers and traders, as well as colonial officials and military men. The first railway line from Swakopmund (the most important port) to Windhuk (the colonial capital) was completed in 1902, and by 1904 an additional line from Swakopmund to Otavi was under construction. The ownership of land and cattle steadily shifted from Herero to white hands. In 1897, a rinderpest (cattle plague) epidemic devastated the Herero economy, which was wholly oriented around cattle farming. As the Herero began to sell off parts of their "tribal lands" and herds, they were frequently swindled by unscrupulous traders.[87]

The years before the outbreak of the war were characterized not only by these ongoing transactions but also by a complete failure of justice for the African population. Most Germans felt as if they were members of a "master race," free to punish the Africans physically and to assault their women and girls. Whites seldom faced sanctions, although their behavior crassly contradicted the protection and friendship treaties that were supposed to guarantee respect for existing Herero traditions and customs. Courts usually handed down only mild punishments (when trials took place at all), even when Africans were murdered.[88]

Horst Drechsler sees the process of expropriation and the African population's utter lack of rights as key reasons for the "long-planned uprising" of the Herero.[89] His assessment contradicts the official depictions of the German General Staff, which sought to mask the Europeans' misbehavior by emphasizing the "warlike" and "freedom-loving" nature of the Herero.[90] Jan-Bart Gewald has recently argued that there was no long-planned Herero "uprising." Instead, he posits that the war was sparked by the overreaction of Germans in Okahandja—particularly the division head, Lieutenant Rolf Zürn, who wrongly interpreted the behavior of the Herero in the first days of January as preparations for an imminent attack, and ordered his troops to open fire on the Herero on 12 January.[91]

Whatever sparked the war, it caught the Germans by surprise. In early January, Governor Leutwein and much of the seven-hundred-man colonial force were in the southernmost part of the colony, attempting to put down a "revolt" of the Bondelswarts Nama. Because Hereroland was only sparsely occupied by German troops, the Herero successfully asserted their control in the first two weeks of the war. A few fortified strongholds where the Germans—settlers and military men—had retreated were the only exceptions. In this first phase of the war, the Herero plundered white farms and businesses, but they neglected to exploit their superiority in a military sense. They did not attack the strongholds where the whites had retreated, nor did they permanently destroy the railroad line between Swakopmund and Windhuk, which would have made waging war in the heart of the colony impossible for the Germans. The main telegraph line was broken, but quickly restored.[92]

In the first weeks of the war, the Herero killed around 120 Germans. Most were settlers on remote farms who were caught unaware by events and could not retreat to a protected location in time. These murders were the basis for numerous horror stories that spread like wildfire throughout Germany and the colony, demonstrating great staying power. The tenor of the reports was that all whites—men, women, and children—whom the Herero got their hands on had been brutally murdered and mutilated. In fact, with very few exceptions, only German men were killed. Samuel Maharero, Paramount Chief of the Herero, had ordered that "Englishmen, Basters, Bergdamaras, Namas, Boers," and missionaries be spared.[93] Moreover, the Herero chiefs were said to have jointly decided not to kill women and children, and there are several documented cases of Herero escorting German women to the next German outpost.[94] But the tales of horror had an enduring effect and later influenced the treatment of the Herero in the concentration camps.[95]

Until the end of the war, the call to avenge supposed atrocities, especially against women and children, remained a central motif in interactions with the Herero, long after their military defeat. The enemy had to be punished harshly, as the words of Captain Gudewill demonstrate: "The harshest punishment for the enemy is necessary as atonement for the countless, vicious murders, and as a guarantee for a peaceful future."[96]

The impression left by the horrific tales of slaughtered women and children was amplified by the traditional Herero style of fighting, as Isabel Hull describes:

> They took no prisoners. They used large knives or clubs (*kirris*) to kill wounded enemy soldiers. When they lacked bullets, they made their own out of scrap metal and glass, which left jagged, often fatal, wounds. They ritually mutilated corpses, which caused the Germans to surmise (probably incorrectly) that they had tortured the wounded. They stripped the dead of their uniforms and wore them themselves. Herero women hid in the thornbushes and encouraged their menfolk with chants, which the German soldiers found chilling and which fed the myth that Herero women participated in killing.[97]

It seems likely that stories about murdered whites and the "barbaric" Herero style of fighting reinforced the colonizers' racist stereotypes and confirmed military leaders' presumptions that they were dealing with "wild beasts," for whom the rules of "civilized warfare" did not apply. The later commander-in-chief, General Lothar von Trotha, thus asserted: "A 'humane' war cannot be waged against 'subhumans.'"[98]

German response to the outbreak of war was immediate. The colonial force's Fourth Company under Lieutenant Franke, which had been on its way south, was promptly sent back to Hereroland. Within just a few weeks, it succeeded in liberating all important sites, securing the Germans' position in the center of the colony for the time being. Support from marines on the cruiser *Habicht*, which had been off Cape Town at the beginning of January, arrived on 18 January 1904. The corps were immediately sent to the neighboring German colony to restore damaged communication lines. Governor Leutwein landed in Swakopmund on 11 February. He had swiftly made peace with the Bondelswarts, then boarded a ship in the English Cape Colony so he could return to the area of crisis as quickly as possible. Reinforcements came from the mother country in February and March: 1,576 men, 10 pieces of artillery, 6 machine guns, and 1,000 horses.[99]

These troops—around 2,500 men in all—were directed to crush the Herero. Berlin denied Leutwein any kind of negotiating authority, depriving him of the means that he had successfully used in the past to resolve all previous disputes. The leadership in Berlin pushed for a clear military victory to restore German prestige. But the German forces were not entirely prepared for this mission. The new arrivals, in particular, paid for their lack of knowledge about the land and local ways of waging war. The East Section under Major Glasenapp, comprised entirely of new arrivals, was nearly wiped out in two ambushes. Another fundamental problem was the Germans' struggle to supply their own troops in a land where everything had to be imported, then transported hundreds of kilometers without any meaningful infrastructure, in order to reach their own men. Without enough food, clean water, or medical supplies, the remainder of the East Section was overcome by a typhoid epidemic and unable to fight. The Main Section under Leutwein also struggled under considerable difficulties. After beating the main Herero force at Onganjira on 9 April, they were forced to retreat after a new skirmish at Oviumbu on 13 April. Running low on ammunition after hours of fighting, Leutwein agreed with the majority of his officers and ordered the troops back to Okahandja. This decision was incomprehensible to the leadership in Berlin.[100] The cult of the offensive defined European and especially German military doctrine, both in the colonies and on the continent.[101] Under no circumstances could an army of superior Europeans be permitted to give in to "half-naked savages." Leutwein was removed from his post as commander-in-chief and replaced by Lieutenant General Lothar von Trotha.[102]

A transition of power that had begun in the first days of the war was now complete. In early February, Kaiser Wilhelm II had already identified the war as a threat to national security, placing its resolution in the hands of the General Staff under Count Alfred von Schlieffen—thereby relieving the Imperial Colonial Office of its sole responsibility for the conflict. While still at sea on his way to the crisis area, Trotha declared martial law. This gave him decision-making authority not only in military but also political affairs. Although Leutwein kept the office of governor until the end of November 1904, he was effectively disempowered and entrusted only with administrative duties. Thus, until Trotha's dismissal in November 1905, German South-West Africa was a military dictatorship, nominally led by Chief of Staff Schlieffen in Berlin, but in practice by the colony's commander-in-chief, Lothar von Trotha.[103]

Trotha had made a name for himself as an uncompromising colonial officer in East Africa and during the Boxer Rebellion in China. The expectation in Berlin was that he would refuse to negotiate and thus end the Herero war militarily. Trotha planned a decisive battle at the Waterberg mountain, where the Herero had retreated after the skirmishes with Leutwein's forces in April. Leutwein, too, had envisioned a key battle at the Waterberg. But while Leutwein sought to deal the Herero a crippling blow in order to engage in subsequent negotiations, Trotha's aim was a battle of encirclement, à la Sedan (the decisive victory in the Franco-Prussian War of 1870/71). The opponent would be militarily "annihilated,"[104] and the defeated Herero taken prisoner.[105]

After months of preparation, when Trotha had assembled around 1,500 men in six sections around the Waterberg, the day of the battle arrived on 12 August. The German forces did succeed in defeating the Herero, but the Herero broke through the encirclement at its weakest point, in the southeast, and fled east into the Omaheke Desert. And so Trotha's plan failed. Following standard military procedure, he ordered his forces to pursue the Herero. But they had to turn back in early October because they were unable to follow the Herero far enough into the sandveld. Trotha ordered his forces to cordon off the Omaheke, and on 2 October 1904 he delivered his infamous "extermination order":

> The Herero people must leave the land. If they do not do so, I will force them with the Groot Rohr [cannon, J. K.]. Within German borders every Herero, armed or unarmed, with or without cattle, will be shot dead. I will no longer take in women and children, I will drive them back to their people or have them shot at.[106]

Today, most historians interpret General von Trotha's proclamation as an "order for genocide."[107] Because questions about the genocidal nature of the war in South-West Africa have dominated historical research of the past decades and played a central role in the discussion of the camps over the course of the war, I will consider them more closely here.

The central question of the debate is whether the annihilation of the Herero was intended by the relevant German colonial authorities. Trotha's extermination order appears to affirm this. Every Herero on German soil was supposed to be killed. And even though a subsequent order specified that "shooting at women and children is to be understood as firing over their heads, so as to force them to run away,"[108] they were being forced into the Omaheke, where they would inevitably die of thirst, or at least that is what the Germans expected.

Some scholars—for example, Brigitte Lau—have suggested that Trotha's proclamation was merely a "successful attempt at psychological warfare," and that at the time the word *Vernichtung* (usually translated as "annihilation," "extermination," or "destruction") meant "breaking the power of the enemy to resist, not killing off one by one."[109] But this interpretation falters when the extermination order is placed within the context of further statements by Trotha. On 4 October 1904, he wrote to Chief of the General Staff Alfred von Schlieffen that he believed "the nation must be destroyed as such," and that he strictly rejected a negotiated peace.[110] Just three weeks later, in a letter to Leutwein, he confirmed: "Sealing off the colony's eastern border and terrorizing every Herero who presents himself will continue, as long as I am in the land. The nation must perish. Since I failed to destroy them with guns, it must happen like this."[111] The "psychological warfare" argument is difficult to uphold within the context of this internal communication between German officials. Moreover, the word *vernichten* can hardly refer to breaking the enemy's military capabilities, since at the time of these remarks, around two months after the Battle of Waterberg, the Herero no longer posed a military threat.[112] The nation itself was the target of destruction. Trotha's classification of the conflict with the Herero as a "race war"[113] implies that, for him, it could end only with the complete eradication of the "savages" in a Social Darwinistic sense.

The perception of the conflict as a "race war" contradicts another recently formulated objection to the genocide thesis. Boris Barth has suggested that Trotha's order can also be interpreted as a call for "ethnic cleansing" rather than genocide, since the general threatened to annihilate only those Herero who did not want to leave the territory.[114] But this interpretation does not fit with the life-or-death conception of a "race war." Rather, internal communications suggest that annihilation was the primary goal. In the previously cited letter to Schlieffen, Trotha writes: "I believe that the nation must be destroyed as such, or, if this is not possible using tactical strikes, it must be expelled from the land operatively and by means of detailed actions."[115] Here, expulsion seems more like a fallback strategy if the primary goal of annihilation proved unattainable on practical grounds. It is also questionable whether the Germans actually saw the escape of the Herero as a realistic option. This would have meant crossing through the Omaheke Desert, which the German military had long considered impassable, into British-controlled Bechuanaland.[116]

Trotha's policies at the end of 1904, which were expressed most radically in the proclamation of 2 October, aimed to physically destroy the Herero.[117] However, the presumption that Trotha arrived in the colony with a set plan to exterminate the "rebels" seems less plausible. Before the Battle of Waterberg, he had ordered the construction of large detention camps in Okahandja that could hold eight thousand people, a figure that corresponded to the maximum estimates of the number of Herero fighters[118]—a clear sign that he was not thinking about extermination at this time. And during his previous colonial postings, Trotha had not been known as a proponent of total annihilation practices.[119]

A structuralist approach[120] coupling the genesis of annihilation policies with the development of the war—as persuasively presented by Isabel Hull—is much more plausible. The Battle of Waterberg was a key turning point. Despite the official spin of later military histories, the battle was not a success. The Herero fled and were not utterly defeated, as demanded by the European theory of the "decisive battle." All combatants had not been captured and compelled to surrender unconditionally.[121] The course of the fighting raised two questions: How should the war be brought to an end? And how should the battle's disappointing outcome be handled? Trotha rejected the possibility of a negotiated peace out of hand; he saw this as a sign of weakness toward the "natives" and an invitation for another "uprising" in the future. Instead, in line with contemporary military doctrine, he ordered that the fleeing Herero be pursued into the desert, in order to reengage them in battle and claim final military victory. A successful pursuit presented the opportunity not to have to concede failure at the Waterberg.

But Trotha still did not seem to intend that all Herero should be exterminated. Immediately after the Battle of Waterberg, he again expressly forbade the killing of women and children, although he ordered the execution of all armed men.[122] Even so, the killing of all captured Herero, regardless of age or sex, became the dominant practice during the pursuit. As long as the pursuit in the desert continued, it seems plausible—as Isabel Hull suggests—that the colonial force's insufficient supply of food and water precluded the taking of prisoners.[123] In addition, enormous strains—hunger, thirst, disease, fear, and disappointment at failing to defeat an "inferior" opponent—may have heightened the German soldiers' willingness to use violence.[124] On 13 September 1904, Trotha himself ordered that women and children who were asking for water should be forcibly expelled.[125] Around this time, he must have solidified his intent to end the war by wholly annihilating the Herero.[126] When the utter exhaustion of his troops forced him to call off the pursuit on 30 September, without having reengaged the Herero in a serious confrontation, the last remaining possibility for military victory was to destroy the opponent by sealing off the desert.[127] As depicted in the jargon of the official military history: "The waterless Omaheke was to complete what German weapons had begun: the annihilation of the Herero people."[128] Two days later, Trotha announced this plan in the proclamation of 2 October—the extermination order. The eradication of the Herero, which had effectively begun during the pursuit, now became official policy.

It remained so until the beginning of December 1904, when Trotha was directed by Berlin to soften his approach. His plans for annihilation were not well liked in the colony or in Berlin. And although a missionary named Elger had reported on the mood in South-West Africa after the beginning of war that "one hears, in this respect, nothing else but: 'clearing out, hanging, gunning down to the last man, no pardon,'"[129] most settlers appeared horrified when Trotha actually put these words into action. Not least, they needed the Herero as cheap labor to operate their farms, and they did not share Trotha's opinion that in a settlement colony like German South-West Africa "the European can work to sustain his family on his own."[130] Both Governor Leutwein and settlement commissioner Paul Rohrbach opposed Trotha's annihilation policy, emphasizing the grave economic consequences that the colony would suffer.[131] The Rhenish missionaries, who had been active in the area since 1842 and did not want to lose their field of work, also lobbied on behalf of the "natives."[132] And even the colonial armed force was not entirely comprised of those who called for "shooting one hundred of these beasts dead for every fallen man," or for "encircling and shooting [the Herero] with guns, until it's all over."[133] Especially the "old Africans," military men who had been in the colony for a longer time, criticized Trotha's "horrific and foolish policies" and demanded a change in strategy.[134]

Critics in Germany also voiced their concerns. Social Democratic representatives August Bebel und Georg Ledebour led the denunciation of German military atrocities in the Reichstag. Responding to letters from soldiers in the combat zone who reported that no prisoners were being taken, Bebel had already sought clarification from the Colonial Department in March 1904. If the reports were correct, Bebel argued, this kind of fighting was "not only barbaric," but "bestial."[135] After learning about the extermination order, Ledebour not only called for Trotha's dismissal, but pushed for him to account for his actions in court.[136] And the Rhenish Mission repeatedly voiced its criticism of colonial policy in Berlin.[137]

These critiques played a role in encouraging Berlin to get involved in Trotha's war plans.[138] On 23 November, Chief of Staff Schlieffen wrote a long letter to Bernhard von Bülow, the German chancellor, explaining that "the intent of General v. Trotha [the annihilation of the Herero, J. K.] is to be commended. He just does not have the power to carry it out." Although the chief of staff shared Trotha's analysis that the conflict was a "race war" that could end only with the "annihilation" of one party, he also argued that Trotha should be instructed to save the lives of those Herero who surrendered.[139] Bülow, who had become aware of the extermination order only through Schlieffen's letter, sprang to action. On 24 November, he appealed to the Kaiser and urged him to intercede. Using unusually strong language, Bülow argued that Trotha's proclamation ought to be revoked. It was "contrary to the principles of

Christianity and humanity," exceeding what was "appropriate for the demands of justice and the reestablishment of German authority." He then pointed out that "eradication" (*Ausrottung*) was infeasible, and that it would "severely impair the colony's potential for development." In addition, Trotha's order would "harm Germany's reputation among the civilized nations and feed foreign agitation against us."[140] Five days later, Wilhelm II approved the suspension of the extermination order.[141] It took until 8 December before Schlieffen and Bülow agreed on a new course of action and Trotha could be notified by telegram that "mercy should be shown toward the Herero who voluntarily surrender and ... their lives spared, with the exception of the leaders and those directly guilty."[142] The news was immediately passed on to the Herero in the field and announced to the German troops:[143] the planned mass murder of the Herero had come to an end.

The policy of mass extermination had been in place for nearly three months, from early to mid-September through early December. Why was it not stopped earlier? Did Berlin support Trotha's actions, at least for a time, thereby enabling the murder of thousands of Herero in the sandveld? There is no doubt that Schlieffen fundamentally agreed with Trotha's actions, and also that he backed them for a certain period of time. But this period of time may have been much shorter than the two months that is often presumed in the historical literature.[144] It is unclear when Schlieffen first heard about Trotha's proclamation. In the letter from 4 October that is quoted above, Trotha sent Schlieffen the proclamation and reported on his plans, but it is not clear when the letter arrived in Berlin. Given its length, and because it included at least one enclosure, it was presumably sent by ship. The letter would not have reached Berlin until six weeks later, probably in mid-November.[145] Whether Trotha also cabled the General Staff cannot be determined, because the relevant files from the General Staff were destroyed in World War II. There is no such telegram in the archives of the Imperial Colonial Office, or in the archives of the Imperial Naval Office, where the General Staff generally forwarded Trotha's telegrams. Moreover, Trotha could not have cabled Berlin at the beginning of October, because poor weather in the colony had interrupted communications for days.[146] And in his letter from 4 October, he stated that "for the time being" he had, "on his own responsibility, undertaken and executed ... a certain rigorous treatment of all parts of the nation"—which implies that to this point he had not yet informed Berlin about the extermination order.[147] Thus, if one considers the long delay in communications, there is reason to conclude that Schlieffen did not back Trotha for two months, but only for several days.

Bülow learned about Trotha's proclamation only through Schlieffen's letter on 23 November. A letter from Leutwein to Bülow that contained the text of the extermination order had been sent by ship and was still en route at the end of November.[148] Given Bülow's energetic intervention at the end of the month, he presumably would have taken action earlier, had he known about the happenings in South-West Africa. But once again, slow channels of communication hindered a speedy response.

The Kaiser's position on the extermination question cannot be determined. Drechsler has interpreted the five-day window of hesitation before Wilhelm agreed with Bülow to revoke the proclamation as quiet affirmation of Trotha's approach: "Wilhelm II was evidently reluctant to abandon Trotha's policy of annihilation."[149] By contrast, Gunter Spraul notes that on these days the Kaiser was in Upper Silesia and occupied with more urgent problems, and that he had, in any case, already lost interest in the events in South-West Africa back in April. This could explain the delayed response.[150]

Belated intervention from Berlin made the radical policy of annihilation possible in the colony, but this should not necessarily be interpreted as affirmation of Trotha's actions. Slow channels of communication between the colony and metropolis gave Trotha considerable room for maneuver. Schlieffen supported Trotha, but presumably only for a few days, because he probably did not learn about the extermination order until mid-November. Bülow vehemently opposed the mass killing. He was unable to take action sooner only because the letter from his subordinate Leutwein, which would have kept him informed about the happenings in the colony, was still en route. And whatever Wilhelm II may have thought about Trotha's policy, he did approve the intervention to change it—not right away, but soon.

It should be noted that the repeal of Trotha's proclamation also provides a powerful argument against Isabel Hull's thesis that the "final solution" in South-West Africa occurred because the constitution of Imperial Germany isolated the military from external criticism, structurally hindering opposition to internal military extremism.[151] Because this is exactly what happened. Criticism in the Reichstag and in the press prepared the way for Schlieffen, and especially Bülow, to push successfully for intervention. Checks and balances were unquestionably weaker in Germany than in more liberal neighboring states, but they were nevertheless strong enough to stop the process of annihilation.

The correction of Trotha's policy from the German capital was accompanied by another instruction that would decisively influence the course of the colony in the following years. On 11 December, the chancellor wired Trotha that "for now, the idea is not to create reservations ... for the provisional feeding and sheltering of the rest of the Herero people," as the general had presumed, "but rather, concentration camps."[152] And although the Omaheke remained cordoned off until March 1905, with patrols continuing to search the area for Herero, the fighting in the center of the colony drew to a close at the end of 1904. Until the official end of the war in 1907, the fate of the Herero would be determined by concentration camps, as we will see in the pages ahead.

## *The War with the Nama*

The situation looked quite different in the south of the colony. On 3 October 1904, the Witbooi Nama rose up under the leadership of the charismatic *kaptein*[153] Hendrik Witbooi. In years past, the influential old Witbooi leader had fought at the side of the German colonial power on multiple occasions. Now, other Nama groups—the Fransman, Red Nation, Veldschoendragers, and northern Bethanie—successively took up his call to join the "uprising." In addition, numerous Bondelswarts Nama in the Great Karas Mountains joined the "rebels" under Jacob Morenga,[154] who had not yet laid down their arms after the Bondelswarts war of 1903. Although the outbreak of the war in the south took the Germans completely by surprise, by acting quickly they were able to contain the "rebellion." The Bondelswarts in Warmbad were interned and—like the Nama groups in the north, the Topnaar and Swartboois—promptly disarmed. At the same time, by dispatching messengers quickly, the district commissioner from Keetmanshoop was able to hold off the Nama in his division from entering the war—either permanently (the southern Bethanie and Berseba), or at least for the time being (the Veldschoendragers and northern Bethanie). He was also able to warn the white settlers of the impending danger.[155] Thus, all settlers in the Keetmanshoop district managed to escape to secure locations in time to save themselves, while in the Gibeon district, around forty whites were murdered by the Witbooi in the first days of the war. Like the Herero in the north, the Nama killed only men and only Germans (with the exception of a few Boers). Women and children were spared and escorted to the vicinity of the German strongholds.[156]

    The outbreak of war in the south had not only taken the Germans by surprise; the war had apparently not been planned for long by the Witbooi, either. It is otherwise hard to explain why the Witbooi waited until October to attack—after the Herero resistance had already been broken in the north, so a large number of German soldiers were available to fight in the south—or why at the Waterberg the Witbooi had still sent an auxiliary contingent to support the Germans against the Herero.[157] As with the Herero war, the General Staff's official history sought to present the "love of freedom" and "warlike nature" of the so-called "Hottentots" as reasons for the outbreak of this subsequent war. Horst Drechsler, however, emphasizes that "systematic expropriation" and poor treatment by the colonizers played a decisive role here, too.[158] Multiple factors contributed to the "uprising." First, there was open discussion that the Nama would be next in line after the suppression of the Herero; this must have been highly unsettling for the Nama. Second, nineteen of the one hundred Nama who had fought with the German forces at the Waterberg had fled, arriving in Gibeon in mid-September and reporting to Hendrik Witbooi about the brutality of the Germans' campaign. And third, the "prophet" Skipper Stürman had come to the Witbooi from the Cape Colony in June 1904. As a representative of the "Ethiopian movement,"[159] he preached that the time had come for liberating Namaland, a message that drew the attention of Hendrik Witbooi.[160]

The Nama war differed fundamentally from the fighting in the north. The Nama were not cattle farmers like the Herero, but lived mostly from hunting, raising small animals, and scavenging root vegetables and herbs.[161] "As an itinerant people of hunters and gathers," Walter Nuhn writes, "who placed little stock in worldly goods, they waged war like they hunted wild game, the kudu, the springbok, or ostrich; they lured their opponents into an ambush that was typically shaped like a half-circle or horseshoe, almost always along a path their opponents had been driven toward because they were unfamiliar with the land. Then the Nama attacked from secure cover."[162] As experienced riders and excellent marksmen, armed mostly with modern breech-loading rifles, they waged an effective guerrilla war. In contrast to the Herero, who always sought to protect their relatively immobile cattle herds, the Nama avoided open battle. They set ambushes and confronted their opponents only when they felt they held a clear advantage. They knew how to disengage with their enemy and scatter in all directions, convening anew at a designated watering hole. They posed a constant threat to German lines of reinforcement, certainly the weakest link of the German military apparatus.[163]

For German soldiers who were unfamiliar with the land, the Nama were "more fearsome enemies ... than the Hereros," as all contemporary observers emphasized.[164] Moreover, the colonial force also suffered from a shortage of provisions in the arid south. The barren land produced nothing. Everything had to be carried in from the coast. But because there was still no railway line in the south in 1904, the undertaking was extraordinarily difficult, costly, and inefficient. Some supplies came from Lüderitzbucht, the only port in the south, and then were carried by oxcart along the Baiweg (Bay Road) to Keetmanshoop. This route went through an approximately 120-kilometer-long stretch of the Namib Desert. The entire route was 350 kilometers and so long that nearly the entire load of an ox- or donkey cart was consumed by the animals and drivers. Other supplies came from the north, via the railroad from Swakopmund to Windhuk, and then were carried on to Gibeon by oxen. This transport route was just as expensive and could only reach the northern part of Namaland. Finally, some goods were brought in via the Cape Colony. This was not only extremely costly, but at times prohibited by British authorities. Thus, the supply network for the German forces was extraordinarily precarious; on multiple occasions, all operations had to be temporarily halted because of a shortage of supplies.[165]

In order to resolve the supply problem in the south, construction on a new railway line from Lüderitzbucht to Kubub (and later, all the way to Keetmanshoop) began at the end of 1905—much too late, in the eyes of many military officials. Trotha had already called for railway construction at the end of 1904,[166] but the Reichstag had declined to approve the necessary funds. Only at the end of 1905, when rinderpest broke out along the Baiweg, did the construction of at least a partial line come to seem inevitable.[167] The extension once again sparked debate in 1906, setting the stage for the so-called "Hottentot elections." The result was a parliament that supported Germany's colonial undertakings, and it immediately approved the extension of the railroad to Keetmanshoop.[168]

Another great problem for the German counter-guerrilla fighters was the proximity of the British border. Neither the Germans nor the British were able to maintain effective control over the long frontier that stretched for hundreds of kilometers, separating South-West Africa from the Cape Colony in the south and from British Bechuanaland in the east. British territory offered a secure hinterland for the Nama—a site for relocating their *werfts*,[169] for escaping German pursuers, and also a place where cattle seized from the Germans could be traded for supplies, especially ammunition.[170] The existence of this hinterland was a key difference from the guerrilla fighting in the South African War, which otherwise largely resembled the constellation in South-West Africa. As we will see in the pages ahead, this difference was significant for the use of concentration camps as an anti-guerrilla instrument.

These circumstances allowed around 2,000 to 2,500 Nama guerrilla fighters to uphold a successful resistance effort in the colony against as many as fifteen thousand German soldiers for more than two-and-a-half years. The Nama did not fight as a unified force. There was no single leader who presided over all of the Nama communities, although Hendrik Witbooi held a certain influence beyond the Witbooi Nama because of his great prestige.[171] The Nama fought in separate groups, which were always reconfiguring. The most important of these were led by Hendrik Witbooi, Cornelius Frederiks (one of the Bethanie leaders), and Jacob Morenga.[172]

Colonel Berthold von Deimling was entrusted with the campaign in the south during the first weeks of the Nama "uprising," as Trotha was still in Hereroland. Deimling's forces attacked Hendrik Witbooi in Rietmond on 4 December, dealing the Witbooi serious losses. In order to avoid full military defeat, Hendrik's people fled in haste. They left behind a considerable amount of cattle, weapons, and ammunition, in addition to Hendrik's personal belongings and correspondence. As Horst Drechsler writes, the win would prove to be a Pyrrhic victory, as the Witbooi became more mobile without the encumbrance of their few possessions, transitioning to guerrilla warfare once and for all.[173]

Nama evasiveness meant that the German forces had to divide up and encircle their opponents in concentric operations, in order to compel them to fight. This tactic harbored significant risk, as quickly became apparent during the next confrontation with the Witbooi. In the battle of Great Nabas on 2 January 1905, the main Witbooi force of 1,200 men attacked one of the German sections that was marching in isolation. Without the help of the other German troops, the 223-man section was nearly wiped out, able to push ahead to the next watering hole only after a desperate assault. With twenty-two dead and forty-seven wounded German soldiers, the battle at Great Nabas brought the greatest German losses of the entire Nama war.[174]

The colonial forces experienced a similar fiasco while battling Morenga in March. Trotha had ordered a halt to operations because of supply difficulties, but Deimling ignored his superior and attacked Morenga in the Great Karas Mountains. Morenga responded to the three German sections' concentric approach by using his strongest force to attack the weakest German section at Auob on 10 March. It would have been wiped out had it not managed to retreat under the cover of night. Eleven soldiers were killed, and eight wounded. The section lost one-third of its fighting force. The next day, the remaining German sections did defeat Morenga's men, but succeeded only in dividing them, so that now—like the Witbooi—they operated in smaller groups that were harder to apprehend.[175]

On 21 April, Trotha took over the command in the south, after sickness compelled Deimling to return home to Germany. Only one day later, the general made the following proclamation in Gibeon to the "Hottentot people":

> The powerful, great German Kaiser wants to grant mercy to the Hottentot people, sparing the lives of those who surrender voluntarily. Only those who murdered whites at the beginning of the uprising, or who ordered others to do so, will forfeit their lives in accordance with the law. I announce this to you and say, moreover, that the few who do not submit will meet the same fate as the people of the Herero ... You should come with a white cloth on a stick, with your entire *werft*, and nothing will happen to you. You will receive work and food until the end of the war, when the great German Kaiser will make new arrangements for the territory. Anyone who believes that he will find no mercy should emigrate, because if he is seen on German territory, he will be shot at, until all are destroyed.[176]

Although Trotha threatened the Nama with destruction, referring to the fate of the Herero, the threat was only directed toward those who did not want to surrender voluntarily or who had participated in the murder of Europeans. This was an evident contrast with the extermination order against the Herero, which excluded any possibility of surrender and offered all Herero only two alternatives: death or fleeing the colonial territory. Unlike the proclamation to the Herero, this later proclamation can hardly be interpreted as an order for genocide. There was no official policy of extermination toward the Nama.

Trotha's proclamation was not a success. Its misinterpretation by colonial authorities in Warmbad resulted in the release of Bondelswarts who had been interned since the beginning of the war, and they immediately joined the guerrillas.[177] In the subsequent months of fighting, Trotha claimed few victories. Mostly inconclusive campaigns against Cornelius Frederiks (an extraordinarily flexible and agile guerrilla leader who was also the son-in-law of Hendrik Witbooi), and then against Morenga, were followed by equally fruitless peace negotiations. An unexpected victory against the Witbooi came only in October.[178] The Witbooi had escaped the German forces by retreating for several months into the Kalahari in the east of Namaland, returning to the Gibeon district in June because they faced a shortage of water. The Germans turned up the pressure on the Witbooi by occupying all of the area's water sources. During a Witbooi attack on a supply wagon near Vaalgras on 29 October, a bullet hit Hendrik Witbooi in the thigh, and he died soon thereafter. The death of their *kaptein* led to the collapse of the Witbooi forces, who surrendered to the Germans in the following weeks. The Germans later brought the Witbooi to concentration camps.[179]

Hendrik's death allowed Trotha, who was under growing criticism for his unsuccessful operations in the south, to leave South-West Africa at last.[180] On 19 November 1905, he set sail for Germany from Lüderitzbucht. The military dictatorship that had existed in the colony since Trotha's arrival came to an end, and separate civilian and military spheres were restored. Dr. Friedrich von Lindequist, the former vice governor, who had also served as consul general in Cape Town, now returned to South-West Africa to become the new governor. Colonel Cai Friedrich Theodor Dame provisionally assumed the top military command.[181]

Under Dame's leadership, the Germans successfully "neutralized" their next opponent in early 1906. Because of the immense supply problems in Namaland, Cornelius Frederiks had long evaded pursuit and posed an ongoing threat to smaller supply columns and patrols. But he was under tremendous pressure by the end of January. His men surrendered in two waves, in mid-February and early March.[182]

This left the Bondelswarts under Kaptein Johannes Christian in the far south of the colony as the Germans' only major opponents. In September 1905, Christian had joined up with Morenga in the Great Karas Mountains, taking over the command of his group of mostly Bondelswarts.[183] Morenga and Christian parted ways in April 1906, and soon thereafter German forces attacked, seriously wounded, and pursued Morenga all the way to British territory, where he was taken into custody by British authorities.[184]

Colonel Deimling, who assumed the post of commander-in-chief on 23 June, now adjusted the strategy of the German forces to match the fighting style of the Bondelswarts in this "smallest of small wars."[185] As a first step, he ordered the consolidation of all German-owned livestock in well-secured locations in the quiet northern regions of Namaland. He hoped to cut off the Bondelswarts from their food supply, luring them into hopeless raids on military strongholds. He halted concentric operations, which had led to a third fiasco for the German troops in Hartebeestmund, following the skirmishes at Great Nabas and in the Karas Mountains in October 1905. Instead, he introduced flying columns that tenaciously pursued opponents as soon as they appeared in the open to attack a secure post.[186] Fresh troops relieved these columns at predetermined sites, allowing the enemy to be hunted down until the point of exhaustion.[187]

Deimling's new strategy was a success. After different German columns pursued Johannes Christian in August and killed nearly all of his men, peace negotiations with the *kaptein* began in October. The peace treaty of Ukamas/Heirachabis was signed on 23 December. The Bondelswarts gave up their weapons, but they were guaranteed freedom in certain "locations."[188] Unlike the other Nama, they were not brought to concentration camps as prisoners of war. Numerous Bondelswarts groups submitted to this treaty in the following weeks, including some who had fled to British territory and were only now returning.

And so the most important opponents of the German colonial power were defeated, and the state of war was lifted on 31 March 1907. A few smaller Nama guerrilla units remained in the field; the most significant of these groups was led by Simon Cooper. Morenga, too, resurfaced. He was freed by English authorities after the end of the war in South-West Africa, but after he made moves to resume fighting, he was apprehended on British soil in a joint German-British operation and killed in battle.[189] Cooper, who had signaled his support for peace at the beginning of 1907, retreated deep into the Kalahari even before the negotiations were over. In March 1908, he was apprehended by an expedition of camel riders but escaped soon thereafter. He later negotiated a treaty with British authorities.[190]

And so the war in South-West Africa finally came to an end. It had cost Imperial Germany 585 million marks and more than two thousand lives.[191] Estimates suggest that 66 to 80 percent of the sixty to eighty thousand Herero, and up to 50 percent of the twenty thousand Nama lost their lives in this conflict.[192] A substantial portion died in the concentration camps that will be investigated more closely in the pages ahead.

## Notes

1. For more on the prehistory of the South African War, see Iain R. Smith, *The Origins of the South African War, 1899–1902* (London, 1996), 14–37; Nasson, *South African War*, 1–5 and 21–25; and Thomas Rodney Hope Davenport and Christopher Saunders, *South Africa: A Modern History* (New York, 2000), especially 194–222.
2. Smith, *Origins*, 37–69.
3. On the Jameson Raid, see ibid., 70–104; Pakenham, *Boer War*, 1–5; and Cord Eberspächer, "'Albion zal hier dietmaal zijn Moskou vinden!': Der Burenkrieg (1899–1902)," in Klein and Schumacher, *Kolonialkriege*, 185.
4. Milner to Chamberlain (8 July 1898), quoted in Pakenham, *Boer War*, 64.
5. Smith, *Origins*, 415 and 417–23.
6. Ibid., 419 and 423.
7. Ibid., 414.
8. On the ultimatum, see ibid., 372–81; and Nasson, *South African War*, 35.
9. Smith, *Origins*, xi; and Eberspächer, "'Albion,'" 186.
10. Eberspächer, "'Albion,'" 186. On the different positions, see Hartesveldt, *The Boer War*, 2–10; and most recently, Nasson, *The War for South Africa*, 21–63.
11. Smith, *Origins*, xi.
12. Pakenham, for example, speaks of "Milner's War." See Pakenham, *Boer War*, 9–122.
13. Smith, *Origins*, 1–2. See also Pakenham, *Boer War*, 572–73; and Kessler, *Black Concentration Camps*.

14. Smith, *Origins*, 1–2. For the military side of the first phase of the war, see Pakenham, *Boer War*, 100–175.
15. Quoted in Smith, *Origins*, 2.
16. On the division of the war into different phases, see Erwin A. Schmidl, "Der Zweite Anglo-Burenkrieg 1899–1902: Ein Rückblick nach 100 Jahren," *Österreichische Militärische Zeitschrift* 38, no. 2 (2000): 180.
17. For a less critical assessment of Buller than was held by most of his contemporaries, see Pakenham, *Boer War*, xvii and 457–58.
18. Spies, *Methods of Barbarism*, 17.
19. On Roberts's offensive, see Pakenham, *Boer War*, 309–460; and Kruger, *Goodbye Dolly Gray*, 223–365. On the annexation of the Boer republics, see Spies, *Methods of Barbarism*, 55–61.
20. Milner to Roberts (21 June 1900), quoted in Spies, *Methods of Barbarism*, 179.
21. On the transition of power in British military leadership, see ibid., 179–82.
22. Spies, *Methods of Barbarism*, 18.
23. Pakenham, *Boer War*, 491–93.
24. Spies, *Methods of Barbarism*, 180–82; Pakenham, *Boer War*, 492.
25. This was the name for male citizens of the Boer republics. Between the ages of sixteen and sixty, they were required to defend their country in case of war.
26. On Roberts's proclamations, see Spies, *Methods of Barbarism*, 21–51.
27. Ian van der Waag, "Boer Generalship and the Politics of Command," *War in History* 12, no. 1 (2005): 15–43.
28. Spies, *Methods of Barbarism*, 105; Pakenham, *Boer War*, 472.
29. Schmidl, "Anglo-Burenkrieg," 184; Nasson, *South African War*, 205. On the guerrilla phase, see also Bossenbroek, *Boer War*, especially part 3.
30. Spies, *Methods of Barbarism*, 183; Pakenham, *Boer War*, 470–82 and 485–86.
31. Spies, *Methods of Barbarism*, 106–12.
32. Proclamation no. 5 of 1900 (16 June 1901), quoted in Spies, *Methods of Barbarism*, 106.
33. On early instances of farm burning, see ibid., 38–39.
34. Ibid., 124–25.
35. Ibid., 125.
36. Ibid., 124.
37. Copy of telegram from Milner to Chamberlain (16 December 1901), National Archives London (NAL), Colonial Office (CO) 417/327, p. 722.
38. Spies, *Methods of Barbarism*, 124. See also Fransjohan Pretorius, "The Fate of the Boer Women and Children," in Pretorius, *Scorched Earth*, 40.
39. Quoted in Spies, *Methods of Barbarism*, 126.
40. Ibid., 127.
41. Kelly-Kenny to Roberts (8 September 1900), quoted in ibid., 128.
42. Telegram from Roberts (13 September 1900), quoted in ibid., 128.
43. Bruce Hamilton to Roberts (29 September 1900), quoted in ibid., 129.
44. Kitchener, "Circular Memorandum, No. 27" (7 December 1900), quoted in ibid., 189.
45. On the drives, see ibid., 207 and 254; as well as Pakenham, *Boer War*, 493–94.
46. Kitchener, "Circular Memorandum to all commanding officers, No. 29" (21 December 1900), National Archives Pretoria (NAP), Provost Marshal's Office, Army Headquarters, South Africa (PMO) 70, P 29.
47. Arthur Conan Doyle, *The War in South Africa: Its Causes and Conduct* (Leipzig, 1902), 233.
48. Spies, *Methods of Barbarism*, 307–8; and Pakenham, *Boer War*, 547–48. The most important work on the participation of the black African population is Warwick, *Black People*. See also Nasson, *Abraham Esau's War*.

49. Pakenham, *Boer War*, 488; and Spies, *Methods of Barbarism*, 219–28.
50. Milner to Violet Cecil (8 March 1901), quoted in Pakenham, *Boer War*, 487.
51. Pakenham, *Boer War*, 489–91 and 499.
52. Kitchener to Brodrick (22 March 1901), quoted in ibid., 500. Particularly with respect to the concentration camps, it is often suggested that the intent of the British Empire was to exterminate the Boer population. I will explore this question in greater depth in the Chapter 2 section "Deliberate Annihilation?"
53. Pakenham, *Boer War*, 499; and Spies, *Methods of Barbarism*, 227.
54. Kitchener to Brodrick (28 June 1901), NAL, Public Record Office (PRO) 30/57/22, pp. 116–23.
55. Nasson, *South African War*, 210.
56. Chamberlain to Brodrick (20 August 1901), Cadbury Research Library Birmingham (CRLB), Joseph Chamberlain Papers (JC), 11, 8/40. On Kitchener's proposals more broadly, see Spies, *Methods of Barbarism*, 255–59; Pakenham, *Boer War*, 500; and Nasson, *South African War*, 210.
57. Spies, *Methods of Barbarism*, 255–61.
58. Pakenham, *Boer War*, 497–99.
59. Ibid., 537.
60. Ibid., 534–50; and Nasson, *South African War*, 210–12. On the different types of blockhouses, see Johan Hattingh, "The British Blockhouse System," in Pretorius, *Scorched Earth*, 226–41; and Darrell Hall, *The Hall Handbook of the Anglo Boer War* (Pietermaritzburg, 1999), 213–15.
61. Nasson, *South African War*, 210–11; and Pakenham, *Boer War*, 547–48.
62. This was the name for Boers who wanted to fight until the bitter end.
63. Nasson, *South African War*, 213–16. On broader Boer collaboration with the British, see Grundlingh, *The Dynamics of Treason*.
64. Pakenham, *Boer War*, 548.
65. Ibid., 536 and 554–55; Spies, *Methods of Barbarism*, 268–72.
66. Pakenham, *Boer War*, 534–36; Spies, *Methods of Barbarism*, 273.
67. On Smut's raid on the Cape Colony, see Pakenham, *Boer War*, 532–33 and 567–68.
68. Pakenham, *Boer War*, 568. On the Boers' situation at the beginning of 1902, 565–70. See also Nasson, *South African War*, 229–30.
69. Pakenham, *Boer War*, 551–52; Nasson, *South African War*, 230–31.
70. Nasson, *South African War*, 228 and 230–31.
71. On the conditions of the peace treaty, see Pakenham, *Boer War*, 563–64.
72. Ibid., 575–77; and Nasson, *South African War*, 284–85 and 288.
73. The expression comes from Rudyard Kipling's famous poem "The White Man's Burden." On Great Britain's many small colonial wars in the Victorian era, see Donald Featherstone, *Victorian Colonial Warfare, Africa: From the Campaigns against the Kaffirs to the South African War* (London, 1993). On the difficulties of defining an "imperial" or "colonial" war, see Dierk Walter, "Warum Kolonialkrieg?," in Klein and Schumacher, *Kolonialkriege*, 14–43, and "Imperialkriege: Begriff, Erkenntnisinteresse, Aktualität (Einleitung)," in *Imperialkriege von 1500 bis heute: Strukturen—Akteure—Lernprozesse*, ed. Tanja Bührer et al. (Paderborn, 2011), 1–29; as well as Henk L. Wesseling, "Colonial Wars: An Introduction," in *Imperialism and War: Essays on Colonial Wars in Asia and Africa*, ed. Johannes A. de Moor and Henk L. Wesseling (Leiden, 1989), 1–11.
74. Nasson, *South African War*, 241–43 and 251–53.
75. Kitchener to Brodrick (June 21, 1901), quoted in Spies, *Methods of Barbarism*, 256.
76. Surridge, "The Politics of War: Lord Kitchener and the Settlement of the South African War, 1901–1902," in Cuthbertson, Grundlingh, and Suttie, *Writing a Wider War*, especially 220–21 and 228.

77. Spies, *Methods of Barbarism*, 3–7; and Stephanus Burridge Spies, "The Hague Convention of 1899 and the Boer Republics," in Pretorius, *Scorched Earth*, 168–77.
78. See, for example, Hull, *Absolute Destruction*, 134–37 and 145–46; and Walter, "Warum Kolonialkrieg?," 35.
79. On this assessment, see Nasson, *South African War*, 283–84.
80. Pakenham, *Boer War*, 571.
81. Hartesveldt, *Boer War*, 32–33.
82. Pakenham, *Boer War*, 538.
83. Ibid., 538–39.
84. Nasson, *South African War*, 244–46.
85. Spies, *Methods of Barbarism*, 152, 296, and 324–29.
86. But not a "white man's war" in the sense of not involving Africans.
87. On the practices of the traders, see Jon M. Bridgman, *The Revolt of the Hereros* (Berkeley, 1981), 50–51. On the early years of German colonial rule in Namibia, see Bley, *Kolonialherrschaft*, 18–185; and Drechsler, *Südwestafrika*, 27–130.
88. Drechsler, *Südwestafrika*, 132–36.
89. Ibid., 131 and 143.
90. Großer Generalstab, *Die Kämpfe der deutschen Truppen in Südwestafrika* (Berlin, 1906), vol. 1, 4.
91. Gewald, *Herero Heroes*, 142–56. For a critique of this interpretation, see Eckl, *"S'ist ein übles Land hier,"* 24–28.
92. On the events in the first weeks of the war, see Hull, *Absolute Destruction*, 10–13; Bridgman, *Revolt*, 68–80; and Walter Nuhn, *Sturm über Südwest: Der Hereroaufstand von 1904—Ein düsteres Kapitel der deutschen kolonialen Vergangenheit Namibias* (Koblenz, 1989), 54–76.
93. Quoted in Drechsler, *Südwestafrika*, 144. For more on this order, see Gewald, *Herero Heroes*, 156–61.
94. Such a decision was mentioned by the Herero under-chief Daniel Kariko. See Union of South Africa, *Report on the Natives*, 57.
95. In Chapter 2, see the section "German South-West Africa: 'Pacification,' Labor, and Penal Camps."
96. Captain Gudewill to the Chief of the Admiralty Staff (4 February 1904), BA-MA, RM 3/v. 10263, p. 38, quoted in Zimmerer, "Krieg, KZ und Völkermord," 48.
97. Hull, *Absolute Destruction*, 11.
98. "Brief aus Deutsch-Südwestafrika," *Berliner Lokalanzeiger* no. 358, 2 August 1904.
99. On the reinforcements, see Bridgman, *Revolt*, 87.
100. On the course of the war before Leutwein's dismissal, see Hull, *Absolute Destruction*, 13–22; and Nuhn, *Sturm über Südwest*, 77–199.
101. Hull, *Absolute Destruction*, 22; Charles E. Callwell, *Small Wars: Their Principles and Practice* (London, 1906), 150.
102. There are contradictory reports as to whether Trotha was selected by Wilhelm II, Schlieffen, or the chief of the military cabinet, General Dietrich Graf von Hülsen-Haeseler. See Bley, *Kolonialherrschaft*, 191–92; Susanne Kuß, *Deutsches Militär auf kolonialen Kriegsschauplätzen: Eskalation und Gewalt zu Beginn des 20. Jahrhunderts* (Berlin, 2010), 83; and Paul Leutwein, *Afrikanerschicksal: Gouverneur Leutwein und seine Zeit* (Stuttgart, 1929), 139. I am grateful to Christoph Kamissek for this reference.
103. Bley, *Kolonialherrschaft*, 195–203; and Hull, *Absolute Destruction*, 12 and 24–25.
104. In the words of Captain Bayer, who was present at the Waterberg battle, "annihilation" (*Vernichtung*) in this context still meant "that not everything should be razed, but only that the resistance of the enemy must be broken so he can no longer regroup for battle." Quoted in Nuhn, *Sturm über Südwest*, 202–3 (note 1). Matthias Häußler,

too, argues in a recent article that the goal at this point was military, not genocidal, annihilation. Matthias Häußler, "From Destruction to Extermination: Genocidal Escalation in Germany's War against the Herero, 1904," *Journal of Namibian Studies* 10 (2011): 55–81, and *Der Genozid an den Herero: Krieg, Emotion und extreme Gewalt in Deutsch-Südwestafrika* (Weilerswist, 2018), 104–18.
105. On the differing visions for the Waterberg battle, see Hull, *Absolute Destruction*, 27–39; and Bley, *Kolonialherrschaft*, 202–3. Some authors believe that Trotha was already planning complete physical eradication of the Herero at Waterberg—see, for example, Drechsler, *Südwestafrika*, 157. Zimmerer argues that upon arriving in the colony, Trotha firmly intended to engage in genocidal extermination. Jürgen Zimmerer, "Annihilation in Africa: The 'Race War' in German Southwest Africa (1904–1908) and its Significance for a Global History of Genocide," *Bulletin of the German Historical Institute* 37 (2005): 53.
106. Proclamation by Lothar von Trotha (2 October 1904), Bundesarchiv Berlin-Lichterfelde (BAL), Reichskolonialamt (R 1001)/2089, p. 7.
107. Horst Gründer, *Geschichte der deutschen Kolonien* (Paderborn, 2004), 122.
108. Proclamation by Lothar von Trotha (2 October 1904), BAL, R 1001/2089, p. 7.
109. Lau, "Uncertain Certainties."
110. Lothar von Trotha to the Great General Staff (4 October 1904), BAL, R 1001/2089, pp. 5–6. Trotha underscores the need to destroy the nation three times in this letter.
111. Lothar von Trotha to Theodor Leutwein (27 October 1904), BAL, R 1001/2089, p. 29. The original German text ("Wenn es mir nicht gelang, sie durch die Geschütze zu vernichten, so muß es auf diese Weise geschehen") is sometimes interpreted in the subjunctive tense ("If I fail to destroy them with guns, it must happen like this").
112. Hull, *Absolute Destruction*, 44–45.
113. Trotha to the General Staff (4 October 1904), BAL, R 1001/2089, pp. 5–6.
114. Barth, *Genozid*, 130.
115. Trotha to the General Staff (4 October 1904), BAL, R 1001/2089, pp. 5–6. Here, the original German text ("wenn dies durch taktische Schläge nicht möglich war") is grammatically ambiguous and can also be understood in the past tense ("since this was not possible using tactical strikes").
116. Schlieffen wrote: "It was once believed that this Omaheke was a desert where people would drop like cattle, at least at the present time of year." Alfred von Schlieffen to Bernhard von Bülow (23 November 1904), BAL, R 1001/2089, pp. 3–4. For a rejection of the interpretation of these events as "ethnic cleansing," see Christoph Kamissek, "Lernorte des Völkermordes? Die Kolonialerfahrung des Generals Lothar von Trotha in Ostafrika, China und Südwestafrika (1894–1907)," (unpublished thesis, Humboldt University of Berlin, 2007), 51–53.
117. According to the criteria of most definitions of genocide, these policies were genocidal.
118. Paul Rohrbach, *Aus Südwest-Afrikas schweren Tagen: Blätter von Arbeit und Abschied* (Berlin, 1909), 167; and Hull, *Absolute Destruction*, 43.
119. Kamissek, "Lernorte des Völkermordes," 54–126. For Trotha's ideas on fighting the war, see also Häußler, who was allowed to work with the general's private papers. Häußler, *Genozid*, 154–97.
120. The binary opposition between structuralist (or functionalist) and intentionalist explanations comes from Holocaust studies. Intentionalist scholars emphasize that the intent to murder European Jews was present already in—or even before—1933, and that this intent was gradually translated into action after Hitler's seizure of power. Structuralists, by contrast, assert that a "cumulative radicalization" occurred only over the course of the war. Lower-ranking officials played a decisive role in initiating the extermination of the Jews, and thus a central order from the Führer may not have triggered the "Final Solution." For a brief summary of these positions, see

Barth, *Genozid*, 79–81. For a more thorough discussion, see Hans Mommsen, "Forschungskontroversen zum Nationalsozialismus," *Aus Politik und Zeitgeschichte* 14–15 (2007): 14–21. Structuralist and functionalist interpretations have subsequently been applied to other cases of mass murder. See, for example, Donald Bloxham, "The Armenian Genocide of 1915–1916: Cumulative Radicalization and the Development of a Destruction Policy," *Past and Present* 181, no. 1 (2003): 141–91.
121. Bley, *Kolonialherrschaft*, 202–3; Hull, *Absolute Destruction*, 42–43.
122. Hull, *Absolute Destruction*, 49.
123. Ibid., 44–55. See also Maximilian Bayer, *Mit dem Hauptquartier in Südwestafrika* (Leipzig, 1909), 179–80 and 188.
124. Hull, *Absolute Destruction*, 51, 134–37, and 143. Matthias Häußler and Trutz von Trotha have recently argued that habituation to genocidal violence came from the soldiers—in other words, "from below"—over the course of the war, reinforcing radicalization "from above" by General von Trotha. Matthias Häußler and Trutz von Trotha, "Brutalisierung 'von unten': Kleiner Krieg, Entgrenzung der Gewalt und Genozid im kolonialen Deutsch-Südwestafrika," *Mittelweg 36* 21, no. 3 (2012): 57–89.
125. Hull, *Absolute Destruction*, 53.
126. Ibid., 52. Häußler believes that this point came even later. He suggests that Trotha realized only in October/November 1904 that sealing off the Omaheke would lead to mass Herero deaths. Only then, according to Häußler, did the cordoning policy become genocidal. Trotha had previously believed that the majority of Herero were beyond his reach in British territory; the extermination order was initially an attempt to use terror ("subjugating practices of annihilation") to keep the Herero from returning to German territory. Häußler, "From Destruction to Extermination." See also Häußler, *Genozid*, chapter 4.
127. Hull, *Absolute Destruction*, 55–56.
128. Generalstab, *Kämpfe*, vol. 1, 132.
129. Ortschronik Karibib, Archives of the Evangelical Lutheran Church in the Republic of Namibia (ELCRN), V.12, p. 13.
130. Trotha's diary, quoted in Jürgen Zimmerer, *Deutsche Herrschaft über Afrikaner: Staatlicher Machtanspruch und Wirklichkeit im kolonialen Namibia* (Hamburg, 2001), 38. On the criticism from settlers, see Leutwein, *Afrikanerschicksal*, 127.
131. Rohrbach, *Aus Südwest-Afrikas schweren Tagen*, 160–61, 165, 169–70, 176–78, and 192–95; and Leutwein, *Elf Jahre Gouverneur*, 525. See also Drechsler, *Südwestafrika*, 164–65.
132. Drechsler, *Südwestafrika*, 168.
133. Quoted in ibid., 148.
134. For example, Ludwig von Estorff, *Wanderungen und Kämpfe in Südwestafrika, Ostafrika und Südafrika 1894–1910* (Wiesbaden, 1968), 116.
135. August Bebel in the Reichstag on 17 March 1904, 60th meeting, *Stenographische Berichte über die Verhandlungen des Reichstags* 1903/05, vol. 3, 1891–92.
136. Georg Ledebour in the Reichstag on 25 May 1905, 192nd meeting, *Stenographische Berichte* 1903/05, vol. 8, 6159; and Ledebour in the Reichstag on 2 December 1905, 5th meeting, *Stenographische Berichte* 1905/06, vol. 1, 92. Center Party representative Matthias Erzberger, who is often depicted in historical literature as a critic of Germany's military leadership, defended Trotha against Ledebour's attacks. Matthias Erzberger in the Reichstag on 25 May 1905, 192th meeting, *Stenographische Berichte* 1903/05, vol. 8, 6177.
137. On the broader criticism in Berlin, see Gunter Spraul, "Der 'Völkermord' an den Herero: Untersuchung zu einer neuen Kontinuitätsthese," *Geschichte in Wissenschaft und Unterricht* 12 (1988): 718–20; and Nuhn, *Sturm über Südwest*, 310–11.

138. See, for example, the telegram from Bernhard von Bülow to Kaiser Wilhelm II (6 December 1904), BAL, R 1001/2089, pp. 19–20.
139. Schlieffen to Bülow (23 November 1904), ibid., pp. 3–4.
140. Bernhard von Bülow to Kaiser Wilhelm II (24 November 1904), ibid., pp. 8–11.
141. Telegram from Schoen to the Foreign Office (29 November 1904), ibid., p. 13.
142. Telegram from the Great General Staff to Lothar von Trotha (8 December 1904), ibid., p. 48. Negotiations between Schlieffen and Bülow involved raising the bounty for Herero leaders and the role of the missions. See Hull, *Absolute Destruction*, 64–65.
143. See the telegram from Lothar von Trotha to Bernhard von Bülow (9 December 1904), BAL, R 1001/2089, p. 53; and the Kompanie Brockdorff war diary (11 December 1904), Bundesarchiv-Militärarchiv (BA-MA), Landstreitkräfte der Kaiserlichen Marine (RM 121), 435, vol. 2.
144. Spraul, "Der 'Völkermord' an den Herero," 719.
145. Hull, *Absolute Destruction*, 63, note 85.
146. Telegram from the Great General Staff to the Imperial Naval Office (3 October 1904), BA-MA, Reichsmarineamt (RM 3), 4287–92, p. 165.
147. Trotha to the General Staff (4 October 1904), BAL, R 1001/2089, pp. 5–6.
148. Theodor Leutwein to the Colonial Department (28 October 1904), ibid., 21–22. See also Hull, *Absolute Destruction*, 63.
149. Drechsler, *Südwestafrika*, 167. Bülow's memoirs also support this interpretation. Bernhard Wilhelm von Bülow, *Denkwürdigkeiten* (Berlin, 1930), vol. 2, 21.
150. Spraul, "Der 'Völkermord' an den Herero," 718–20.
151. Hull, *Absolute Destruction*, 2 and 182–93.
152. Telegram from Bernhard von Bülow to Lothar von Trotha (11 December 1904), BAL, R 1001/2089, p. 54.
153. *Kaptein* is the generally accepted title for the highest political office of the Nama.
154. Morenga, who had made a name for himself in the "Bondelswarts uprising" of 1903, was the son of a Nama father and a Herero mother.
155. On the containment of the "uprising," see Nuhn, *Feind überall*, 62–64.
156. Ibid., 64–65.
157. Ibid., 56.
158. Generalstab, *Kämpfe*, vol. 2, 1; and Drechsler, *Südwestafrika*, 177–78. "Hottentot" was the name that Germans of the time typically used for the Nama, with clearly pejorative connotations.
159. The "Ethiopian movement" was a Christian movement that coalesced in southern Africa at the end of the nineteenth century, directed against the colonial churches of the European missionaries.
160. Drechsler, *Südwestafrika*, 178–80. On the causes of the "uprising," see also Bühler, *Namaaufstand*, 157–81; and Nuhn, *Feind überall*, 56–58.
161. Nuhn, *Feind überall*, 161.
162. Ibid., 73.
163. On the fighting style of the Nama, see ibid., 73–75; and Drechsler, *Südwestafrika*, 183.
164. G. Auer, *In Südwestafrika gegen die Hereros: Nach den Kriegstagebüchern des Obermatrosen G. Auer* (Berlin, 1911), 194. See also Generalstab, *Kämpfe*, vol. 2, 185; and Berthold von Deimling, *Südwestafrika: Land und Leute – unsere Kämpfe – Wert der Kolonie: Vortrag, gehalten in einer Anzahl deutscher Städte* (Berlin, 1906), 12.
165. On the supply problems, see Nuhn, *Feind überall*, 75 and 206–10; and Bridgman, *Revolt*, 140–41.
166. Generalstab, *Kämpfe*, vol. 2, 35. See also Drechsler, *Südwestafrika*, 184.
167. On the approval of the first partial railway line, see Nuhn, *Feind überall*, 205–10.

168. After a budget amendment was rejected by the Social Democratic and (Catholic) Center party delegations, along with the Polish minority, the Kaiser dissolved the Reichstag and called for new elections. On the "Hottentot election," see Ulrich van der Heyden, "Die 'Hottentottenwahlen' von 1907," in Zimmerer and Zeller, *Völkermord in Deutsch-Südwestafrika*, 97–102.
169. *Werft* was a contemporary expression for African settlements. Here, the term refers to the family of the guerrilla fighters, along with their cattle and other possessions—in other words, all people and things belonging to the settlement.
170. Nuhn, *Feind überall*, 74, 106, and 139. For more details, see also Jonas Kreienbaum, "Guerrilla Wars and Colonial Concentration Camps: The Exceptional Case of German South West Africa (1904–1908)," *Journal of Namibian Studies* 11 (2012): 89–90.
171. Nuhn, *Feind überall*, 27.
172. The two most thorough depictions of the war (Nuhn, *Feind überall*; and Bühler, *Namaaufstand*) focus on the groups of these three leaders.
173. Drechsler, *Südwestafrika*, 183. See also Nuhn, *Feind überall*, 81–85; and Bühler, *Namaaufstand*, 226–29.
174. On the battle at Great Nabas, see Bühler, *Namaaufstand*, 230–35.
175. On the battles against Morenga, see ibid., 235–42.
176. Generalstab, *Kämpfe*, vol. 2, 186.
177. Nuhn, *Feind überall*, 127.
178. On the campaigns against Morenga and Cornelius in the first half of 1905, see Bühler, *Namaaufstand*, 245–55.
179. On Hendrik's death and the surrender of the Witbooi, see ibid., 255–70; and Nuhn, *Feind überall*, 167–80.
180. The criticism from Paul Leutwein, son of the former governor, was particularly withering. Leutwein, *Afrikanerschicksal*, 170. See also Nuhn, *Feind überall*, 175.
181. Nuhn, *Feind überall*, 176. See also Bley, *Kolonialherrschaft*, 200.
182. Bühler, *Namaaufstand*, 291–94.
183. Ibid., 270–71; and Nuhn, *Feind überall*, 156.
184. Nuhn, *Feind überall*, 220–25; and Bühler, *Namaaufstand*, 277–85.
185. BA-MA, Nachlässe (N) 559, "Von der alten in die neue Welt," Lebenserinnerungen des Generals der Infanterie Berthold von Deimling, vol. 3, 21–22.
186. On the defeat at Hartebeestmund and the problem of concentric operations, see Nuhn, *Feind überall*, 196–204.
187. Generalstab, *Kämpfe*, vol. 2, 290–91; Nuhn, *Feind überall*, 235–36; and Bühler, *Namaaufstand*, 296.
188. "Locations" were residential areas that the colonial power had granted for the Africans' use, but without rights of ownership.
189. Bühler, *Namaaufstand*, 310–17.
190. Nuhn, *Feind überall*, 185, and 254–64; and Bühler, *Namaaufstand*, 318–28.
191. Bley, *Kolonialherrschaft*, 193.
192. Such estimates can be found in Drechsler, *Südwestafrika*, 213–14; Hull, *Absolute Destruction*, 88–90; and Schaller, "Kolonialkrieg," 147. It is, however, important to recognize that these estimates are not based on verifiable or straightforward statistics. On this dilemma, see Lau, "Uncertain Certainties."

## Chapter 2

# The Purpose of the Camps

In order to understand the camps' purpose for the colonial powers, we must look carefully at the period of time when the first camps formed. The motives for constructing a camp system are important indicators of its function. But this approach alone is not sufficient. A central conclusion of the scholarship on National Socialist camps also applies to the colonial camps—all camps are not the same, and their functions can change dramatically over time.[1] Thus, the Norvals Pont and Bethulie camps differed particularly with respect to their internal functioning and day-to-day operations. And in the midst of the guerrilla war in June 1901, Norvals Pont served an altogether different purpose than after the peace settlement in June 1902. These considerations should be kept in mind as we direct our attention to the early phase of the South African camps, in the second half of 1900.

## South Africa: Refugee, Internment, and "Education" Camps

The first camps, established at the end of 1900, were officially "refugee camps," where Boers who had surrendered could voluntarily take shelter with their families.[2] Many burghers had turned themselves in after the capture of Bloemfontein. After swearing an oath of neutrality, they returned to their farms, where British authorities proved unable to control or protect them effectively. Boer commandos roamed the land and urged their former allies to return to arms, under threat of retribution if they were unwilling to do so voluntarily.[3] Protecting the surrendering Boers thus became a question of military necessity, a problem that led to the establishment of the camps.

## *Protection for Boer Refugees*

At the beginning of September 1900, Lieutenant General Sir Thomas Kelly-Kenny—who held the Bloemfontein command at this time—informed Lord Roberts that he supported the establishment of "refugee camps" in Bloemfontein and Kroonstad "for loyal farmers threatened by Boers. If you approve, I will sketch out proposals. I think although an expense and a little risky it is a necessity."[4] In his next letter, he elaborated:

> The change for the better in attitude of farmers during recent movements of enemy suggests that we should offer protection. Will provide tents and rations if required; camps under police control here and at Kroonstad. A military officer to supervize [sic] and a few farmers employed to work at it. The refugees not to be prisoners but must comply with our disciplinary and sanitary orders. Many farmers latterly came in for protection and gave valuable information. They are very tired of the constant raids of the enemy.[5]

Roberts had turned down similar plans in the past, but now he accepted the proposal and even suggested that additional camps could be built in the Transvaal.[6] An official announcement followed on 22 September: "All burghers now captured or surrendering are prisoners of war. . . But burghers who surrender voluntarily may be assured that they will not be sent out of South Africa. . . A camp for such as voluntarily surrender is being formed in Pretoria [and] at Bloemf[ontein]."[7]

In fact, it appears that the first camps already existed at this time. According to Emily Hobhouse, the first camp was established near Mafeking in July 1900;[8] a camp in Bloemfontein followed soon thereafter.[9] By the end of year, as Hobhouse reported, there were camps in Johannesburg, Standerton, Klerksdorp, Potchefstroom, Krugersdorp, Heidelberg, Vereeniging, and Irene (in the Transvaal), as well as in Heilbron, Vredefort Road, Kroonstad, and Norvals Pont (in the Orange River Colony). Camps in Pietermaritzburg and Howick (Natal) and Port Elizabeth (Cape Colony) rounded out the list.[10]

Some of these camps no longer arose under the aegis of Lord Roberts, but formed only after Lord Kitchener had relieved him as commander-in-chief in South Africa on 29 November 1900. Kitchener shared Roberts's

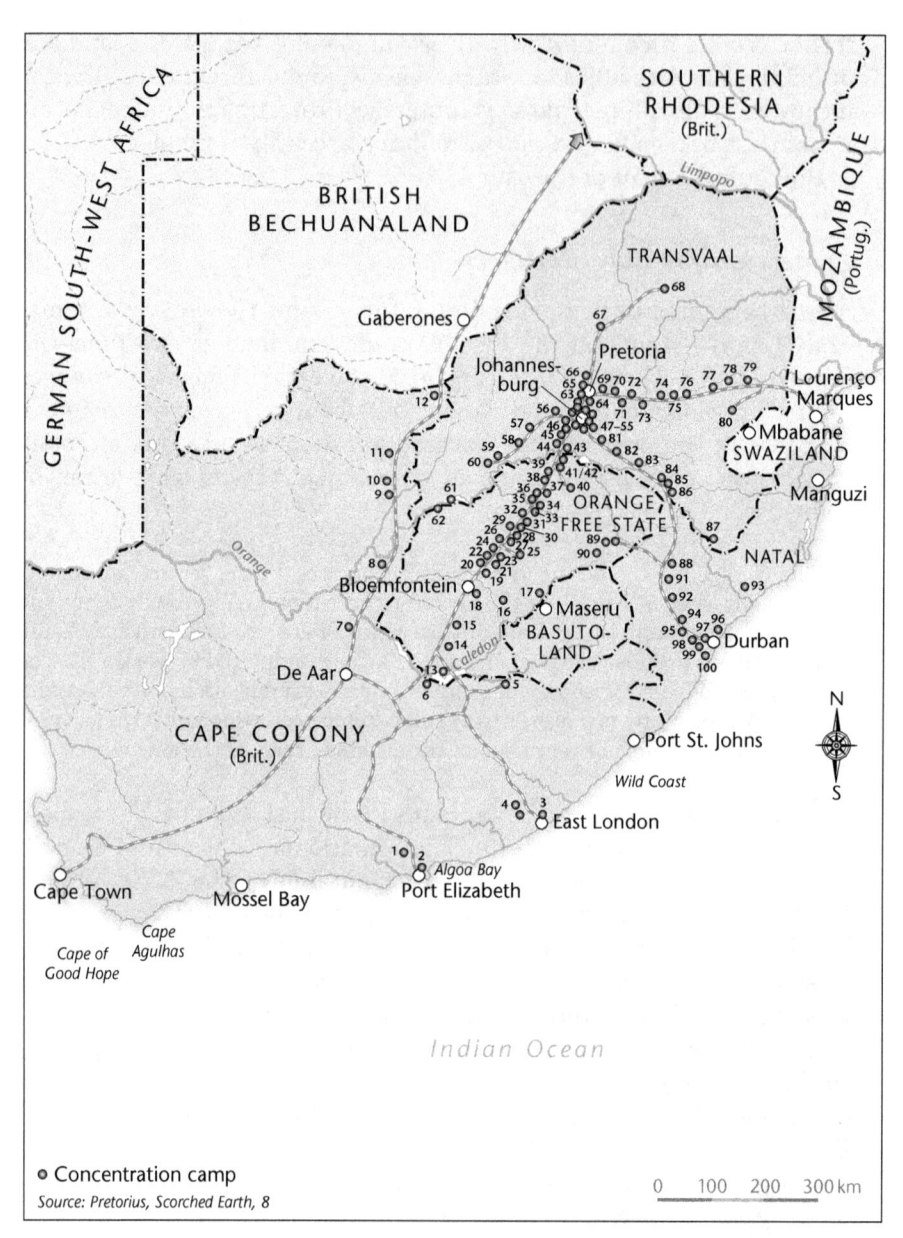

**Map 2.1.** Concentration camps in the South African War (© Peter Palm, Berlin/Germany, used with permission).

*The Purpose of the Camps*

*Key to Map 2.1*

☐ = "White" camps   ■ = "Black" camps

1. Uitenhage ☐
2. Port Elizabeth ☐
3. East London ☐
4. King William's Town/Kabusi ☐
5. Aliwal North ☐■
6. Norvals Pont ☐
7. Orange River Station ☐■
8. Kimberley ☐■
9. Taungs ■
10. Dryharts ■
11. Vryburg ☐
12. Mafeking ☐
13. Bethulie ☐
14. Springfontein ☐
15. Edenburg ■
16. Thaba 'Nchu ■
17. Ladybrand ☐
18. Bloemfontein ☐■
19. Allemans Siding ■
20. Houtenbek ■
21. Eensgevonden ■
22. Brandfort ☐■
23. Vet River ■
24. Smaldeel ■
25. Winburg ☐■
26. Welgelegen ■
27. Virginia ■
28. Rietspruit ■
29. Ventersburg Road ■
30. Holfontein ■
31. Geneva ■
32. Bosrand ■
33. America Siding ■
34. Honingspruit ■
35. Serfontein ■
36. Roodewal ■
37. Kroonstad ☐■
38. Koppies ■
39. Vredefort Road ☐■
40. Heilbron ☐■
41. Wolwehoek ■
42. Taaibosch ■
43. Vereeniging ☐■
44. Meyerton ■
45. Witkop ■
46. Kliprivier ■
47. Klipriviersberg ■
48. Natalspruit ■
49. Bezuidenhout Valley ■
50. Boksburg ■
51. Rietfontein West ■
52. Bantjes ■
53. Brakpan ■
54. Springs ■
55. Nigel ■
56. Krugersdorp ☐■
57. Frederikstad ■
58. Potchefstroom ☐■
59. Koekemoer ■
60. Klerksdorp ☐■
61. Bloemhof ☐
62. Kromellenboog ☐
63. Irene ☐
64. Olifantsfontein ■
65. Meintjeskop ☐
66. Vanderhovensdrift ☐
67. Nylstroom ☐
68. Pietersburg ☐
69. Van der Merwe Station ■
70. Elands River ■
71. Bronkhorstspruit ■
72. Wilge River ■
73. Balmoral ☐■
74. Brugspruit ■
75. Groot Olifants River ■
76. Belfast ☐■
77. Middelburg ☐■
78. Elandshoek ■
79. Nelspruit ■
80. Barberton ☐
81. Heidelberg ☐■
82. Greylingstad ■
83. Standerton ☐■
84. Platrand ■
85. Paardekop ■
86. Volksrust ☐■
87. De Jagersdrift ☐
88. Kaffirfontein ■
89. Ladysmith ☐
90. Harrismith ☐■
91. Colenso ☐
92. Mooi River ☐
93. Eshowe ☐
94. Howick ☐
95. Pietermaritzburg ☐
96. Pinetown ☐
97. Merebank ☐
98. Wentworth ☐
99. Jacobs ☐
100. Isipingo ☐

view that the camps should serve as protection for the surrendering Boers. On 9 May 1901, he wrote: "it is the only way to settle the country and enable the men to leave their comrades and come in to their families without being caught and tried for desertion."[11] In this view, the Boers were responsible for their own internment. Because Boer leaders threatened to punish all burghers (and their families) who refused to join the commandos, Kitchener informed Louis Botha, Commandant-General of the South African Republic: "I have no other course open to me, and am forced to take the very unpleasant and repugnant steps of bringing in the women and children."[12] However, internment no longer concerned only the families of those who had surrendered: "It became necessary to bring in families of men on commando to enable them to join them by surrendering."[13]

## *Combating Guerrillas*

But the camps were useful to Kitchener not only as safe havens for war-weary Boers. Additional military and strategic considerations played a role. Three weeks after assuming his high post, Kitchener instructed his commanding officers in a confidential memorandum:

> The General Commanding in Chief is desirous that all possible measures shall be taken to stop the present guerrilla warfare. Of the various measures suggested for the accomplishment of this object, one which has been strongly recommended and has lately been successfully tried on a small scale, is the removal of all men, women and children and natives from the district which the enemy's bands persistently occupy. This course has been pointed out by surrendered burghers, who are anxious to finish the war, as the most effective method of limiting the endurance of the guerrillas as the men and women left on farms, if disloyal, willingly supply burghers, if loyal, dare not refuse to do so.[14]

Thus, not only surrendering Boers, but all residents of certain areas, were to be brought to the camps.

Internment fit within the overall concept of scorched earth policy, whereby land was to be systematically cleared of all resources that might assist guerrilla units. This included removing all people who could help the Boer commandos—voluntarily or not—by relaying information, supplying food and clothing, or providing shelter. For Kitchener, every farm was "an intelligence agency and a supply depot."[15] In March 1901, he reported with satisfaction to London:

> The refugee camps for women and surrendered boers are I am sure doing good work ... The women left in farms give a complete intelligence to the

boers of all our movements and feed the commandos in their neighbourhood. When they are brought in to the railway they settle down and are quite happy they may give some intelligence but it is very little.[16]

Like Weyler in Cuba, Kitchener adopted his scorched earth policy and controls over the local population in order to render operations impossible for enemy guerrillas, robbing them of support and systematically starving them until they capitulated.[17] But this idea did not come into play only under Kitchener's command, despite enduring depictions of Kitchener as the lone "father" of the British concentration camp.[18] Already in October 1900, different district commissioners in the Orange River Colony had urged the removal of all women and children from rural areas because they were passing along information to the Boers.[19] In addition, certain districts were to be stripped of all means of sustenance.[20] And lists drawn up by the British authorities in the different concentration camps identify numerous persons with close male relatives "on commando" who were already interned under Roberts's command.[21] They had not turned themselves in willingly, and the British often considered them "undesirables."[22]

The British authorities also pointed to humanitarian motives as grounds for establishing the camps. On 2 August 1901, Colonial Secretary Chamberlain told the House of Commons that the camps were the only humane alternative to leaving women and children alone on the "desert veld."[23] And Kitchener emphasized in his letters that families who would otherwise starve should be brought to the camps.[24] Pro-British authors accepted this explanation. For Arthur Conan Doyle, internment in camps was "the most humane plan possible."[25] Doyle was less concerned about saving Boer families from starvation in districts that had been "cleared" than about protecting them against attacks by the black population.[26]

However, it is unlikely that humanitarian considerations played a decisive role in the creation of the camp system. For one, as long as there was still no systematic "clearance strategy" under Roberts's command, the British forces had taken precisely those actions that were later tarred as "inhumane." They had left families—whose houses they had burned down and whose provisions they had confiscated or destroyed—alone on the "desert veld," without worrying about their sustenance. In addition, Kitchener emphasized that the treatment of refugees and "undesirables" in the camps should not be the same:

> The women and children brought in should be camped near the railway for supply purposes, and should be divided into two categories, viz.:—1st, Refugees, and the families of neutrals, non-combatants, and surrendered bur-

ghers; 2nd, Those whose husbands, fathers, or sons are on commando. The preference in accommodation, etc, should, of course, be given to the first class.[27]

The establishment of lesser food rations for the second group was an expression of these categories. Until the different ration levels were eliminated, presumably because of critical inquiries in Parliament in March 1901, the "undesirables" received no meat, less coffee, and smaller amounts of sugar.[28] For Kitchener, the camps were an instrument of punishment that allowed harsh living conditions to be inflicted upon the families of Boer guerrilla fighters.[29] If the camps had actually been established for humanitarian reasons, this unequal treatment would not have occurred. The camps came into being as military measures in a counter-guerrilla war. Burridge Spies accurately summarizes the calculus:

> The concentration camp system inaugurated by Roberts and extended by Kitchener formed part of the strategic measures employed to end Boer resistance. The establishment of the camps enabled the authorities to clear the country of civilians—both white and black—whose presence on the farms was considered to be undesirable from a military viewpoint ... They were also created to provide surrendered burghers with a guarantee that they would be safe from being compelled to fight again by their compatriots in the field. This surety, together with the knowledge that they would not be taken away from their districts would, it was anticipated, cause more Boers to lay down their arms. An added inducement to burghers to stop fighting would be provided, it was felt, by the fact that the only way they could see their families who had been brought into the camps would be by surrendering.[30]

Thus, the camps were meant for refugees as well as for those who were involuntarily interned; in both cases, the intent was to end the guerrilla war. Within the "refugee camps," the number of those who were interned against their will soon overtook those who had come voluntarily. A glance at the camp registers confirms this. In October 1900, around sixty-two persons whose male relatives were "on commando" or prisoners of war were interned in the Bloemfontein camp. However, the clear majority—162 persons—belonged to families whose men accompanied them to the camp, and who were presumably seeking protection from the Boer commandos.[31] But already in November, still during Roberts's command, the proportions shifted. A total of 246 new arrivals belonged to families whose men accompanied them to the camp, while 331 came without men who were old enough to bear arms. These women and children usually had male relatives who were "on commando" (134) or prisoners of war (126). Some were widows or lived alone. In any case, they did not come to the camps because their men were tired of fighting and feared retribution from the guerrillas.[32] During her visit to the Kroonstad camp in February 1901, Emily Hobhouse reported that there were few "true" refugees: "As these people [true refugees, J. K.] are quite in a minority, it is wholly absurd to call the Camps by their name, 'Refugee'. . . The people who were in reality taken as prisoners of war occupy the centre and great bulk of the Camp."[33]

The military function that Roberts and Kitchener linked to the camp system is clear—the camps were supposed to help end the guerrilla war. But were they actually effective in this respect? Thomas Pakenham suggests that the opposite was true. In his view, Kitchener's final halt on the policy of concentration was one of the deciding factors that led to the hopeless military situation of the Boer commandos in early 1902. Beginning in December 1901, the commander-in-chief directed his officers not to send any more people to the concentration camps. This meant that guerrilla fighters now had to look after their own relatives, insofar as they had not already been interned by the British forces before December. In devastated areas, this became a considerable handicap for the fighters.[34] Conversely, therefore, one can argue that the camps significantly increased the resilience of the Boer commandos by freeing them of the responsibility to provide for their families.[35]

Although this argument is plausible for the early phase of the guerrilla war, Bill Nasson correctly observes that, in the long run, the camps certainly played a part in ending the war.[36] To begin, the camps were part of the British scorched earth policy that gradually wore down the Boer commandos, making it difficult for them to keep up their resistance. Anxiety about the well-being of loved ones in the camps also played a role. During the peace negotiations in Vereeniging, different delegates pointed to conditions in the camps as an urgent reason for ending the war. Schalk Burger, for example, argued:

> I say it is my holy duty to stop this struggle now that it has become hopeless, and not to allow one more man to be shot and not to allow the innocent, helpless women and children to remain any longer in their misery in the plague-stricken concentration camps.[37]

Some delegates also feared that camp life could lead to the moral degeneration of Boer women. One delegate asserted that "our female sex stands under the influence of the enemy, and is beginning to deviate from the morals of our forefathers and that deviation touches the root of our national existence."[38]

There is one fact, however, that speaks against the argument that Boer guerrillas' concern for the well-being of their interned families significantly increased their readiness for peace. By the time that peace negotiations began in Vereeniging in May 1902, the mass mortality in the camps, which had reached its peak in October 1901, was long over. The death rate in the camps was now lower than in some large European cities. Boer delegates no longer had to fear for the survival of their loved ones. But it is unclear whether they knew that conditions in the concentration camps had improved. Given the abundance of expressions of concern for the internees, it seems plausible that this was, indeed, a reason for ending the war.[39]

## Social Engineering

The concentration camps for whites had a clear military function at the time of their inception. They were part of a strategy for combating the guerrillas, which was supposed to encourage Boer combatants to lay down their weapons in exchange for protection from intimidation by their former brothers in arms. Above all, however, the camps were part of a military "clearance strategy," which sought to denude the land of all resources that could help guerrilla fighters wage war. As a military measure, the administration of the camps was initially placed in military hands. Lieutenant Colonel Flint was responsible for their overall administration, while Major Armstrong attended to their finances. Oversight of individual camps was placed in the hands of officers from the staffs of the district commissioners.[40] This changed, however, at the beginning of 1901. On 19 January, the military governor of the Transvaal, General John G. Maxwell, informed Lord Milner that "with regard to the camps . . . the Commander in Chief has put the entire responsibility on the Civil side." And so Maxwell asked the high commissioner for assistance with personnel: "Will you select for Camp Superintendents ten real good men of experience in dealing with large bodies of men from amongst the refugees waiting to come up?"[41] In the Orange River Colony, camp superintendents were coordinated by Captain Arthur Grant Trollope, chief superintendent of the refugee camps, who reported, in turn, to Hamilton Goold-Adams, the colony's deputy administrator. In the Transvaal, the director of burgher camps—first Major Goodwin, then (briefly) H. B. Papenfus, followed by W. K. Tucker in May 1901— was responsible for oversight. This general superintendent reported to Maxwell, the military governor. The camps in Natal and the Cape Colony remained, for the time being, under military administration.[42]

Different reasons were given for the reorganization. At first, it was said that Kitchener could not spare any officers to work in the camps.[43] In November 1901, Maxwell retrospectively explained that the military officers were overwhelmed by the situation in the camps: "this excellent officer [Flint, J. K.] was not able to compete with the influx of women and children and their requirements."[44] In any event, Kitchener encountered no objections from Milner with respect to the transfer of responsibilities; Milner believed that the camps were better off in the hands of civil authorities who could devote more time to their administration.[45]

As Spies notes, the reorganization of early 1901 did not place the camps completely under civil authority, so the military was not relieved of all responsibility for the camps. With respect to the camps' internal administration, the civilian superintendents were in fact accountable only to their civilian superiors. But the situation looked different outside the camp gates. Throughout the entire war, external protection remained the responsibility of military authorities, who likewise determined whether a camp should be moved and where new camps were built. The military controlled access to the camps and continued to send a growing number of civilians to them, often without informing the superintendents in advance. Kitchener was, moreover, the direct superior of General Maxwell, who oversaw the Burgher Camps Department in the Transvaal. The same was not true for Goold-Adams in the Orange River Colony—although here, too, Kitchener had the last word over the colony's administration as long as it remained at war.[46] This particularly affected the allotment of railroad transport capacity, a responsibility that the commander-in-chief reserved for himself, and which was of central importance to supplying the camps.[47]

Until mid-November 1901 Kitchener remained in the best position to control the entire camp system.[48] One reason for this was Milner's absence because of his trip to London between May and August 1901. The high commissioner, the most important civil authority in the land, could have assumed supervisory oversight, but during these months Kitchener represented the high commissioner, in addition to his responsibilities as commander-in-chief. Even after Milner's return, he and the Colonial Office remained insufficiently informed about conditions in the camps. They did receive monthly reports from Goold-Adams about the camps in the Orange River Colony, but detailed monthly accounts from the Transvaal camps went only from Maxwell to Kitchener, and then on to the War Office. For this reason, Secretary of State for War Brodrick continued to answer questions from the lower house of Parliament about the concentration camps even after 18 February, the day that the civilian superintendents assumed their duties.[49] Only in November did all parties agree to consolidate all responsibility for the camps within the Colonial Office, and Secretary Chamberlain could assure Milner: "You are now, I understand, receiving all reports relating to the refugee camps and are in a position to exercise full control of the arrangements for all camps."[50]

Thus, responsibility for the concentration camps shifted from military to civil authority in two stages—in the first months of 1901, and then in November of the same year.[51] The essential military function of the camps in the counter-guerrilla war remained in place throughout this transition, but now other functions were possible too, as will be examined below.

As high commissioner, Lord Milner had a different perspective on South Africa and the camps than the commander-in-chief. Kitchener's duties ended with the conclusion of the war, so his view of the concentration camps was limited to their military function. Milner, by contrast, had to think beyond the war and consider postwar conditions. His long-term goal was to strengthen the Anglo-Saxon element in South Africa with a settlement program that sought to funnel more British settlers into the colony. The calculus was that an anglicized South Africa, unlike one dominated by Afrikaners, would be bound firmly to the British Empire.[52] The camps presented a unique opportunity to further Milner's project of anglicization. In the camps, large numbers of the Boer population, who were otherwise scattered across the land, were directly subject to state authority. Deputy Commissioner Goold-Adams stated that "the Refugee Camps afforded such an opportunity of reaching the country children as would never occur again, and one, therefore that must not be allowed to pass unutilised."[53] Milner elaborated that the present moment was "an unequalled opportunity of teaching children English, and bringing them under influence which will promote future harmony of races."[54]

Anglicization was promoted in the schools, which were established in the different camps around the same time as the gradual transition to civilian administration. With the exception of religion, all school subjects were taught in English. Edmund Sargant, the acting director of education for the annexed Boer republics, opened the first camp school in Norvals Pont at the beginning of February 1901, and by the middle of that year there were schools in most of the camps. In early 1902, hundreds of teachers from Great Britain, Canada, Australia, and New Zealand were sent to South Africa to fill openings in different schools across the land, especially in the camps.[55] *The Times* described the responsibilities of the new educators:

> Their work will not be limited to imparting merely knowledge to Dutch children. They should realize that they have been permitted to assist, and very materially, in the cause of the Empire, and by winning with ready sympathy and tact the hearts of the people, both young and old, they will contribute as much as can the wisdom of statesmen towards securing lasting peace for South Africa.[56]

The camp schools and their promotion of the English language sought to bind the next generation of Boers more closely to the Empire, thereby fostering an enduring peace in South Africa under the British flag. The English language was also to serve as a "vehicle of progress and modernity,"[57] opening doors to the wider world and introducing children to "those ideas which belong to the civilization of the twentieth century."[58] Camp schools, and the English language in particular, were seen as "tools of modernisation," to borrow the words of Elizabeth van Heyningen.[59]

The "modernization"[60] of internee hygiene assumed particular prominence. Most of the superintendents and doctors agreed that the Boers, who were accustomed to a rural lifestyle, were deeply ignorant of all standards of personal hygiene and averse to the use of sanitary facilities. One camp doctor even asserted that "if you tried to wash them you would cause an insurrection in the Camp."[61] Emphasis on the internees' lack of cleanliness figures prominently in nearly all of the official reports from the camps, whether they were written by superintendents, doctors, or traveling inspectors. These statements must naturally be interpreted with caution. Living conditions in the camps made personal cleanliness difficult; at times no soap was available at all.[62] Given the mass mortality in the camps in 1901, many camp officials may have been tempted to downplay their own responsibility by assigning blame for the masses of deaths on the behavior of the internees. But there was an evident conflict between the expectations of camp personnel, who had been primarily socialized in industrialized Victorian society with its awareness of public health, and the traditions of Boers who were mostly raised on farms.[63] Thus many camp officials attempted to inculcate the internees with Victorian standards of hygiene, "civilizing" them according to the Victorian model and transforming them into "modern" humans of the twentieth century. A. A. Allison, superintendent of the Heidelburg camp, summarized this mission: "I have much trouble in making the people observe hygienic rules, but under the circumstances, and taking into consideration the kind of people they are, their behaviour is satisfactory, and I have hopes of teaching them to conduct themselves in a more civilised manner than they have been accustomed to."[64]

In taking over the camps, the civilian administration under Lord Milner implemented a program of social engineering that was supposed to turn unruly and "backward" Boers into anglicized, modern, and—especially—loyal subjects of the British crown.[65] Looking ahead to the postwar era and the Boers' dominant position in independent South Africa after 1910, the project of anglicization and assimilation must be deemed a failure. The assumption that camp schools would make the former Boer republics British within one generation proved "wildly overoptimistic."[66] The influence of the camp experience on hygiene and health care is also debated.[67] After the war, these "modern" practices were promoted by various organizations and journals like *Die Huisvrou* and *Die Boerevrou*, and by the 1920s they were firmly embedded within the Boer population.[68] It can hardly be determined whether or not the camps were influential in this respect.

## The Black Camps: Anti-Guerrilla Weapon and Pool of Labor

Large numbers of Africans were also interned alongside Boer civilians. Why did the British colonial power seek to concentrate these members of the population who were actually neutral? Like the camps for whites, "black camps" (as they are often identified by scholars) were initially part of the British military's strategy for combating guerrillas. On 28 August 1900, in an early proposal for establishing camps to protect the surrendering Boers, the intelligence officer H. R. Abercrombie already envisioned that this policy could be extended to "natives."[69] And in Kitchener's central memorandum from 21 December, the African population was explicitly included in the policies of "clearance" and concentration. They were to be removed, like the Boer population, from districts that were threatened by commandos. The commander-in-chief concluded: "With regard to natives, it is not intended to clear Kafir locations, but only such Kafirs and their stock as are on Boer farms."[70] This restriction was repeated in the subsequent instructions for "clearing" farms. In practice, however, large areas were "cleared" of African as well as Boer families.[71] And this often affected families who lived in African settlements, not only on Boer farms.[72] Only the larger reserves were left untouched, presumably because the British military believed they could defend themselves successfully against the incursions of Boer commandos.

At the end of September 1901, shortly after taking over the administration of the black camps, Captain G. F. de Lotbinière offered this summary of internment practice:

> I found that the Native Refugee question had become a serious matter in its development and was assuming enormous proportions: for the whole of the Transvaal and Orange River Colony were being swept by Columns with orders to bring in all Natives excepting those found in the Native Reserves near Pietersburg and along the Northern boundaries of the Transvaal and those located on the lands of the Maroka District around Thaba'Nchu (which is the great Native centre for the Orange River Colony).[73]

The goal of "clearing" the land of Africans, as with the Boers, was to cut off the commandos from all sources of sustenance. If the British military saw every Boer farm as a potential "intelligence agency" or "supply depot," they similarly worried that the dwellings of blacks could serve as "barracks" for guerrilla units. So these, too, had to be razed to the ground, and all food supplies confiscated so they would not be requisitioned by commandos.[74]

It did not matter that the African population was often hostile toward the Boers. The commandos used force, or at least the threat of force, in order to extract food and information from African settlements. The numerous raids led some Africans to leave their homes without British intervention, so they might find protection near British stations.[75] Much more often, however, Africans were driven from their homes and brought to the railroad lines by British troops systematically combing through individual districts.[76] Thus, much more than Boer civilians, the black and colored people of South Africa (who were actually neutral) found themselves caught "between the devil and the deep sea," to borrow the well-known words of Emily Hobhouse.[77]

Left alone by the railroad lines, the Africans gradually settled in groups near British military posts and the white concentration camps. By mid-1901, a mutually dependent relationship had developed between white and black camps in the Orange River Colony.[78] Africans took jobs in the Boer camps, such as cleaning the grounds and particularly the latrines, for which they received food and (increasingly) wages in return. Early on, the black camps began to be administered by superintendents of the neighboring white camps, and thus officially stood under the purview of the Department of Refugees. By June, nine black camps, which housed about 15,500 Africans, had come together in this way.[79] In the Transvaal, by contrast, there is persuasive evidence—despite the assertions of older scholarship—that no camps for blacks were officially administered by the Burgher Camps Department until mid-1901.[80] In fact, the Department was apparently not allowed to accept "refugee Kaffirs," as a telegram from Heidelburg indicates.[81] Kitchener had ordered that all male "natives" were to be turned over to the next army department, so the superintendents of the Boer camps had to appeal to the Army Labour Depot in Johannesburg if they wanted African workers. The families of the male workers were left mostly to fend for themselves and settled near the railroad lines where the British columns had brought them.[82] However, some black camps had formed in the Transvaal before mid-1901. Spies mentions Heidelburg, Standerton, Nigel, and Potchefstroom.[83] But these sites—as Kessler depicts—were not administered from the white camps, as in the neighboring colony. In Heidelburg, for example, the district commissioner oversaw the camp. In Nigel, some "native refugees" lived alongside Boer internees, but it was not an official camp and not overseen by the Burgher Camps Department.[84]

Since the beginnings of concentration for the black and colored population, the military effort to deprive Boer guerrilla fighters of all resources went hand-in-hand with an additional motive for establishing black camps—access to cheap black labor, which the military and railroad depended upon enormously during the war.[85] Just a few years later, a similar constellation played an important role in the concentration camps of South-West Africa. In his frequently cited December memorandum, Kitchener had already declared: "They [the resettled natives, J. K.] will be available for any works undertaken, for which they will receive pay at native rates."[86] In fact, nearly all African men who were able to work and were interned by the British forces soon worked for the army or in the Boer camps.[87]

When the first Witwatersrand mines resumed operations in May 1901, the economic function of the black camps became even more prominent. One year earlier, after the capture of Johannesburg, eight to nine thousand African mineworkers had entered the service of the British army and the Imperial Military Railway, but now they returned to the different mines. Kitchener ordered that the departing workers be replaced by "native refugees," and he assigned de Lotbinière "to take charge of all Native Refugees brought to the Railway Line from their Kraals by the troops, and to find employment for as many able-bodied men as possible in the various Departments of the Army."[88] De Lotbinière, a Canadian officer in the Royal Engineers, headed the newly created Department of Native Refugees, which had assumed responsibility for all resettled Africans in June. Before this point, the Africans had been mostly left to fend for themselves near the railroad lines of the Transvaal. On 1 September, responsibility for the black camps in the Orange River Colony also shifted to de Lotbinière's department.[89] The consolidation of the Department of Native Refugees in mid-1901 brought the phase of the "original black camps" (as Kessler calls them) to an end, ushering in a second phase of the concentration camps for blacks and coloreds, which was distinguished by a growing emphasis on economic concerns.[90]

Kessler, who has studied the history of the black camps most intensively to this point, disputes that economic motives played a role in the expansion of concentration policy. His thesis is that "the Department of Native Refugees, like the original black concentration camps, was part of the overall anti-guerrilla strategy of Lord Kitchener, and that these camps were formed for purely military reasons."[91] According to Kessler, replacing two thousand mineworkers in May 1901 hardly required the establishment of a Department of Native Refugees with around fifty camps.[92] The department was much more urgently needed to provide for the tens of thousands of Africans who were already displaced, and especially for those who would follow after the intensification of clearance measures in July 1901.[93]

First and foremost, the camps were part of Kitchener's counter-guerrilla strategy. But there is no plausible reason why they could not have had a dual function. Kitchener might have been able to drum up two thousand mineworkers without the help of the new department. But that was only the beginning. After one month, de Lotbinière had arranged for these workers to return to the mines—but then he had to reassign the remaining six to seven thousand African mineworkers, who had served the army and railroad since May 1900.[94] Overall, statistics from the Department of Native Refugees show that the demand for African labor was high. In many cases, more than 75 percent of all interned men were employed; most worked for the government, but others worked for private individuals or in the camps themselves. According to de Lotbinière, these were very favorable statistics: "a very fair proportion of men were kept employed, after an allowance has been made for the sick and aged, and those who were prevented from one cause or another." They were joined by numerous women and children, who likewise found employment.[95] It seems reasonable, therefore, that de Lotbinière's explanation of his department's function should not be ignored out of hand: "Our first consideration was the supply of native labourers to the Army."[96] Without the British counter-guerrilla strategy, of course, the African population presumably would not have been interned in camps, regardless of how great the army's demand for labor was. But from the very beginning, Kitchener's military scheme was associated with plans to exploit the labor of the concentrated black population. So, both motives played a role. And the economic function of the black camps became more prominent with the reopening of the first mines, the rising demand for labor, and the related establishment of the Native Refugees Department.

De Lotbinière also expected that the camps would have a positive effect on postwar South Africa. He oversaw a far-reaching change to the black camps shortly after his department was established; this will be examined more closely in the pages ahead. The very large camps, mostly in the Orange River Colony, were dissolved, and the residents were sent to much smaller camps along the railroad lines. By the end of the war, there were more than seventy black camps in the new colonies.[97] The internees—mostly women, children, and old men because nearly all younger men who were fit to work had found employment elsewhere—were now expected to farm the land, so they would be able to support themselves in the future. Contemporary imperial ideology held that this was very important so the "natives" would not grow lazy by receiving free food and shelter and subsequently relapse into poverty. De Lotbinière described the "problem" as follows:

> The native character required some such treatment, for it would be wrong and inadvisable to feed them gratis for nearly two years, when their natural instincts and habits lead them to cultivate their own food requirements which occupation comes as second nature, and in so doing they would improve instead of deteriorate physically and morally if fed free.[98]

Maintaining the labor force of the concentrated black and colored population was also of great importance to the colonial power. Many of the internees had come from white farms, where their labor would be needed again after the war's end. In this respect, the Native Refugee Department saw them as an economic asset: "our aim having been from the beginning to look upon the natives as an asset of the farming industry, and to preserve them as far as possible for this industry."[99] The department worked not only to maintain the black and colored internees' fitness for labor (a mixed success at best, given camp mortality rates), but also to redistribute them among white farmers after the war. This frustrated those Africans who had hoped to receive allotments of land that they could farm on their own—particularly after Chamberlain's lofty promise that Great Britain was also waging war to improve the situation of the "native races."[100] Moreover, the British wanted to prevent former "farm hands"[101] from migrating to the cities after the war. Instead, in postwar society Africans were to return to the place that they had already occupied before the war—as cheap labor in the service of white farmers.

Here, too, one can speak of a kind of social engineering. With respect to the black camps, this did not mean altering the population in a deliberate way, but rather conserving existing conditions. The undertaking involved change in only one respect. As part of the imperial project of anglicization, British farmers who resettled in South Africa after the war's end were to be accommodated wherever possible. This meant that black workers were to be transferred from Boer to British farms.[102] De Lotbinière did, however, later concede that while his department had succeeded in preserving "native farm labourers" in the Transvaal, taking care of the new settlers was not always possible.[103]

## *Deliberate Annihilation?*

The Boer camps have been ascribed another purpose, particularly in the popular memory of the Afrikaner population—the purpose of annihilation. In her 1901 report, Emily Hobhouse had already warned that "to keep these Camps going is murder to the children."[104] The political opposition in England also drew from this topos. The Welsh member of Parliament, Lloyd George, for example, compared the actions of the British army with those of King Herod, who had tried "to crush a little race by killing its young sons and daughters."[105] In the book *Should We Forget?*, published shortly after the war, the Boer author Elizabeth Neethling spoke of the "extermination camp of Volksrust."[106] And by the 1930s, the myths of glass or poison in the camps' sugar rations had been firmly lodged in the collective memory of the Afrikaners.[107] The international press also depicted the camps as sites where Boers were deliberately annihilated. The *Alldeutsche Blätter*, for example, opined that Great Britain "intended to eradicate the Boer people." Boer women and children had been interned in concentration camps so they would "slowly starve and die of other diseases."[108]

The high mortality in the camps appears to support the thesis that one purpose of the camps was annihilation. Shortly after the war, P. L. A. Goldman attempted to calculate the precise number of whites who died in the camps. His tally of 27,927 casualties, including around 22,000 children under the age of sixteen and more than 4,000 women, is the figure most frequently cited in historical literature. More recently, some historians have questioned Goldman's methods of calculation, which may have counted some deaths twice. Elizabeth van Heyningen has lowered the estimated number of deaths to around 25,000.[109] Other scholars, by contrast, maintain that Goldman's estimate was too low. Stowell Kessler, for example, argues that camp records were not always kept in an orderly way, particularly in the periods of the highest mortality, so not all deaths are included in the official statistics. The significant number of deaths that occurred en route from the farms to the camps must also be considered. And no death statistics exist from the period of military administration, between September 1900 and February or March 1901. Thus, Kessler concludes that mortality in the white camps must have been significantly higher than the figure calculated by Goldman.[110]

Such scholarly disputes aside, a comparatively rich source base allows us to estimate the number of deaths with considerable certainty at a value between 25,000 and 30,000. A comparable empirically based estimate is not possible for any of the other cases in this study. Definitive statements about the overall mortality of the black camps in the South African War are much harder to make. Peter Warwick has drawn from various archival sources to document 14,154 deaths in the black camps.[111] Kessler uncovered further evidence and includes 21,042 people in his extensively researched list of deceased persons.[112] Given the numerous gaps in documentation, however, mortality in the black camps was probably much higher, likely reaching proportions comparable to the Boer camps.[113]

If we accept that during the war around 140,000 whites and 140,000 blacks were interned in different camps,[114] the aforementioned figures suggest an approximate overall mortality rate of 18 to 21 percent over the entire existence of the camps. Particularly during the period of the greatest mortality in the second half of 1901, contemporary observers could have easily developed the impression that all internees would soon perish. In October, the monthly death rates in the white camps reached nearly 3 percent. Extrapolated for the entire year, this would be a death rate of more than 34 percent, and in the Orange River Colony, nearly 41 percent.[115] In some camps, the internees would have died out within a year had the mortality continued unabated; in Mafeking, the death rate in October was 8.5 percent.[116] In Brandfort, the October death rate reached 9.6 percent.[117] If the pace of deaths had held constant, the Brandfort internees would have died out altogether in just ten months. Mortality in the black camps did not peak until two months later. In December 1901, it reached 38 percent, well above the highest value for the Boer camps.[118]

Despite this extreme mortality, there is no documentary evidence that could plausibly suggest that the goal of leading British authorities was the annihilation of the camp internees. It was clear from the outset that both the Boer and the black and colored population would remain part of South Africa after the war. Even Kitchener's idea (as radical as it was unrealistic) for resettling recalcitrant Boers and their families in Fiji or Madagascar was not a program for physical destruction. And the plan was, in any case, rejected as nonsensical in London. The mortality in the camps is better explained by factors such as disinterest or logistical difficulties, not as deliberate murder by neglect, as will be shown in greater detail in the pages ahead.

The annihilation thesis is even more untenable when one considers the reactions of the civil authorities at the end of 1901. After Emily Hobhouse had stirred up the British public with her reports from the South African camps in the middle of the year, and a measles epidemic raised mortality to unprecedented heights in October, Milner and Chamberlain were alarmed. Communications between the high commissioner and the colonial secretary indicate a firm resolve to reduce the masses of deaths in the Boer camps with all available means.[119] This resolve was expressed by directions like the following to the responsible parties on the spot: "I can only urge you to cram into the camps as fast as possible, and damning the cost, whatever is possibly wanted either to improve hospital accommodation or the comforts for the sick or to raise the general health of the inmates."[120] Plans for annihilating camp internees sound different.

## *Repatriation*

With the end of the war on 31 May 1902, the main function of the camps for both whites and blacks became obsolete. The camps had fulfilled their purpose as counter-guerrilla measures. But some of the camps remained in existence until the beginning of 1903. They became key instruments of repatriation for members of the population who had been driven from their homes, deported as prisoners of war, or sent to distant regions as combatants. It is telling that this functional transformation was also accompanied by a change in how the camps were financed. After some initial disputes, the cost of the camps had been covered by the military, but after 1 January 1903 the financial burden shifted to civil authorities.[121] The black camps were initially funded and administered by the military, but immediately after the war's end they were taken over by the civilian administration, which oversaw repatriation.[122]

First, the camps served as sites of reunification for families who had been separated. The burghers who surrendered at the war's end went to camps where their families were detained. This was also true for many of the thirty-three thousand or more prisoners of war, many of whom had been sent overseas[123] and could return to South Africa only after some delay. Wherever possible, all internees were transferred to the camps that were closest to their original place of residence.[124]

Depots were established in the white camps to provide families with the essentials they needed to return to their farms; a tent, bedding, and one month's food rations were provided at no cost.[125] In addition, families had the opportunity to purchase further supplies at reasonable prices.[126] In some places, garages were set up to repair vehicles that were urgently needed for transporting internees back to their original places of residence.[127]

Those who could provide for themselves and their families without much additional government support were the first to leave the camps. Others had to wait until the necessary preparations could be made for repatriation. Unlike during the war, however, the administration no longer held them against their will in the camps. Burghers who were fit for work, but without farmland, were ultimately resettled with their families in Burgher Land Settlements (Transvaal), where land was made available to cultivate, or else they were hired by relief works that gave them a source of income (Orange River Colony).[128]

In this way, the number of camp internees shrank quite rapidly. Of the nearly seventy thousand Transvaalers who were living in concentration camps in Natal and the Transvaal at the end of the war, only twenty thousand remained at the end of October. By the beginning of 1903, the number of internees in the Transvaal camps had dropped to 1,452, while the camps in Natal were practically empty. The administration transferred the Natal internees back to camps in the Transvaal, so they could then return to their homes. By the beginning of January, only five camps remained in the Transvaal (one for every district), where stragglers were still housed for several more weeks. Finally, on 7 February, the last internees left these temporary residences.[129] The repatriation process proceeded similarly for internees in the camps of the Orange River Colony and the Cape Colony. Of the just under 40,000 internees at the war's end, only 11,800 remained at the end of October, even counting the more than 8,500 prisoners of war who temporarily passed through the camps.[130] By the beginning of 1903, there were just 1,866 internees, and after mid-January only two camps remained in operation.[131] Camp administrators mostly auctioned off or sold the shuttered camps' inventory.[132] Brandfort, the last concentration camp of the South African War, closed at the end of March 1903.[133]

A similar functional transformation occurred with the black camps after the end of the war. The men, who had been primarily employed by the army, were immediately sent back to the camps so they could be repatriated together with their families, which led to a temporary rise in the camp population.[134] And so the black camps not only lost their military purpose in the counter-guerrilla war, but also their second function, as a source of labor for the British army. Instead, the 115,000[135] Africans in the camps of the two new colonies were supposed to return as quickly as possible to the farms of the white population. This would provide whites, who were returning back home, with an urgently needed workforce to restore agricultural production. It was also hoped that quickly repatriated blacks would be able to cultivate their own fields in the coming season (beginning in September), thereby freeing them from government assistance as soon as possible. To this end, they were given a modest amount of seeds for planting and agricultural equipment at no cost.[136]

At first the repatriation process proceeded slowly, and only a few hundred "native refugees" were released from the camps in the first two postwar months. The pace of repatriation picked up only after a larger number of Boer farms had been reoccupied. Another important factor was the liberalization of redistribution procedures. Farmers initially had to apply to camp administrators for the transfer of African workers, but soon employers and employees were allowed to negotiate for themselves. African families were not compelled to return to their old employers, although many did. Those who had sympathized with Great Britain during the war often preferred to work for British settlers or authorities. As de Lotbinière intended, however, they were not supposed to exit the camps permanently without arrangements to work for whites.[137]

The exodus from the camps picked up speed in August. At the end of October, there were only 3,800 blacks in the camps in the Transvaal, and 23,583 in the Orange River Colony.[138] One month later, the authorities closed all of the black camps in the Transvaal. In the Orange River Colony, the process effectively came to an end by the end of January 1903. Only seventy-seven persons, who were old and sick, were not yet repatriated.[139]

## *Periodization of the History of the Camps*

A rough periodization of the history of the South African concentration camps is possible based on the camps' evolving functions and broader organizational changes. The following four phases can be distinguished for the Boer camps.

**First phase—Mid-1900 to February/March 1901.** During this period the military established and administered the first camps for Boers. The function of these early camps was purely military. Commanders-in-Chief Roberts and Kitchener hoped that large numbers of war-weary Boers would surrender if they and their families could find protection in concentration camps from the vengeance of Boer commandos. Above all, military leaders expected that clearing large swathes of land and interning residents would deprive guerrilla units of sustenance and compel them to surrender.

**Second phase—February/March to October 1901.** Civilian superintendents assumed control of individual camps, but control over the entire camp systems was not yet transferred to civil authorities (Milner and the Colonial Office) in a systematic way. The Boer camps simultaneously assumed a secondary function. From this point forward, they also served as instruments of social engineering, a means of teaching internees how to become "modern," anglophile subjects of the British Empire. During this phase, the number of internees skyrocketed—from 32,234 in the Transvaal and Orange River Colony in March, to 99,529 at the end of July.[140] Measles and other epidemics spread, and mortality rose to new heights. Emily Hobhouse informed the British public about the catastrophic situation in the camps, but efforts to combat these conditions were partial at best.

**Third phase—November 1901 to May 1902.** Milner and Chamberlain now assumed control over the entire camp systems. This transition did not change the function of the camps, but it improved their conditions decisively. There were hardly any new admissions, internee numbers remained constant, and mortality fell significantly by the beginning of 1902.

**Fourth phase—June 1902 to March 1903.** With the end of the war on 31 May 1902, the concentration camps lost their main military function. Until the last camps closed in early 1903, they became repatriation centers where families were reunited, outfitted with necessary supplies, and sent back to their farms.

Periodization for the African camps is more difficult because of insufficient sources. Only the following three phases can be reasonably distinguished.

**First phase—End of 1900 to Mid-1901.** British forces combating guerrillas also "cleared" the land of the African population and brought the deportees to railroad lines. It was here that unofficial black camps formed, usually in the vicinity of British military posts and white concentration camps. In the Orange River Colony, these unofficial camps were soon taken over by the superintendents of the Boer camps. Alongside the "original" black camps' military function, which was part of British scorched earth policy, the interned black population was quickly put to work by the military and in neighboring Boer camps.

**Second phase—Mid-1901 to May 1902.** The military's Department of Native Refugees took over all black camps, leading to the formation of numerous "official" concentration camps for Africans in the Transvaal. The economic function of the camps gained importance. The department systematically sent the men off to work as wage earners, dissolving the large camps and redistributing the women, children, and adults over the age of seventy to smaller camps, where they worked the land. Major de Lotbinière, who oversaw these changes, promised to protect the black population from pauperization while preserving their availability to work on the farms of white settlers after the war. This was the third function of the black camps. As in the Boer camps, the number of internees and the rate of deaths climbed dramatically through the end of 1901. But in contrast to the white camps, the mortality crisis did not lead to comparable improvements in camp conditions.

**Third phase—June 1902 to the beginning of 1903.** With the end of the war, the black camps not only lost their primary military function, but also their secondary economic one. The military immediately transferred employed black workers back to the camps, which now served (like the white camps) as centers of repatriation. Many of the motives for establishing the South African camps—combating guerrillas, social engineering, punishment, procurement of labor, and, finally, repatriation—soon reappeared with differing emphases in the neighboring colony.

## German South-West Africa: "Pacification," Labor, and Penal Camps

Less than two years after the last concentration camps closed in South Africa, institutions by the same name were established in the neighboring German colony. Did the German colonial power pursue the same goals as Great Britain during the South African War? In the previous section, I dispelled the interpretation of the South African camps as instruments for deliberately annihilating the interned population. This interpretation has, however, come to dominate research on the camps in German South-West Africa. According to this view, mass death in the camps was the logical continuation of the genocidal annihilation of the Herero in the Omaheke, as infamously depicted in General Lothar von Trotha's proclamation of 2 October 1904.[141] Some authors even speak of "extermination camps."[142] Given the dominance of this argument, I will begin by examining the plausibility of such an assessment.

### *The Dimensions of Mass Death: Deliberate Annihilation?*

The number of deaths certainly encourages this kind of interpretation. Statistics from the command of the colonial forces indicate that overall mortality in the South-West African camps between October 1904 and March 1907 was 45.2 percent; among a total of 15,000 interned Herero and 2,000 Nama, there were apparently 7,682 deaths.[143] But these figures cannot be correct. The number of Herero and Nama who became prisoners of war—a category that includes men, women, and children—must have been significantly higher. After the end of 1904, once Berlin had directed Trotha to grant mercy to surrendering Herero, those who

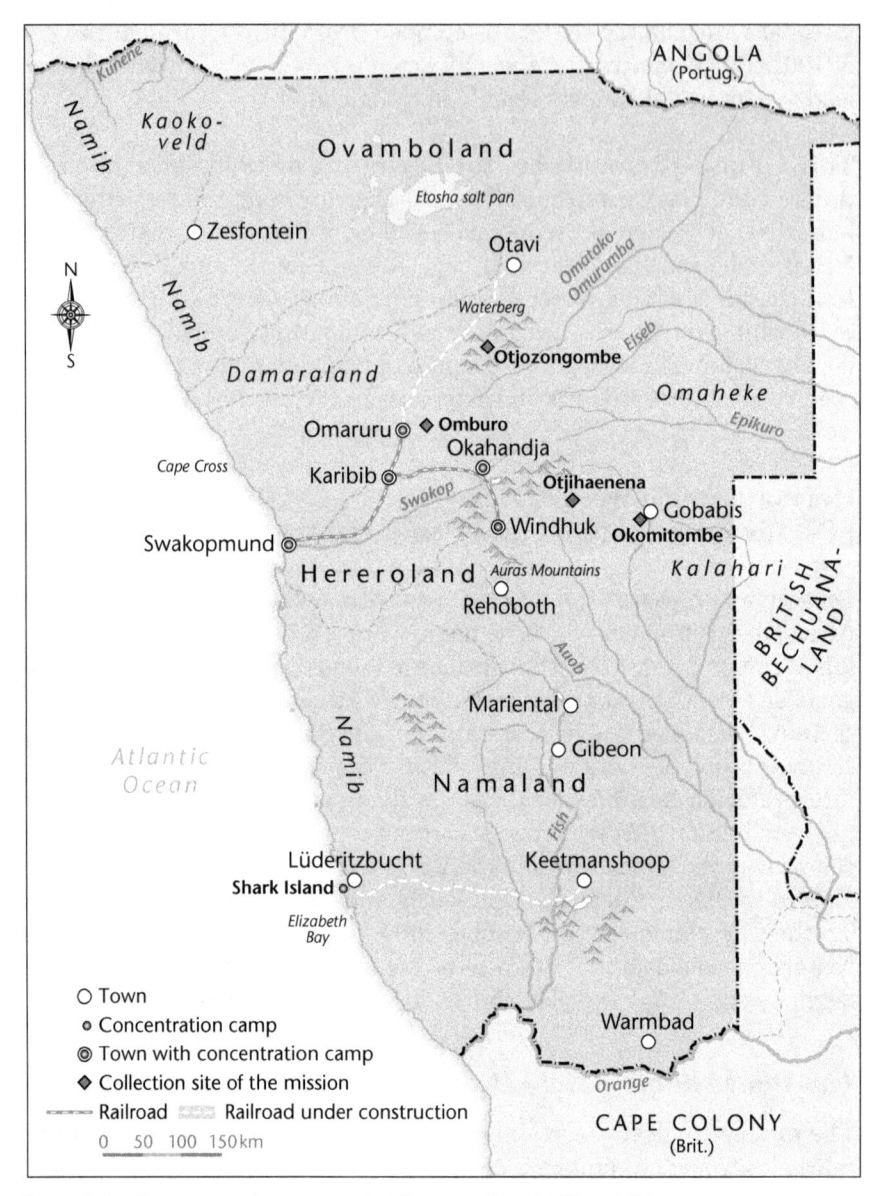

**Map 2.2.** Concentration camps in German South-West Africa
(© Peter Palm, Berlin/Germany, used with permission).

turned themselves in were interned in newly established concentration camps. By the time that the civilian governor Lindequist replaced Trotha as the colony's top leader in mid-November 1905, the number of captured Herero had already climbed to more than eight thousand.[144] Many had left the field in response to the Rhenish mission's mediating efforts, surrendering voluntarily either to the German authorities or to the privately operated Otavi railroad. The missionaries Eduard Dannert, Wilhelm Eich, and Willy Diehl had already joined different military patrols in December 1904, so that they could encourage roaming Herero to turn themselves in. Disappointed by the brutal military actions that had made dialogue between the missionaries and Herero practically impossible, the missionaries were not optimistic about their chances for success, although they prevailed in the end. "Native messengers" were sent into the field to spread the word that the Herero would be granted mercy, and that the missionaries stood by this pledge. There were apparently many Herero who continued to trust the missionaries; thousands quickly surrendered, particularly in Omaruru and Okahandja.[145] Military patrols still combed the area but took few prisoners, particularly in the first weeks after the lifting of Trotha's "extermination order." When a *werft* was "cleared" (*aufgehoben*)—in other words, when a Herero settlement was attacked—more Herero were apparently killed than were captured.[146] The company commander Count von Brockdorff admitted that "the way things proceeded stood in contradiction to the proclamations that promised mercy."[147] The forces seemed to have difficulty translating the change in policy from annihilation to concentration into practical action. Over the course of 1905, however, the approach of the patrols appears to have gradually changed. After a coordinated "cleansing" of Hereroland in September, the German military counted 250 Herero dead and 750 prisoners.[148]

Concentration of the Herero received new attention under the new governor, Friedrich von Lindequist, who issued a proclamation that the Herero would "be treated fairly."[149] He suspended the horseback patrols in Hereroland and encouraged the Rhenish mission to set up collection sites, which were sometimes also called "concentration camps."[150] These were established at old mission sites and staffed with missionaries who sent "native patrols" into the field to search for Herero settlements. The patrols were to convince the Herero—if necessary, by armed force—to turn themselves in at the mission stations. Missionaries fed and sheltered detainees at the expense of the military, although there were no soldiers present at the mission sites. As soon as the detained Herero had regained some strength (they were typically emaciated upon arrival), they were sent to military concentration camps. This manner of concentration proved highly effective. Between December 1905 and March 1907, 12,253 Herero turned themselves in at the four collection sites—in Otjihaenena and Omburo, and later Otjozongombe and Okomitombe.[151]

If one adds this number to the more than eight thousand prisoners of war at the end of 1905—considering, too, that other Herero must have surrendered outside of the missionary collection sites between December 1905 and March 1907—it becomes clear that the total number of Herero war prisoners must have easily exceeded twenty thousand. In addition, the more than eight thousand Herero in German custody at the end of 1905 were not identical to the number who had originally been taken prisoner, as hundreds had already died in the camps by this point. In Swakopmund alone, there were around eight hundred Herero deaths over the course of 1905; in Karibib, there were 212.[152] There are no numerical records for the other sites with concentration camps in 1905, but the proportion of internees who died in Lüderitzbucht was said to have been even higher than in Swakopmund. There were, however, significantly fewer prisoners in Lüderitzbucht than in Swakopmund in 1905.[153] Numerous deaths also occurred in the remaining camps—Omaruru, Windhuk, and Okahandja—if not to the same extent as in the coastal towns.[154]

The estimated numbers of interned Nama were likewise far too low. By 5 February 1906, there were already 2,353 Nama prisoners of war; they were joined soon thereafter by another 300 Nama who surrendered with Cornelius Frederiks of Bethanie.[155] On the basis of these figures, a total of around 25,000 (not 17,000) prisoners of war appears realistic.

The number of internees thus deviates widely from official records. What this means for the number of deaths is, unfortunately, unclear. It is conceivable that the recorded number of deaths is correct, which would mean—given the much higher number of internees—that the proportional mortality rate is lower (30.7 percent) than officially reported. But it is also possible that the number of survivors is correct, which would mean that mortality was much higher among prisoners of war (around 16,000 casualties), with a proportional mortality rate of 64 percent. In either case, the statistics do not include deaths that occurred after 31 March 1907, the date that the war officially ended. The camp with the highest death rate, on Shark Island near Lüderitzbucht, was in fact evacuated around this time—but many camps continued to operate, some into 1908. At least 184 internees died between 8 April and 17 October 1907 in the so-called "Boer camp" in Lüderitzbucht, where prisoners of war from Shark Island were transferred.[156] And statistics from an annual medical report indicate that a total of 641 internees died between May 1907 and 1 April 1908, the date when Herero were no longer detained as prisoners of war.[157] Moreover, records from the Karibib camp appear to include deaths only from 1905, but the *Gefangenenkraal* continued to exist, and of course internees continued to die there.[158]

Whether the mortality rate was 30, 45, or 64 percent, proportionally speaking it clearly exceeded that of the camps in the South African War. The disparity is even starker if one focuses on the sites and time periods of the greatest numbers of deaths. On Shark Island, 1,203 of around 2,000 interned Nama died in less than seven months, from mid-September 1906 to the end of March 1907. If the Nama had remained on the island under these conditions, instead of being transferred to the mainland in April, they would have presumably all died within one year—that is, by September 1907. In December 1906, the mortality rate climbed to around 18 percent, well above the highest monthly death rate (9.6 percent) in one of the white camps in South Africa.[159] The disparity with the black camps must have been narrower, since the maximum monthly mortality in the black camps was significantly higher than in the Boer camps. But there is a lack of detailed numbers that could facilitate more precise comparisons between individual camps.[160]

Given these numbers, it seems justifiable to call Shark Island an "island of death,"[161] supporting David Olusoga's and Casper W. Erichsen's assertion that "here, on the southern edge of Africa, the death camp was invented."[162] But the South African case shows that large numbers of deaths are not necessarily the result of a deliberate annihilation strategy. The number of deaths is only one factor in assessing whether or not the concentration camps in South-West Africa were intended as instruments for intentionally murdering internees. The central question is what function the camps served for the Germans, and whether or not the camps were conceived as sites of planned murder.

Practically all firsthand sources speak against a positive answer to the second part of this question. As we have already seen, the order to establish concentration camps was directly linked to the intervention of Berlin against Trotha's annihilation policy. On 8 December 1904, Trotha was directed to grant mercy to surrendering Herero, and three days later Imperial Chancellor Bülow ordered the construction of "concentration camps for the provisional accommodation and maintenance of the rest of the Herero people."[163] Given Bülow's vigorous intercession with the Kaiser to revoke Trotha's proclamation, it can be assumed that the chancellor genuinely sought the "maintenance of the rest of the Herero people." Trotha was not pleased about the order from Berlin; he wanted to refuse "the responsibility for supervising larger concentration camps" outright, especially after he was forbidden from holding the

Herero men in chains. He asked to be relieved by a civilian governor.[164] He nevertheless had to defer to orders from Berlin, and there is some evidence that he eventually accepted the departure from his annihilation strategy.[165] He otherwise would not have agreed to release war prisoners who were unfit to work, or orphan children, to the Rhenish mission.[166] In May 1905, the mission alerted Berlin to the high mortality of internees in Swakopmund, suggesting that sick Herero be transferred to the interior of the colony, where living conditions were healthier.[167] German authorities rejected this proposal because of the shortage of workers on the coast, but Trotha's deputy governor, Hans Tecklenburg, announced that shelter and provisions for the Herero would be improved wherever possible, and that only the strongest families would be sent to Swakopmund and Lüderitzbucht. In principle, Tecklenburg believed that prisoners of war should suffer during their internment, since it would teach the Herero a lesson and deter them from future resistance. But in expressing this position he did not want to be perceived as supporting "the proclamation of General Lieutenant v. Trotha from 2 October of the previous year."[168] Instead, with these words he explicitly distanced himself—and also the practice of interning prisoners of war in the concentration camps, which was the subject of his letter—from the previous annihilation of the Herero in the Omaheke. With respect to the camps in Okahandja, the missionary Philipp Diehl also recognized a change in policy: "The government is making every effort to keep the people alive, insofar as this is within its powers, which is progress compared to earlier, when one wanted to rid the world of them all."[169]

Historical scholars have taken two approaches to demonstrate that the mortality in the camps was planned. Casper Erichsen argues that the civilian governor, Friedrich von Lindequist, knowingly allowed the Nama to die in the infamous concentration camp on Shark Island in order to reduce the costs of deporting them to another colony later, as the following memorandum supposedly shows:[170]

> Since at present the Hottentots have been securely accommodated on Shark Island and are performing very useful work there, in my view the question of deportation can still be postponed somewhat. Perhaps one could wait to see how the situation develops, especially whether the numbers to be deported might be limited, so that expenses will not be too high.[171]

But the memorandum is much more indicative of how deporting the Nama had apparently become less urgent once their custody on the island was secure.[172] The Colonial Department had, in any case, already decided against deporting all captured Nama to other colonies on 28 July 1906, several months before Lindequist's memorandum. The only option under consideration was sending away some of the leaders (*Groß- und Vorleute*) and their families to South Seas islands.[173] Thus, the suggested "limitation," or "reduction," of deportees no longer applied to the masses who were interned on Shark Island.

A second argument for classifying the camps as sites of planned genocide has been taken up by Jürgen Zimmerer.[174] He cites the Rhenish Missionary Society's chronicle for Lüderitzbucht, which states that the local commander (*Etappenkommandant*), Captain Zülow, had asked the commander-in-chief, Colonel von Deimling, to transfer the prisoners of war from Shark Island to the mainland. This appears to have occurred during the time of the greatest mortality on the island, in the South-West African summer of 1906–07, when the missionary Karl Emil Laaf, who was stationed in Lüderitzbucht, worried: "If things continue this way, it won't take long until the people die out completely."[175] According to the chronicle, the response to Zülow's request was "that as long has he (Deimling) has any say in the matter, no Hottentot would be allowed to leave Shark Island alive."[176] But the chronicle, which was compiled many years later,[177] is not precise enough on this point—as other records demonstrate.

The files of the Rhenish mission suggest that Commander Zülow did not ask Deimling to evacuate Shark Island until February or March 1907—after he had been requested to do so by the local missionaries Laaf and Hermann Nyhof.[178] Before this point, Shark Island had already been partially cleared, by Deimling's order. In a letter from 26 December 1906, Tobias Fenchel, the head of the Rhenish Missionary Society's Nama mission, reported on a conversation with Deimling:

> Then I told him [Col. v. Deimling] about the conditions on Shark Island and asked him if he couldn't bring the hundreds of women and children who were unnecessarily dying there to another site. He said: "It hadn't occurred to me that there are actually more women than men there. Certainly, I'll take steps immediately ... I now want to remove all Herero from Shark Island, if possible, also all Hottentot women and children who don't have men or parents there ... and I want to bring the dangerous prisoners [apparently the Nama men, J. K.] to a healthy location, I don't know where yet."—Yesterday evening he asked me to accompany him home, and then said: "I've already telegraphed Lüderitzbucht about the women. There will have to be negotiations about the men."[179]

In fact, the Herero and numerous Nama women and children were transferred from Shark Island to the aforementioned Boer camp on the mainland at the end of January 1907.[180] This transfer appears to have been at least partially revoked due to protests from the men who remained on Shark Island, and from the missionary Laaf, who feared that the Nama women would be molested by whites on the mainland.[181] In February, Deimling again announced that he had sent the Nama women and children (who were unaccompanied by men) from Shark Island to the mainland, and that he wanted to take them to the healthier northern region of the colony as soon as the state of their health allowed.[182] The deputy governor Oskar Hintrager spoke out vehemently against this plan and remarked that the security of the colony ought to carry more weight than "reasons of humanity."[183] But Deimling was not swayed. He stood by his decision, pointing to the persistently high mortality:

> In light of this condition [the high mortality, J. K.], I do not think I should ignore considerations of humanity, insofar as they are permissible without endangering the security of the colony. I can't see a danger to the colony in transferring around 150 unaccompanied, sick and weak Hottentot women, and their children younger than ten years old, in kraals to Okahandja and Windhuk.[184]

These are certainly not the words of an officer who was seeking the physical destruction of all internees on Shark Island. The refusal to vacate Shark Island, as noted in the chronicle, applied only to Nama men.[185] And the question of whether this refusal actually corresponded to Deimling's wishes, or was instead more of a concession to Hintrager, ought to be considered with Fenchel's account in mind. According to Fenchel, Deimling had announced that he wanted to send the dangerous (male) prisoners to another secure location.

An intent to annihilate can be assumed most readily for Deimling's antagonist, Oskar Hintrager. In his dispute with the commander-in-chief, he explained that he "did not want to make the case" for "annihilating the Hottentots in question," but then he argued against the partial clearance of Shark Island:

> Given the dangers posed by this opponent, and as long as the land is so sparsely settled by whites who are able to ride and shoot, I feel that only full measures can be of use to us, unless we are willing and able to maintain a larger number of forces in the land. I believe these considerations are, at the moment, more important than attending to the current shortage of native workers in the land, and also [more important] than reasons of humanity. For the sake of its rule in South Africa, England considered the deaths of 20,000 women and children, during a very long period of detainment in the concentration camps, to be unavoidable.[186]

Hintrager apparently did believe that mass death on Shark Island—in effect, the physical destruction of a large part of the Nama—was an acceptable tradeoff for the colony's security. For Hintrager, annihilation was not an end in and of itself; it was costly, and certainly not the original goal of detention, but it could be tolerated as the lesser of two evils.

Hintrager was unable to mobilize much support for this view. As already mentioned, Deimling arranged for the Herero, and also the Nama women and children who were unaccompanied by men, to be taken from Shark Island to the Boer camp, where mortality dropped quickly. Conflict arose once again in April 1907. Ludwig von Estorff, who had in the meantime become commander-in-chief, refused to take responsibility for this "hangman's duty," referring to the mortality on the island. He ordered all prisoners of war to be moved to the mainland, including the Nama men.[187] Hintrager again voiced his opposition, pointing to the threat to the colony's security—but to no avail.[188] Around this time, State Secretary Bernhard von Dernburg became the head of the newly established Colonial Office. He approved the evacuation of Shark Island and wanted to know why the colonial government (*Gouvernement*) had not reported the masses of deaths in Lüderitzbucht earlier.[189]

It is clear from these events that the evidence that has been repeatedly cited to prove an intent to annihilate does not hold up. Moreover, the conflict over the evacuation of Shark Island shows that Isabel Hull's explanation of the mass death as a consequence of European—and particularly, German—military culture is only partially accurate. It was not the "hidden basic assumptions" of military doctrine that turned the involved officers into advocates of a "final solution," unable to be effectively stopped by civilian authorities.[190] Rather, it was the military officers Deimling and Estorff—in a reversal of roles—who asserted themselves against the civilian Hintrager, in order to stop the impending annihilation of the Nama. These roles had already been evident in the peace negotiations with various Nama groups. In talks with the Witbooi at the end of 1905, and with the Bondelswarts at the end of 1906, it was the commanders-in-chief—first Dame, then Deimling—who were prepared to accept far milder terms than Governor Lindequist in order to end the war.[191] A similar constellation was present during the South African War. In February and March 1901, Kitchener lobbied for a negotiated peace, while the civilian high commissioner Milner wanted to accept only unconditional surrender.

## *"Pacification"*

If the concentration camps were not intended to be instruments of extermination, what was their purpose? Why were they built? To answer this question, we must first consider the wartime situation. Although the coordinated military resistance of the Herero was broken after the

Battle of Waterberg, pursuing the Herero into the Omaheke Desert did not achieve the intended total military victory. Leaders in Berlin not only objected to Trotha's annihilation strategy and the cordoning of the Omaheke for humanitarian and economic reasons; they also did not believe this approach would encourage the colony's ultimate "pacification."[192] A fear was that the Herero would slip through the cordon of the German forces, back to the center of the colony, in order to wage a drawn-out guerrilla war. Imperial Chancellor Bülow thus emphasized to the Reichstag in early December 1904 that the most pressing task in Hereroland was "to restore law and order, security for life and property, in the devastated area."[193] Concentrating and controlling the Herero in camps was to serve this purpose.

But the guerrilla war that was feared in Hereroland did not come to pass. The only threat to security and peace that the German authorities encountered was frequent cattle theft by impoverished Herero. An incident in October 1905 is a typical example. A group of 100 to 150 Herero were sighted in the field and then fled. Since the group possessed hardly any cattle, local military authorities feared that they would be driven by "hunger, because of their lack of provisions, to resort to cattle theft instead." The responsible commander asked the Rhenish mission to send out a "native" messenger to encourage the people to turn themselves in.[194] Successfully collecting the Herero did appear to be an effective defense against cattle theft. A missionary chronicle for Omaruru reports that there were almost no instances of stolen cattle in the region since the cooperative district officer, Captain von Brockdorff, ensured the detainees were well treated and thereby encouraged thousands of Herero to surrender voluntarily. In the vicinity of Windhuk, by contrast, there were numerous raids around the same time.[195] The aforementioned collection stations of the Rhenish mission, which the colonial governor had encouraged since the end of 1905, can also be seen as part of these "pacification" efforts.

Detention of the Nama, however, was more important for "pacifying" the colony than detention of the Herero, as the "uprising" in the south was in no way defeated in 1905–06. Beginning in November 1905, larger groups of Nama fell under German control. Around four hundred thirsty Witbooi women and children surrendered at the beginning of the month, after German forces cordoned off the local watering holes. The Witbooi were taken to Keetmanshoop.[196] In the following weeks, additional Nama groups, who were demoralized by the death of Hendrik Witbooi, entered into peace negotiations and surrendered.[197] Although the Witbooi under Samuel Isaak were not initially considered prisoners of war and continued to live in a free *werft* in Gibeon, Lindequist wanted all other Nama kept under watch behind barbed wire.[198] Then in February 1906, the colonial force moved all Nama out of Gibeon and Keetmanshoop, marching them under close watch to the concentration camps in Hereroland. This was "necessary for political reasons, but primarily because of difficulties with provisions that existed in the south."[199] The political reasons presumably involved the hope that the Nama would be easier to control in unfamiliar surroundings—a well-known stratagem from the colonial context. Colonial auxiliary forces were usually deployed in areas that were unfamiliar to them, so their loyalty would not be at risk.[200] In the case of the deported Nama, the distance from home decreased the risk that they might flee and rejoin the "rebels."[201] So the Witbooi came to Windhuk, and the Veldschoendragers to Osona near Okahandja.[202] After three hundred more Bethanie under Cornelius surrendered in February and March 1906, they were taken north by boat and interned in Karibib.[203]

Discussions about deporting and securely detaining the captured Nama reveal how important it was for both the civilian administration and the military to keep them under control. Especially after the escape of some Nama prisoners of war, Governor Lindequist and Commander-in-Chief Deimling pressed for the speedy deportation of all Nama to other colonies.[204] After Berlin decided against the deportation of entire "tribes," Deimling suggested that at least the leaders could be removed from the region. The rest could simultaneously be taken to Shark Island; otherwise, it was to be feared that "without the oversight and influence of the tribal leaders, even more escapes" would occur.[205] Despite minimal personnel, Shark Island was considered a high-security camp that was impossible to escape. "One machine gun on the bridge, a sentry guarding the only entrance to the island was enough to seal it off."[206] The goal was to prevent any chance of escape because, as Oskar Hintrager explained, "the escape of each one of the very embittered prisoners [can] cause renewed unrest and hostilities."[207] For Hintrager, this thought ballooned into a larger security paranoia, as evident from the aforementioned discussion about evacuating Shark Island. The colonial power's need for security was great enough that at the beginning of 1907 only the Herero (who had been largely defeated since the end of 1904) and Nama women and children were allowed to return to the mainland from Shark Island. The men were considered so dangerous that they were not allowed to leave the island even to work or fetch water.[208]

Thus, one function of the camps in German South-West Africa was to help bring the war to an end by securely detaining prisoners of war and "pacifying" the land. Ending the war—as already described—was also a goal of the camps in South Africa, but there was nevertheless an important distinction between the two cases. Concentration camps in the South African War were part of a scorched earth policy that sought to "cleanse" the land of everything that could support the guerrilla fighters. And this included the civilian population. The goal was to hinder the operations of mobile commandos, who were beyond the reach of British forces in the vast South African veld, and so to compel their ultimate surrender. In South-West Africa, there was no guerrilla war in Hereroland to necessitate such an approach. In the south of the colony, the German forces did have to contend with mobile guerrilla units. But the guerrillas were not supported by a settled civilian population. Nama noncombatants either accompanied the guerrilla fighters or crossed into British territory in the south or the east. In both cases, they were beyond the reach of the German military and could not be interned. Unlike the civilians in South African war zones, Nama civilians did not supply the guerrillas with food, information, or munitions. The fighters acquired their provisions by attacking German convoys, and especially by trading captured cattle in the German-British border region, which was difficult to police. During the war, numerous traders were on the move there, looking for deals. A scorched earth strategy that sought to destroy the land's meager resources would have been senseless in this context.[209]

There is a noteworthy exception. Some of the Bethanie Nama, as mentioned above, joined the war under Cornelius Frederiks. A smaller group remained at peace in their home region with the old *kaptein* Paul Frederiks. But after a German convoy was attacked by guerrilla fighters near Bethanie in November 1905, and the four Bethanie Nama who were leading the wagon train joined the attackers, even those who had remained at peace were subsequently interned in a new concentration camp in Bethanie.[210] They were kept under close watch because "there was reason to assume that the people sympathized with the rebels."[211] The purpose of this "concentration camp for loyals,"[212] as it was called by the mission inspector Spiecker, was (as in South Africa) to hinder all contact between guerrillas and civilian sympathizers. A foremost concern was stopping the spread of sensitive information—about German transport convoys, for example.[213]

Bethanie was, however, an exception. As a rule, the concentration camps in South-West Africa prevented only those Herero and Nama who were already in German hands from rejoining the "rebels." In this sense, the camps resembled conventional prisoner of war camps, like those for combatants in the South African War. In South-West Africa, tellingly, all concentration camp internees—women, children, and older people alike—were identified as "prisoners of war." In South Africa, this label was reserved for the fighting men who normally were not sent to "concentration camps," but instead were interned elsewhere or deported. Concentration camp internees were not officially considered prisoners of war.[214]

## Forced Labor and "Educating to Work"

The camps had an economic as well as military function. Since the beginning of the war, the colonial economy had suffered from a massive shortage of labor. Numerous Herero and Nama had given up their positions to join the "rebellion."[215] At the same time, the war rapidly increased demand for cheap black labor, especially for unloading ships in the coastal towns of Swakopmund and Lüderitzbucht. All kinds of commodities—troops, weapons, foodstuffs, and so forth—were needed to wage war and feed the German population (and later, the internees). With the arrival of around fifteen thousand soldiers, the white population of the colony grew by about 300 percent. Nearly all provisions had to be brought in by ship and unloaded because there was almost nothing in the colony.[216] The military transported goods from the coast to the interior by railroad, and then sometimes further on carts led by oxen and donkeys in order to supply the troops in the field. Here, too, the colonial power needed workers, particularly for the construction of new railway lines to replace inefficient transport by oxen. Construction of the Otavi railroad in the north, and the railroad from Lüderitzbucht to Keetmanshoop in the south, demanded thousands of workers. Other construction projects included efforts to keep the ports in Swakopmund and Lüderitzbucht operational and increase their capacity. And the military itself needed many workers in a variety of areas. Nearly all officers employed so-called *Bambusen*, adolescent "native boys" who worked as personal servants.

The answer to this worker shortage was forced labor by prisoners of war. On 13 January 1905, Imperial Chancellor Bülow instructed Trotha that "the surrendering Herero are to be placed in concentration camps at different sites in the territory, where they can be guarded and put to work."[217] Some Herero women, whom the Germans had detained in Swakopmund at the beginning of the war, already seem to have been compelled to work at the port in 1904.[218] The number of prisoners of war who were forced to work in Swakopmund multiplied rapidly at the beginning of 1905, with the start of the Herero concentration. But more than twenty thousand prisoners of war were still not enough to cover the labor shortage of the colonial economy. The files of the colonial administration are full of petitions, mostly from private individuals, requesting the referral of "native workers"; these petitions were mostly denied because there were not enough prisoners.[219] After railroad construction began in the south at the end of 1905, and the construction company, Lenz & Co., called for many hundreds of Herero workers, male prisoners of war were no longer supposed to be released to private individuals.[220] One sign of the colonial economy's excessive reliance on forced labor is how local authorities compelled not only healthy adults to work, but in many cases, also children and the sick.[221] Sunday, once a day of rest, increasingly became a normal workday,[222] and work continued through the night.

By the time that Friedrich von Lindequist became governor, at the latest, labor procurement had become a central focus of concentration policy. The massive shortage of workers must have encouraged Lindequist to offer the Herero new incentives for turning themselves in. Lindequist's proclamation of 1 December 1905 ought to be understood within this context. Lindequist promised fair treatment and the establishment of mission-run collection sites, as well as an end to military patrols and guaranteed low wages, at least for the most "diligent" prisoners. Before long, thousands of Herero had surrendered at the mission stations. As soon as they were fit to work, they were released to concentration camps that were operated by the *Etappenkommando*, the rear military command that was responsible for staging and provisioning behind the front lines. The concentrated Herero promptly received new work assignments from the district and division offices of the colonial government.

As the exploitation of Herero labor assumed ever greater importance, security concerns remained central to the handling of the captured Nama, as their aforementioned move to Shark Island demonstrates. With the Nama, security concerns and the desire to exploit internee labor were evidently at odds. For security reasons, Nama men were not allowed to leave Shark Island, even for work. And their construction work on the island soon had to be halted altogether, because nearly all Nama prisoners fell sick due to the dire living conditions.[223] But even in this situation, the *Etappenkommando* preferred to contend with the labor shortage rather than relocate the captured Nama in a healthier location. Security came first.

The systematic exploitation of forced labor was intended to relieve the extreme shortage of workers. In addition, the colonial power also wanted to "educate" the internees to become good workers. The commander responsible for the prisoners of war, Colonel Dame, instructed the relevant authorities in August 1905:

> It is anticipated that the political situation of the colony will compel us to treat the rebels ... as prisoners of war for the foreseeable future. Thus, alongside supervision, the colonial force is taking on the often more difficult task of educating the people to work (*die Leute zur Arbeit zu erziehen*), in order to ensure they remain a useful element for the further development of the colony in the future.
>
> And so, in addition to handling resisters with the necessary discipline and severity, there must be proper concern for the physical well-being of the people and for their moral upbringing.[224]

He continued by resolutely opposing the frequent mistreatment of the internees and asserted: "We are not slaveholders who use the foreman's whip."[225]

And barely a year later, Governor Lindequist hailed the advantages of educating the Herero on how to work:

> Putting the Herero to work while they are prisoners of war is very beneficial to them, yes, they are indeed fortunate to be learning to work before their full freedom is restored, as they would otherwise presumably continue to roam about the land indolently, scraping together a miserable existence after they lost their entire cattle holdings.[226]

This goal was particularly evident in efforts to teach captured Herero boys a trade. Because it was in the colony's interest "to send people as apprentices to master tradesmen, so there will be more, and less expensive, workers in the trades," the *Etappenkommando* asked the colonial government to find suitable instructors in August 1905.[227] By mid-November, it was reported that the first six young Herero had begun their apprenticeships.[228] Around the same time, young Herero prisoners of war were sent to Catholic and Protestant missions in order to learn a trade. The success of their training was to be evaluated through the submission of sample work.[229]

These efforts to "educate" the prisoners can be understood in another context as well. In waging war, the colonial power wanted to confiscate the cattle and land of their defeated enemies in order to dissolve "the tribal organization of the Herero and Nama" and to eliminate them as a "factor of political power."[230] Africans were to become "dependent wage earners" in postwar society—as Jürgen Zimmerer depicts in his study of the "Native Ordinances" of 1907.[231] This social engineering project began before 1907. Many elements of these policies were already evident before the war, and the Native Ordinances themselves developed out of a conference in September 1905.[232] The camps provided an opportunity to accelerate and intensify the process of social transformation. Significant parts of the 1907 ordinances were anticipated in the camps.

The pass and control system was first designed for prisoners of war; as early as 1905, prisoners were issued pass badges and identification numbers to make them easier to monitor. Efforts to "educate" the internees through forced labor were simultaneously part of the attempt to turn Africans into a dependent working class.

There are few parallels in the Boer camps for the forced labor of internees. There are, however, significant parallels with the South African black camps. The degree of compulsion was significantly higher in German South-West Africa, as will be shown in greater detail in the pages ahead. On the other hand, both contexts share the fundamental idea that internees could be a source of urgently needed labor, especially for the military. Moreover, in both cases the colonial power believed that labor would prepare the camp internees for their life in postwar society. While the intent in South Africa was to hinder the physical and moral "degeneration" of blacks, so they could resume their work as farmhands after the war, efforts in South-West Africa were oriented toward the compulsory "education" of workers who would be dependent on whites. Both cases can be understood as attempts to engineer the future roles of black workers in colonial society—on one hand, to conserve, and on the other, to change the status quo.

## *Punishment*

As already depicted, the murder of white settlers in the first days of the Herero and Nama "uprisings" drove settlers and military officials to call for revenge. "The strictest punishment is necessary to atone for the countless cruel murders and as a guarantee for a peaceful future,"[233] Captain Gudewill asserted. And this punishment could be exacted in the concentration camps. Deputy Governor Tecklenburg's remarks from early 1905, about the suffering and mass death in the Swakopmund *Gefangenenkraal*, can be understood in this sense:

> The more the Herero people feel the consequences of the uprising on their own bodies, the less they will long for a repetition of the uprising for generations to come. Our actual successes in battle have made a lesser impression on them. I assume that the period of suffering they are enduring will have a more lasting effect.[234]

Both Gudewill and Tecklenburg associated the moment of retribution with the establishment of lasting peace in the colony. In their eyes, punishment was a necessary pedagogical instrument for inculcating the Herero and Nama with the unmistakable lesson to never again think about "rebelling" against white rule. In this sense, punishment in the camps was to be understood as a deterrent, as an "investment" in the colony's future security.

Punishment was also a motive for Governor Lindequist. Referring to the murder of District Commissioner von Burgsdorff in the first days of the "uprising," he explained to the imprisoned Witbooi on 13 March 1906: "For such crimes, death awaits, and each one of you deserves to be sentenced to death." He nevertheless put mercy before justice, because the Witbooi had not been aware of the gravity of their actions. If they worked, remained on good behavior, and did not think about fleeing, then they would be treated well in return.[235] The close connection between compulsory labor and the punishment motive is apparent in the following quotation from the rear commander:

> The *Etappenkommando* entirely agrees that impoverished settlers who have incurred heavy losses in the uprising should be supported by the contribution of female prisoners of war, without remuneration . . . The *Etappenkommando* has no objections if the people who destroyed the happiness of a family and threatened its material existence is compelled to help rebuild the latter, without remuneration.[236]

The desire to punish internees played a much larger role in South-West Africa than in South Africa; it was certainly present in the South African Boer camps, but advocated with much less vehemence.

## *Periodization of the History of the Camps*

The annihilation of internees was not an intended goal of the concentration camps in South-West Africa, although scholars have frequently asserted otherwise. The purpose of the camps—from the perspective of the colonial power—was instead to "pacify" the colony, to procure labor, to punish internees, and also to "educate" them to be good workers. These four motives remained relevant throughout the entire existence of the camps, although they were sometimes at odds. While the security argument took priority for the interned Nama, the economic motive gained importance, especially for the captured Herero, after Lindequist's arrival in the colony. Lindequist also breathed new life into the "collection" of Herero in the field, particularly through the establishment of mission-run collection stations, which led to a significant rise in the internee population—from around 8,000 in November 1905, to 16,420 at the end of 1906.[237] The history of concentration camps in South-West Africa can thus be divided into a first phase under Trotha (January to November 1905), and a second phase under Lindequist (November 1905 to 1907–08).

## Notes

1. See, for example, Nikolaus Wachsmann, "The Dynamics of Destruction: The Development of the Concentration Camps, 1933–1945," in *Concentration Camps in Nazi Germany: The New Histories*, ed. Jane Caplan and Nikolaus Wachsmann (London, 2010), 17–43.
2. Spies, *Methods of Barbarism*, 162.
3. The monthly reports of the district commissioners in the Orange River Colony provide a good overview of the problem. See, for example: District Commissioner Boshof and Jacobsdahl to the Military Governor (7 November 1900), Free State Archives Bloemfontein (FAB), Military Governor Bloemfontein (MGB) 2; and District Commissioner Hoopstad to the Military Governor (31 October 1900), FAB, MGB 3.
4. Kelly-Kenny to Roberts (7 September 1900), NAL, War Office (WO) 105/20, T 40/30, TA 48, quoted in Spies, *Methods of Barbarism*, 160.
5. Kelly-Kenny to Roberts (9 September 1900), ibid.
6. General Brabant was the first to suggest that camps could be established for surrendering Boers in May 1900. The intelligence officer Abercrombie and Lord Milner later made similar proposals. See Spies, *Methods of Barbarism*, 43–44 and 154–60; and Kessler, "South African War," 55–59.
7. Telegram to Military Governor Bloemfontein (22 September 1900), FAB, MGB 7.
8. Hobhouse, *The Brunt of the War*, 33.
9. According to one source, this camp was established in August. See "Report on the Schools Established in the Refugee Camps of the Orange River Colony" (13 June 1901), NAL, CO 417/325, vol. VII, pp. 348–56 (here, p. 351).
10. Hobhouse, *The Brunt of the War*, 356. It is not clear whether the camps in Vredefort Road and Howick began operation in December 1900 or January 1901. See also Spies, *Methods of Barbarism*, 161–62.
11. Herbert Kitchener to St. John Brodrick (9 May 1901), NAL, PRO 30/57/22, pp. 10–17.
12. Herbert Kitchener to St. John Brodrick (6 December 1901), NAL, WO 32/8064.
13. Telegram from Herbert Kitchener to St. John Brodrick (25 June 1901), NAL, WO 32/8061.
14. "Circular Memorandum No. 29" (21 December 1900), NAP, Military Governor Pretoria (MGP) 258, p. 17.
15. Telegram from Herbert Kitchener to St. John Brodrick (20 December 1900), NAL, PRO 30/57/22, quoted in Paula M. Krebs, "'The Last of the Gentlemen's Wars': Women in the Boer War Concentration Camp Controversy," *History Workshop Journal* 33 (1992): 41.
16. Herbert Kitchener to St. John Brodrick (7 March 1901), NAL, PRO 30/57/22, pp. 166–81.
17. Smith and Stucki, "The Colonial Development of Concentration Camps."
18. See the entry for "Transvaal" in *Encyclopædia Britannica*, vol. 27 (London, 1927) 207. Pakenham also presents the concentration camps as Kitchener's idea: Pakenham, *Boer War*, 493–94. Spies mentions the tendency of many contemporaries to contrast Roberts' mild-mannered temperament with Kitchener's recklessness. Within this scheme, Kitchener was the likelier candidate for the role of the camps' sole inventor. See Spies, *Methods of Barbarism*, 333–34.
19. District Commissioner Boshof to Military Governor Bloemfontein (29 October 1900), FAB, MGB 2.
20. See, for example, Benson to Trollope (20 October 1900), FAB, MGB 4 and the draft of a reply to the Secretary Municipal Committee, Wepener, ibid.

21. See, for example, FAB, Superintendent of the Department of Refugees, Orange River Colony (SRC) 73.
22. See, for example, Officer Commanding Refugee Camp to Military Governor Bloemfontein (7 February 1901), FAB, SRC 1. See also Hobhouse, *The Brunt of the War*, 117; and Pretorius, "The Fate of the Boer Women and Children," 41.
23. Spies, *Methods of Barbarism*, 200.
24. Kitchener to Brodrick (6 December 1901), NAL, WO 32/8064; and Kitchener to Brodrick (25 June 1901), ibid., WO 32/8061.
25. Arthur Conan Doyle, *The War in South Africa: Its Causes and Conduct* (London, 1902), 105.
26. Ibid., 95. For similar arguments, see Martin, *The Concentration Camps*, 5–15.
27. "Circular Memorandum No. 29" (21 December 1900), NAP, MGP 258, p. 17.
28. Telegrams from St. John Brodrick to Herbert Kitchener (21 February 1901 and 27 February 1901), NAL, WO 32/8061. See also Spies, *Methods of Barbarism*, 214–16. On the early rationing, see John G. Maxwell, "To the Feeding of Indigent Boers, Pretoria" (1 December 1900), NAL, WO 32/8008.
29. Heyningen, *The Concentration Camps*, 76 and 124; Nasson, *The War for South Africa*, 243–44; and Forth, *Barbed-Wire Imperialism*, 163.
30. Spies, *Methods of Barbarism*, 205.
31. Of course, it is possible that some of these families did not come to the camps voluntarily, but were instead removed from their farms by British forces.
32. These figures are not exact. Some entries are difficult to decipher; others are incomplete. Even so, the figures do give a sense of the numerical proportions. See FAB, SRC 70–72.
33. Hobhouse, *Report*, 6.
34. Pakenham, *Boer War*, 548.
35. Nasson, *The War for South Africa*, 246.
36. Ibid., 247.
37. Quoted in Spies, *Methods of Barbarism*, 320.
38. Quoted in ibid.
39. Ibid., 317–20. See also Nasson, *The War for South Africa*, 247.
40. John G. Maxwell to Alfred Milner (draft) (13 November 1901), NAP, MGP 133, pp. 53–70. See also Spies, *Methods of Barbarism*, 209.
41. Telegram from John G. Maxwell to Alfred Milner (19 January 1901), NAL, CO 291/27, p. 211. Here, "refugees" means the so-called *Uitlanders*, generally British subjects, who had fled from Johannesburg to the coast before the beginning of the war. Many were now waiting to be allowed to reenter the Transvaal.
42. Spies, *Methods of Barbarism*, 210–11.
43. John G. Maxwell to Colin MacKenzie, Military Governor of Johannesburg (12 January 1901), NAP, MGP 207, pp. 108–9. On the reasons for the reorganization, see also Spies, *Methods of Barbarism*, 210.
44. Maxwell to Milner (13 November 1901), NAP, MGP 133, p. 57.
45. Alfred Milner to Joseph Chamberlain (14 March 1901), NAL, CO 417/323, pp. 748–49. See also Alfred Milner to Joseph Chamberlain (13 February 1901), ibid., pp. 63–66.
46. Spies, *Methods of Barbarism*, 211–12.
47. Kessler, "South African War," 138–43.
48. Spies, *Methods of Barbarism*, 213.
49. See the draft to St. John Brodrick (16 November 1901), NAL, CO 417/335, pp. 186–89. On Milner's insufficient oversight, see also Milner to Chamberlain (13 February 1901), NAL, CO 417/323, pp. 63–66.
50. Telegram from Joseph Chamberlain to Alfred Milner (16 November 1901), NAL, CO 417/335, p. 182.

51. *The Times History* first depicted this transfer of responsibility in two stages. See Leo Amery, ed., *The Times History of the War in South Africa 1899–1902* (London, 1909), vol. 6, 25.
52. Denoon, *A Grand Illusion*, 32–40; Zietsman, "The Concentration Camp Schools," 90–93.
53. Report on the Civil Administration of Orange River Colony since September 1901, NAL, CO 224/7, p. 527.
54. Telegram from Alfred Milner to Joseph Chamberlain (9 September 1901), NAL, CO 224/4, pp. 175–76.
55. On the camp schools, see Riedi, "Teaching Empire"; and Zietsman, "The Concentration Camp Schools."
56. "Education in the New Colonies," *The Times*, 27 December 1901.
57. Riedi, "Teaching Empire," 1320.
58. "Report of the Acting Director of Education for the Half-Year ending June 30th, 1901," NAL, CO 291/29, pp. 180–81.
59. Heyningen, "A Tool for Modernisation?"
60. "Modernization" is a loaded term with problematic implications. Only from a British perspective was the modernization, or civilization, of Boer society deemed essential. For a critique of the term "modernization" and modernization theories, see Dipesh Chakrabarty, *Provincializing Europe: Postcolonial Thought and Historical Difference* (Princeton, 2000); and Frederick Cooper, *Colonialism in Question: Theory, Knowledge, History* (Berkeley, 2005).
61. Kendal Franks, "Report on the Burgher Camp of Potchefstroom," NAP, Secretary of the Governor of the Transvaal (GOV) 261.
62. Hobhouse, *Report*, 7. See also "Complains [sic] by Refugees Re lack of Soap," FAB, SRC 3, no. 511.
63. Even some of the Boer doctors in the camps had studied at British universities and were influenced by the British culture of medicine and hygiene. See Elizabeth van Heyningen, "'Fools Rush in': Writing a History of the Concentration Camps of the South African War," *Historia* 55, no. 2 (2010): 15; and Heyningen, "Women and Disease."
64. "Monthly Report for July 1901 on Burgher Camp Heidelburg," NAP, GOV 261.
65. Here, social engineering refers to the planned intervention in a society in order to realize a certain kind of social order. For more on this term, see Thomas Etzemüller, "Social engineering als Verhaltenslehre des kühlen Kopfes: Eine einleitende Skizze," in *Die Ordnung der Moderne: Social Engineering im 20. Jahrhundert*, ed. Thomas Etzemüller (Bielefeld, 2009), 11–39. On social engineering in the colonial context, see May, *Social Engineering*; and Schaller, "Kolonialkrieg," 189–95. The "civilizing mission" can be seen as a specific colonial version of social engineering. On the concept of the civilizing mission, see Barth and Osterhammel, *Zivilisierungsmissionen*; and Jürgen Osterhammel, *Die Verwandlung der Welt: Eine Geschichte des 19. Jahrhunderts* (Munich, 2009), 1172–88.
66. Riedi, "Teaching Empire," 1343. See also Heyningen, "A Tool for Modernisation?," 10.
67. See the debate between Heyningen und Pretorius in Heyningen, "A Tool for Modernisation?" and "Fools Rush in"; as well as Pretorius, "A Debate Without End."
68. Heyningen, "A Tool for Modernisation?," 9. See also Pretorius, "A Debate Without End," 48.
69. Stowell V. Kessler, "The Black and Coloured Concentration Camps," in Pretorius, *Scorched Earth*, 133–34.
70. "Circular Memorandum No. 29" (21 December 1900), NAP, MGP 258, p. 17.

71. "Circular Memorandum No. 31" (15 March 1901), ibid, pp. 17–18; and "Circular Memorandum No. 37" (17 May 1901), ibid., pp. 21–22.
72. See, for example, Stowell V. Kessler, "The Black Concentration Camps of the Anglo-Boer War 1899–1902: Shifting the Paradigm From Sole Martyrdom to Mutual Suffering," *Historia* 44, no. 1 (1999): 123.
73. G. F. de Lotbinière to Alfred Milner (30 September 1901), NAP, Secretary for Native Affairs (SNA) 59, pp. 91–100.
74. Telegram from District Commissioner Heidelburg to John G. Maxwell (26 July 1901), NAP, MGP 109, pp. 148–49.
75. See, for example, the telegram from Legality to the Secretary Native Affairs Department (27 January 1902), NAP, SNA 15, pp. 72–73. See also de Lotbinière to Milner (30 September 1901), NAP, SNA 59, p. 92.
76. On these "sweeps," see the table in Kessler, "The Black and Coloured Concentration Camps," 137; and B. E. Mongalo and Kobus du Pisani, "Victims of a White Man's War: Blacks in Concentration Camps During the South African War (1899–1902)," *Historia* 44, no. 1 (1999): 153.
77. Hobhouse, *The Brunt of the War*, 102.
78. The common scholarly distinction between "white" and "black" camps is not entirely correct, as Liz Stanley rightly notes. Africans who were the servants of Boer families also lived in the Boer camps, a fact that is masked by the term "white camps." With this caveat in mind, I will nevertheless continue to use these terms, since they are the widely accepted designations for two camp systems that were clearly distinct from one another. See Stanley, *Mourning Becomes*, 209.
79. Kessler, "South African War," 81–86 and 95–96.
80. The assumption that black camps in the Transvaal were also administered by the superintendents of nearby white camps can be found in Mongalo and Pisani, "Victims of a White Man's War," 150; Jacob Saul Mohlamme, "African Refugee Camps in the Boer Republics," in Pretorius, *Scorched Earth*, 112; Warwick, *Black People*, 149; and Spies, *Methods of Barbarism*, 247–48.
81. Telegram from District Commissioner Heidelburg to John G. Maxwell (17 February 1901), NAP, MGP 73, p. 21.
82. Kessler, "South African War," 87.
83. Spies, *Methods of Barbarism*, 208.
84. Kessler, "South African War," 89–90. On Heidelburg, see the telegram from District Commissioner Heidelburg to John G. Maxwell (22 June 1901), NAP, MGP 101, pp. 187–89.
85. Denoon, *A Grand Illusion*, 14.
86. "Circular Memorandum No. 29" (21 December 1900), NAP, MGP 258, p. 17.
87. Kessler, "South African War," 107–8.
88. De Lotbinière to Milner (30 September 1901), NAP, SNA 59, pp. 91–100.
89. Ibid.
90. Kessler, "South African War," 76–160.
91. Ibid., 111.
92. Ibid., 112.
93. Ibid., 127.
94. De Lotbinière to Milner (30 September 1901), NAP, SNA 59, p. 93.
95. "Final report of the work performed by the Native Refugee Department of the Transvaal from June 1901 to December 1902," NAP, Transvaal Administrative Reports (TKP) 135, pp. 1–2.
96. Ibid., 1.
97. Mongalo and Pisani, "Victims of a White Man's War," 149.

98. De Lotbinière to Milner (30 September 1901), NAP, SNA 59, p. 94.
99. "Final Report Native Refugee Department Transvaal," NAP, TKP 135, p. 7.
100. Nasson, *The War for South Africa*, 67.
101. De Lotbinière to Milner (30 September 1901), NAP, SNA 59, p. 99.
102. Ibid., pp. 99–100.
103. "Final Report Native Refugee Department Transvaal," NAP, TKP 135, p. 7.
104. Hobhouse, *Report*, 4. But Hobhouse did not believe that the British government supported a deliberate policy of annihilation.
105. Quoted in Warwick, *Black People*, 145.
106. Elizabeth Neethling, *Should We Forget?* (Cape Town, 1902), 33.
107. Elizabeth van Heyningen, "The Concentration Camps of the South African (Anglo-Boer) War, 1900–1902," *History Compass* 7, no. 1 (2009): 26; and Pretorius, *Scorched Earth*, 63. On the interpretation of the camps as sites of genocide, see Albert Grundlingh, "The Anglo-Boer War in 20th-Century Afrikaner Consciousness," in Pretorius, *Scorched Earth*, 242–65.
108. *Alldeutsche Blätter* (28 September 1901), 11/39, pp. 2–3, quoted in Bender, *Der Burenkrieg und die deutschsprachige Presse*, 107.
109. See, for example, Heyningen, "Costly Mythologies," 496 and 507. On Goldman's methods, see Liz Stanley and Helen Dampier, "The Number of the South African War (1899–1902) Concentration Camp Dead: Standard Stories, Superior Stories and a Forgotten Proto-Nationalist Research Investigation," *Sociological Research Online* 14, no. 5 (2009).
110. Kessler, "South African War," 132–34.
111. Warwick, *Black People*, 145.
112. Kessler takes the entire period of the camps' existence into consideration, from the end of 1900/beginning of 1901 until the end of 1902, well after the conclusion of the war. In addition to deaths in the black camps, his figures include Africans who died in the white camps while working as servants. See Kessler, "South African War," 245–52 and appendix 6.1.
113. The death records that remain for the original black camps in the Orange River Colony are extremely spotty. For the period before the Native Refugee Department took over the black camp in Brandfort, only three of eight monthly mortality statistics remain. For Kroonstad, there are figures for one month only. There are no statistics at all for the period after November 1902, although the last black camps did not close until the beginning of 1903. And not all superintendents of white camps recorded the deaths of black and colored residents. Finally, Kessler notes that no numbers are available for the "informal camps" that formed along the railroad lines in the Transvaal, before de Lotbinière's department took over the camps for blacks in the Transvaal in June 1901. The mortality among their approximately fifteen thousand occupants must have been enormous. Since the informal camps were not administered by British officials, it is debatable whether deaths that occurred there should be included in estimations of camp mortality. But these camps were, of course, also a product of British scorched earth policy. See ibid., 245–52.
114. This figure comes from the number of white (110,000) and black or colored (115,000) internees at the end of the war, in addition to the 25,000 to 30,000 members of each group who died in the camps. Strictly speaking, the group of persons who were already allowed to leave the camps during the war should also be added to these numbers. But this group was presumably not large, so it can be overlooked in a rough calculation of the total number of internees.
115. Cd. 853, *Further Papers Relating to the Working of the Refugee Camps in the Transvaal, Orange River Colony, Cape Colony, and Natal* (London, 1901), 124.

116. "Statistical Return for Inmates sick and Deaths in Burgher Camps Transvaal for month ending 31st October 1901," NAL, CO 417/327, p. 104.
117. Cd. 853, *Further Papers*, 124.
118. See the tables in Warwick, *Black People*, 151.
119. CRLB, JC, 13, 1; and CRLB, JC, 14, 4/2.
120. Milner to Goold-Adams (4 December 1901), BLO, MP 173, pp. 245–48.
121. "Refugee Camps, Cost of Maintenance" (14 March 1901), NAL, CO 417/323, pp. 747–58; Under Secretary of State, War Office, to Under Secretary of State, Colonial Office (10 August 1901), NAL, CO 417/334, p. 202; Cir. F. 31, Financial Controller to Superintendent Irene, Middelburg, Potchefstroom, Standerton (19 December 1902), NAP, GOV 270; Mongalo and Pisani, "Victims of a White Man's War," 174.
122. "Final Report Native Refugee Department Transvaal," NAP, TKP 135, p. 7.
123. It was less expensive to house prisoners in Ceylon, India, Bermuda, or St. Helena. Moreover, the British wanted to break the morale of those who continued to fight, and also to demonstrate the Empire's size and might. See Nasson, *The War for South Africa*, 234–35.
124. "General Report of the Burgher Camps of the Transvaal and Natal" (10 March 1903), NAP, TKP 135. See also George Bailey Beak, *The Aftermath of War: An Account of the Repatriation of Boers and Natives in the Orange River Colony 1902–1904* (London, 1906), 29–30 and 122–40.
125. "Instructions to Superintendents of Burgher Camps," NAL, CO 291/39, pp. 598–99.
126. "Monthly Report on the Orange River Colony Refugee Camps for the month ending July 31st 1902" (14 August 1902), NAL, CO 224/8, p. 77.
127. "Monthly Report on the Orange River Colony Refugee Camps for the month ending August 31st, 1902" (16 September 1902), ibid., p. 302.
128. "General Report of the Burgher Camps of the Transvaal and Natal" (10 March 1903), NAP, TKP 135; and "General Report on Burgher Land Settlements (Transvaal)," ibid. See also Beak, *The Aftermath of War*, 43 and 138–42.
129. "General Report of the Burgher Camps of the Transvaal and Natal" (10 March 1903), NAP, TKP 135.
130. See the monthly reports for the Orange River Colony camps for May, October, and November: NAL, CO 224/7, pp. 667–94; NAL, CO 224/8, pp. 600–13; and NAL, CO 224/11, pp. 9–25.
131. "Monthly Report for December on ORC Camps" (19 January 1903), NAL, CO 224/11, pp. 129–44.
132. See, for example, "Monthly Report for February 1903 on ORC Camps" (17 March 1903), NAP, GOV 276.
133. Ibid.
134. "Final Report Native Refugee Department Transvaal," NAP, TKP 135, p. 7; and Mongalo and Pisani, "Victims of a White Man's War," 173.
135. Monthly reports for May 1902 recorded 55,696 "native refugees" in the Transvaal, and 60,004 in the Orange River Colony. Of these "native refugees," 10,052 were employed outside the camps in the Transvaal, and 6,634 in the Orange River Colony. These workers did not enter the camps until after the war's end, creating a temporary increase in the camp population. See NAP, SNA 44, pp. 66–76.
136. "Final Report Native Refugee Department Transvaal," NAP, TKP 135, pp. 7–8. See also Despatch, "Repatriation of Native Refugees" (23 July 1902), NAP, SNA 45, pp. 92–103; and Mohlamme, "African Refugee Camps," 125–30.
137. "Repatriation of Native Refugees" (23 July 1902), NAP, SNA 45, pp. 92–103; "Repatriation of Native Refugees" (6 June 1902), NAP, SNA 31, pp. 115–22; "Final Report

Native Refugee Department Transvaal," NAP, TKP 135, pp. 7–8; and Mohlamme, "African Refugee Camps," 126–27.
138. "Final Report Native Refugee Department Transvaal," NAP, TKP 135, p. 2; "Statement Shewing [sic] Number of Inmates Repatriated During the Eight Months—1st June, 1902, to 31st January, 1903," FAB, Secretary to the Orange River Colony Administration (CSO) 149, 1652/03.
139. "Return for the month of November 1902" (21 January 1903), NAP, SNA 98, pp. 104–7; Statement, FAB, CSO 149, 1652/03.
140. See Table 3.1 in the Chapter 3 section "Cities of Tents and Huts: Structural and Spatial Organization of the Camps."
141. Jürgen Zimmerer, "Kriegsgefangene im Kolonialkrieg: Der Krieg gegen die Herero und Nama in Deutsch-Südwestafrika, 1904–1907," in *In der Hand des Feindes: Kriegsgefangenschaft von der Antike bis zum Zweiten Weltkrieg*, ed. Rüdiger Overmans (Cologne, 1999), 292; Zeller, "'Wie Vieh,'" 242; and Zeller, "'Ombepera i koza,'" 76.
142. Olusoga and Erichsen, *The Kaiser's Holocaust*, 10; and Madley, "From Africa to Auschwitz," 446.
143. "Sterblichkeit in den Kriegsgefangenenlagern in Südwestafrika," BAL, R 1001/2140, pp. 161–62.
144. At the end of May, Trotha had already reported 8,040 captured Herero. Lothar von Trotha to the Great General Staff (8 June 1905), BAL, R 1001/2118, pp. 122–24. On 1 December, Dame calculated the total number of prisoners to be 8,814, including 684 Nama. Telegram from Cai Dame to the Great General Staff (2 December 1905), BAL, R 1001/2137, p. 92.
145. On the missionaries' efforts, see Ortschronik Omaruru, ELCRN, V.23.1, pp. 304–7; Wilhelm Eich to Johannes Spiecker (4 January 1905), Archiv der Vereinten Evangelischen Mission (AVEM), Rheinische Missionsgesellschaft (RMG) 1.609, pp. 2–7; and Wilhelm Eich to Johannes Spiecker (7 March 1905), ibid., pp. 13–18. On the arrival of the Herero in Okahandja, see 1904/1905 annual report, NAN, Distriktsamt Okahandja (DOK) 117 S.14.Q vol. 1, pp. 40–41.
146. Trotha announced, for example, that a total of thirty-nine Herero were killed during the "clearance" of three Herero *werfts* on 11 and 22 December 1904. He made no mention of prisoners. See the announcement by Lothar von Trotha (26 December 1904), BWI 403 E.V.2 spec. vol. 2, p. 65.
147. Ortschronik Omaruru, V.23.1, p. 306 and pp. 305–7. See also the papers of Kurt von Frankenberg und Proschlitz, who reported numerous shootings even after the lifting of the extermination order: NAN, AACRLS 70, pp. 123–33.
148. Telegram from Lothar von Trotha to the Imperial Chancellor (11 October 1905), BAL, R 1001/2136, p. 162; and telegram from Lothar von Trotha to the Great General Staff (12 October 1905), BAL, R 1001/2118, p. 172.
149. Notice from Friedrich von Lindequist (1 December 1905), BAL, R 1001/2119, p. 14.
150. See, for example, "Deutsch-Südwestafrika: Die Hereros nach dem Kriege—Falsche Politik," *Berliner Tageblatt*, 11 February 1908; and Jahresbericht 1905/1906, NAN, DOK 117 S.14.Q vol. 1, p. 51.
151. This figure comes from adding together the numbers from the four collection sites in Otjihaenena (4,829 detainees), Omburo (4,497), Otjozongombe (1,824), and Okomitombe (1,103). See Wilhelm Diehl to Johannes Spiecker (20 September 1906), AVEM, RMG 1.664, p. 86; August Kuhlmann to the missionary society, "Abschluß der Sammelarbeit" (31 July 1906), AVEM, RMG 1.644a, pp. 49–52; Wilhelm Eich to Johannes Spiecker (1 November 1906), AVEM, RMG 1.609e, pp. 25–26; Wilhelm Diehl to the fathers of the mission (28 May 1907), AVEM, RMG 1.664, pp. 75–77.

152. Heinrich Vedder, 1905 annual report (15 January 1906), ELCRN, VII.31.5, pp. 239–40. For Karibib, see "Sterblichkeit in den Kriegsgefangenenlagern," BAL, R 1001/2140, pp. 161–62.
153. Wilhelm Eich to Heinrich Vedder (14 June 1905), ELCRN, VII.31.1, pp. 395–98. See also "Bericht über eine Reise (25. 7.–9. 8.) nach Lüderitzbucht" (10 August 1905), AVEM, RMG 1.644a, pp. 33–41. Kuhlmann speaks of around five hundred prisoners in the camp on Shark Island near Lüderitzbucht.
154. "Sterblichkeit in den Kriegsgefangenenlagern," BAL, R 1001/2140, pp. 161–62.
155. Cai Dame to the Great General Staff (8 February 1906), BAL, R 1001/2138, pp. 41–42. On the surrender of Cornelius's people, see the telegram from Richard Volkmann (19 February 1906), NAN, Zentralbureau des Gouvernements (ZBU) 2369 VIII.G, p. 66; and telegram from Georg Maercker to Friedrich von Lindequist (3 March 1906), ibid., pp. 75–76.
156. See the unfortunately incomplete weekly reports from the garrison doctor to the district office in Lüderitzbucht between 15 April and 7 October 1907, in NAN, Bezirksamt Lüderitzbucht (BLU) 165 O.6, and NAN, BLU 166 O.7.
157. "Bericht über Sanitätsdienst und Gesundheitsverhältnisse im Berichtsjahr 1907/08" (5 July 1908), NAN, ZBU 833 H.I.I.5 vol. 2, p. 19. It is difficult to determine how complete these figures are.
158. "Sterblichkeit in den Kriegsgefangenenlagern," BAL, R 1001/2140, pp. 161–62. On the question of internee numbers, see also Hull, *Absolute Destruction*, 89.
159. "Sterblichkeit in den Kriegsgefangenenlagern in Südwestafrika," BAL, R 1001/2140, pp. 161–62.
160. The corresponding monthly report on the "native refugee camps" in the Orange River Colony from December 1901, the month with the highest mortality in the black camps, is not part of the archival holdings.
161. Johannes Spiecker to Tobias Fenchel (8 May 1907), ELCRN, II.5.2.
162. Olusoga and Erichsen, *The Kaiser's Holocaust*, 10.
163. Telegram from Bernhard von Bülow to Lothar von Trotha (11 December 1904), BAL, R 1001/2089, p. 54.
164. Lothar von Trotha to Bernhard von Bülow (14 January 1905), ibid., pp. 120–21.
165. Bülow did not relieve him of responsibility. See telegram from Bernhard von Bülow to Lothar von Trotha (21 January 1905), ibid., pp. 124–25.
166. Lothar von Trotha to Etappenkommando (14 March 1905), BAL, Kaiserliches Gouvernement in Deutsch-Südwestafrika, 1884–1915 (R 151 F) 82097, D.IV.L.3 vol. 1, p. 40.
167. BAL, R 1001/2118, p. 112.
168. The proclamation that he refers to is the extermination order. See Hans Tecklenburg to the Department of Colonial Affairs (3 July 1905), ibid., pp. 154–55.
169. Philipp Diehl, "Konferenzbericht über Okahandja von Januar 1904 bis September 1906" (September 1906), ELCRN, I.1.22, pp. 173–80, here 177–78.
170. Erichsen, *"The Angel of Death,"* 120.
171. Memorandum from Friedrich von Lindequist (12 December 1906), BAL, R 1001/2090, p. 100.
172. See also Drechsler, *Südwestafrika*, 211. Erichsen's interpretation may have been encouraged by his English translation of the phrase "ob nicht die Deportation auf eine geringere Zahl beschränkt werden kann," which he renders as "whether the numbers to be deported might be *reduced*" [my emphasis, J. K.]. See Erichsen, *"The Angel of Death,"* 120.
173. On the question of deportation, see NAN, ZBU 2369 VIII.G, pp. 80–92.
174. Zimmerer, *Herrschaft über Afrikaner*, 47.

175. Karl Laaf to Johannes Spiecker (20 December 1906), AVEM, RMG 1.656a, p. 43.
176. Chronik Lüderitzbucht, ELCRN, V.16, pp. 26–27.
177. The page that is cited above features a photo that is dated 29 June 1913, and the chapter covers the period until 1920. See ibid., 26 and 31.
178. Hermann Nyhof to the Deputation of the Rhenish Missionary Society (22 April 1907), AVEM, RMG 2.509a, pp. 347–52, here 347–48.
179. Letter from Tobias Fenchel (26 December 1906), BAL, R 1001/2140, p. 18.
180. Karl Laaf to Johannes Spiecker (25 January 1907), AVEM, RMG 1.656a, pp. 38–41.
181. Ibid. See also "Aufzeichnungen für den Reichstag über die kriegsgefangenen Eingeborenen auf den Haifischinseln [sic]," BAL, R 1001/2140, pp. 157–60. All of the Herero seem to have remained in the Boer camp.
182. Berthold von Deimling to the Colonial Government (19 February 1907), NAN, ZBU 2369 VIII.G, p. 96.
183. Oskar Hintrager to Berthold von Deimling (22 February 1907), ibid., pp. 97–98.
184. Berthold von Deimling to the Colonial Government (25 February 1907), ibid., pp. 99–100.
185. See also Nyhof to Deputation (22 April 1907), AVEM, RMG 2.509a, pp. 347–48.
186. Hintrager to Deimling (22 February 1907), NAN, ZBU 2369 VIII.G, pp. 97–98.
187. Telegram from Ludwig von Estorff to the Command of the Colonial Forces Berlin (10 April 1907), BAL, R 1001/2140, p. 88.
188. Telegram from Oskar Hintrager to the Foreign Office (10 April 1907), ibid., p. 87.
189. Telegram from Bernhard Dernburg to the Deputy Governor (11 April 1907), ibid., p. 89.
190. Hull, *Absolute Destruction*, 91–196.
191. On the conflicts surrounding the peace negotiations, see Bühler, *Der Namaaufstand*, 264–70 and 300–8; and Nuhn, *Feind überall*, 238–42.
192. See Schlieffen to Bülow (23 November 1904), BAL, R 1001/2089, pp. 3–4. See also Hull, *Absolute Destruction*, 64.
193. Bernhard von Bülow in the Reichstag on 5 December 1904, 105th meeting, *Stenographische Berichte* 1903/05, vol. 5, 3376.
194. Georg Maercker to Wilhelm Eich (10 November 1905), ELCRN, VII.11.3, pp. 152–53.
195. Chronik Omaruru, ELCRN, V.23.1, p. 311.
196. Great General Staff to the Navy (2 November 1905), BA-MA, Admiralstab der Marine (RM 5), vol. 6055, pp. 25–26; and Great General Staff to the Navy (20 November 1905), ibid., 70–73.
197. Bühler, *Der Namaaufstand*, 264–70.
198. Friedrich von Lindequist to Kommandantur Keetmanshoop (12 December 1905), NAN, ZBU 2369 VIII.G, p. 40. See also "Allgemeine Gesichtspunkte über Unterbringung und Behandlung der kriegsgefangenen Hottentotten" (16 February 1906), ibid., p. 56.
199. Great General Staff to the Navy (11 February 1906), BA-MA, RM 5, vol. 6055, pp. 365–66.
200. Thomas Morlang has identified numerous examples of this approach in the German colonial empire. See Thomas Morlang, *Askari und Fitafita: "Farbige" Söldner in den deutschen Kolonien* (Berlin, 2008), 13, 16, and 46. See also David Killingray, "Guardians of Empire," in *Guardians of Empire: The Armed Forces of the Colonial Powers c. 1700–1964*, ed. David Kilingray and David Omissi (Manchester, 1999), 14–16.
201. Thus, the division head Strahler from Okahandja (in Hereroland) argued for sending the Herero to the south, and for sending Nama war prisoners northward in return, since no Nama had yet escaped from his division. See Strahler to the District Office Windhuk (13 July 1906), NAN, DOK 27 E.2.E vol. 1, pp. 10–12.

202. Friedrich von Lindequist to the Colonial Department (17 April 1906), BAL, R 1001/2138, p. 150. See also "Allgemeine Gesichtspunkte über Unterbringung und Behandlung der kriegsgefangenen Hottentotten" (16 February 1906), ibid., p. 56.
203. Telegram from Cai Dame to the Great General Staff (1 April 1906), BAL, R 1001/2138, p. 94.
204. Friedrich von Lindequist to the Foreign Office (10 July 1906), NAN, ZBU 2369 VIII.G, p. 83.
205. Berthold von Deimling to Friedrich von Lindequist (7 August 1906), ibid., p. 87.
206. BA-MA, N 559, vol. 3, p. 19.
207. Oskar Hintrager to the Foreign Office (10 April 1907), BAL, R 1001/2140, p. 87.
208. Karl Laaf to Johannes Spiecker (21 October 1906), AVEM, RMG 1.656a, pp. 46–47.
209. See the reflections on this topic in Susanne Kuß, "Kriegführung ohne hemmende Kulturschranke: Die deutschen Kolonialkriege in Südafrika (1904–1907) und Ostafrika (1905–1908)," in Klein and Schumacher, *Kolonialkriege*, 225–26.
210. They had already been sent to Kubub, Umub, and other locations because of supply problems around Christmas 1905. See Bühler, *Der Namaaufstand*, 207. After Cornelius surrendered in March 1906, the military released the internees. See *Berichte der Rheinischen Missions-Gesellschaft* (BRMG) 63 (1906): 203.
211. BRMG 63 (1906): 34.
212. "Missionsinspektor Spiecker. Visitationsbericht Bethanien. Stichworte. Vom 27. 11.–2. 12. 1906," AVEM, C/h 6a, quoted in Bühler, *Der Namaaufstand*, 206.
213. On the Bethanie and their internment, see Bühler, *Der Namaaufstand*, 203–8.
214. Even when some observers described them as such, as in Hobhouse, *Report*, 6.
215. Chronik Windhuk: Herero/Ovambo 1904–1949, ELCRN, V.37, p. 25.
216. On the practically nonexistent production of food in South-West Africa, see "Der Herero-Aufstand, II," *Militär-Wochenblatt* 19 (1904): 485–91, especially 489.
217. Bernhard von Bülow to Lothar von Trotha (13 January 1905), BAL, R 1001/2089, pp. 116–17.
218. All Herero men in Swakopmund were sent to South Africa as mineworkers in the first days of the war. The women remained in Swakopmund and were interned; photographs suggest that they were already enlisted to work in 1904. See Gewald, *Herero Heroes*, 188–89; and Zeller, "'Wie Vieh,'" 227. Major Stuhlmann reported that almost all prisoners fled from Swakopmund to nearby Walvis Bay in July 1904, but they were brought back by steamship. NAN, Private Accessions (A) 109, pp. 30–31.
219. See, for example, the holdings of the district office in Windhuk: BWI 406 E.V.8 spec. vol. 2.
220. Georg Maercker to the Imperial Gouvernement (18 January 1906), ibid., vol. 1.
221. Heinrich Vedder to Johannes Spiecker (private) (1 August 1905), AVEM, RMG 1.660a, pp. 68–76.
222. This especially displeased the missionaries, since attending worship services and Sunday school became more difficult. See, for example, ibid.; Wilhelm Eich to Johannes Spiecker (2 December 1905), AVEM, RMG 1.609d, pp. 122–28; and Laaf to Spiecker (25 January 1907), AVEM, RMG 1656a, pp. 38–41.
223. See the related documents in NAN, Hafenbauamt Swakopmund (HBS) 52 4/1.
224. Circular order from Cai Dame (27 August 1905), ELCRN, VII.11.3, pp. 157–59.
225. Ibid.
226. Colonial Government for South-West Africa to the Colonial Department (17 April 1906), BAL, R 1001/2119, pp. 42–44.
227. Colonel Cai Dame to the Colonial Government Windhuk (9 August 1905), BAL, R 151 F, D.IV.L.3 vol. 1, pp. 99–100.
228. Etappenkommandantur to the Colonial Government Windhuk (14 November 1905), ibid., p. 107.

229. Etappenkommandantur to the Rhenish Missionary Society [Windhuk] (16 October 1905), ELCRN, II.11.11, p. 197; and Etappenkommandantur to the Rhenish Missionary Society (18 October 1905), ibid., p. 196.
230. Zimmerer, *Deutsche Herrschaft über Afrikaner*, 57.
231. Ibid., 282.
232. Ibid., 69–76.
233. Captain Gudewill to the Chief of the Admiralty Staff (4 February 1904), BA-MA, RM 3/v. 10263, p. 38, quoted in Zimmerer, "Krieg, KZ und Völkermord," 48. The English translation is taken from Zimmerer and Zeller, *Genocide in German South-West Africa*, 44.
234. Hans Tecklenburg to the Colonial Department (3 July 1905), BAL, R 1001/2118, pp. 154–55.
235. "Ein ernstes Wort an die Witbois," *Afrika-Post: Zeitschrift für deutsche Interessen in Afrika* 19, no. 8 (29 April 1906), quoted in Bühler, *Der Namaaufstand*, 269.
236. Etappenkommando to the District Office Windhuk (9 April 1906), NAN, BWI 407 E.V.8.spec. vol. 4.
237. Telegram from Oskar Hintrager to the Foreign Office (12 December 1906), BAL, R 1001/2139, p. 85.

## Chapter 3

# How the Camps Functioned

The goals that Great Britain and Imperial Germany pursued by establishing concentration camps were explored in the previous chapter. In both cases, the intent of the camps was not to kill internees. So how can we explain the mass death in the camps? This question provides a kind of crosscheck to the previous remarks about the motives of internment. To find answers, we must consider how the sites of internment functioned and look closely at conditions and day-to-day life in the camps.

## South Africa: Between "Gypsy Camps" and Improvised Towns

Particularly in South Africa, the circumstances that brought people to the camps strongly influenced their life as internees, so we must first examine these circumstances before turning to the camps themselves and the different aspects of how they functioned.

### *Burning Farms: The Journey to the Camps*

For most Boers who were interned in British concentration camps after the end of 1900, the road to internment began with the burning farmhouses that they had occupied just hours before. L. March Phillips, a British soldier in Rimington's Guides who personally condemned the destruction of farms, recounted his experiences:

> I had to go myself the other day, at the General's bidding, to burn a farm near the line of march. We got to the place, and I gave the inmates, three women and some children, ten minutes to clear their clothes and things out of the house, and my men then fetched bundles of straw and we proceeded to burn it down. The old grandmother was very angry. She told me that, though I was making a fine blaze now, it was nothing compared to the flames that I myself should be consumed in hereafter. Most of them, however, were too miserable to curse. The women cried and the children stood by holding on to them and looking with large frightened eyes at the burning house. They won't forget the sight.
>
> I give you this as a sample of what is going on pretty generally. Our troops are everywhere at work burning and laying waste, and enormous reserves of famine and misery are being laid up for the future.[1]

Many of the details in his depiction correspond with numerous testimonials by Boer women that were published in the years and decades after the war, particularly by Emily Hobhouse and Elizabeth Neethling. British troops, sometimes accompanied by armed Africans, would approach a farm and order its evacuation. The amount of time that was granted for leaving varied from place to place; sometimes it was five minutes, sometimes two days.[2] This period of time was immensely important, determining whether or not a family was able to take along the most essential items for its journey and subsequent residence in the camps. Transportation was sometimes insufficient for bringing along bedding, clothing, cooking utensils, or food.[3] Different reports mention how personal belongings were plundered or wantonly destroyed. One letter states: "At Winburg there were a number of families less fortunate than ourselves ... These people had been able to bring nothing with them. One of these women, in my presence, told the military that when she tried to save some of her children's clothing the soldiers threw these back into the flames."[4]

Some scholars have questioned the accuracy of the Boer women's testimony.[5] But official British accounts confirm that deportees were often given little opportunity to bring along even the most essential items for life in the camps. A memorandum from 19 March 1901 states: "There have been many women brought in to Refugee Camps who have been given no time to collect their personal effects. The Deputy Administrator would be glad if officers could see that these people are allowed to bring necessaries with them. The expenditure on clothing alone for refugees is a large item."[6] An inventory from the camp in Bloemfontein shows that newly arrived internees had brought along only a fraction of the necessary blankets and cooking utensils.[7]

Once the families had left their houses as ordered, they were loaded onto wagons with their few possessions, and the journey began. Eye-witness accounts of Boer women depict the grueling conditions of these transports, which often carried all families from an entire area on long wagon trains into "Babylonian captivity."[8] In the usually uncovered wagons, passengers were subjected to the extremes of the South African climate with little protection: scorching heat during the day, nightly temperatures below freezing in the winter, storms, and downpours that drenched everything in the rainy season. The journey took days, sometimes several weeks, and occasionally continued by train—usually in open cattle or coal cars that also offered no protection from the weather. Food rations might not be distributed for days, or there might not be any fuel for cooking. Under these circumstances, there were already numerous deaths en route to the camps.[9] A letter reprinted by Emily Hobhouse describes:

> A certain train arrived from Potchefstroom full of females all loaded in open trucks, and three women confined in the open trucks in the midst of children. On arrival at Braamfontein Station it was found that one had died under confinement, together with the baby. Others on alighting at the station fainted from sheer exhaustion. We have arranged with the authorities and got permission to send refreshments to the station when trains arrive, as the poor are without anything to eat for days.[10]

And a German missionary summarized the ordeal as follows:

> The evacuations usually occurred in an exceedingly careless way; the English came and ordered the missionaries and their families to prepare for departure straightaway, leaving them no time to bring along sufficient clothing or food, leaving them outdoors day and night to suffer frost and hunger along the way, leaving them to fend for themselves as best they could, then bringing them to one of the camps, where they likewise found no abundance.[11]

It is noteworthy that British officials attributed the high mortality in the camps, at least in part, to the internees' poor health upon arrival. A report by the chief superintendent of refugee camps in the Orange River Colony asserted: "The privations endured by numbers of these people owing to the depletion of supplies in the country seriously undermined their health prior to their arrival in the Refugee Camps."[12] And British officials repeatedly emphasized that mortality among new arrivals was especially high.[13] Insofar as the newcomers' poor health was explained at all in British reports, it was usually attributed to the insufficient food supply in the countryside. Pro-Boer sources also accepted this interpretation. Johanna van Warmelo-Brandt, a volunteer nurse in the Irene camp and a passionate advocate of the Boer cause, assumed that her patients' frail health was the result of the miserable conditions in their home district of Zoutpansberg.[14] British reports noted that internees who had first joined a Boer commando in the field before being apprehended by British forces and sent to the next camp were in an especially pitiful state.[15]

These assessments are apt, but they neglect a significant point. The poor health and high mortality among new arrivals in the camps can also be attributed to the aforementioned circumstances that they endured in transit, including inadequate provisions and lack of protection against the elements. Commander-in-chief Lord Kitchener must have been aware of these problems, as he had to remind his officers to leave people in their homes until necessary precautions could be taken—not only for transporting goods, but also women and children in delicate health.[16]

The tribulations of the journey naturally varied from case to case; some columns took better care of deportees than others, and the weather was unpredictable. The distance that had to be traveled was an especially important factor. Some camps reported that "the Refugees on arrival are mostly fairly well clothed, and with few exceptions have the wherewithal for tent life."[17] In these cases, the responsible British columns had presumably allowed Boer families enough time to pack and had provided transportation, and the district had not been cut off from the chain of supply for a longer period of time. Most reports, however, emphasized the newcomers' impoverished and weakened state.

The journey to the camps was quite different for the *hendsoppers* (literally, "hands-uppers")—those who had placed themselves voluntarily under British protection. They were not driven from their farms on short notice, so they had more time to plan and bring along essentials, insofar as their transport capacity allowed. Emily Hobhouse wrote: "They are put in the best marquees, and have had time given them to bring furniture and clothes, and are mostly self-satisfied and vastly superior people. Very few, if any of them, are in want." On their way to the next camp, some of these genuine "refugees," as Hobhouse called them, joined the columns that forcibly deported the remaining families.[18] But remarks about the privileges of the *hendsoppers* by pro-Boer authors should be interpreted with caution. *Bittereinders*—those burghers and their families who wanted to fight until the "bitter end"—usually demonstrated open revulsion for those who had surrendered. And because these authors were either *bittereinders* or sympathized with them, it can be assumed that they overemphasized the favored treatment of the *hendsoppers*. The *hendsoppers* were, however, usually in better condition when they arrived in the camps, as British sources also confirm.[19]

Even after detainees had arrived at camp, their time in transit was by no means over. There was a regular exchange of persons between camps. At the end of 1901, several thousand internees were transferred from overcrowded camps in the Transvaal and Orange River Colony to camps in Natal or the Cape Colony, and they had to be transported back after the war's end. The Pietersburg camp was even transplanted completely from northern Transvaal to Natal.[20] But even before this, transfers were undertaken for a variety of reasons—to accommodate people in their home districts, to relieve overcrowding, to remove troublesome detainees, and also to reunite family members.[21] If the internees themselves asked to be transferred, they were expected to pay for their own transportation; such movement between camps was not always permitted.[22] Moving people between camps exacerbated the spread of infectious diseases, a problem that contributed to a fatal measles epidemic.[23]

Transport between camps occurred almost exclusively by train, since the camps were generally located near railroad lines.[24] Transit times were usually shorter than the long wagon rides that had followed the burning of farms. On the railroad lines, it was easier to ensure that deportees were adequately fed. Thus, transport within the camp system was presumably not as strenuous as the journeys that marked the beginning of internment.

Very little information exists on how Africans were transported to the black camps. Most Africans, like the majority of Boer families, were forcibly deported after British forces had destroyed their homes in order to clear the land.[25] They would have endured many of the same tribulations as the deported whites. Because of the military's limited transport capacity, most of their food reserves were destroyed, and they could take only a small portion with them. The military had often already confiscated their cattle.[26] British military provisions for transporting African deportees must have been even more deficient than for Boer families; at least, this would seem to be the case, given that the black camps received significantly fewer resources. Like the Boer *hendsoppers*, some Africans did approach the British lines voluntarily, primarily to seek protection from hostile Boer commandos, but also because British forces had destroyed their homes.[27] Similar to the "genuine" Boer refugees, they must have been better equipped when they arrived in the camps. The railroad not only carried Boer internees, but after the division of the original black camps in mid-1901, the railroad helped to redistribute their residents among smaller camps as part of the new agricultural program.[28]

## *Cities of Tents and Huts: Structural and Spatial Organization of the Camps*

The scene that newcomers experienced upon arriving in the camps varied widely. It is tempting to generalize about impressions gleaned from the best-known photographs of the camps. These photographs (see Figure 3.1) depict long, straight rows of white bell tents, interspersed with a few larger rectangular tents, or "marquees."[29] But if we consider how dramatically the number of internees fluctuated in individual camps, it is evident that the camps' appearance must also have changed greatly over time.

The Krugersdorp camp would have looked very different in May 1901, with 1,531 internees, than in October of that same year, with 5,488. The type of construction favored by individual camps also varied over time—as seen in the Johannesburg camp in the Transvaal, and Pietermaritzburg in Natal. The Johannesburg camp was located on the grounds of the Turffontein racecourse, and families were initially sheltered below the two grandstands and in the stalls. Camp administrators soon built six additional large barracks to house the many new arrivals, and 370 bell tents were erected in March 1901.[30] In Pietermaritzburg, the military began building simple wooden-frame houses with waterproof linen for walls, and with doors and windows, early on. These houses replaced used tents and were considered a "great success."[31] A smaller number of similar structures were built in the Aliwal North camp, as depicted in Figure 3.2.[32]

Despite local differences, it is possible to discern some general tendencies in the architecture of the camps and its evolution over time.

**Figure 3.1** The Norvals Pont camp, outfitted with bell tents and marquees (© War Museum of the Boer Republics, used with permission).

**Figure 3.2** Huts in the Aliwal North camp (© War Museum of the Boer Republics, used with permission).

In general, there was identifiable movement away from simple, cheap, temporary structures toward more elaborate, permanent structures. This process corresponded to the change in administrators' attitudes toward the camps. When the "refugee camps" were taken over by civilian superintendents in early 1901, their superiors emphasized the need to administer the camps in a cost-effective way. Major Goodwin, general superintendent of the Transvaal camps, underscored this priority twice in his instructions to the new superintendents.[33] Similarly, the rules for the Orange River Colony camps stated: "Superintendents will bear in mind that the strictest economy should be observed and that the camps are of a temporary nature."[34] The assumption was that the camps were short-term institutions, so large investments in their infrastructure were unnecessary. This attitude changed over the course of the year. As the guerrilla war dragged on, it became apparent that the camps would continue to exist for the foreseeable future. The maxims of their administration likewise changed. After Emily Hobhouse returned to England from South Africa and drew attention to the mass death in the concentration camps in mid-1901,[35] reducing mortality rates took priority over cost management. A "Ladies Commission" under Millicent Garrett Fawcett was sent to South Africa by Secretary of State for War Brodrick to report on the situation in the camps and to formulate suggestions for improvement; most of the commission's proposals were implemented promptly.[36] And most significantly, after the number of deaths in the white camps reached a record high in October, Milner ordered that all efforts should be made to reduce mortality, regardless of cost.[37]

In the early phase from mid-1900 to early 1901, most camps were only a cluster of used military tents. Latrines (sometimes only a board over a trench), and tents or other spaces for storing and distributing food rations, were among the small camps' earliest "amenities."[38] New facilities were added as internee numbers grew, especially after Kitchener introduced his coordinated "sweeps" and civilian authorities took control. The superintendents and their staff needed offices, which were often housed in the large rectangular tents known as marquees. By April 1901, private firms—especially Poynton Bros.—had set up shops in nearly all of the camps so internees could acquire blankets, clothing, and food in addition to the usual rations.[39] The Department of Education erected large tents, or sometimes brick structures, to serve as schools, which opened in all of the camps in 1901.[40] Vegetable gardens were planted in many camps after mid-1901.[41] Because of the camps' continued growth and especially the high rate of sickness, the construction of hospitals was unavoidable. The Kroonstad camp already had a hospital in February, and one opened in Irene in March. The camp in Krugersdorp, which was established in April, did not open its hospital until the end of June.[42] These facilities expanded steadily in order to treat the growing number of sick internees.[43] Over time, they often moved out of large tents into warmer, sturdier buildings.[44] The hospitals, which often included a pharmacy and living quarters for medical personnel, were usually fenced in.[45]

The camps themselves were not fenced for some time, which seems difficult to reconcile with the typical image of a concentration camp. In March 1901 the general superintendent reported that "no camp [in the Transvaal] is enclosed by a fence."[46] Over the course of the year, however, policy in the colony changed, and barbed-wire fences were erected—especially wherever camps were not surrounded by blockhouses, which had first been constructed to protect the railroad lines from guerrilla attacks.[47] In the Orange River Colony, Goold-Adams continued to insist that camps were better without fences, so internees did not feel like prisoners. Aside from exceptional cases like Kimberley, the concentration camps under his direction were not fenced with barbed wire.[48] Within the camps, however, superintendents frequently erected barbed-wire enclosures to serve as "prisons" for punishing internees who violated camp rules.[49]

Camp sanitation also evolved. The superintendents expanded the system of latrines, replacing the trenches with more hygienic latrines with buckets that could be emptied. They built bathhouses and laundries, as well as facilities for boiling drinking water, disinfecting laundry from the hospitals, and eliminating excrement that had been contaminated by typhoid. On the recommendation of the Fawcett Commission, engineers were hired to drill wells and even install sophisticated plumbing systems in some of the Transvaal and Orange River Colony camps.[50]

Over the course of 1901, the camps received thoroughly modern infrastructure, which frequently surpassed that of neighboring settlements. The camps became makeshift towns, in some cases with populations larger than the nearby locales.[51]

Development toward increasingly complex and permanent camp architecture could also be seen in the internees' dwellings. For a long time, most camps consisted of an assemblage of tents, but—particularly after the mortality crisis at the end of 1901—camp administrations increasingly turned to huts instead. As mentioned above, huts had already been tried out successfully in some of the camps in Natal. Kitchener saw to it that the new overflow camps on the coast of Natal and the Cape Colony were consistently outfitted with huts. And in the established camps of the annexed Boer republics, the old tents were also replaced en masse.[52] This change significantly improved the situation of the internees. The secondhand tents frequently leaked, and two or three often had to be layered on top of one another in order to provide any meaningful protection from the elements. The tents were even less suitable during the dry winter months, when temperatures at night fell below freezing. Families frequently slept on the ground, even in times of extreme cold. Pneumonia brought on by measles was one of the most common causes of death, certainly related to the tents' insufficient warmth.[53] Doctors had repeatedly warned that the tents would become a problem in the South African winter.[54]

The gradual investments in camp infrastructure should not, however, distract from the often grave structural deficiencies that persisted well into the second half of 1901. Dwellings were always overcrowded. In extreme cases, a bell tent (later limited to five occupants) might have housed up to twenty people.[55] The number of latrines was often insufficient,[56] and hospitals lacked the capacity to accommodate the many sick residents.[57]

This had to do, above all, with continuously rising internee numbers. Emily Hobhouse noted in April 1901: "If only the camps had remained the size they were even six weeks ago, I saw some chance of getting them well in hand, organizing and dealing with the distress. But this sudden influx of hundreds and thousands has upset everything, and reduced us all to a state bordering on despair."[58] Table 3.1 illustrates the rapid growth of internee numbers, especially between March and August 1901.

There were not enough tents in South Africa for what would soon be more than 100,000 homeless persons. Construction materials like wood and corrugated iron were also not always available. These essential commodities had to be imported from overseas. Thousands of tents came from India and England,[60] but they took weeks to arrive in the ports of Natal and the Cape, which in turn lacked the capacity to unload all of the ships quickly. Materials were often trapped in the coastal towns because of the single-track railways' limited transport capacity, and military needs took priority—a problematic constellation that also affected the supply of food, clothing, and fuel, as will be discussed more thoroughly below. A similar situation later arose in German South-West Africa.[61] Only at the end of 1901 were transport problems alleviated to the extent that the camps could be supplied more reliably.[62] The situation became less dire; although in January 1902 (following a tour of inspection through various camps) Major Thomson still reported that "the cry throughout all the Camps is for more tents, wood and corrugated iron."[63]

**Table 3.1** Internee numbers in the Transvaal and Orange River Colony (ORC) camps between March and December 1901.[59]

| Month | Transvaal | ORC |
| --- | --- | --- |
| March | 20,671 | 11,563 |
| April | 23,812 | 19,296 |
| May | 37,939 | 24,887 |
| June | 45,659 | 31,694 |
| July | 62,479 | 37,049 |
| August | 65,500 | 42,107 |
| September | 65,314 | 44,572 |
| October | 63,707 | 45,306 |
| November | 62,325 | 45,083 |
| December | 61,961 | 43,755 |

Exacerbating the shortage of accommodations was that the British forces often did not give camp administrators advance notice before bringing a new group of "refugees"—often hundreds at a time—to one of the camps. Local superintendents could not make any advance preparations, so new arrivals had to fill already crowded tents, camp in their wagons, or sleep in the open for days.[64] The archives contain numerous complaints about the commanders' uncooperative behavior, even in the period after 15 December 1901, when Kitchener had officially halted the transport of civilians to concentration camps.[65] The problem seems to have been quite widespread.

Overcrowded tents were not only due to logistical problems. According to another explanation for the camps' deficient conditions, overcrowding was also the result of a fundamental administrative problem, especially in the early phase of the camp system. The camps were administered solely by the military until the beginning of 1901, and even afterwards, military doctors, superintendents, and inspectors continued to play an important role. Without much reflection, they tended to bring soldierly camp routines to the concentration camps and their civilian residents, who were mostly women and children. Small children initially received the same food rations as British soldiers, despite their different nutritional needs.[66] And fifteen people were expected to live in a single bell tent because this was the number of soldiers who slept in one tent.[67] The military administrators apparently did not consider the difference between living in a tent for a longer period, and merely spending nights there before moving on.[68] After the British officers acquired more experience managing concentration camps, an understanding emerged that Boer families should not be treated like soldiers. Each family was to be assigned their own bell tent—and large families with more than five members could even have two—so that a maximum of five persons would occupy one of the small bell tents.[69]

There is no evidence of a comparable evolution from cheap, temporary structures to better and more permanent ones in the black camps; a dearth of sources is just one of the reasons. Neither the South African, the British, nor the international public engaged in a meaningful discussion about conditions in the black camps, which might have moved the British administration—as with the debate sparked by Emily Hobhouse about the white camps—to reconsider its fundamental assumptions. A change that did occur once the Department of Native Refugees took control of the black camps in mid-1901 was a steady decline in spending for the African internees. One reason was the movement toward self-sufficiency within the new agricultural program;[70] implementation of this scheme also affected the appearance of the camps. Both the large camps for the African population in the Orange River Colony (which until this point had been administered by Chief Superintendent Trollope) and the unofficial black camps in the Transvaal were divided, and internees were resettled in smaller camps on abandoned farms. At the end of July 1901, the ten original black camps in the Orange River Colony housed 22,713 Africans—or on average, 2,271 persons each.[71] In October, after the division of the camps (and despite growing internee numbers overall), a total of twenty-four camps sheltered an average of 1,831 internees each. In January 1902, there were twenty-eight camps with an average of 1,631 internees each.[72] In the Transvaal, an average of 1,565 persons each lived in the twenty camps that existed in October 1902.[73]

Moving the camps and reducing their size brought, at most, a gradual transformation in their structural organization. As before, "native refugees" had to construct their own dwellings with locally available materials. Because the type and availability of materials differed from place to place, the quality of dwellings in the individual camps must have been very different. The two black camps on Vredefort Road provide an example. While the West camp, which was close to a white camp, had "excellent patrol tents or huts made of boughs and thick thatches," the huts in the more remote East camp were covered only with sacks.[74] Sometimes superintendents distributed corrugated iron for the roofs of the huts, but more often old sacks were employed for this purpose.[75] The improvised dwellings must have left a very different impression than the symmetrical rows of white tents in many white camps; one inspector even compared the Edenburg black camp to a "large gipsy encampment."[76]

The lack of materials meant that many huts were not weatherproof. Dr. Pratt Yule, Medical Officer of Health in the Orange River Colony, saw this as an advantage because better ventilation fostered good health.[77] Belief in the importance of fresh air was a fixture of medical culture at this time.[78] But Yule's assessment was the exception, not the rule. In numerous reports, the accommodations—which did not correspond to the standards of the "natives'" own settlements—were identified as an important reason for the high mortality in the camps.[79] And the little information that is available on the causes of death for interned Africans indicate that pneumonia was a significant factor.[80] Dwellings that did not provide sufficient protection against the elements were no doubt partially responsible.

Camp administrators approved the distribution of tents only in exceptional cases, usually favoring less costly alternatives.[81] As a rule, tents were reserved for white internees; at best, old and used tents were passed on to blacks. The superintendent of the white camp in Heilbron provides a characteristic example. After requesting used tents for the nearby black camp, he noted: "I have requisitioned for another 20 good tents in the event of other whites being brought here."[82] Under no circumstances were good tents permissible for "native refugees."

The example demonstrates how clearly the British administration adhered to the principle of favoring whites over blacks in the camp system, too. Although camp administrators often portrayed the Boer internees as backwards, uncivilized, and having "gone native,"[83] they never placed the Boers on the same level as African internees. Rather, the different treatment of the two groups institutionalized the old racial order, which persisted after the war.

In the black camps, simple trenches usually served as latrines.[84] There were small shops, as in the white camps.[85] And some of the early Orange River Colony camps even had small hospitals, before these camps were divided in August and September 1901. The hospital in the Bloemfontein black camp was initially comprised of two tents, one of which served as a pharmacy, in February 1901. By April, it occupied five full tents because so many internees had fallen sick.[86] That same month, a hospital consisting of one marquee and one bell tent opened alongside the Edenburg camp.[87] These were probably the only hospitals in the original black camps, but the existence of others cannot be ruled out altogether because of the gaps in documentation.[88] In Edenburg, a second large tent also served as a schoolhouse, and in the Rietfontein camp in the Transvaal, internees built two churches.[89] Camp administrators attempted to use these facilities to provide for basic needs so internees would not need to leave the camps and could be more efficiently controlled; the arrangement resembled the "compound system" for housing workers in the South African mines.[90]

Dividing and relocating the original camps in order to implement the agricultural program tended to worsen, not improve, camp infrastructure. Resettlement had to take place quickly, so internees could cultivate their allotted parcels of land at the appropriate time. Another problem was inadequate space in the protected areas near the railroad lines for setting up the camps. As a result, internees built their dwellings under time pressure and too close together. In the original black camps, care had been taken to arrange the huts symmetrically, with a sufficient buffer of space between them, but now these ground rules of sanitation were frequently violated.[91] The Native Refugee Department did not encourage reform or better distribution of living quarters in the black camps until the end of 1901—only after the planting was completed, and the dire conditions had already led to extremely high mortality.[92]

The few hospitals appear to have been abandoned after the division of the camps. Captain Wilson Fox's report on his tour of inspection through nearly all of the black camps in the Orange River Colony describes every camp that he visited—but no hospitals. It is unlikely that he would not have mentioned any hospitals that existed.[93] Appropriately, then, de Lotbinière's final report states that camp authorities fought disease not through "ineffective" medical treatments but more so by relying "on splitting up the camps, on improving the water supplies, and, better still, the food supplies."[94]

Official British documentation does not indicate whether the camps for Africans, like many white camps, were fenced with barbed wire. A German mission report states that the black camp near Rietfontein was surrounded by barbed wire and guarded by soldiers.[95] However, we cannot say for sure if this was always the case.

## *Reform through Public Pressure: Provisions in the Camps*

The paradigm shift in the administration of the white camps was also evident in the provision of necessities such as food, clothing, and medicine.

### Clothing, Blankets, and Furniture

Many families could bring to the camps only what they wore on their bodies because of limited transportation options and not enough time to pack. They were supposed to receive essential provisions upon arrival. Chief Superintendent Trollope explained: "Clothing is supplied by Government to all destitute Refugees, who are unable, through poverty, to pay for the same." A committee—comprised of the camp's superintendent and three internees—was supposed to oversee distribution.[96] At first, other entities were also allowed to distribute aid; the best-known example is the South African Women and Children Distress Fund, which Emily Hobhouse represented on her trip to South Africa. But on 30 April 1901, General Maxwell ordered that all aid for the Transvaal camps had to go through the superintendents.[97] This included donations from foreign organizations. Persons with the financial means to acquire their own clothing, blankets, and other utensils were supposed to rely on their own resources, which is why shops were set up in all of the camps. Superintendents also used these stores to purchase items for the needy.[98]

In practice, this system of aid struggled under considerable challenges. Commodities that were needed by newcomers were often simply unavailable. This was especially true during the phase that lasted until about March 1901, when many camps did not yet have stores where families with means could purchase essentials.[99] But even afterwards, stores often sold out as soon as new shipments of goods arrived and before all internees had received adequate supplies.[100] And not only private shops ran out of goods regularly; local camp administrations also had difficulty obtaining essentials.

In July 1901, General Maxwell remarked that "it is sometimes impossible to supply the immediate wants for a few days as we cannot possibly foresee what the demand will be or where."[101] In part, this was because the military did not reliably inform camp administrators how many people it would be sending, when, or where. It was also difficult to predict whether new arrivals would be adequately outfitted, and thus what kinds of provisions were needed. The most serious problem, however, was that the transport system could not keep up with wartime demands, and this resulted in chronic shortages. On 12 April 1901 Chief Superintendent Trollope complained:

> The alottment [sic] of trucks viz 6 to my contractor was for about 7000 Refugees. There are now over 24,000. I do not at present ask for more trucks to be allotted, but for the trucks allowed to be despatched in accordance with promise of Q.M.G. Army Head Quarters vide telegram Q5006. Otherwise my Refugees will be left without supplies. If I had not put in slightly more than 14 days Reserve Rations at each camp, I should undoubtedly be in difficulties at the present moment.[102]

Trollope found himself in the difficult situation of having to provide for three times as many internees with the same number of railroad cars as before. And even these cars did not reach the camps as planned but only after great delay, which nearly led to a catastrophic famine.[103]

The transport situation was similarly precarious in the Transvaal. Military Governor Maxwell described the problems of 1901:

> Railway transport at this time was precarious and uncertain, owing to the action of the Boers in blowing up bridges, culverts and holding up trains; all night traffic was suspended and we were face to face with a most difficult + intricate problem. The Army had to have its food, remounts + multifarious stores, there was a large civil population to feed, increasing pressure was brought to bear to bring up [British, J. K.] refugees from the Coast, an embryo civil administration was gradually being organised and on top of all indigent and sometimes starving boers [sic] were pouring into camps all over the Transvaal and Orange River Colony ... As the columns operated so the camps grew, in some camps such as Middelburg they literally poured in, as this centre was the dumping ground of columns operating all over the Eastern Transvaal.
> At times it was almost impossible to keep pace with the influx and provide them with the barest necessity of life, the superintendent was driven to his wits ends.[104]

According to Maxwell, strains on the transport system came not only from the extreme demands placed on the rudimentary railway network to supply military men, civilians, and internees, but especially from the Boers' regular attacks on British trains. In effect, Maxwell made the Boer commandos responsible for shortages in the concentration camps—an argument that can also be found in the historical literature.[105]

Boer attacks on the railroads certainly hindered provisioning the camps, but a more decisive factor was military control over the allocation of transport capacity; supplying the troops with war materials took absolute priority. After Goold-Adams complained about the transport situation, the responsible quartermaster general did ensure that in February 1901 priority was given to train cars carrying supplies for the camps in the Orange River Colony.[106] But this was little more than lip service. In April, the state of provisioning was just as critical. Of the twenty cars that were designated each week for the civilian population of the Orange River Colony (from which the camps were also to be supplied), only half actually arrived. The other half were redirected to move troops in the Transvaal. Kitchener personally refused to increase the transport share for civilians, an urgently needed step that Goold-Adams had requested on behalf of the camps.[107]

According to Stowell Kessler, it would have been easy for Kitchener to provide the camps with much more transport capacity. Kitchener promptly organized a large number of train cars for the division and relocation of the black camps in mid-1901, even though the railway lines were simultaneously needed for numerous troop movements. Kessler speculates that 154 cars were available to move the Orange River Colony's "native refugees" in August alone, while only twenty to thirty cars each week were dedicated to supplying the colony's entire civilian population. Since more transport capacity was available, Kessler argues that Kitchener's refusal to send more cars to the camps must have been a policy of "deliberate neglect."[108] His estimate of the number of cars that were used for the relocation of the black camps must be viewed with caution, however. It cannot be ruled out—as de Lotbinière explained—that the internee transfer occurred in "empty railway trucks moving North as opportunity affords without affecting the ordinary railway traffic."[109]

The railroads were overburdened, and so military decision makers naturally gave priority to military needs. Contemporary military doctrine demanded such an approach.[110] This—and not the deliberate neglect of internees—was the reason for the sometimes deficient provisions in the concentration camps.

The transport problems extended well into 1901, as did the ongoing referral of internees without advance notice, which meant that those who arrived in the camps with little or nothing suffered most from the lack of provisions. There was a constant shortage of blankets and clothing to protect against the cold. In many camps, furniture was in short supply because wood was so scarce. Some schools could not accommodate all students because there were not enough desks and chairs.[111] In its final report from December 1901, the Fawcett Commission called on camp administrators to provide more bedframes so fewer internees would have to sleep on the ground.[112] Sleeping on the ground in often leaky tents, without adequate clothing or blankets, must have driven up the number of sick internees, especially in the cold winter months.

The state of provisioning in the black camps can be only partially pieced together through the available sources. The structural problems of limited transport capacity and the referral of internees without advance notice were clearly relevant there, too.[113] But it is unclear whether camp administrators made any serious efforts to provide interned Africans with clothing, blankets, or other essentials. An April 1901 inspection report for the Edenburg camp stated: "There is practically no expense in connection with the settlement save the rations."[114] No money was apparently spent for clothing or blankets, although a letter from the Doorn Kop "native refugee" camp demonstrates the urgent need for these items. The commandant reported that the majority of internees were "badly in want of clothing," and he asked where articles of clothing might be obtained.[115] Unfortunately, the documents do not reveal how the chief superintendent responded to this request, and whether the clothes were actually delivered.

The state of provisioning in the Orange River Colony in no way improved when the Department of Native Refugees took over the black camps in mid-1901. Almost a half year after the change in administration, the superintendent of the black camps in the Orange River Colony wrote that the first load of clothing had just—in January 1902—been distributed among the camps.[116] Things were better in the Transvaal, where the Department procured blankets and clothing soon after the camps formed, in mid-June 1901, but items were donated to the needy only in exceptional circumstances. Internees usually had to purchase the articles at cost in the camps' small stores. In all, the African internees in the Transvaal spent nearly £5,550 on blankets and clothing through December 1902.[117] By comparison, the administration of the Transvaal burgher camps (which housed a comparable number of internees) spent £13,200 on clothing in just one year.[118] And then there were the internees' own purchases and the donations of aid organizations. The comparison to the Boer camps, which were also under-resourced, shows how poorly appointed the black camp internees were. The high number of deaths from pneumonia in the black camps was probably caused by a combination of insufficient shelter and the lack of clothing and blankets.

## Nourishment

Food was central to the health of camp internees. All white internees in the Boer camps received rations at no cost, although these were deemed to be completely inadequate by many observers. In February 1901, for example, a church committee complained to foreign consuls about the food that was distributed to internees. Reverend Bosman worried that the current ration system would result in slow starvation.[119]

Provisions in the early phase of the camps were decidedly meager. General Superintendent Tucker later reflected that more substantial provisions were simply impossible because of the difficult transport situation.[120] In the Transvaal, Military Governor Maxwell determined that internees would receive only one pound of flour a day, as well as small amounts of salt, sugar, and coffee. Refugees who had voluntarily turned themselves in additionally received one pound of meat twice a week.[121] Rations were better in the Orange River Colony. Beginning in January, "refugees" received 5 1/4 pounds of meat per week, while even "undesirables" received two pounds. Significantly, children under the age of six were granted a small amount of condensed milk.[122] The unequal treatment of different internee groups came to an end after critical inquiries in Parliament.[123] After 27 February 1901, "undesirables" in the Transvaal were also supposed to receive meat.[124] On 8 March, the administration in the neighboring colony followed suit by introducing uniform rations for all internees, regardless of age—although the new rations were not as substantial as what adult refugees had previously received.[125]

British officials were also well aware of the inadequate provisions in the camps. As early as December 1900, Walter Hely-Hutchinson, the governor of Natal, warned about the consequences of meager rations. After he had a prison doctor evaluate the rations that Maxwell had approved (and that were presumably adopted in Natal as well), he wrote to Milner: "It is none of my business: but as it has come to my notice I think you would like me to draw up your attention to the matter. It would be awkward if scurvy was to break out amongst the 'innocent Boer refugees.'" Over a longer period of time, he warned, the rations for "undesirables" would endanger the internees' health.[126] The British doctor T. S. Haldane drew similar conclusions about the different ration levels that remained in place until the end of 1901. He wrote in a letter to the *Westminster Gazette*: "On looking over the diets specified in the Blue Books, I have been able to come to no other conclusion than that grave mistakes have been made as regards their sufficiency." The amount of calories in the rations would not cover minimum daily needs.[127] He did not believe that the inadequate food supply was intentional, but rather that it arose from the uncritical adoption of military rations:[128]

> I feel little doubt that the miscalculations have had their origin in official ideas as to the amount of food required by a soldier. The diets of the Concentration Camps seem to have been calculated by comparison with the food allowance which still constitutes the so-called "daily ration" of a British soldier on a peace footing. In the case of the inmates of the Concentration Camps, a certain addition has even been made to this "daily rations," in order, ap-

parently, to leave no doubt as to the sufficiency of the allowance ... Nothing but seething discontent, an enormous death-rate, and very great expenditure in hospitals, doctors, nurses, "medical comforts," etc., can be expected in Concentration Camps with a dietary calculated on the same scale as the miserable official allowance to the British soldier. A soldier can supplement his ration out of his scanty pay, but a "refugee" in a Concentration Camp, and without money, is in a very different position.[129]

A second problem arose from the orientation toward soldiers' rations that were intended for grown men. They were wholly inadequate for parts of the camp population. The lack of milk in the Transvaal rations was particularly unfortunate because small children had difficulty tolerating the foods they were given. The Ladies Commission cut to the heart of the problem: "Wherever a community of little children is found who have to be fed without fresh milk, fresh vegetables, or eggs, and sometimes without fresh meat, then a high death-rate will follow as certainly as night follows day."[130] Children suffered constantly from diarrhea, particularly during the early phase of the camps. A February 1901 medical report from the Kroonstad camp stated: "The prevalence of fatal diarrhea amongst children is due to the food, bread and meat is not a suitable food for these children in hot weather and they are not used to it. I give condensed milk when required, but cow milk is very scarce and we have not sufficient for hospital use."[131] At the end of the month, the doctor reported that of the twenty-five deaths in the camp, 65 percent were the result of diarrhea in children under five years of age.[132]

Another cause of diarrhea was improperly cooked food. In some camps, there was no locally available firewood. Internees made do with coal, which was eventually distributed as part of their rations. But coal was difficult to ignite without more flammable materials.[133] And fuel rations were not always sufficient, as the Fawcett Commission criticized.[134] In fact, wood and coal provisions were a problem that persistently beset the camp administration. Even after the greatest crises had been resolved by the start of 1902, monthly reports still noted the shortage of fuel.[135]

If the early rations did not seem sufficient on paper, they were even less so in practice. Transport problems meant that food deliveries did not reach their destinations on time, and that some rations could not be distributed.[136] The archives contain numerous complaints about spoiled or unusable food. Providing meat for the camps was difficult, particularly in the winter months when grasslands were scarce and cattle herds grew leaner.[137] The administration began to deliver canned meat instead, but the lack of fresh meat did away with the rations' last source of Vitamin C.[138] It is hardly surprising that numerous cases of scurvy were diagnosed after mid-1901,[139] and that by the end of the year the camps had turned to imported frozen meat.[140] Emily Hobhouse summed up the inadequate provisions in the early phase of the camps: "Either of these [rations, J. K.] was sufficiently small, but when, as I constantly found, the actual amount given did not come up to the scale, it became a starvation rate."[141] Moreover, the constant malnourishment made the internees more susceptible to diseases that spread in the camps, especially measles.[142]

In the second half of 1901, the Fawcett Commission urged further changes to the rations. A half-pound of rice was to be given out weekly, in order to add more variety to the internees' diet, and small children were supposed to receive a daily bottle of milk. Boiled water and condensed milk were mixed in the camp pharmacy, so bottles could be distributed ready to drink. British officials alleged that Boer mothers who mixed their own bottles did not heed the correct proportion of water and milk, and that milk that was too thick or too thin caused many of the problems with diarrhea.[143] Finally, the Ladies Commission recommended vegetables or lime juice in the summer to prevent scurvy, and additional fat rations in the winter.[144]

All of these suggestions were accepted and implemented, but criticism from within the British ranks persisted as the mortality crisis continued to escalate. On 12 December, Dr. Pratt Yule (Medical Officer of Health) and Dr. Whiteside Hime (Medical Inspector of Refugee Camps) wrote a critical report about rationing in the Orange River Colony camps. They concluded: "It [the ration, J. K.] does not even supply the physiological minimum of nutrient necessary for the maintenance of health." Granting "medical comforts," as had long been common practice in all of the camps, could only partially mask the inadequate rations. These were items prescribed by a doctor—especially food and drink like dairy products, jam, or alcohol—that were supposed to help recuperation or have a preventive effect. Hime and Yule considered them "necessary articles of food" for certain age groups (especially milk or soup for children and the elderly), but a sufficient supply of such commodities was not guaranteed in all camps. They also emphasized the importance of regularly providing vegetables and fats.[145]

In January 1902, rations in both new colonies were adjusted once more. The new rations introduced a much wider spectrum of foods, and varying provisions for different age groups. The standard foodstuffs—flour, meat, salt, sugar, and coffee—continued to be distributed in similar amounts as before, but now there were vegetables, lime juice, jam, and fat, in addition to rice and milk. Meat rations were eliminated for small children, but instead they received more milk, soup, and easily digestible fare such as oatmeal, rice, maizena (cornstarch), and flour.[146]

Thus, within one year provisions for the white camp population had significantly improved and reached an acceptable level. In Natal, this had even been the case since early 1901. The coastal colony's comparatively few camps were administered by the military until October 1901. Early on, they had received food rations that approached the standard of the more substantial provisions that came to the Transvaal and the Orange River Colony in 1902. The Natal camps were presumably easier to supply because they were closer to key ports.[147]

Provisioning for African internees was based on entirely different principles. Unlike white internees, "native refugees" were supposed to pay for their own food to the greatest possible extent. Men who were fit to work were not supposed to be in the camps, but in the employ of different army departments wherever possible. The British authorities retained £1 of their monthly wages to cover the costs of supporting their families in the original black camps of the Orange River Colony. Only those camp internees who did not have a working family member, and who were unable to work themselves, received provisions at no cost.[148] This approach corresponded to the prevailing British philosophy of relief for the poor—that aid should be given only in return for work. It was otherwise feared that the needy would lapse into pauperism.[149] De Lotbinière's explanation of rationing policy in the "native refugee" camps was that "cases of destitution will have to be helped, but, at the same time, the Government is anxious to avoid a heavy expenditure in relief, which may tend to create a spirit of laziness, and a pauperising of the natives."[150]

Provisions in the African camps were characterized by the same deficiencies as those for the interned Boers—only these deficiencies were far more radical. The official rations were a pared-down version of the early rations for whites. Instead of flour, there was corn, corn flour, unsifted flour, or "Kaffir corn" (millet). Black internees received one pound of meat each week, and salt, coffee, and sugar in smaller amounts than was typical for whites.[151] Daily rations cost 4 1/2 pence for adults and 3 1/2 pence for children—around half of the 8 1/2 pence that was spent on white internees' rations in the Orange River Colony in July 1901.[152] Over time, this discrepancy grew considerably, indicating that the black camps were run far more frugally than those for the whites. The administration of the camps clearly shows that the Africans remained a second-class population in the eyes of the colonial power. It made no difference that they were not the "enemy" (unlike the Boers), and that one of the official British reasons for waging war was to improve the Africans' standing.[153]

The enormous transport problems also hurt the black camps' provisioning. As the weakest link in the supply chain, consequences for these camps were particularly severe. In February 1901, the superintendent of the Edenburg camp reported under the rubric of "Food Supplies": "These were very irregular at the beginning of the month, indeed I had to get 1000 lbs biscuits from the supply officer here, as shown in my accounts, to keep the natives from starving."[154] In May, the general officer commanding in Kroonstad spoke of starving "native refugees."[155] And in June, the commanding officer in Rhenoster asked Chief Superintendent Trollope to arrange for the distribution of rations because all of the food for Africans in this newly formed camp had already been consumed.[156]

Transport problems also hindered the distribution of foodstuffs that were especially important as "medical comforts" for children, the elderly, and the sick. After receiving only a small portion of the medical supplies that he ordered, the superintendent of the Edenburg camp complained: "Particularly no disinfectant has come and no condensed milk and considering the number of ailing children there are this latter is urgently required."[157] In the black and white camps alike, many children suffered from diarrhea because they could not tolerate the food they were given.[158] Adequate milk provisions were gradually introduced in the Boer camps, but this does not appear to have been the case in the African camps. In March 1901, the Boer camp in Bloemfontein reported that cases of diarrhea in children were declining significantly, and that seventy-five cows were now available to provide milk for the hospital and all children under two years old.[159] The superintendent's report from the local black camp had a very different tone: "Regret to state that there seems to be considerable sickness among children in Camp, said to be Infantile Diarrhoea; but the Doctor hopes to cope better with that when he receives the necessary medical comforts, for which a Requisition is sent."[160] Medical reports of the following weeks show that this hope was unrealized; numerous children continued to fall sick and die of diarrhea.[161]

Transport problems were not the only reason why the food that African internees received was worse in practice than on paper. Superintendents sometimes overruled rationing guidelines if they felt that the meager official rations were apparently still too much. The February report from Edenburg states, for example: "I fed wifes and families of boys engaged by Remounts, from whose wages £1 for month is deducted, according to scale, except that I did not consider it necessary to issue coffee[,] sugar and similar luxuries." The Edenburg superintendent distributed only flour or corn to the other internees.[162] But even the daily flour rations, at one pound, were 33 percent less than the prescribed amount.[163] He did not approve full rations until 1 April.[164]

The provisioning system in the black camps changed fundamentally after the Department of Native Refugees took control in mid-1901. In

July, de Lotbinière, the head of the new department, worried that the number of "native refugees" could soon double as a result of the scorched earth strategy being systematically implemented by Kitchener's forces. This would inevitably lead to famine—a realistic prognosis, given the already overburdened railroad system. He therefore asked the commander-in-chief "to allow the families of all Native Refugees to be located on deserted farms along the railway lines in the areas now protected by our troops, where, during the approaching rainy season of September, October and November 1901, they might cultivate and grow sufficient food for their own consumption."[165] De Lotbinière went on to explain that this step would save money that could be used elsewhere to provide for the internees; it would also provide relief for the railroads and effectively prevent the "degeneration" of the African people by giving them a sensible occupation.

Kitchener agreed, and the smaller groups of "native refugees" that had gathered along the railroad lines all over the Transvaal, where they had been dropped off by the military, were promptly moved to nearby locations with arable land. They were to be outfitted with seeds, agricultural equipment, and draft animals, so they could support themselves as soon as possible.[166] The internees were able to obtain grain at cost from the camp administration until the harvest of May and June 1902. Families of men who were working for the military or on cultivation projects paid only half. And the needy could receive one-and-a-half pounds of corn flour for free from the Department of Native Refugees (children under twelve received one pound). All internees received a quarter-ounce of salt at no cost.[167]

In August, after this agricultural program had been enacted throughout much of the Transvaal, de Lotbinière began to direct his attention toward the Orange River Colony. Here the scheme was more difficult to implement because old, large camps had to be dissolved and all internees transported by train to the northernmost parts of the colony. Only in the north were the soil and climatic conditions suitable for growing crops successfully without irrigation. Most internees had been resettled by mid-September. Only the Orange River and Kimberley camps in the Cape Colony, which were also administered by the Orange River Colony, were still awaiting relocation.[168]

The agricultural program strongly resembled the cultivation zones (*zonas de cultivo*) in Cuba that were supposed to allow the *reconcentrados* to support themselves. The scheme succeeded only in part. The first harvest in the Transvaal produced around twenty thousand sacks of millet, corn, and pumpkins; the produce belonged to the internees, but some was sold to local authorities. The yield was below average, but—

according to de Lotbinière—it nevertheless facilitated the internees' speedy repatriation. The agricultural program was hindered by many of the same problems as in the Cuban cultivation zones; as on the Antilles island, suitable land was scarce in areas that were militarily secure. The women, children, and old men who worked the land usually did not have proper tools. Not all of the fields could be plowed because draft animals were in short supply, and "much of the work had to be done in the old native fashion, with Kaffir pick and hoe."[169] Dry conditions and the destruction wrought by British forces also played a role.[170] If cultivation succeeded in a particular area, chances grew that guerrilla fighters would raid the associated camp in order to obtain desperately needed provisions.[171] The attempt to grow animal feed, potatoes, and vegetables for the army (which began in January and February 1902) was a total failure. The two thousand acres that were planted yielded almost nothing.[172]

Until the first harvest in mid-1902, internees continued to depend on external provisions. This posed a large problem. In the final report of the Transvaal Department of Native Refugees, de Lotbinière admitted: "Owing to the very limited truckage obtainable, great delays ensued before ample provision could be made to stock all the camps."[173] And in January 1902, he summarized the situation in the Orange River Colony: "At first great difficulty was experienced in providing trucks from the Coast to meet requirements." The food supply was "very precarious."[174] Inspectors repeatedly reported on complaints that black internees were not getting enough food, particularly meat. One inspector attributed numerous cases of illness to the consumption of cattle that had died from rinderpest.[175] These criticisms are apt, as grain was initially the only provision in the camps that were overseen by the Department of Native Refugees; the diet in the camps was in no way sufficient to maintain the health of internees. Rations even skimpier than in the original black camps certainly contributed to the high mortality following the introduction of the agricultural program.[176]

Provisions in the black camps appear to have improved somewhat around the turn of 1902. On 18 January 1902, de Lotbinière wrote that his department had succeeded in securing some dairy cows for the camps, and that the previous difficulties with transport and supply had now been satisfactorily resolved.[177] Only this phase of the camps' development corresponds with what the department's final report touted as its general "health policy"; improving the food supply became the primary strategy for reducing high mortality.

> Cows were hired or bought, when possible, and fresh milk issued, large quantities of tinned milk, bovril [a meat extract, J. K.], corn-flour were issued free, and a store was opened in each camp to enable the natives to purchase, at

cost price, flour, sugar, coffee, Boer meal, clothing and other Kaffir requisites. The milk and food, in my opinion, did more good than anything else.[178]

In fact, around this time the Department of Native Refugees embraced a change in thinking that distantly resembled the white camp administrators' response to the high death rate several months before. The cost-cutting imperative was relaxed, and superintendents were called upon to introduce measures that would halt the masses of deaths. In February 1902, after completing a tour of inspection through the black camps of the Orange River Colony, Superintendent Wilson Fox noted:

> I found that many Superintendents were rather afraid of acting on their own responsibility on the matter of issuing free comforts to some of the destitute, such as milk, maizena etc., but they are all warned that should they think it desirable they must issue what they think necessary, submit their lists to the Medical Officers and get them sanctioned at their next visit. I told them the Government would rather stand the loss of a few pounds than of several lives, and I think now that we shall see our death rate absolutely normal in a very short time.[179]

This shift in thinking occurred later than in the white camps, in part because the height of the mass death in the black camps happened later as well—in December, rather than October, 1901. The transport situation also improved at the end of 1901, easing competition over scarce resources among the different departments, and within this context the Native Refugee Department was finally able to procure the necessary commodities for its camps. In January 1902 de Lotbinière prevailed over the director of supplies in Pretoria, who wanted to take all of the dairy cows from the black camps near Harrismith. The latter argued that the needs of sick soldiers in Pretoria ought to take priority over the needs of black camps. Military Governor Maxwell decided that the cows would stay with the internees—a decision that would have been difficult to imagine a few months earlier.[180]

## Medical Care

Medical care was precarious in the black and white camps alike. Two problem areas were particularly evident in the Boer camps. First, it was difficult to maintain sufficient capacity—with respect to supplies and personnel—for treating the sick. Second, conflicts between internees and medical personnel prevented the healthcare system from functioning effectively.

Transport difficulties meant that the hospitals initially did not receive enough medicine, equipment, or beds for the sick. In June 1901, Bethulie and Aliwal North still had received no "hospital comforts," and in the latter camp there was not even a real hospital—a situation that Chief Superintendent Trollope sought to change.[181] The medical officer for the Bloemfontein camp saw the hospital's inadequate capacity for patients with infectious diseases as one of the main reasons for the high death rate. The infirmaries offered insufficient protection against the weather, a second pharmacy was needed, and medical personnel were overworked and in short supply.[182]

Hiring additional medical staff was difficult. Deputy Administrator Goold-Adams complained about the "deficiency of Medical Officers to take charge, the Military having drained South Africa of those who are suitable."[183] In February 1901, he asked High Commissioner Milner to send fifteen loyal nurses from the Cape to the new camps in the Orange River Colony, but this proved to be infeasible. Want ads were placed in the daily newspapers, and wages raised.[184] Military and district doctors filled in to care for the patients in the camps, and untrained women were hired as nurses.[185] But military doctors who specialized in treating battle wounds were not particularly suited for treating sick women and, especially, children.[186] Emily Hobhouse's earlier report on medical care in the Kimberley camp summed up the situation: "No nurse; an empty, unfurnished marquee, which might be a hospital; overcrowded tents; measles and whooping-cough rife; camp dirty and smelling; an army doctor, who naturally knows little of children's ailments."[187] Despite these problems, some camps with competent personnel managed to keep the rate of infection low. In other camps—like Mafeking and Bethulie—inadequate resources played a major role in the mass death.[188]

Medical assistance came from England. The first requests for personnel went out as early as May 1901.[189] Lord Milner called upon doctors and nurses to come from Great Britain, especially after the Fawcett Commission recommended a significant increase in personnel.[190] Soon thereafter, around fifty doctors and more than one hundred nurses arrived in South Africa.[191] By May 1902, the camps were so well staffed that the general superintendent of the Natal camps wrote that he did not know what to do with all the nurses from England, and he offered ten to the other colonies.[192]

In the second half of 1901, some camps were still reporting inadequate medical supplies. In the Mafeking camp in September, for example, basic medications were in short supply, the pharmacy was too small, and the medical staff was overwhelmed.[193] Thus when the measles epidemic reached Mafeking, it ushered in one of the highest monthly death rates in any of the Boer camps. Many other camp hospitals, however, were functioning well by this time. By 1902, Governor Henry McCallum's assessment of the Natal camps was likely valid almost everywhere: "Dr.

Hime, who is my principal medical officer for Burgher Camps, accompanied me and could not suggest any important improvements: the measures adopted for dealing with enteric and other infectious diseases being quite up to date, including provision for super-heating apparatus, boilers, and destructors for enteric stools, bed pans, etc."[194]

The second factor that thwarted effective medical care in the camps was the difficult relationship between primarily British medical personnel and Boer internees. Elizabeth van Heyningen has persuasively depicted the interaction between these two groups as a "clash of medical cultures."[195] By the second half of the nineteenth century, knowledge about the role of bacteria and the importance of a sterile environment for surgery were well-established in Great Britain, reinforcing convictions that cleanliness was the key to health. The hospital simultaneously became an accepted site of treatment.[196] The roots of Boer medical culture, by contrast, lay in seventeenth-century Europe, the milieu of the Boers' ancestors. In South Africa, this medical culture was presumably influenced by the practices of the colonized Africans. Equilibrium of the four humors—blood, phlegm, yellow bile, and black bile—was considered vital to good health. Sickness arose through an imbalance in the four humors, which could be treated through practices such as bloodletting.[197]

These fundamentally different medical cultures had entirely different approaches to healing, and the reports of British camp doctors and administrators devoted a great deal of space to condemning the Boers' "quack remedies." Dangerous practices such as the use of dogs' blood or cow dung as medicine, and painting bodies with poisonous paint, received much attention.[198] Internees who refused to air out their tents were criticized for making them a "hot-bed for the breeding of disease germ."[199] In the eyes of a Victorian middle class that was obsessed with cleanliness, the Boers' reluctance to use latrines—among other "dirty habits" that encouraged disease to spread—was a cardinal sin.[200] In addition, Boer mothers were said to neglect their sick children. All in all, the Boers' own behavior was deemed largely responsible for the mortality in the camps.[201]

Conversely, many internees viewed the hospitals as sites of institutionalized murder. Elizabeth Neethling reported on medications that supposedly led to patients' deaths.[202] The Boers believed that typhoid patients, in particular, were certain to die of starvation because they did not receive solid foods in the hospital. As a countermeasure, family members attempted to smuggle in food, which in turn hindered successful treatment.[203] Patients refused to take prescribed medications.[204] Mothers hid sick children so they would not be sent to the "dangerous" hospital, where they could sometimes see visitors only once a week. The hiding of sickness was a major frustration for camp administrators. When those who were ailing did not receive treatment, their chances of recuperation fell. Above all, the "hidden" sick threatened to infect their fellow internees and contribute to the spread of epidemics.[205]

The mutual mistrust ebbed over time. Many internees came to recognize that sick people actually did get better in hospitals, and they gradually let down their resistance to the institution. In mid-1901, British reports began to note that the fear of hospitals had diminished.[206] Likewise, Boer patients presumably had a harder time escaping the influence of camp doctors. By mid-1901, all camps had introduced a system of daily tent visitation to identify the sick and, if necessary, send them to infirmaries. "Probationers"—young Boer women from the ranks of the internees, who earned a small wage by working as auxiliary nurses in the hospitals and camps—must have played an influential role in bringing doctors and Boers closer together. British officials explicitly saw them as multipliers, who were to learn the basics of medical care in the camp hospitals and then pass these on to "their people."[207] Other intermediaries between the medical cultures included Boer nurses from elsewhere who helped in the camps, pastors, and Boer camp doctors.[208]

In sum, medical care in the Boer camps underwent a familiar arc of development. Johannes Otto's characterization of the early hospitals as "primitive first aid facilities" is certainly apt. Their inadequacy contributed to the mass death that occurred in the camps.[209] In contrast to Otto, however, we should also emphasize how the situation changed over time. By the beginning of 1902, at the latest, the medical sector had overcome its problems with supply and personnel, and the debilitating conflicts between medical personnel and internees had abated. The medical system was now relatively stable.

As with other resources, medical care was worse in the black camps, and it seems to have declined further after their division into many smaller camps in mid-1901. With few exceptions, the original camps were administered by the nearby Boer camps, whose doctors also provided limited care for the black internees. In Brandfort, the camp doctor received blacks who lived in the white camp as the servants of interned Boers, as well as those who were internees in the neighboring black camp. But these internees had to come to the Boer camp, which was a full mile away, and they could not be admitted to the hospital.[210] There was little help for Africans who were seriously ill. In Aliwal North, the two camps were five miles apart. Trollope initially turned down multiple requests to hire an additional doctor, which meant that the black camp had practically no medical care. In June 1901, another doctor was finally engaged.[211] In Heilbron, by contrast, the doctor for the Boer camp also had an examination room in the black camp, so he was more accessible for African internees.[212] Overall, however, the medical care that was already deficient for white internees was appreciably worse for Africans.

The early black camps in Bloemfontein, Edenburg, and Thaba 'Nchu, which were not administered together with a Boer camp, received their own medical facilities. A doctor began working in the Bloemfontein camp as early as December 1900, and before long he presided over an infirmary with multiple tents.[213] Edenburg was initially served by a local military doctor and the civilian district surgeon on an alternating basis. British authorities set up a camp hospital only after an outbreak of bubonic plague in the Cape Colony because they were afraid that the disease would spread.[214] This shows—as Kessler persuasively argues—that medical care for Africans was deemed necessary only when its absence could endanger whites or the labor supply.[215] In Thaba 'Nchu, where the camp was located in the great "native reserve," African internees could consult a doctor who worked in the town of Thaba 'Nchu.[216]

The rudimentary medical care got worse after the Native Refugee Department took control of the camps. Camps were divided hastily, and almost no medical precautions were taken so that the planting foreseen by the new agricultural program would occur on time. More doctors were needed than before in order to meet the needs of many small camps. But doctors who had previously treated the black internees remained in the Boer camps. Instead, local military doctors were supposed to visit the black camps on a regular basis. In the Orange River Colony, these visits were supposed to occur at least twice a week, and in the Transvaal, once a day,[217] but the few inspection reports we have suggest that this did not happen. Following his visit to the camps in the Harrismith district, the resident magistrate wrote:

> The next complaint was that they were dying and could get no medicine. I told them I would try and arrange for a medical man to visit the camps more frequently.
> 
> I strongly recommend that a Resident Medical Officer be appointed for native work alone. The present arrangement is very unsatisfactory. Dr. Beor who attends the Boer Camp here cannot possibly do the work. The distance is too great and he cannot give the people proper attention: a large number of children is dying from want of proper treatment.[218]

After another tour of inspection several weeks later, Superintendent Wilson Fox reported that it had been more than one month since the last doctor visited the camp in Roodevaal. He promptly arranged for a doctor to come at least once a week.[219] But this, too, fell short of his own recommendation of at least two weekly visits. The incomplete monthly reports of the Department of Native Refugees suggest that doctors' visits to the Orange River Colony camps were comparatively rare. A total of £98 was spent on doctors' fees in October 1901, and in November, only £80.[220] Since £1 was the cost of one doctor's visit to a camp,[221] we can establish that in October each of the twenty-six camps was visited by a doctor an average of 3.77 times. In November, after the addition of two more camps, the average fell to 2.86. Thus, a doctor came to the black camps in the Orange River Colony less than once a week. The situation was different in the Transvaal. The Transvaal reports indicate significantly higher expenses for medical officers; two to three visits per camp per week appears realistic.[222] This may be one reason why mortality in the Transvaal camps for Africans was lower than in the neighboring colony. Even so, the frequency of doctors' visits was much lower than in the Boer camps. And most significantly, there were not enough infirmaries, nurses, or medical supplies—especially in the first weeks after the division, when transport problems were extreme.[223]

## *Work, School, Free Time: Daily Life in the Camps*

The internees in the Boer camps, mostly women and children, spent a great deal of time securing enough to eat every day. Depending on how well food distribution was organized in their particular camp, it could take hours to obtain the basic rations that were usually given out once a week. For meat, internees often had to return each day to the distribution site. Wherever water was scarce, they might stand in line at wells or dams, which were supposed to facilitate access to water from nearby rivers, from morning to night. And they spent long hours collecting wood and cow dung, or digging up roots, because of inadequate fuel rations.

Each family prepared its own meals, often with improvised cooking tools. Only over the course of 1901 did superintendents set up public ovens and soup kitchens that made food preparation simpler and more efficient. Washing clothes under difficult circumstances was another time-consuming household task. There were no laundry facilities, especially in the early phase of the camps, and soap was hard to come by.[224]

The few men in the camps who were fit to work were expected to do so. They could receive wages, and often better rations, if they held certain jobs—for example, as camp police, guarding the camp entrances and enforcing camp rules, or as corporals, keeping order in their camp sections, or distributing rations. Sometimes they took positions in nearby towns, or they participated in public works projects, which meant they were removed from their camp's ration list. This could be a first step toward leaving the camp permanently, because the British administration sometimes granted self-sufficient internees the right to resettle in the next town. Women were also encouraged to look for paid work outside the camps. But they also held positions within the camps, especially as auxiliary nurses (probationers).[225] Camp financial records show that many internees worked for pay. Internee wages were the second-largest expense item, after the cost of rations.[226] The Ladies Commission reported that some camp superintendents paid more than 150 internees.[227]

In addition, all internees were required to work without compensation for the general welfare of the camp, although local practices varied. The Fawcett Commission reported that healthy men in Bloemfontein had to work six hours a day. In Norvals Pont, it was three hours. There was no work requirement in Johannesburg, except for members of the "scavenging gang," who were responsible for sanitation.[228] The commission advocated for standardized work practices within each colony in its general recommendations. In the Natal camps, the commission recommended that every adult male perform three hours of "compulsory labour, for the good of the camp." In the Orange River Colony, the commission even advised nine hours per day.[229] Internee jobs included setting up tents, brickmaking, shoe repair, woodworking, and gardening. Women were generally exempt from labor requirements, but worked in some cases nevertheless, although they were not paid by the superintendents. They offered sewing or tailoring classes, for example, in order to teach other internees. Young people sometimes received professional training in workshops within the camps.[230]

The emphasis on work was presumably based on two considerations. First, it helped to keep the camp system running as economically as possible. Second, it reinforced basic assumptions behind charity for the poor and "native policy" in the British Empire; recipients of aid were expected to work, otherwise they would become lazy and degenerate. General Superintendent Goodwin elaborated on this thought in one of his early circular letters:

> You know the average of the men and women now under your charge are very resourceful, and if tactfully encouraged will do a great deal to help themselves, whilst if allowed they may sink into an absolutely hopeless and helpless frame of mind. This is the worst that can happen to them, therefore, even if it entails a slightly higher cost on our Government (which I think unlikely) I would prefer to see them encouraged to work, rather than be led to expect everything to be done for them whilst in Laager.[231]

The Ladies Commission identified the same problem in Mafeking: "We noticed many men and women sitting in a melancholy way, doing absolutely nothing, with their hands before them. They would be much happier if they could be induced to work."[232]

This raises the question whether, and to what extent, British camp administrators perceived and treated interned Boers like colonized Africans.[233] Kitchener's depiction of the Boers as "uncivilized Afrikaner savages with only a thin white veneer,"[234] who occasionally revealed their full "native savagery"[235] in the concentration camps, suggests such an interpretation. In this view, the Boers had been "kaffirized" during their isolated, rural existence and regressed into barbarism.[236] The danger of Europeans in the colonies "going native," an established topos in colonial discourse, was projected onto an entire people.[237]

British actors also drew upon the image of the European lower classes as a means of classifying the Boer camp population. The Boer internees' resistance to the camp hospitals reminded the Fawcett Commission of "the more ignorant of the English poor."[238] For Inspector Kendal Franks, the misery and filth in the overcrowded camps resembled the conditions in the "residences of the poor in the British Isles, such as Whitechapel, St. Giles, and the Liberties in Dublin."[239] This context, too, explains the efforts to put internees to work. British welfare policy made aid contingent upon work—as in the workhouses.[240]

British camp administrators therefore viewed Boer internees through a prism of European poor relief and "native policy," overlapping principles that informed their interactions with the Boers. The categories of class and race are often intertwined and interdependent, as advocates of Critical Whiteness Studies emphasize.[241]

Even so, there was an enormous difference in how British actors treated the Boer and African populations. The supposed "degeneration" of the Boers did nothing to change this. Although recent scholars of colonialism have emphasized that "the otherness of colonized persons was neither inherent nor stable,"[242] the racial classification of African internees remains relevant. "The rule of colonial difference,"[243] as Partha Chatterjee calls it, also held sway in the camps. In the dichotomous world of the colony, the Boers belonged to the dominant group, and they would continue to do so in the future. The handling of the mortality crisis demonstrated the sharp distinction between the two groups. Conditions in the Boer camps outraged the British public, leading the British government to funnel tremendous resources toward improving the situation, while mass death in the camps for Africans—as in German South-West Africa—was met with indifference. To borrow the words of Helen Fein, the racist conceptions of the colonizers, as disparate and fluid as they were in individual cases, ensured that the interned Africans were excluded from the "universe of obligation." The African internees did not belong to those "whom we are obligated to protect, to take into account, and to whom we must account."[244] There was, by contrast, a moral obligation to help suffering Boers.

Daily life in the camps changed decisively for children and young people in the first half of 1901, as Edmund Sargant, the acting director of education, gradually introduced schools in all of the camps. These new institutions complemented or replaced the small private schools that had already been established by internees. With the exception of religion classes, instruction took place entirely in English, usually beginning around 8:30 a.m. and ending around 1:00 p.m. However, the scarcity of school buildings, furniture, instructional materials, and teachers often meant that half of the children were taught in the morning, and the other half in the afternoon, in order to accommodate more students. This shortened the school day for everyone.[245] Student numbers grew quickly. In the camps of the Orange River Colony alone, where just under 14,000 school-age children lived, the number of students rose from 2,001 in May 1901, to 9,440 in November 1901, and finally reached 12,666 in May 1902. Thus, the number of students in the camps was significantly higher than the school population ever had been in the former Orange Free State.[246] In the Transvaal, 3,633 persons attended the camp schools in June 1901, and 12,046 in November. The peak number of attendees (17,213) was reached in May 1902; this was 3,000 more persons than the largest school population ever in the former South African Republic.[247] Average daily attendance was, however, significantly lower, not least because of the high rate of sickness. Some camp schools even closed temporarily because of the measles epidemic.[248]

Attending school was voluntary and free of charge, although in some cases "school corporals"[249] persuaded parents to send their children to school. Sargant believed that compulsory schooling was counterproductive because it could lead to parental resistance, a position that he successfully asserted over the objections of the Fawcett Commission.[250] Internees initially mistrusted the schools, especially given the dominance of English-language instruction. Internees did, however, constitute a majority of the teachers during the war, which helped to overcome skepticism.[251] Parents came to appreciate school as a useful distraction for their children from the death, sickness, and hunger in the camps.[252] Most teachers were Boer women (often under a male principal), so the British goal to promote "anglicization" in the schools was never fully realized. The situation changed only when three hundred educators arrived from Great Britain, Australia, and New Zealand at the beginning of 1902, but by this point little could be accomplished before the camps were dissolved.[253]

Educational opportunities were offered not only for children but also for adults. A twenty-seven-year-old might sit next to a six-year-old at school. School administrators held special classes for adults in order to keep up with demand.[254] "Lantern lectures" on the British Empire were intended to appeal to adults, and kindergartens occupied the youngest children.[255]

Educational offerings such as workshops and sewing classes gradually expanded after February 1901, which helped to relieve the monotony of camp life that was repeatedly described in testimonial literature.[256] In her report from mid-1901, Emily Hobhouse complained that "the camp life is felt to be purposeless and demoralising." She called for more recreational activities,[257] which were introduced in some cases. Soon after the civilian administrators had assumed control of the camps, Chief Superintendent Trollope remarked in March 1901: "The Camps are made as favourable as possible under the circumstances, the inhabitants are not treated like prisoners, and every encouragement is given to such games as cricket and football; Government in some cases having supplied cricket requisites etc."[258] But recreational opportunities remained limited as long as transport routes remained overburdened, waiting in line for food rations and water took hours or days, and epidemics kept internees sick in bed or caring for relatives.[259] This gradually changed. Tennis courts and soccer fields were built, and there were even track and field competitions[260] and cricket matches between teams from different camps.[261]

At the end of 1901, the Transvaal camp administration directed its superintendents to organize special Christmas celebrations or picnics for all of the children.[262] Beginning in December, the Merebank camp superintendent sent several convalescent children each day by train to the nearby coast, so they could recuperate on the beach. He explained: "This should help them a good deal and be a nice change."[263] Members of the Fawcett Commission reported that the Johannesburg camp had a tea and coffee shop, and they also observed different groups playing cards.[264] With respect to the later phase of the camps, Arthur Martin's assessment is correct: "Life within the camps, even when conditions did not permit of [sic] passes out, was not altogether dull. Musical societies, dramatics, reading rooms, home industries, carpentry, games and sports were all encouraged. Concert parties visited the camps and every means of interesting the occupants was attempted."[265]

There were religious activities, too. In early 1901, ministers of the Dutch Reformed Church who had taken an oath of allegiance to Great Britain began to work in the Orange River Colony camps. They were paid by the camp administration. They were joined by pastors of other churches, some of whom visited the camps regularly.[266] In the Transvaal, Military Governor Maxwell began to hire camp chaplains somewhat later, in July 1901. When the Fawcett Commission toured the colony between September and November, most camps did not yet have a permanent chaplain. Religious services were conducted in the meantime by church elders or visiting pastors, as in the few Orange River Colony camps that did not yet have a camp chaplain.[267] Ministers held worship services and daily prayer meetings, coordinated Sunday schools, and performed baptisms and confirmations. Demand was so great that the available facilities were often too small, and religious services were held outdoors as weather permitted. Elira Wessels writes that a spiritual revival occurred after conditions in the Bloemfontein camp improved at the end of 1901; attendance at morning devotions doubled, reflecting the internees' "thirst" for the word of God.[268]

It is difficult to make definitive statements about daily life in the black camps. The brief reports of British officials provide little information, and there are no testimonials because the internees themselves were usually unable to write. Emily Hobhouse and the many other visitors who raised awareness about the misery in the Boer camps generally did not set foot in the camps for Africans.[269] More recently, B. E. Mongalo and Kobus Du Pisani have drawn upon interviews that were conducted eighty years after the South African War to create a portrait of the black camps; their interviews, however, tell us more about the memory of the camps than conditions at the time. The authors conclude that "the life of the black people in the camps was the typical life of a manual labourer in the case of men and either domestic servant or a crop cultivator in the case of women."[270]

Of course, cultivating crops defined many women's lives only after the introduction of the agricultural program in mid-1901. There were no farms in the original black camps, which were satellites of Boer camps. African women often worked for the white internees as laundresses, maids, or nurses.[271] African men did all kinds of sanitation work in the Boer camps; they removed garbage, cleaned latrines, and performed other tasks that were not assigned to white internees.[272] But even in this early phase, most grown men did not stay together with their families in the camps but instead worked elsewhere for the military or private employers. They visited the camps every three months or so before starting a new assignment. British authorities also arranged for several hundred children to work as servants in private homes.[273]

Opportunities to work in the Boer camps went away once the black camps divided and moved near the railroad lines. Agricultural work became more important, and women, children, and old men worked in the fields every day. Some men found paid work as "plough boys," helping with the few available plows and draft animals in order to cultivate the land.[274] Others worked as armed sentries in order to protect the camps from Boer attacks. There were 850 black sentries by the end of the war.[275] And some men worked in the camps as assistants of white administrators and police.[276] In January 1902, about one thousand men were employed in the Orange River Colony camps alone. Another four thousand men were engaged by station commanders to build "local defence works" and thus could still live in the camps.[277]

Work must have dominated the daily routine of the black internees.[278] Obtaining water and fuel, washing, and cooking all took time. As in the white camps, standing in line for rations remained very time-consuming, at least until the harvest was brought in. According to a Honingspruit camp report from December 1901, the distribution of rations took up to two entire days every week.[279] In Vredefort Road, it was four days.[280]

Nothing is known about recreation in the black camps, although religion and school did play a role. Shortly before the war's end, the director of education Edmund Sargant proposed establishing schools in the black camps, too. De Lotbinière opposed this idea because he feared that "the introduction of a new element into each Camp in the shape of Schoolmaster or Clergyman of some denomination would only tend to unsettle the natives' present system of control, and weaken the hands of my Superintendents."[281] There were, however, local efforts to introduce these very elements. In the Belfast camp, a "native evangelist" directed a school with the approval of the local superintendent.[282] In Honingspruit, a "schoolmaster for the camp" even had his own assistants.[283] And a German missionary wrote that the church leader Matthäus Komane led Sunday morning and evening prayers in the Rietfontein camp. Missionary Jordt, who was initially not permitted to enter the camp, sent an evangelist and three "native teachers" to hold worship services, to accept around one hundred children as students, and to give baptismal instruction to sixty more. After repeated requests from the internees, the local commander finally allowed the missionary to settle in the camp.[284]

## Hendsoppers, Bittereinders, *and Khakis:*
*Social Relations in the Camps*

Social relations also influenced daily life in the camps. Three groups dominated social life in the Boer camps: khakis, or British officials; *hendsoppers*, refugees who had come to the camps voluntarily; and *bit-*

*tereinders* who had come to the camps against their will and whose male relatives were usually either "on commando" or prisoners of war. Conflict between the two internee groups appears repeatedly both in British sources and Boer accounts of camp life. In a letter from the camp in Howick, for example, one internee criticized the *hendsoppers* who swore an oath of allegiance to the British crown:

> I always bore an ill-feeling towards them, but now I simply loathe them. They all have sons, brothers, and fathers still fighting, and how can they face them after this? But I believe the women here gave them a good bit of their mind, and the result is that they shun us, and simply stick to their tents.[285]

And one of the first British reports from the Transvaal stated:

> It is disquieting to find that in most camps the wives and families of burghers still fighting think of and treat contemptuously those whose immediate male relatives (having surrendered) have taken the oath of neutrality, and I must report that the congregation of all classes in the same camps has materially increased the difficulty of management.[286]

One of the most immediate problems that arose from the conflict was the unequal distribution of aid. So, for example, Johanna van Warmelo, a volunteer auxiliary nurse in Irene, unambiguously sympathized with the *bittereinders*. She wrote in her diary that she went from tent to tent and passed along donations only to needy families whose men were "on commando." She did her best to avoid contact with the *hendsoppers*, let alone to provide them with care, although this was not always possible.[287] Van Warmelo surely spoke for the majority of the involuntary internees when she declared: "Oh, how we loathe those hands-uppers! More than Khakis and capitalists and anything else objectionable."[288]

On the other side, *hendsoppers* performed much of the paid work in the camps, which gave them some power over the *bittereinder* majority.[289] A war prisoner recalled the behavior of *hendsoppers* who worked as police in the Bethulie camp: "Every day I had to hear or see how these poor women, girls and even small children were most abominably treated, badly handled or scolded and cursed by these same self-imagined gentlemen."[290] Some *hendsoppers* acted as spies, reporting the anti-British remarks of other internees to the administration.[291] In some camps, internees reported that the voluntary refugees received preferential treatment in the distribution of clothing.[292] As with the different ration levels in the camps' early phase, this unequal treatment must have exacerbated conflict between the two groups.[293] Placing the distribution of relief items in British hands was a logical solution. The Fawcett Commission report stated:

> Speaking generally, we found that for positions of authority in the camps, especially where the distribution of gifts or favours of any kind was concerned, the people decidedly preferred an Englishman or Englishwoman to one of themselves. Constant charges of favouritism, in such positions, were preferred against their own people.[294]

The commission thus recommended that all donations be coordinated by the superintendent, who then frequently assigned this task to a British "relief matron."[295] This was surely an important step toward a more effective system of distributing aid.

The aversion between voluntary and involuntary internees may also partially explain another phenomenon that frequently appears in British sources—the refusal to help other residents of the camps. From Aliwal North, Inspector Kendal Franks complained about the "sympathy for the sick and helpless which in these camps is so conspicuously absent, even when their own kith and kin are the afflicted ones.—Examples of this have come painfully to my notice in nearly all the camps I visited."[296] Malnourishment, particularly among internees who did not have enough money to supplement their rations, certainly contributed to the widespread apathy and reluctance to help others. The human body responds to a lack of nutrients by minimizing all activity.[297] The experiences of deportation—often beginning with the burning of farms—and internment claimed lives in most families; some were practically annihilated. This added to the trauma and social isolation of many internees.[298] Daily life in the camps could be so exhausting that little energy remained for helping others,[299] and in fact there were repeated instances of theft.[300] Even so, camp society was not entirely atomized. The memoirs of Boer internees feature numerous examples of great generosity, which belonged to camp life as much as the indifference to others' suffering.[301]

The social fabric of the camps changed over time. Many Boer men joined scout units and fought alongside the British in the final phase of the war. They were identified as "joiners." In order to protect these men and their families from the animosity of *bittereinders*, the British moved them to special joiner camps—such as Meintjeskop, near Pretoria—or to their own sections of the camps. They were frequently permitted to move into houses in nearby towns.[302] In addition, the mood of the involuntary internees may have slowly changed. Some women probably hoped that the war would end soon, and that their men would lay down their arms. In early 1902, Henry McCallum reported on the mood in the Pietermaritzburg camp:

> There is quite a change in the feelings of women in the Pietermaritzburg Camp since my last visit. Then the "hands-uppers" were held in contempt by

the majority. Now the opposite feeling is apparent, the women for the most part being anxious that their male relatives still in the field should surrender and accept the inevitable.[303]

Nevertheless, widespread expressions of disappointment over the peace agreement suggest that the majority of internees remained confirmed *bittereinders*, and that the conflict with the *hendsoppers* was in no way over.[304]

*Bittereinders* and *hendsoppers* were not immutable categories, however, and internees in the camps sometimes shifted allegiances. These shifts accompanied changes in living conditions, reminding us that the internees did enjoy a certain freedom of action. Women who wrote letters to their men still on commando, asking them to lay down their arms—or who were at least willing to contribute to the functioning of the camps—earned the trust of camp administrators, and in the early phase of the camps they could be upgraded from "undesirable" to "refugee" rations.[305] Men swore oaths of neutrality or even allegiance, accepting positions such as camp police in order to secure additional income for their families, thereby supplementing insufficient food rations and significantly improving their chances for survival.[306]

There were, however, options beyond collaboration[307] with the British authorities. Running away was one. Even former *hendsoppers* sometimes fled and became *bittereinders* by rejoining a commando.[308] Internees wrote petitions to the superintendents, general superintendents, and even Lord Kitchener; they demanded better conditions and mobbed the offices of local camp administrators.[309] Others looked for help outside the camps, asking friends and relatives to take them into their homes to increase their chances of being released.[310] Internees from abroad appealed to consuls from their home countries to negotiate their release.[311]

While not as toxic as relations between *bittereinders* and *hendsoppers*, relations between involuntary internees and khakis (British military and camp personnel) were still fraught. Great Britain was responsible for deportation, internment, and the glaring inadequacies of the camp system up until the end of 1901—and so was chiefly responsible for the mass death. The conflict between British and Boer traditions of medicine heightened tensions between internees and medical personnel, occasionally even erupting in physical violence.[312] It is important to recognize, however, that Boer-British relations were very different in the individual camps. One internee praised the superintendent in Standerton, P. C. Jonas: "Later on we got a new Superintendent who could speak no Dutch; he treated us very well and earned the gratitude of Standerton Camp."[313] By contrast, Johanna van Warmelo derided Superintendent

Scholtz in the Irene camp as the "biggest jingo that ever lived."[314] The relationship between a superintendent and internees ultimately said little about the former's ability to lead a camp effectively. Sometimes it was precisely the well-liked superintendents whose friendly demeanor hindered their management of problems in the camps. The Bethulie superintendent, Russell Deare, was well-liked but—according to Elizabeth van Heyningen—also responsible for the decidedly poor conditions in his camp. Heyningen writes: "The Boers themselves valued 'kindness,' but it was 'firmness' that kept the mortality rate low."[315]

Relations were worst with the superintendents of Boer descent, who were necessarily perceived by the camps' *bittereinder* majority as *hendsoppers* or joiners. The Fawcett Commission reported:

> The Englishman is, generally speaking, more successful as a camp superintendent than the man of Dutch or Boer parentage; the bitterest complaints addressed to us in camp against superintendents were directed against men of Dutch origin. The people would say they preferred a "Verdomnde Rooinek" [damned redneck] to a "Schelm" [rogue] of a Boer.[316]

Relations were simpler with camp personnel of Boer descent who did not carry the stigma of *hendsoppers*. This was especially true of women. Auxiliary nurses and teachers seem to have been generally accepted, and the volunteer nurses who came to Irene from Pretoria were practically revered.[317] The same could be said of some male prisoners of war, who were sometimes transferred to the concentration camps after mid-1901. According to Johanna van Warmelo, internees in the Irene camp greatly admired Dr. Andries Christoffel Neethling[318] and some of the camp chaplains, although their close relations to the *bittereinders* raised suspicions among the camp administration. Numerous ministers were banned from the camps because they were viewed as political agitators.[319] A similar fate befell the volunteer nurses in Irene after protracted disputes with the various superintendents.[320]

These measures were part of a general trend toward greater administrative centralization in order to better control the camps. Actors in the camps who were once quite independent—including volunteer relief committees from nearby towns, pastors, and representatives of philanthropic organizations such as Emily Hobhouse—were either shut out of the camps completely or officially integrated as a member of staff, which placed them more directly under the superintendent's control. The same was true for the British military. In response to complaints about "immoral" liaisons between soldiers and Boer women, the camps were declared off-limits to military men.[321] On one hand, this policy offered protection from rape; on the other, it removed the option of trading with soldiers, who could supply needy internees with in-demand goods. Prostitution, too, was mostly lost as a means of earning money.[322] Generally speaking, and insofar as we can trust the depiction of relations between internees and representatives of British colonial power in the testimonial literature, average British soldiers, or "Tommies," enjoyed a better reputation among internees than British officers.[323]

Except when under quarantine, camp society was not completely cut off from the outside world. Private individuals could request permission to visit, and a certain contingent of internees could regularly leave the camps to go to the next town.[324] There was correspondence by mail, even if all letters were subject to censorship.[325]

Conflicts occurred not only between internees and camp personnel but also among the personnel. The Fawcett Commission noted: "During the two-and-a-half days the Commission spent at Irene officials repeatedly complained to them of each other. Mr. Esselin [the superintendent, J. K.] complained of the Ladies' Committee; the Ladies' Committee complained of Mr. Esselin; the Assistant Superintendent complained of the Superintendent, and so on."[326] There were frequent disputes between superintendents and doctors over their respective authority—which is hardly surprising, considering that the doctors were higher-paid but formally subordinate to the superintendents.[327] Particularly during the measles epidemic, the camp personnel was chronically overworked, heightening the potential for conflict.[328] Many became sick themselves, died, or left their positions. Qualified replacements were hard to find, and persons without proper qualifications sometimes filled vacant positions.[329] All of these factors hindered effective camp administration and so indirectly contributed to the high mortality.

In contrast to the white camps, reconstructing social relations in the camps for Africans is hardly possible because of the meager documentation. British authorities sometimes observed conflicts between different groups in the camps. An inspector at the Harrismith camp reported that "the Fingoes and Zulus do not like being together." He recommended eventually placing the groups in two separate camps.[330] This seems to have corresponded to an overall strategy because camps for certain "tribes" are mentioned elsewhere.[331] It is impossible to know how prominent such conflicts were in the life of the camps.

Relations between internees and the white personnel could be difficult. De Lotbinière believed that regular camp inspections were essential in order to protect internees from administrators, explaining: "Further, I find from experience that constant expecting [*sic*, should be "inspecting," J. K.] is essential as the only means of keeping the Military supplied with labour, the cultivation work moving, and a close check and supervision over the subordinate Staff to prevent them defrauding the natives."[332]

Because there are hardly any written sources from African internees, one might assume that they were insignificant as historical actors. But even the few surviving British documents show that this impression is deceptive. African internees complained to inspectors about shortages in the camp, sometimes successfully,[333] and they sent letters of protest to high-ranking British authorities.[334] They organized religious and educational programming themselves, and they even succeeded in bringing missionaries they knew before the war to the camps, although this contradicted the official position of the Department of Native Refugees. Internees could accept or turn down paid positions, particularly with the military or private employers. And not least, many black internees decided to flee.[335]

## *Summary*

Life in the Boer camps changed significantly over time, as the previous sections in this chapter show. The camps were characterized by persistent shortages well into 1901, but this situation gradually changed. By the beginning of 1902, death rates had fallen below the level of large European cities, and some aspects of camp life—above all, schooling—could be considered an improvement over rural life in the Boer republics.

The ubiquitous shortages—of clothing, food, shelter, medical care, and sanitary facilities—were largely responsible for the mass death of 1901. British authorities had not intended to create a situation in which the interned Boers slowly perished; it was, rather, the result of a number of different factors. These included overburdened transport routes, the prioritization of military traffic, and the initial directive to civilian administrators to save money wherever possible. The scarcity of qualified personnel, particularly in the medical field, led to inadequate medical care in the camps and deficiencies in organization. Disputes among the camp personnel—as well as with and between the different internee groups—hindered efficient administration. The uncritical adoption of military guidelines (fifteen persons per tent, soldiers' rations) in civilian camps also had a negative effect. Kitchener's disinterest, finally, discouraged faster improvements to the catastrophic situation in the camps.

British authorities were not, however, responsible for all of the causes of the mass death. The hygiene practices of many Boers—often described by British camp doctors as "dirty habits"[336]—encouraged the spread of epidemics in the overcrowded camps. And the frequent disregard of doctors' orders could have fatal consequences. But these were not the main reasons for the high mortality, despite the assertions in many British reports.[337] The administration's own missteps were much more consequential, as was a factor beyond the control of both British and Boer actors—the measles epidemic that had already broken out in South Africa in 1899. Because measles was not endemic to the former Boer republics, the sickness not only afflicted children, but the entire population. As in other parts of the world, first contact with measles was especially fatal. The virus spread rapidly because there was hardly any resistance, and the concentration of so many infected persons led to a particularly severe form of the disease. British authorities had not foreseen any of this when they set up the camps. Relatively little was known about viruses at the turn of the century; measles were considered an "act of God."[338] But British internment policy increased the rate of mortality. The epidemic spread faster in the camps than it would have in a sparsely settled area. And the malnourishment of the internees was a key reason why so many cases of measles resulted in death.[339]

Similar factors contributed to mass death in the black camps—insofar as we can draw conclusions based upon the sparse documentation. The disinterest of British authorities and shortages of practically everything appear to have been even more pronounced than in the Boer camps. Significantly, there was no public outcry comparable to what Emily Hobhouse unleashed with her reports on the Boers' suffering, which ultimately led to improvements in the Boer camps. Any appeal that would have publicized conditions in the black camps would have been unlikely to provoke a meaningful response in European societies that were governed by racist principles. Life in the black camps did change significantly over time, especially after their division as part of the new agricultural program, but radical improvements never came.

## German South-West Africa: Scarcity, Disinterest, Compulsory Labor

Annihilating internees was not the declared purpose of the concentration camps in German South-West Africa, any more than in South Africa. But here, too, the question necessarily arises: why did mass death occur in the camps of the German colony? To find answers, we must look to the experience of the Herero and Nama in the concentration camps. How did the camps function? What did day-to-day life and conditions in the camps look like for the prisoners of war?

## *Walking Skeletons: The Journey to the Camps*

The military, which was responsible for administering the camps, blamed the high mortality on the internees' miserable condition when they were first taken prisoner or transferred.[340] Mission sources affirm this assessment. A history of Omaruru describes the surrendering Herero:

> Most of the people who came in from the field were such wretched figures that one had to ask: How could the people even make it to here? The small children, especially, awakened the deepest sympathies. Their bellies were often distended and misshapen, the rest of their bodies completely emaciated and covered with drooping skin. One is often moved to see how a starving mother still cares for her child, who is usually wracked with diarrhea, with tender concern . . . These are wretched figures, the likes of which will never be seen again in this lifetime.[341]

In Windhuk, missionary Friedrich Meier recorded similar observations: the people arrived "draped in rags or naked, emaciated to their bones."[342]

But the Africans' poor condition upon imprisonment was not enough to explain the mass death. For one, many Nama—unlike the majority of the Herero—were in good health when they surrendered to the German forces. A missionary named Eisenberg wrote about the Nama who surrendered in Berseba: "Their outward appearance did not suggest . . . many privations, but rather genuine well-being."[343] But the mortality of the Nama on Shark Island was higher than in every other camp. Second, the death rate of Herero prisoners who were permanently sent to work for private companies was often far lower than in the concentration camps of the military forces. Thus, only 6 of 115 Herero (5.2 percent) who were compelled to work for the Woermann shipping line in Swakopmund died between 22 April and 22 May 1905, while 181 of 1,281 Herero (14.1 percent) died in the military prison camp between 22 April and 26 May. One explanation for the difference is that the prisoners who worked for Woermann were better housed and fed.[344]

A further explanation for the high mortality points to the conditions under which the prisoners of war were brought to the camps. After the extermination order was lifted in December 1904, Herero in the field were encouraged—in part, by the missionaries—to surrender, and then were brought to concentration camps in the larger towns (*Etappenorten*). Missionary Eich, who had traveled to Epukiro in the eastern part of the colony for this "labor of peace," reported on the conditions there. At first, prisoners received a good amount of flour and rice, and five days' rations for the march to Windhuk. But when more soldiers arrived and additional provisions did not, the situation changed. Once there was no longer enough food, the Herero received no more rations, and they had to try to survive on whatever they could scavenge. Consequently, only 100 of 278 prisoners made it to Windhuk. Most presumably died on the days-long march—undertaken six to seven hours every day. According to Eich, around fifty Herero perished on another march from Otjombinde.[345]

This brings us to a central factor that contributed to the mass death. Whenever there was a conflict between the interests of the prisoners and those of the military—or in general, any Europeans—the latter always prevailed. Food shortages were chronic in South-West Africa; soldiers in the field rarely received more than two-thirds of their designated rations. Shortages always hit the interned Herero and Nama first and hardest. Thus, when there was no longer enough food in Epukiro, resources were taken from the Herero and given to the soldiers instead.

Conditions seem to have improved in later transports. In February 1906, when all detained Nama were supposed to be brought from Gibeon and Keetmanshoop to Hereroland, groups of five hundred to seven hundred persons were assigned to empty transport columns. Women, children, and the sick could travel in oxcarts; only men had to march. The people were not treated roughly, and their stamina set the pace of the march. Nevertheless, security was tight. Provisions were cooked in advance and only distributed day by day, in order to discourage stockpiling and escapes. Sentries were ordered to shoot any Nama who attempted to escape.[346]

The other large marches began at the Rhenish Missionary Society's collection sites, which began to appear in Hereroland in December 1905, and they ended at the closest towns and their associated camps. Detainees were not initially escorted by German soldiers, but by Herero "native patrols," who had been tasked by the missionaries with combing the surrounding area and luring their fellow Herero to collection sites.[347]

Once prisoners of war arrived in the concentration camps they were usually done marching, but they were still moved to different locations. There was a great deal of traffic between the various camps.[348] In 1905 most prisoners were brought from the camps in eastern Hereroland—Omaruru, Okahandja, and Windhuk—to Swakopmund and to the Otavi railroad. In early 1906 the German authorities sent a large number of Herero to Lüderitzbucht, to put them to work on a new railroad construction project. Their old jobs were filled by recently surrendered Herero. The captured Nama were brought north in February 1906, and they moved to Lüderitzbucht in September. About one year later, the few survivors were sent back north to Okawayo. These movements took place in open train cars and on Woermann steamships.[349]

Because difficulties with provisions eased once prisoners were transported by railroad, it appears that mortality was not unusually high on these later transports. Documents from the colonial administration and the mission do not point to large numbers of deaths. Nevertheless, the many transfers—as in South Africa—may have contributed to mass death because prisoners of war carried infectious diseases from one camp to another. According to an official medical report, this is what happened when prisoners were taken from the mission collection site in Otjihaenena, where dysentery had broken out in early 1906, to the concentration camps in Hereroland. Once space became available in the Windhuk "native lazaretto" in mid-1906, the Germans began isolating "dysentery-contaminated prisoner transports" from Otjihaenena and Okomitombe in a special section of the lazaretto—with good results.[350] Over time, this strategy had also succeeded in the South African camps. By far, the sickness that cost the most internee lives in South-West Africa was scurvy, which was not an infectious disease, in contrast to the measles epidemic in South Africa.

## Gefangenenkraale: *Structural and Spatial Organization of the Camps*

The camps where the prisoners of war were taken shared two common structural features. First, they were either secured by a rampart of thorn branches (as in Windhuk), or by a barbed-wire fence (as in Swakopmund). The sea provided a natural barrier on Shark Island near Lüderitzbucht. The prisoners were sheltered on the far end of the island, and a triple layer of barbed wire blocked access to the other side, where a military hospital was situated. The so-called *Einkraalung*[351] was intended to stop the internees from escaping, and to address the colonial power's need for security. It also cut off the internees' contact with the outside world. Only military guards were allowed to enter. Even police who were sent by the civilian administration could enter the camps only with the permission of the local military commander.[352] But the ban on whites in the camps does not always appear to have been strictly enforced.

A second shared structural feature was that the prisoners' dwellings were usually constructed from locally available materials.[353] This was usually sufficient for building the traditional round huts called *pontoks* in the colony's interior. But on the barren coast, "no native has a plank or a tree branch that could be used for this purpose," as the missionary Vedder wrote. His assessment of living conditions in the Swakopmund camp continued:

Most of the huts in the government *werfts*, where the prisoners now live, are worse than deficient. A few huts are built from wood and corrugated iron and offer acceptable protection against the harsh, damp sea wind; inside, two bunks are stacked on top of one another, just high enough for lying down and sitting up a bit. But most of the houses consist only of poles nailed with sackcloth for walls and a roof, and they offer no protection to speak of at night.[354]

Living conditions were also miserable in Lüderitzbucht, as the missionary Kuhlmann reported:

How do the Hereros live? The whole island consists of compact rock masses, which only now and then display a thin layer of sand and earth. So the people don't have a chance to drive poles or wooden planks into the ground in order to build a hut. Now and then, one comes across a makeshift hut with loosely propped supports that will be knocked over by a strong wind. This is why they usually lean pieces of wood at an angle against the rock walls, and then cover them with sacks. But there aren't enough of the latter, so the sight of the huts is more than bleak. Others even live outdoors, in the cold, damp sea air they aren't used to at all . . . Still others make their beds between the rocks.[355]

But it was precisely along the coast where better lodging was needed; temperatures were significantly cooler on the coast than in the interior because of the cold Benguela Current. The unaccustomed cold was a terrible problem for the prisoners, as indicated by one of the few surviving documents actually written by an internee. Samuel Kariko, an evangelist with the Rhenish mission in Lüderitzbucht, lamented: "It is very difficult for me, my body is weak and it is very cold. I don't know how I should stay."[356] Many prisoners of war, who were often inadequately clothed, came down with deadly cases of pneumonia in the cold coastal areas. Vedder described the situation in Swakopmund:

You can only imagine how adversely this lack of protection against the nighttime cold affects [the internees'] health. "Ombepera i koza"— "the cold is killing me" is the complaint that I hear every day, whenever I enter the *werft*. And this expression is literally true. In one night, people catch pneumonia and are already dead the next morning.[357]

Vedder further complained that a shortage of housing meant that thirty to fifty men, women, and children from different families all had to live in one room, and he asked the district office to change this.[358] And the Rhenish mission critically noted that some camps—especially Okahandja—had huts that were too close together, which could be catastrophic in the case of a fire or epidemic.[359]

Conditions improved slightly over time. At a conference of the Rhenish mission in October 1905, it was reported that the prisoners' living conditions in Swakopmund were no longer as deficient. Internees were allowed to build their own dwellings and live in them with their families, and in the cold months they could request "more effective cover" for the wooden frames draped with sackcloth.[360] With the coming rainy season, more had to be done to weatherproof dwellings in other locations,[361] but the rear commander did agree to expand the *Gefangenenkraale* and widen the distance between *pontoks*.[362] Different photographs of the camp near the old fortress in Windhuk show that the *pontoks* were reordered as the camp grew. Initially pushed together in a cramped space (Figure 3.3), the tents later stood in orderly rows (Figure 3.4). The new layout marked a break with the traditional circular arrangement of Herero huts. Gesine Krüger sees this change as a symbolic disruption of traditional Herero structures, a reflection of the colonial power's declared goal to rob the Herero people of their own organization and turn them into a dependent proletariat.[363]

On Shark Island, makeshift shacks were gradually replaced with tents, although these did not always protect against the cold (Figure 3.5).[364] Here the colonial administration—especially the *Etappenkommando*, which was responsible for prisoners of war—did make a limited effort to improve camp conditions and reduce mortality.

The fenced-in area of the camps included not only the internees' dwellings but also a large space where they presumably gathered before work. The grounds of some concentration camps also held other facilities. On Vedder's suggestion, a provisional church was constructed in

**Figure 3.3** The concentration camp near the old fortress in Windhuk (© National Archives of Namibia, no. 1843, used with permission).

**Figure 3.4** Postcard of the reordered concentration camp near the old fortress in Windhuk (© National Archives of Namibia, no. 11495, used with permission).

**Figure 3.5** The concentration camp on Shark Island near Lüderitzbucht (© National Archives of Namibia, no. 9780, used with permission).

Swakopmund, along with a thirty-meter-long infirmary built from corrugated iron.[365] In Windhuk, the colonial power set up a similar "native lazaretto" in three large tents "near the kraal."[366] It steadily expanded to accommodate growing demand. At the height of the hospital's expansion in early 1906, it was the largest institution of its kind in the colony, with room for five hundred patients. As soon as space was available, the personnel divided up the patients by ailment into different sections of the facility, in order to prevent infection. But this was not always possible, especially in the early phase of internment, and many sick persons were housed in an extra "sick department" within the camp itself.[367] Sometimes the sick and the healthy were jumbled together in the *pontoks* of the camp, significantly heightening the risk of infection.[368] Other locations—including Okahandja and Lüderitzbucht—also had separate "native lazarettos," which were likewise fenced and guarded.[369] We should therefore amend Susanne Kuß's assertion that the Germans interned not only prisoners of war in the concentration camps but also free women who suffered from sexually transmitted disease.[370] The women were detained against their will, but not in concentration camps; instead, they were usually held in outside lazarettos.

Another distinctive characteristic was the spatial separation between Herero and Nama prisoners of war. In Windhuk, another camp was built for the Nama, presumably when a larger group was brought to Hereroland in early 1906.[371] On Shark Island near Lüderitzbucht, where Herero as well as Nama were interned, the *Etappenkommando* divided the camp into two separate zones.[372]

Overall, the architecture was very provisional; camps could be quickly erected and then taken back down. This was hardly surprising, given the general reluctance to dedicate more resources to the prisoners of war. The camps were not conceived as long-term accommodations. In 1905, it already seemed plausible that internment would end in the foreseeable future.[373] Camps might need to move at any time, as Trotha had already stated in his first instructions to camp administrators: "If there is an outbreak of infectious disease, the camps must immediately be moved several kilometers into the bush, and the old camp burned down."[374] In fact, several camps were resituated—including those in Omaruru, Swakopmund, and Windhuk.[375]

The provisional character of the South-West African camps recalled those in South Africa—especially the black camps, where internees had to construct their own dwellings with inadequate materials. But even the Boer camps with their distinctive tent architecture and initially makeshift facilities could in no way meet the internees' needs. Inadequate facilities contributed to the high mortality in the camps for blacks and whites alike. The paradigm shift near the end of the war—from provisional to increasingly permanent facilities—became the most significant architectural difference between the Boer camps and those for blacks in South Africa and South-West Africa. This new way of thinking, and the resolve to improve camp housing, was only rudimentarily present in the concentration camps for Africans in both colonies.

## *From Total Deprivation to Scarcity: Provisions in the Camps*

Inadequate clothing also contributed to the prisoners' high mortality. The Herero, in particular, often came from the Omaheke nearly naked. "If they had received the necessary clothing, perhaps some of the deaths in Swakopmund, where the prisoners were sent, could have been prevented because many of them came down with pneumonia," the missionaries' chronicle for Omaruru asserted.[376] But in early 1905, local military authorities did not provide the Herero with enough warm clothing or blankets to protect against the cold in Swakopmund or Lüderitzbucht. The coastal towns did not even have enough fuel to compensate for this shortfall.[377] Numerous prisoners of war fell victim to inadequate protection against the cold coastal climate.

The food supply was likewise deficient. Detainees initially received only rice, then some "meat from fallen animals," and a little coffee now and then. The Herero were unaccustomed to rice, and it overwhelmed their digestive organs, particularly when it was not fully boiled because of the shortage of cooking pots and firewood. Hundreds collapsed and died from an inadequate diet.[378]

Medical care was also completely deficient. In early March 1905, the missionary Vedder did report that around thirty prisoners were treated with opium after eating spoiled bacon—so there was apparently limited access to medical treatment. But the "native lazarettos," where the prisoners of war were supposed to receive medical care, were not established right away. In Karibib, the missionary Elger had run a lazaretto even before the Africans were interned,[379] but Swakopmund did not have a lazaretto until May 1905,[380] and Windhuk, only at the year's end.[381] Prisoners who were unable to work were not sent to the missionaries for care until mid-March 1905.[382]

The chaotic early months in the concentration camps have come to be characterized by cadaverous prisoners of war who lacked nearly everything, resulting in mass death. In most camps mortality was highest in the first half of 1905, and it tapered off toward the end of the internment period. A statistical overview from the command of the colonial forces indicates that the highest monthly mortality for Swakopmund

(16.91 percent) and Okahandja (5.72 percent) occurred in June 1905. The lowest mortality for both sites (around 1 percent) occurred toward the end of the internment period.[383] A leading cause of the early chaos was certainly that German authorities had not counted on so many Herero turning themselves in, so they were ill-prepared to provide for thousands of prisoners.[384] The military's fundamental disinterest in coordinating provisions for the prisoners also played an important role. The military saw combat as its foremost responsibility. Maintaining the supply chain and taking care of prisoners did not bring military honors, as officer Franz Xaver Epp noted in his diary, so these duties were neglected.[385] Trotha himself was a good example of how the priorities were set. He would have gladly turned down "responsibility for supervising the larger concentration camps."[386] But Berlin did not allow this, so he pushed responsibility for provisioning down to individual troops and stations and simultaneously emphasized that "readiness for further operations in the east and provisioning of the forces must not suffer under any circumstances."[387]

The internees' food, clothing, shelter, and medical care gradually improved. These improvements were a clear sign that the responsible authorities did not intend to murder the internees, as the missionary Philipp Diehl observed: "The government is making every effort to keep the people alive, insofar as this is within its powers, which is progress compared to earlier, when one wanted to rid the world of them all."[388] The command distributed blankets, so every prisoner on Shark Island possessed at least one by August 1905.[389] Some internees received old military uniforms,[390] and in February 1906 rear commander Lieutenant Colonel Karl Ludwig von Mühlenfels approved an order of standard blue canvas uniforms for convicts from Germany.[391] The military also ordered women's clothing, which were not part of its own inventory.[392] Significantly, the prisoners now received clothing before they reached the cold coast. Mühlenfels's predecessor, Major Maercker, determined that the prisoners should be "carefully furnished with clothing and blankets" while still in the colony's interior, in addition to receiving "2 days' food rations (generously measured)." His expectation was that "only people who were vigorous and fit to work" would be sent to the coast.[393]

Instead of rice, the colonial forces began to distribute flour, which was easier to digest. This improved the health of many prisoners, even if it did not fully resolve their dietary problems. Over time, large numbers of internees came down with scurvy because of an unvarying diet that lacked basic nutrients. The *Etappenkommando* responded with further adjustments to the prisoners' rations, which will be discussed more below.

The "native lazarettos" began treating patients in the second half of 1905. They often expanded several times before they could accommodate all of the sick. An official medical report stated that the hospitals were well-furnished. In Windhuk, four to five teams of white medics worked with thirteen black helpers. But the medical personnel did not provide costly treatment, underscoring the German colonial power's reluctance to dedicate greater resources to the internees. This was a radical difference with the Boer camps in South Africa after the end of 1901.

Once the civilian administration in South Africa had taken over the camps, efforts to bring down the high mortality completely overshadowed the question of cost for some time. This affected not only medical care but also food rations. However, the disparity in provisioning between the camps of South Africa and South-West Africa did not exist from the start, despite Isabel Hull's assertion to the contrary. According to Hull, the lowest meat ration in the Boer camps was five times higher than what prisoners of war in South-West Africa received. She concludes that rations in the German *Gefangenenkraale*, in contrast to those in the British camps, were intentionally designed to produce extreme suffering, hunger, sickness, and death.[394] In fact, as Table 3.2 demonstrates, early rations for the "undesirable" Boers in the Transvaal included no meat at all, and also in other respects they lagged behind the German camps' rations. Only over the course of 1901, and especially after the reforms of January 1902, did provisions in the Boer camps surpass those for detained Herero and Nama. Thus, the difference in rationing had more to do with different reactions to mass death than with original allowances. German response to the mortality crisis more closely resembled British policy toward black internees. In both cases, reluctance to dedicate meaningful resources toward improving conditions for internees was combined with a conviction that existing conditions were good enough. Only a minority of black camps in South Africa even had a hospital, as described above. Despite the German colonial power's refusal to properly equip the lazarettos, these facilities did improve the situation of interned Herero and Nama. Mandatory smallpox vaccinations helped to contain the affliction, which had been rampant among detainees. And the simple act of separating and isolating those who were sick reduced the spread of lethal diseases.[396]

The Rhenish Missionary Society played a large role in improving conditions in the camps. Missionaries witnessed the internees' misery firsthand and usually visited the camps daily. Many missionaries felt responsible for the prisoners' well-being, not least because they had par-

**Table 3.2** Selected official rations for adults in the concentration camps of South Africa and South-West Africa.[395]

|  | GSWA 1905 | GSWA 25 April 1906 | Transvaal 1 Dec. 1900 Class A | Transvaal 1 Dec. 1900 Class B | ORC 8 March 1901 | ORC 16 Jan. 1902 | Natal 1901 | ORC 15 Feb. 1901 Africans |
|---|---|---|---|---|---|---|---|---|
| Flour | 3,500 g | 2,800 g | 3,178 g | 3,178 g | 2,384 g | 2,384 g | | |
| Rice | or 3,500 g | or 2,800 g | | | | 227 g | | |
| Bread | | | | | | | 3,178 g | |
| Potatoes | | | | | | | 1,589 g | |
| Corn / Millet | | or 2,800 g | | | | | | 4,767 g |
| Meat | 300 g | 300 g | 908 g | | 1,589 g | 1,589 g | 1,816 g | 454 g |
| Salt | 210 g | 210 g | 112 g | 112 g | 196 g | 196 g | 98 g | 49 g |
| Sugar | | 280 g | 336 g | 224 g | 392 g | 392 g | 392 g | 56 g |
| Coffee | 280 g | 210 g | 168 g | 112 g | 196 g | 196 g | 196 g | 14 g |
| Milk | | | | | 1/12 can | 1/12 can | | |
| Fat | 210 g | 350 g | | | | 196 g | | |
| Lime juice | | | | | | 112 g | | |
| Jam | | | | | | 227 g | | |
| Vegetables | | 140 g | | | | if available | | |
| Tobacco | | 1 plug | | | | | | |

ticipated directly in the surrender of many Herero. Mission Inspector Spiecker wrote to Wilhelm Eich, head of the Herero mission:

> I was pleased that you have already made arrangements so that the Herero who are sick and in need of help will be cared for. This is a solemn responsibility, which we should not shirk in any way. In my view, the government's responsibility is to pay for sustaining the Herero, even if we gladly perform the work. So please be sure to keep precise records of the funds that are spent, and whenever you feel the moment is right, from time to time, perhaps monthly, calculate expenses for the government and request reimbursement. But even if the government declines to fulfill this duty, we cannot and must not turn away from this solemn duty of mercy. The financial situation of our

mission is very grave, but the Lord will compensate us for our efforts. Herein you also have—as mentioned—full freedom of movement.[397]

Taking up their own call, the missionaries distributed blankets and clothing to prisoners in need. Items were collected in Germany and promptly sent to the colony. In Swakopmund alone, missionary Vedder gave out around eight hundred articles of clothing to approximately eleven hundred prisoners of war in the first half of 1905.[398] The mission headquarters in Barmen continuously sent crates of clothing to other concentration camps and to the mission's collection sites, which had been active since the end of 1905. Missionaries also tried to improve the prisoners' diet. In Lüderitzbucht, the missionaries Laaf and Nyhof gave out "Boer flour," coarsely ground flour that was easier for the prisoners to digest. In Swakopmund, Vedder distributed tea and milk, especially to the weakest children. And missionary Elger collected fresh lemons for patients with scurvy in his lazaretto in Karibib. But all of these efforts were just a drop in the bucket. Even after diverting the fees they collected for baptisms, missionaries lacked the funds to help on a larger scale.[399]

In addition, missionaries cared for sick detainees. This became a major area of responsibility after 14 March 1905, when Trotha ordered that prisoners of war who could not work would be sent to the Rhenish mission. In Okahandja alone, missionary Eich received 795 such detainees between 14 April 1905 and 4 May 1906. They were sheltered in a separate, unguarded "kraal," where their care was overseen by Eich's wife. Seriously ill prisoners seem to have been sent to a "native lazaretto."[400] The system functioned similarly in Windhuk, where missionary Meier assumed responsibility for around 120 detainees who could not work in May 1905. Their mortality declined significantly under the care of his wife, who was assisted by another prisoner of war.[401] Sometimes family members were recruited to care for sick prisoners, as in Elger's lazaretto in Karibib.[402] The *Etappenkommando* provided the usual prisoners' rations; any other food had to come from the mission.[403]

Orphaned children who were not taken in by captured family members were sent to the mission. The Rhenish mission built an orphanage in Otjimbingwe, and missionaries stationed in different locations also provided shelter to children.[404] Trotha's initial determination that only the Rhenish mission would care for the Herero was overturned in September 1905. From this point on, the Protestant mission had to contend with Catholic "competition." Half of the orphans and prisoners of war who were unable to work were henceforth sent to the Catholic mission of the Oblates of Mary Immaculate.[405]

Mission and military efforts to improve living conditions in the camps succeeded in bringing down prisoner mortality from its early heights. Missionary sources emphasize that conditions improved substantially after the first terrible weeks, and particularly over the course of 1905.[406] A new consensus emerged that the prisoners were doing well, perhaps even too well.[407]

But this assessment was mistaken. Mortality was lower, but still high. Internees died less often because of the cold coastal climate, or because they could not tolerate the food. Instead, most fell victim to scurvy, a sickness caused by the Vitamin C deficiency that came from the camps' unvarying, nutrient-poor diet. The role of vitamins was not yet understood at the beginning of the twentieth century, although sailors had long known that eating lemons successfully counteracted scurvy. The need to supply ships on the way to India with fruit and vegetables was one of the reasons that Europeans had settled on the South African Cape. This tradition may explain why scurvy was not as prevalent in the South African camps. German doctors, by contrast, did not seem as familiar with the connection between scurvy and the lack of fruit and vegetables. Archival sources reveal substantial confusion about the disease. Dr. Hugo Bofinger, who was responsible for treating the prisoners on Shark Island, published an article entitled "Some Information about Scurvy" in a medical journal after the war; his goal was to improve the state of knowledge about "this rather dark disease."[408] But Bofinger was not able to answer one of the most contentious questions about the ailment—namely, whether or not scurvy was infectious. Julius Ohlemann, a medical officer stationed in the colony, recalled that the high command had promoted the infection theory during the war.[409] Other doctors faulted the prisoners' unvarying diet.[410] Bofinger also recognized the significance of nutrition, but he came to believe that the lack of fat in prisoners' diets was a contributing factor to the many cases of scurvy.[411]

Despite uncertainty over the ailment's causes, German authorities decided to adjust the prisoners' rations. The new governor, Friedrich von Lindequist, agreed with the Medical Office's recommendation to add one hundred grams of dried vegetables to the internees' rations each week. In addition, doctors received citric acid crystals and legumes, and small amounts of condensed milk, dried fruit, and sugar, for treating patients with scurvy. And troops of detained women and children were tasked with scavenging edibles that grew in the wild, or *Feldkost*—especially wild onions, or "onkies."[412] Also, common kitchens for patients were built to encourage the better utilization of resources.

The Medical Office affirmed the "wish to improve provisions for sick natives," but it also observed that "sick soldiers rarely receive fresh lemons anywhere, except in coastal areas and in a few of the towns along the railroad. Likewise, fresh onions, wherever they are available, can be much more beneficial to our sick soldiers, who are constantly coming down with scurvy." Fruit puree or fresh milk for prisoners was similarly rejected on account of the sick soldiers' needs.[413] Under no circumstances could detainee provisions reduce the allowance for German soldiers. This principle was enshrined in Trotha's first instructions for handling prisoners, and it constantly reappeared in all communications about internee provisions. In July 1905, Deputy Governor Tecklenburg rejected the Rhenish mission's proposal to acquire dairy cows so that the prisoners would be better fed, stating: "It would be a crime against our sick soldiers in the lazarettos, against the settlers and their children, to take even one of these dairy cows they so urgently needed."[414] In fact, it was a struggle to provide the soldiers and the rest of the white population with fresh, nutritious food. Except for meat, food production was extremely limited in German South-West Africa, and even this resource grew scarce with the mass death of cattle during the war. All foodstuffs had to be imported, and the limited transport options meant that fruit and vegetables were always in short supply. In this situation, the prisoners received almost no fresh food.

But even when fresh provisions were available, or could have been obtained (for example, on the coast), the *Etappenkommando* still withheld them from the Herero and the Nama. The Medical Office recommended that lemons be given to soldiers on the coast who were sick with scurvy—but not to prisoners of war in the same location, unless they were donated by the mission. To do otherwise would have violated another principle of handling prisoners: internees were supposed to feel like prisoners, so they had to be treated worse than free blacks and, especially, whites.[415] If German soldiers in the interior could not get lemons, then prisoners certainly couldn't, either.

This way of thinking also informed the provisioning of clothing for the Herero in Swakopmund in early 1905. Camp authorities distributed old soldiers' uniforms to the prisoners but recalled them a short time later on the order of the high command. The uniforms were replaced with coarse sacks that offered little protection against the cold.[416] The high command apparently felt that soldiers' clothes were too good for the prisoners. Later on, however, authorities in all of the camps returned to distributing old soldiers' uniforms to the internees.

The aforementioned measures for fighting scurvy were only partially successful in lowering mortality. Later efforts to provide prisoners with fresh milk were ultimately more effective. No new cases of scurvy developed after the surviving Nama were transferred from Lüderitzbucht to

Okawayo (a horse depot near Karibib, with two hundred goats available for the internees' use) in September 1907. And some lazarettos reported success curing scurvy after the beginning of 1908, once milk could again be distributed to "natives" who were suffering from the disease.[417]

Overall, the health of the prisoners steadily improved until the internment of the Herero officially ended on 1 April 1908. There was, however, a significant exception to this trend. In all of the camps, mortality slowly receded after the chaotic first weeks—but on Shark Island near Lüderitzbucht, the worst of the mass death did not begin until September 1906. Here, too, conditions had initially improved after an early phase of high mortality. As late as the beginning of September 1906, Mission Inspector Spiecker reported that the Herero who had been interned on the island for a longer period were relatively well situated and in good health. Only 200 to 300 new arrivals had to sleep outdoors, apparently because the authorities had not been informed in advance that they were coming.[418] Just days later, however, the Germans transferred 1,700 Nama from the north to Shark Island all at once, touching off the mass death that claimed the lives of more than 1,200 Nama through April 1907.

How did the number of deaths shoot upward so quickly? To begin, the colonial power was clearly overextended. If 200 to 300 new arrivals had presented a logistical problem for the authorities in Lüderitzbucht, as Spiecker reported, 1,700 people brought far greater difficulties. The mortality of newcomers was always elevated, as they had to acclimate themselves to local circumstances, and essential supplies were not always on hand.[419] If this were the only explanation, however, the death rate would have gone back down after several weeks. Yet this did not happen. The harsh climate also does not appear to have been the decisive factor. The majority of the prisoners on Shark Island (and in the rest of the colony at this time) died from scurvy.[420]

Within this context, it is noteworthy that the Herero on the island were much healthier than the Nama.[421] Not only had the Herero enjoyed a longer period of acclimatization, but they left the island each day for work and therefore had a chance to obtain additional food—including leftovers from the white residents of Lüderitzbucht.[422] Nama men, by contrast, were not allowed to leave the island at all, and Nama women could leave only to fetch water.[423] In this way, the women may have had opportunities to acquire a little extra food because—according to Dr. Bofinger—they appeared to be somewhat more resistant to scurvy than the men.[424] Remarks on scurvy in the annual medical report of 1907/08 reveal the importance of additional food sources; "natives" who worked in the lazaretto kitchen or had relatives in town had access to better provisions and avoided developing scurvy.[425]

The Nama on Shark Island were the only group of prisoners of war who were not allowed to leave their camp, or at least the island, even to work. Otherwise, they received the same provisions as internees elsewhere—including rice and flour, and meat twice a week. Like the internees in other locations, they received small quantities of legumes, fruit puree, and chocolate. Dr. Bofinger reported on attempts to treat them with citric acid crystals, iron, arsenic, bismuth, and opium, by rinsing, painting, and etching.[426] At the end of 1906, the weekly meat ration was raised from 300 to 1,000 grams.[427] But all of these measures did not successfully address the Vitamin C deficiency. The dried legumes and canned fruit puree were distributed in very small quantities and contained little Vitamin C. Prisoners also had difficulty cooking the legumes because of the shortage of fuel.[428] The lack of access to food outside the camp—a hindrance not shared by other prisoners—seems to be the key difference that explains the high number of scurvy cases and extremely high mortality among the Nama on Shark Island.

## *Prayer and Compulsory Labor: Daily Life in the Camps*

Another factor that significantly influenced internee mortality was the obligation to work—not only for men and women who were deemed fit, but also for children. In November 1906, missionary Vedder reported from Swakopmund that all children above the age of ten were expected to work.[429] And even younger boys worked for German military and civilian officials as *Bambusen*, or child servants.[430] The Germans often compelled sick internees to work, with particularly dire consequences. Some overseers suspected that mere laziness lurked behind all internee claims of sickness. One overseer in Lüderitzbucht singled out supposed "shirkers" among the sick on Shark Island for immediate punishment.[431] In Omaruru, the staff doctor Frey determined that sick Africans who had been sent to the mission for care were in fact healthy, although— as depicted in a mission chronicle—they "were so weak they could not stand."[432] Missionary Vedder's observation was thus hardly surprising: "One sees few sick people because everyone who can still move is forced to work and then dies in the night."[433]

There were, however, significant local differences in how prisoners were handled. These particularly depended on the persons who served as overseers, as well as on the local rear commander (*Etappenkommandeur*) and district commissioner (*Bezirksamtmann*). The number of working hours also affected the prisoners' experience in the camps. In Swakopmund, for example, prisoners worked mornings from 7:00 to 11:00 a.m., and afternoons from 2:00 p.m. to 5:00 p.m.[434] There was no work on Sundays, and sometimes even an additional day of rest, as long as Major Bauer (whom Vedder described as highly accommodating) was rear commander.[435] This changed when a new commander arrived in mid-1905, and prisoners were regularly ordered to work nights and Sundays.[436]

Overall, work on Sunday seems to have increased in the colony over the course of 1905. However, once Governor Friedrich von Lindequist arrived, internees generally received time off on Sunday afternoons.[437] The missionaries had lobbied for this change so the prisoners could participate in religious services. But internees still had to work on Sunday mornings, and often at night.

Prisoners were employed almost everywhere. They worked for the military in officers' clubs, hospitals, clothing depots, and supply columns, and they engaged in public works by building roads and prisons, unloading ships, and removing garbage and human waste. They were also sent to work for private individuals and firms.[438] Large companies such as the Woermann shipping line and the firms responsible for railway construction in the south and north of the colony employed dozens, hundreds, or even thousands of prisoners. On 1 June 1906, for example, 2,302 captured Herero (including 1,128 workers) were overseen by the Koppel company, which was building the Otavi railroad. And on 15 June 1906, 1,302 prisoners were sent to the Lenz company, which was responsible for constructing the southern railroad.[439] These large companies built their own camps for sheltering prisoners. Lenz also assumed responsibility for guarding the prisoners.[440] Both Lenz and Koppel maintained their own lazarettos for sick workers, which also treated the recently transferred prisoners of war.[441] Smaller businesses such as laundries, workshops, and stores also requested prisoners as workers. These prisoners usually lived in one of the concentration camps of the armed forces and were brought to their employers each morning. The *Etappenkommando* and colonial government did, however, allow "individuals, especially farmers, who lived far away and who could ensure the secure custody of prisoners ... to keep prisoners overnight."[442]

All private individuals and firms were expected to take care of their designated workers and families, but also to maintain an appropriate balance: "The people must receive enough food and blankets etc. to be protected against the growing cold, but on the other hand, it should not be forgotten that the people are prisoners who must be fed accordingly." No wages were paid to the workers; instead, beginning 1 April 1905 private employers paid a "rental fee" of fifty pfennigs a day (or a maximum of ten marks per month) to the district office for every transferred prisoner who was fit to work.[443] Directions to private individuals for handling the interned workers clearly demonstrate, on one hand, that the colonial power sought to protect workers' lives, but on the other, that prisoners were to be taught their place in the social hierarchy—significantly below the free blacks, who were paid for their work.

Over time, the German authorities reconsidered the question of fees and wages. After September 1905, rental fees were no longer collected for female prisoners who worked only for households or farms, not commercial employers.[444] Farmers received additional relief; after August 1906 they only had to pay two marks for every male prisoner of war, whereas the maximum fee paid by businesses was set at five marks.[445] Lindequist also gave prisoners the chance to earn a low wage, which was part of his strategy for adding more workers to the colonial economy. He hoped that the prospect of earning a wage would encourage more Herero to surrender. After December 1905, especially talented workers and foremen who had already worked for six months could earn up to five marks per month; women could earn a maximum of three marks. This sum was drawn from the required rental fee. The change in policy simultaneously allowed prisoners to purchase goods with their cash wages.[446] The surviving wage lists for prisoners of war indicate that pay levels rose over time. In January 1906, the building administration paid its prisoners two to five marks per month. Wages climbed as high as eight marks per month in February 1907, and ten marks after November.[447] The Otavi railroad had paid up to ten marks per month since December 1905.[448]

Even so, wages were low and remained so. Free blacks received up to thirty marks per month plus food; African workers from other colonies could even earn between eighty and one hundred marks.[449] The surviving sources do not reveal what prisoners of war bought with their wages, or whether—as in the South African camps—stores operated in the concentration camps, or the extent to which the internees' living conditions improved. There is some evidence that the prisoners used cash to buy clothing.[450] But it seems unlikely that the money did much to improve the internees' diets. On 12 December 1906 the building administration transferred six prisoners with scurvy to the hospital; five of these prisoners had received a wage the previous month.[451] They presumably did not, or could not, spend their money on food that was rich in Vitamin C.

The question naturally arises whether living conditions for prisoners who spent a longer period of time with companies and private individuals were better off than in the military internment camps. This seems to have been the case for prisoners on farms. They were usually better fed, although they often had to work more than in the *Gefangenenkraale*, so some Herero and Nama fled back to the military camps.[452] The farmers' economic interest in preserving prisoner labor was much more immediate than was the case for the military. Since they could not count on receiving new prisoners of war if the old ones fled or died, they had to consider their prisoners' well-being or even satisfaction, to a limited degree. Workers who were known to be mistreated could be taken away.[453] One indication of the better treatment on farms was a report on "native conditions" that noted that the health of prisoners of war had significantly improved "as a result of the better shelter and food with the transfer to private individuals."[454] Even so, some prisoners were badly mistreated, especially on remote farms that were difficult to monitor.[455]

Living conditions also appear to have been better with larger companies than in the concentration camps. Missionary Vedder expressly praised the situation of prisoners who worked for private companies and, particularly, the Woermann line: "Clothing and food are good there, work and treatment is appropriate, living conditions quite good. Thus the number of sick persons is low; there are significantly fewer deaths than in the *Gefangenen-Werft*."[456] And even though we do not know the precise number of deaths with the Otavi railroad, the fact that thousands of Herero voluntarily sought to work there speaks for comparatively good conditions. These Herero circumvented "many an unpleasant experience in the *Gefangenenkraal*," as the mission chronicle for Omaruru states.[457] And missionary Kuhlmann emphasized that the prisoners with the northern railroad were treated well, much better than with the armed forces.[458]

The same could not be said for the southern railroad. Mortality with the southern railroad was not as high as during the worst period on Shark Island (around 18 percent in December 1906) or in Swakopmund (nearly 17 percent in June 1905), but it hovered around 10 percent each month in the winter of 1906. At the start of 1907, it was more than 12 percent—far higher than in all other concentration camps.[459] One explanation for the extraordinarily high mortality on the southern railroad was certainly the extreme physical workload.[460] Mortality in March and April was about 4 percent, but the death rate shot upward in June.[461] Around this time prisoners began to work on Sundays because railroad construction had fallen behind schedule.[462] Night shifts also became commonplace.[463] Food and shelter for the prisoners was apparently acceptable,[464] but medical care was wretched. Of the 757 sick persons who were sent to the Lenz company's lazaretto in Lüderitzbucht between 1 June and 31 December 1906, 637 died.[465]

Prisoners not only worked for the military, civilian authorities, and private companies, but also in the camps themselves. In October 1906, 70 men and 372 women and children resided in the concentration camp in Okahandja. Of these internees, "40 to 50 men, and a very large number of women" worked in the *Gefangenenkraal* itself.[466] They had to clean the camp,[467] fetch water "in large tins (canisters),"[468] or work in the camp's own enterprises. In the Windhuk camp in April 1907, there were shoemaking and tailoring workshops where prisoners repaired the old items of soldiers so these could be distributed to internees. There was also a camp laundry where all of the officers brought their clothes to be washed and ironed, and plans for a trade school for boys and a sewing school for girls.[469]

What happened outside of working hours? Midday breaks were primarily occupied with cooking and eating.[470] On evenings and Sundays, insofar as they were free, religious practice seems to have been especially important. Nearly all of the missionaries reported on the prisoners' "inner pull toward Jesus," which had become more prominent during the war.[471] Missionary Meier from Windhuk remarked that he had never had such attentive listeners, many of whom were moved to tears.[472] Worship services were very well attended and usually took place on Sundays, so the prisoners did not have to work. At first, services usually took place within the concentration camps—either outdoors, presumably in the large open areas inside the fenced compounds, or in separate facilities built for this purpose, as in Swakopmund.[473] Numerous disputes arose between the Catholic and Protestant missionaries after September 1905, once the Catholic mission was also allowed to work with prisoners. All missionaries' access to the camps was subsequently forbidden or at least restricted. The rival parties negotiated various local arrangements: Catholics and Protestants took turns leading services in the camps, or the prisoners chose which mission to visit and marched under military escort to their respective house of God.[474] Reports by the Protestant Rhenish missionaries derisively note that the Herero were not much interested in the Catholic offerings.[475] But the Oblates' lack of success also had to do with the fact that they had not been allowed to work with the Herero before the war, so their presence was less familiar.

Alongside worship services, the Rhenish missionaries offered baptismal instruction and sometimes communion instruction, too. These classes usually took place one or two evenings a week and were likewise well attended.[476] More Africans began to be baptized toward the end of the internment period. Movement between camps, however, made it difficult for students to successfully complete their religious instruction in one place.[477] The mission documented internee participation in the Protestant faith by giving baptismal students special passes that they could present to the missionary in their new camp.[478] The Rhenish mission employed "native helpers" or "evangelists" to serve the religious needs of prisoners along the railroad lines. Sometimes missionaries also traveled these routes, preaching to workers and instructing helpers.[479]

Jan-Bart Gewald persuasively asserts that Christianity was one of the pillars that enabled the reconstruction of Herero society after its destruction in the war. This process began in the camps: "Missionaries, and the faith that they purveyed, brought true spiritual solace, and a way in which a seemingly unintelligible world could be understood." In addition, the missions offered a degree of physical protection and material support in the hostile world of the camps. The missions and their faith became an important touchstone for many prisoners of war.[480]

Alongside religious instruction, the missionaries also offered regular schooling for interned children. In South-West Africa (unlike South Africa), there were no public schools for blacks, and none were established in the camps for interned Herero and Nama.[481] The missions filled this gap, typically employing African helpers as teachers. The missionaries themselves often taught only German or religion. Student numbers were low because older children were expected to work, and nearly all boys served as *Bambusen*.[482] Sometimes there was no instruction at all, as when the children were sent out to hunt for firewood.[483]

Nothing is known about sports or recreation, in contrast to the documentation that exists for the white camps in South Africa. The only festivities that are mentioned in firsthand sources were closely associated with mission work—namely, marriages, which missionaries oversaw in the concentration camps.[484] But the internees must have had their own celebrations. In Omaruru in April 1906, Captain Franke recorded in his diary: "Now it is midnight. The sounds of singing and dancing, mostly prisoners of war, carry over from the native *werfts*—like a call from a bygone era."[485]

Finally, health and medical checks were a daily occurrence, as the following report depicts:

> To begin, every prisoner transport that arrived or departed the camp was examined, and the sick were immediately transferred to the lazaretto; there was also a regular visitation twice a week for all prisoners reporting sick. Until May 1906, all prisoners of war were examined every fourteen days for sexually transmitted diseases; after mid-1906, these examinations were replaced by a weekly health inspection for all prisoners.[486]

## *Violence, Escape, and Collaboration: Social Relations and Room for Maneuver*

The colonial power profoundly disrupted the social relations of internees. Just as prisoners were forbidden from leaving the fenced camps (except under supervision to go to work), civilians were generally kept from entering them. This heightened the emotional duress of being interned behind a cordon of barbed wire. Herero elders in the Swakopmund *Gefangenenkraal* recounted the humiliation of being guarded like oxen behind barbed wire.[487] Some missionaries saw the isolation as another reason for the high mortality in the camps. Their chronicle for Lüderitzbucht described the conditions on Shark Island: "But even more than these wretched conditions [the poor food supply, J. K.], sequestration at the far end of Shark Island contributed to killing the people's desire to live. They grew gradually apathetic to the misery. Three high barbed wire fences separated them from the outside world."[488] This apathy may have been partially responsible for another phenomenon that the missionaries observed: there were hardly any babies. This had not been the case in the field—at least, the Herero had arrived at the mission collection stations with many small children.[489]

Prisoners had the most contact with the personnel who supervised them: one non-commissioned officer, white guards, and some "native" police in every camp. Internees had little reason to expect good relations with their overseers. During the first months of detention, foremen were rarely seen without a *sjambok*, a whip made from hippopotamus hide.[490] Missionary sources are full of references to the serious abuse of prisoners. In response to a query from District Commissioner Kuhn, the missionary Elger described the injured Herero who had come to his lazaretto in Karibib. One had been hit with a hammer; another came with a broken arm.[491] Missionary Kuhlmann described a particularly grisly scene during his visit to Shark Island. An overseer named Benkesser had shot a sick Herero woman five times and let her bleed to death.[492]

The *Etappenkommando* took action to restrain the overseers' violence. In August 1905, Cai Dame urged local rear commanders and other officials to be vigilant in ensuring that "only the officer who held penal authority"—not non-commissioned officers or other guards—could administer corporal punishment.[493] His successor, Major Maercker, reiterated this appeal after missionary Diehl reported that Herero who had been beaten and kicked in the Windhuk camp had fled to the mission collection site in Otjihaenena: "He [Maercker, J. K.] used this opportunity to strictly forbid beatings in the kraals once again, especially by the colored wardens. Neither soldiers, nor colored guards, may carry *sjamboks* from now on. Offenses by the prisoners will be punished by the *Etappenkommandant*." As a matter of principle, he added, beating women was not permitted.[494] But these bans remained ineffective as long as there was no follow-up on site. After the incident on Shark Island, Kuhlmann complained about the overseer Benkesser to the local rear command. Benkesser's superior expressed shock at the missionary's report and announced that there would be consequences. But he had apparently not been to the island in a long time, he was barely informed about conditions there, and so he was hardly in the position to monitor his overseer.[495]

The colonial military's broad disinterest in the prisoners gave the camp personnel—at least in some places—wide berth to live out their fantasies of power. As Isabel Hull aptly states: "Lax administration . . . permitted the ever-present potential for brutality to become real."[496] In other towns, by contrast, the local *Etappenkommandant* closely watched that the prisoners were not beaten.[497] Relations with internees substantially depended on the actions of local authorities, which varied from place to place and over time, due to personnel changes.

There were, moreover, considerable differences in how employers treated their detained workers. Alongside cases of abuse and extreme exploitation, we also find accounts of employers who advocated for their workers. Some employers interceded with the authorities so their workers' families could be reunited, or relatives released from the camps.[498] Some paid higher wages than were officially allowed.[499] In any case, the actions of employers—who were responsible for providing their forced laborers with food and clothing, wages, and sometimes shelter—decisively influenced the living conditions of the Herero and Nama.

While female prisoners were, at least theoretically, exempt from corporal punishment, they were frequent victims of an unsanctioned form of violence: rape. Overseers and other whites were frequent perpetrators.[500] An Italian doctor in the Koppel company's "native lazaretto" in Omaruru reported that a guard had abused a seven-year-old girl. And the camp's guards were apparently aware that railroad workers repeatedly broke into the Herero camp and "took along" women.[501] Not all sexual contact between internee women and whites was forced, to the extent that one can speak of a situation without force in an overarching system of coercion. Missionaries repeatedly complained about the "immorality" of women and girls, revealing the typical racist assumptions that black women were animalistic, promiscuous, and sexually aggressive.[502] Vedder especially ridiculed the Herero women who were interned separately in Swakopmund at the beginning of the war; they behaved "like cattle," asked whites for sex, and occasionally took off for a few hours to make themselves available in the next "native hut."[503] In Windhuk, military authorities set up a "bordello kraal" behind the old fortress, where the "captured Herero girls . . . voluntarily sacrificed themselves to this dirty business," as missionary Wandres described.[504] Money, clothing, and better food appear to have especially motivated interned women to have sexual intercourse with whites.[505] This was one of the few recourses that prisoners had to improve their own living conditions and, often, their chances for survival.

The spread of sexually transmitted diseases can indicate the prevalence of sexual relations—forced or "voluntary"—between white men and black women, especially prisoners of war. Most Europeans believed that practically all black women were infected, which was certainly an expression of racist stereotypes.[506] In Karibib, "more than 70 percent of the female natives who were examined were found to have sexually transmitted diseases, particularly syphilis" in 1904.[507] The explosion in the number of infected German soldiers soon after their arrival in the colony suggests that sexual intercourse with African women was very widespread. Soldiers reported more than 3,300 new infections during the entire period of the war, although the actual number was likely much higher. The spread of sexually transmitted diseases was around five times higher than in the army in Germany.[508] Because there were almost no opportunities in the colony for soldiers to have sex with white women—with the exception of some white prostitutes, who were regularly examined for disease—the infections must have come from sex with Africans.[509] A medical report from April 1906 drew a similar conclusion: "The sharp increase of sexually transmitted diseases in the last 5 months on the northern line of communication was striking. It was apparently related to the increase of prisoners."[510]

The numerous venereal infections posed a large problem for the military, straining the capacity of the lazarettos and reducing the fighting power of the armed forces. Alongside a campaign for using prophylactics during sexual intercourse, there was an attempt to manage the situation by forcibly testing the entire black female population. This upset the prisoners greatly. Transferring Herero from Otjihaenena to Windhuk became extraordinarily difficult, because prisoners feared the examinations for sexually transmitted diseases that were conducted there. Mission Inspector Spiecker also criticized the practice of examinations in Windhuk. They were undertaken "in a nearly open hall, in the presence of all of the women . . . without consideration for modesty."[511] In Karibib, the "natives" responded to the examinations by threatening collective escape into the field.[512]

The general health controls were abolished in mid-1906. They had complicated an already difficult relationship between the black population (especially the prisoners) and the medical personnel of the colonial power, particularly in the "native lazarettos." Internees were understandably frightened to enter the hospitals. Given the high mortality in some lazarettos—particularly those operated by the Lenz company in Lüderitzbucht—there were fears that "whoever enters the lazaretto no longer comes out alive."[513] Statistically speaking, however, the rate of recuperation in the lazarettos was significantly higher than the number of deaths.[514] Mission Inspector Spiecker nevertheless confirmed: "The natives would rather die than be taken to the government lazaretto."[515]

The unfamiliar methods of German doctors, including autopsies to determine causes of death, also contributed to the internees' skepticism.[516] The doctors experimented with different treatments, particularly to fight scurvy, although their scientific curiosity was sometimes greater than their desire to cure patients.[517] Part of colonial medical "research" was preserving specimens for anthropological study. Interned Herero and Nama had to preserve the skulls of deceased fellow prisoners, which were then sent to different research institutes in Imperial Germany.[518] The detached heads were preserved in formalin and sent in soldered tin canisters to institutions that had requested anatomical material from the colony.[519] All of this heightened prisoners' fear of the lazarettos.

German doctors meanwhile decried "the indifference of the native population, particularly in following sanitary guidelines"[520] and pointed to the internees' deficient hygiene as a reason for the high rate of sickness. Dr. Bofinger discussed efforts to introduce modern health practices to prisoners on Shark Island:

> All means were employed to attempt to introduce them to the advantages of general hygiene. They had to get used to defecating only in certain locations, keeping the huts (pontoks) and also the surrounding areas clean. Soap was given to the natives for keeping their clothes and bodies clean ... The extent of the difficulties that all of these efforts encountered can be appreciated only if one is familiar with the indolence and almost entirely deficient sense of cleanliness of the natives, namely the Hottentots. The latter were utterly covered in filth ... Most had to be compelled by force to accept the advantages that were offered to them. No wonder that under such circumstances the fight against scurvy was only partially successful.[521]

The conflict between two medical cultures resembled the one depicted by Elizabeth van Heyningen in the white camps in South Africa. As in South Africa, this conflict surely reduced the efficacy of medical care and contributed to mass death among the Herero and Nama.

The missionaries played an important role in the social network of the camps. They were allowed to enter with special passes that were issued by the German authorities. After some of the camps closed to missionaries because of the conflict between the confessions, prisoners could leave the camps under military supervision to attend worship services and baptismal instruction at the missions. The missionaries also retained some influence in the concentration sites through "native helpers," who were themselves usually prisoners of war and lived in the camps.

The Rhenish missionaries regularly advocated for the internees. They appealed to military and civilian authorities on the prisoners' behalf—to abolish examinations for sexually transmitted diseases, to protest abuse, to reduce work time on Sundays, to improve food and clothing provisions, and so on. In some cases the mission headquarters in Barmen even intervened with the Colonial Department in Berlin—as when missionary Kuhlmann reported on the catastrophic conditions on Shark Island in August 1905.[522] Some interventions were directly motivated by specific requests from internees. In Windhuk, missionary Meier presented a complaint about the mistreatment of various internees to the *Etappenkommando*, adding that the affected internees had asked him "to bring the aforementioned cases to the proper address."[523] It is evident here—and in many other situations—that a relationship of trust usually existed between internees and missionaries.[524] In fact, missionaries were often the only people whom the prisoners could trust at all.

Pastoral care and material aid from the missionaries were naturally important as well. Jan-Bart Gewald has correctly observed that missionaries alleviated some of the suffering in the concentration camps, and that the mortality would have been significantly higher without their engagement.[525] This helps to explain why mortality on Shark Island in early 1905 was higher than in every other camp. Lüderitzbucht was the only site with a large concentration camp, but no stationed missionaries, until December 1905. There was no one who could regularly distribute additional food or clothing, who could care for internees who were unfit to work, or who could have reported the overseer Benkesser's violent acts earlier to the military command.

Nevertheless, the role of missionaries—and particularly the Rhenish mission—was ambivalent.[526] Missionaries had played a key role in detaining the Herero, and they understood that thousands were dying from conditions in the concentration camps. But few missionaries acknowledged responsibility or halted their cooperation. An exception was August Kuhlmann, who could no longer justify his collaboration because Herero were "literally being murdered by their transfer to Swakopmund."[527] If the Rhenish mission had refused to help detain the Herero, fewer people would surely have been interned, and so fewer people would have died in the camps. But this counterfactual thought experiment cannot tell us whether more people would then have starved in the field or been shot by military patrols, or whether the mission would have thereby lost its opportunity to positively influence conditions in the camps.

Because of the lack of the sources, we can draw few conclusions about the prisoners' social relations to one another. The colonial power no longer officially recognized the Herero and Nama *kapteins*, but there was still an elite within the camps whom the administrators and missionaries addressed. Governor Lindequist explained in a speech to the captured Nama: "Of course, there are no longer any *kapteins* among you. But I trust that you, Samuel Isaak, and you, Hans Hendrik, have enough influence over your people to discourage them from further unreasonable acts."[528] And guidelines for handling the captured Nama assigned the former *kapteins* a key role; Samuel Isaak was responsible "for taking care that all orders were precisely followed, and for immediately reporting all irregularities that reached his ears." And "former *kapteins* and field cornets" were to be employed "as foremen and supervisory personnel in larger troops of workers."[529] Among the Herero, the group of elders assumed special importance. They reported unfavorable circumstances to the missionaries, but they also sometimes supported the camp administration—for example, by identifying women who ought to be examined for sexually transmitted diseases, or by reporting plans for escape.[530] There was also a kind of camp foreman. In Windhuk, this was the evangelist Sem, who supervised the camp's sewing school and craftsmen in addition to his religious responsibilities.[531]

Reports about the prisoners' behavior toward one another are highly contradictory. The mission chronicle for Karibib noted that "it was painful to witness how the people were often unsympathetic and unwilling to help one another or the dying. On the other hand, one could also see quite moving love and care."[532] Disputes between the different Herero groups have been documented in the mission collection stations, but we lack information about relations between prisoners in the concentration camps. The Otjihaenena collection station was divided in two parts, in order to separate the Ovaherero and Ovambanderu and to discourage quarrels between them.[533] And missionary Olpp reported that one of his "native patrols" had abused, robbed, and raped the Herero whom they had found.[534] But in the camps, we know almost nothing about relations between ethnic groups. Herero and Nama appear to have been interned separately, insofar as this was possible. The status of the few Bergdamara and San in the large concentration camps of Herero and Nama is unclear. They were presumably interned because the Germans had mistaken them for Herero or Nama, or because they had accompanied Herero and Nama in the field—whether as allies or prisoners.[535]

Older colonial histories have tended to ignore the agency of colonized peoples.[536] But—as other passages in this book have shown—the internees were not passive subjects of the colonial power without room for maneuver. They worked to improve their living conditions in a variety of ways. They formed relationships with whites as *Bambusen*, or as sexual partners or prostitutes, in order to acquire material advantages. They complained about the violence of overseers and other unfavorable circumstances, and they achieved some success, usually with the mission as mediator. District court files reveal that they sometimes even fought back physically against their overseers.[537]

Above all, internees often chose to flee as a means of escaping unfavorable conditions with their employers or the concentration camps. Herero and Nama fled from farmers back to the camps, and from camps back to the field or to the mission collection stations. They also fled from collection stations (especially when they were supposed to be sent to concentration camps), and they fled from lazarettos. Hundreds fled from Swakopmund to the nearby Walvis Bay, hoping to board a ship to South Africa from this British enclave. A numerical example helps to illustrate the extent of these escapes: of the 3,020 prisoners of war who were sent to private employers or the district office in Windhuk between early 1905 and mid-June 1907, 560 took flight.[538] The escapes became so problematic that the colonial power responded with draconian countermeasures. Soon fleeing was punishable not merely by flogging, but also execution.[539] Sending escapees to Lüderitzbucht became an alternative punishment—a prospect so fearful that some prisoners killed themselves before they could be transferred.[540]

## *Summary*

What does the prisoners' day-to-day experience tell us about the causes of mass death in the camps? The German colonial power was clearly overwhelmed by the mass internment of Herero and Nama in the concentration camps. In an area with little food and only rudimentary infrastructure, the Germans were hard pressed to provide even minimal sustenance to thousands of prisoners, many of whom were already emaciated. After an initial period of mass death, the prisoners' situation improved slightly—a consequence of general efforts to protect the lives of prisoners who were urgently needed as future workers. But the colonial power imposed tight restrictions that impeded better provisioning for internees. On one hand, supplies for the German armed forces could not be cut back under any circumstances. On the other, internees were supposed to feel like prisoners, so they were treated and fed worse than whites and free Africans alike. There was not only a lack of will to expend the necessary resources for ensuring the internees' survival. There was also a lack of knowledge about fighting diseases effectively in the camps—most of all, scurvy, which was still seen as something mysterious.

But why were so many prisoners brought to the coast, where mortality was known to be much higher than in the interior? Did this express a genuine will to annihilate? There were three reasons for internment on the coast. First, the most workers were needed here. Second, even rudimentary provisions for thousands of prisoners could be supplied only on the coast. Provisioning was possible to a limited extent along the railroad line, but even the white population and armed forces could hardly be sustained in the south of the colony and, in general, beyond the railroad line.[541] And third, the coast was considered more secure than the interior because it was separated from the center of the colony by the belt of the Namib desert; prisoners on the coast were unlikely to succeed in escaping back to the "rebels."[542] The need for workers and a secure site to detain Herero and Nama were the two reasons why a large number of prisoners were transferred to the coastal towns of Swakopmund and Lüderitzbucht. There was no plan for annihilation. At the end of 1905, the colonial authorities agreed with the Rhenish mission that sick prisoners should be sent from Swakopmund to recuperate in the colony's interior.[543] They were needed in the future as workers and had to be kept alive.

So why, in September 1906, were all of the Nama interned on Shark Island? Why were they held there, even though it soon became evident that they could not survive for long in this setting? Here, too, the security argument proved decisive. The Nama were thought to be much more dangerous than the Herero because their resistance had not yet been broken. When some Nama escaped captivity in Windhuk, Governor Lindequist and Commander-in-Chief Deimling felt compelled to take action, responding in part to pressure from anxious settlers.[544] They transferred the Nama to the only site that was considered secure—the "high-security camp" on Shark Island. Nama men were not allowed to leave the island under any circumstances, which underscores the dominance of security concerns. Finally, the transfer to Shark Island brought a noticeable savings in troops; fewer guards were required on the island than in the camps in the colony's interior, as Colonel Deimling liked to emphasize.[545]

After some weeks, once the extreme mortality among the Nama had become apparent, a discussion began about the (partial) clearance of the island. The missionary Fenchel had alerted Deimling to the conditions on the island. Deimling's lack of awareness about these conditions—insofar as the sources are reliable on this point—can be taken as further indication of the military's disinterest in the prisoners. The security question again figured prominently in subsequent discussions about clearing the island, thereby reaffirming the intended function of internment—the secure custody of prisoners, which had led to the transfer of numerous Herero and Nama to the coast, and also the isolation of the Nama on Shark Island.

Most persons involved in these decisions accepted that the measures would increase the mortality of internees. The interests of the colonizers always came first. The deaths were seen as "just punishment" for the rebels—or at least they could be rationalized in this way. The deaths of black internees earned little notice, corresponding to the racist spirit of the times. In this respect, it is revealing that the Rhenish mission never sought the attention of the German public in its numerous interventions on behalf of the prisoners. No public outcry resembling British society's response to mass death in the white camps of South Africa could be expected. In Britain, too, the mass death of black internees attracted almost no interest.

As in South Africa, internees did not die because the colonial power sought to kill them systematically. The mortality was an unintended consequence of the plan to exploit the labor of the prisoners and to satisfy the colonizers' demands for security. Mortality was compounded by difficulties supplying the colony and fundamental disinterest in the prisoners' well-being—two factors that were also central in South Africa—as well as prioritization of Europeans' needs over those of the prisoners, confusion about scurvy, racist indifference to internee suffering, and the opportunity to view this suffering as fair punishment for "rebellion." All of these factors contributed to the conditions that led to the mass death of Herero and Nama in the camps, particularly during the early phase of internment and again on Shark Island after September 1906.

## Notes

1. Lisle March Phillips, *A Tiger on Horseback: The Experiences of a Trooper & Officer of Rimington's Guides—the Tigers—During the Anglo-Boer War 1899–1902* (Leonaur, 2006), 225.
2. See, for example, Hobhouse, *War without Glamour*, 45–46 and 141; and Hobhouse, *The Brunt of the War*, 59.
3. Hobhouse, *War without Glamour*, 109; and Elizabeth Neethling, *Fünfzehn Monate in den Konzentrationslagern. Erinnerungen einer Burenfrau aus ihrer Gefangenschaft* (Bern, 1902), 16 and 23.
4. Hobhouse, *The Brunt of the War*, 57. There are similar recollections on pages 67 and 70–71; and Hobhouse, *War without Glamour*, 45.
5. See Helen Dampier, "Women's Testimonies of the Concentration Camps of the South African War: 1899–1902 and After," (PhD diss., University of Newcastle, 2005); Stanley, *Mourning Becomes*; and Heyningen, "Costly Mythologies," 505–7.

6. FAB, SRC 3, no. 648. On similar problems in the Transvaal, see General Superintendent of Burgher Camps to the Military Governor, NAL, WO 32/8008. General Superintendent Goodwin, however, believed that the complaints about inadequate opportunities to bring along possessions were valid only in exceptional cases.
7. Two hundred and twenty "refugees" brought along only seventy-six blankets. Superintendent Hume believed that 250 more were needed. Superintendent Hume to Chief Superintendent Trollope (9 March 1901), FAB, SRC 3, no. 497.
8. This was the term used by a Hermannsburg missionary who was personally involved. Georg Haccius, *Aus der Drangsalszeit des südafrikanischen Lüneburg* (Hermannsburg, [1904?]), 7.
9. Neethling, *Fünfzehn Monate*, 19–31; Hobhouse, *Report*; Hobhouse, *The Brunt of the War*; Hobhouse, *War without Glamour*; Haccius, *Drangsalszeit*, 5–9.
10. Hobhouse, *The Brunt of the War*, 72.
11. Georg Haccius, *Die Hermannsburger Mission in Südafrika in und nach dem Burenkriege* (Hermannsburg, [1904?]), 6.
12. Chief Superintendent to the Secretary ORC Administration (12 June 1901), NAL, CO 417/325, pp. 333–47, here p. 338.
13. General Superintendent Tucker to Military Governor Maxwell (19 September 1901), NAP, GOV 262; "Medical Report" (July 1901), Burgher Camp Middelburg, NAP, GOV 261; "Medical Report, Burgher Camp Pietersburg" (31 July 1901), ibid.; Kendal Franks, "Report on Irene Camp" (11 July 1901), NAP, GOV 260.
14. Brandt, *The War Diary*, 267.
15. See, for example, "Monthly Report for Heidelburg Camp" (6 July 1901), NAP, GOV 260.
16. "Cir. Memorandum No. 30" (16 January 1901), NAP, MGP 258, p. 17.
17. Ibid. See also "Monthly Report on Volksrust Refugee Camp for July 1901," NAP, GOV 261. The monthly reports on Barberton und Krugersdorp for July 1901 present a similarly positive picture; all other Transvaal camp reports for July emphasize the new arrivals' poor condition.
18. Hobhouse, *Report*, 10. See also Neethling, *Fünfzehn Monate*, 25.
19. General Superintendent Tucker to the Military Governor (22 February 1902), NAL, CO 417/349, pp. 904–26. See also Spies, *Methods of Barbarism*, 207.
20. Around ten thousand persons were sent to Natal from the Transvaal camps alone, according to the November report of the Burgher Refugee Department. See General Superintendent to the Military Governor (19 December 1901), NAL, CO 417/348, pp. 31–37; and "Monthly Report by General Superintendent January 1902" (22 February 1902), NAL, CO 417/349, pp. 513–19.
21. General Superintendent to the Military Governor (22 March 1901), NAL, WO 32/8008. Smith also emphasizes the porousness between camps and the outside world. See Iain R. Smith, "The Concentration Camps in South Africa, 1900–1902" (paper, International History of Concentration Camps workshop, Dublin, 10 October 2008).
22. "Refugees who have received permission to move from one camp to another must pay own fares," FAB, SRC 5, no. 1427; "Movement of Refugees from one camp to another to be discouraged," FAB, SRC 1, no. 68.
23. Low-Beer, Smallman-Raynor, and Cliff, "Disease and Death," 240. One example of this is the transfer of internees who were infected with measles from Kroonstad to Heilbron at the end of 1901. See the correspondence in NAL, CO 224/7, pp. 59–72.
24. An exception was the small Eshowe camp in Zululand, which was not on a railroad line and was, in any case, an unusual concentration camp. Transport from Eshowe to the camps in Merebank and Wentworth did not occur by train. See Wassermann, *Eshowe*, especially 37 and 54.

25. Kessler, "South African War," 66 and 77.
26. "Final Report Native Refugee Department Transvaal," NAP, TKP 135, 1; and de Lotbinière to Milner (30 September 1901), NAP, SNA 59, p. 92.
27. De Lotbinière to Milner (30 September 1901), NAP, SNA 59, p. 92; and Kessler, "South African War," 72. On the transport of the African population to the camps, see Mohlamme, "African Refugee Camps," 111–12.
28. Kessler, "South African War," 138–43.
29. See also the photographs in Louis Changuin, Frik Jacobs, and Paul Alberts, *Suffering of War: A Photographic Portrayal of the Suffering in the Anglo-Boer War Emphasising the Universal Elements of All Wars* (Bloemfontein, 2003), 119–51.
30. George Turner to the Military Governor (7 March 1901), NAL, WO 32/8008.
31. Lieut-General Commanding Natal District to the Military Governor (21 March 1901), NAL, WO 32/8008. Approximately five hundred people, or around half of the camp's internees, already lived in the houses at this time.
32. Cd. 893, *Report on the Concentration Camps*, 52.
33. General Superintendent, "Cir. A," NAL, WO 32/8008.
34. "Rules for the Guidance of Refugee Camp Superintendents," FAB, SRC 1, no. 103.
35. Pakenham, *The Boer War*, 501–8. On Hobhouse in particular, see Brian Roberts, *Those Bloody Women: Three Heroines of the Boer War* (London, 1991), 122–46 and 164–81; and Andrew J. McLeod, "Emily Hobhouse: Her Feet Firmly on the Ground," in Pretorius, *Scorched Earth*, 198–225.
36. On the Fawcett Commission, see Pakenham, *The Boer War*, 515–18; Roberts, *Those Bloody Women*, 182–203; and Krebs, "'The Last of the Gentlemen's Wars.'"
37. Milner to Goold-Adams (4 December 1901), BLO, MP 173, pp. 245–48. In December 1901, Milner argued that the camps were likely to exist for three more years, and he advocated for the purchase of several hundred huts that could hardly be considered temporary structures. See also Assistant Secretary to the High Commissioner to Major General Sir E. Wood (5 December 1901), NAL, CO 417/348, p. 322.
38. The military camp commanders who oversaw the camps until 1901 left behind almost no records, so very little is known about the early phase of the camps.
39. General Superintendent to the Military Governor (23 May 1901), NAP, GOV 259; Chief Superintendent Refugee Camp to Secretary ORC Administration (12 June 1901), NAL, CO 417/325, pp. 333–47, here pp. 340–41.
40. Zietsman, "The Concentration Camp Schools," 102–3. See also Edmund Sargant to the Secretary to the Orange River Colony Administration (13 June 1901), NAL, CO 417/325, pp. 348–56; Edmund Sargant to John G. Maxwell (Pretoria) (24 July 1901), NAL, CO 291/29, pp. 390–96; and Cd. 893, *Report on the Concentration Camps*, 5.
41. See, for example, the monthly reports on the Transvaal camps for September 1901, which mention gardens several times. NAL, CO 417/335, pp. 332–523.
42. "Hospital Report Compiled by Medical Officer Kroonstad," RC, FAB, SRC 1, no. 69; George Turner to the Military Governor (6 March 1901), NAL, WO 32/8008; "Kendal Franks Report on Burgher Camp Krugersdorp" (31 July 1901), NAP, GOV 261.
43. The Fawcett Commission drew attention to this imperative in numerous camps. See Cd. 893, *Report on the Concentration Camps*, 37, 54, 61, 67, 82, 88, 132, 137, 173, 193, 202, and 208.
44. In Irene, for example, this occurred in July 1901. See "Medical Report for the month of June, Irene," NAP, GOV 260.
45. See, for example, W. M. Brown, "Report Burgher Camp Vereeniging" (12 September 1901), NAP, GOV 262; N. J. Scholtz to the General Superintendent (9 December 1901), NAL, CO 417/348, pp. 61–73; Kendal Franks, "Report on Burgher Camp Springfontein," NAL, CO 417/349, pp. 141–57.
46. General Superintendent to the Military Governor (22 March 1901), NAL, WO 32/8008.

47. On 7 July 1901 Johanna Brandt-Warmelo reported that the Irene camp was enclosed by a barbed-wire fence. Brandt, *The War Diary*, 277. Dr. Kendal Franks noted in his reports that Barberton was fenced in August, while no fence was needed in Balmoral because it was surrounded by blockhouses. See Kendal Franks, "Copy of Report on the Burgher Camp at Barberton" (27 August 1901); and Kendal Franks, "Copy of Report on the Burgher Camp at Balmoral" (21 August 1901), NAP, GOV 262. A fenced enclosure was completed in Standerton in August. "Monthly Report on Burgher Camp Standerton for month of August 1901," ibid.
48. See the correspondence in "Concentration Camps" (17 January 1902), NAL, CO 417/348, pp. 511–42. On Kimberley, see also Hobhouse, *Report*, 10.
49. Hamilton Goold-Adams to Alfred Milner (10 January 1902), NAL, CO 417/348, pp. 519–22; Hobhouse, *The Brunt of the War*, 181, 203, and 251–52; and Elira Wessels, "'A Cage Without Bars'—The Concentration Camp in Bloemfontein," in Pretorius, *Scorched Earth*, 79.
50. Cd. 893, *Report on the Concentration Camps*, 10–12; and General Superintendent to the Military Governor (19 December 1901), NAL, CO 417/348, pp. 31–37. See also Heyningen, "A Tool for Modernisation?," 7–8.
51. Heyningen, "A Tool for Modernisation?"
52. Telegram from Alfred Milner to Joseph Chamberlain (1 December 1901), NAL, WO 32/8061.
53. Chief Superintendent Refugee Camps to Chief Ordinance Officer (9 April 1901), FAB, SRC 4, no. 1136; Hobhouse, *Report*, 12; and "Infantile Mortality in Concentration Camps: reasons suggested for" (12 November 1901), FAB, CSO 44, no. 4103/01. See also Low-Beer, Smallman-Raynor, and Cliff, "Disease and Death."
54. Hobhouse, *Report*, 10; and "Medical Report for May 1901, Burgher Camp Middelburg" (6 June 1901), NAL, WO 32/8009. Goold-Adams, too, did not recommend the bell tents. Hamilton Goold-Adams to Alfred Milner (10 January 1902), NAL, CO 224/7, pp. 40–44.
55. Brandt, *The War Diary*, 226; and Hobhouse, *Report*, 14. See also Wessels, "'A Cage without Bars,'" 66–68.
56. See, for example, "Report for June, Burgher Camp Middelburg" (6 July 1901), NAP, GOV 260; "Report for the month of June 1901, Burgher Camp Volksrust," ibid.; and N. J. Scholtz to the General Superintendent, Burgher Camp Mafeking, NAL, CO 417/348, pp. 53–60. See also the relevant entries in the Fawcett Commission reports, Cd. 893, *Report on the Concentration Camps*.
57. Scholtz to the General Superintendent, Burgher Camp Mafeking, NAL, CO 417/348, pp. 53–60; Cd. 893, *Report on the Concentration Camps*, 13. See also the pages mentioned in note 43 in this chapter.
58. Hobhouse, *Report*, 12.
59. The data for the Transvaal are from "Census return of number of refugees" (22 March 1901), NAL, WO 32/8008; Cd. 819, *Reports, &c., on the Working of the Refugee Camps in the Transvaal, Orange River Colony, Cape Colony, and Natal* (London, 1901), 47; "Total number of Inmates, Sick and Deaths in Burgher Camps Transvaal" (31 May 1901), NAL, WO 32/8009, (30 June 1901), NAP, GOV 260, (31 July 1901), NAP, GOV 261, (31 August 1901), NAP, GOV 262, (30 September 1901), NAL, CO 417/335, p. 342, and (31 October 1901), NAL, CO 417/327, p. 104; "Statistical Return of Inmates, Sick and Deaths in Burgher Camps Transvaal" (30 November 1901), NAL, CO 417/348, p. 39, and (31 December 1901), ibid., p. 794. The numbers for the Orange River Colony are from "Report on Refugee Camps Established for the Benefit of ORC Refugees" (March 1901), NAL, WO 32/8010; "Population on April 30th," FAB, SRC 132; Chief Superintendent to the Secretary to ORC Administration (12 June 1901), NAL, CO 417/325, p. 333, (13 July 1901), FAB, CSO 29, no. 2611/01,

*How the Camps Functioned* 191

and (5 August 1901), NAL, CO 224/4, pp. 103–4; Cd. 819, *Working of the Refugee Camps*, 290; Chief Superintendent Trollope to the Secretary to ORC Administration (8 October 1901), NAL, CO 224/4, p. 539; Cd. 853, *Further Papers*, 123–24; Chief Superintendent Trollope to the Secretary to ORC Administration (11 December 1901), NAL, CO 224/5, p. 444, and (10 January 1902), NAL, CO 417/348, p. 624.

60. See, for example, the telegram from Military, Calcutta to Alfred Milner (28 December 1901), NAL, CO 417/348, p. 313; telegram from Alfred Milner to Viceroy, Calcutta (11 January 1902), ibid., p. 541; Chief Superintendent to Secretary ORC Administration (12 June 1901), NAL, CO 417/325, pp. 333–47, here p. 336; "Tents for RC's in the ORC," FAB, SRC 15, no. 6135.

61. On the problems with obtaining materials for dwellings, see the correspondence in "Concentration camps" (10 January 1902), NAL, CO 224/7, pp. 38–74.

62. See Military Governor, Pretoria to the High Commissioner (21 November 1901), NAL, WO 32/8063.

63. Report by Major W. A. Thomson to the Military Governor, Pretoria (30 January 1902), NAL, CO 417/349, pp. 531–34.

64. Chief Superintendent Refugee Camps to Chief Ordnance Officer (9 April 1901), FAB, SRC 4, no. 1136. For months, some camps had areas where the internees lived in wagons, or in their own "small square tents," for a longer period of time. These were a thorn in the eye of British officials, as they did not make a clean, orderly impression like the rows of white tents. See Kendal Franks, "Copy of Report on the Burgher Camp at Heidelburg" (7 September 1901), NAL, CO 417/335, pp. 355–63.

65. "Notice to be given to Camp Supt. of arrival of Refugees," FAB, SRC 3, no. 616; Chief Superintendent Trollope to Secretary Orange River Colony Administrator (10 February 1902), NAL, CO 417/349, pp. 452–62.

66. See the section on "Reform through Public Pressure: Provisions in the Camps" in this chapter.

67. Major Tribe to Chief Superintendent Trollope (26 March 1901), NAL, CO 224/7, p. 57.

68. This was a criticism of the Fawcett Commission. Cd. 893, *Report on the Concentration Camps*, 17.

69. See ibid.; Chief Superintendent Trollope to Chief Ordnance Officer (16 August 1901), FAB, SRC 15, no. 5670; and "Infantile Mortality in Concentration Camps: reasons suggested therefore" (12 November 1901), FAB, CSO 44, no. 4103/01.

70. The agricultural program will be discussed more thoroughly in this chapter's section on "Reform through Public Pressure: Provisions in the Camps."

71. "Weekly Return. 'B' Coloured" (27 July 1901), NAL, CO 224/4, p. 63.

72. In October 1901 three camps still had more than four thousand internees—Houtenbek, Honingspruit, and Harrismith. Harrismith, with 5,783 persons, was even larger than the largest camp in July (Edenburg, with 4,577 internees). By January 1902, Houtenbek was the largest camp, with 3,574 persons. See ibid.; Native Refugee Department, ORC, "Return for month of October 1901" (October 1901), NAP, SNA 59, pp. 111–12; Native Refugee Department, ORC, "Return for month of January 1902" (January 1902), NAP, SNA 20, pp. 129–32.

73. Native Refugee Camps, "Return for the month of October 1901" (25 November 1901), NAP, SNA 59, pp. 108–10.

74. "Reports on Kronstad, Vredefort Rd. and Brandfort Camps" (15 April 1901), FAB, SRC 5, no. 1304.

75. "Report on Edenburg and Springfontein RC. Report and rough sketch on site for Bethulie Camp. Inspection made by Mr. Daller R[esident] M[agistrate]," FAB, SRC 5, no. 1206; "Appointing white Superintendent at NRC Brandfort," ibid., no. 1359; "White and Native Refugee Camps at Heilbron," ibid., no. 1399.

76. "Report on Edenburg and Springfontein Refugee Camps," FAB, SRC 5, no. 1206.
77. Pratt Yule, "Native Refugee Camps" (17 August 1901), NAL, CO 224/4, pp. 235–38.
78. Heyningen, "British Doctors versus Boer Women: The Clash of Medical Cultures," in Pretorius, *Scorched Earth*, 188.
79. G. F. de Lotbinière to Hamilton Goold-Adams (18 January 1902), NAL, CO 224/7, pp. 557–76, here p. 569; "Health Report Aliwal North," FAB, SRC 5, no. 1163; and "Report on Edenburg and Springfontein RC," ibid., no. 1206.
80. "Health Report NRC B[loemfon]tein," ibid., no. 1252. See also Warwick, *Black People*, 152.
81. See, for example, the correspondence in "Food for Sick Native Refugees at Edenburg," FAB, SRC 2, no. 478. See also Kessler, "Shifting the Paradigm," 142.
82. "White and Native Refugee Camps at Heilbron," FAB, SRC 5, no. 1399.
83. For more on this topic, see the chapter section "Work, School, Free time: Daily Life in the Camps."
84. "Report on Edenburg and Springfontein Refugee Camps," FAB, SRC 5, no. 1206; "Report NRC B[loemfon]tein," FAB, SRC 6, no. 1739; Resident Magistrate to the Secretary to the ORC Administration (26 November 1901), FAB, CSO 48, no. 4353. In some cases, as in Brandfort, there were no latrines at all. See "Report on Kroonstad, Vredefort Rd & Brandfort Camps," FAB, SRC 5, no. 1304.
85. De Lotbinière to Goold-Adams (18 January 1902), NAL, CO 224/7, p. 562.
86. "Monthly Report Native RC," FAB, SRC 2, no. 372; "Report Native Refugee Camp B[loemfon]tein," FAB, SRC 6, no. 1739.
87. "Monthly Report Native RC Edenburg," FAB, SRC 6, no. 1724.
88. Evidence in various reports suggests that certain black camps had no hospital. See, for example, "Report on Kroonstad, Vredefort Rd & Brandfort Camps," FAB, SRC 5, no. 1304; "Appointing white Superintendent at NRC Brandfort," ibid., no. 1359.
89. "Report on Edenburg and Springfontein Refugee Camps," FAB, SRC 5, no. 1206; Georg Haccius, *Lichtbilder aus dunkler Kriegszeit in Transvaal* (Hermannsburg, [1904?]), 13–16.
90. De Lotbinière to Goold-Adams (18 January 1902), NAL, CO 224/7, p. 563.
91. Resident Magistrate to the Secretary to the ORC Administration (26 November 1901), FAB, CSO 48, no. 4353; de Lotbinière to Goold-Adams (18 January 1902), NAL, CO 224/7, p. 569; and "Final Report Native Refugee Department Transvaal," NAP, TKP 135, p. 3. Examples of adequately configured huts in the original black camps can be found in "Report on Edenburg and Springfontein Refugee Camps," FAB, SRC 5, no. 1206; "Report on Vredefort Rd and Brandfort RC's," FAB, SRC 7, no. 1938; "Monthly Report NRC," FAB, SRC 2, no. 372.
92. Resident Magistrate to the Secretary to the ORC Administration (26 November 1901), FAB, CSO 48, no. 4353; and de Lotbinière to Goold-Adams (18 January 1902), NAL, CO 224/7, p. 569; "Final Report Native Refugee Department Transvaal," NAP, TKP 135, p. 3. The problem of cramped construction was no longer mentioned in an inspection report for nearly all of the Orange River Colony camps in February 1902. The issue had presumably been resolved in the meantime. See Superintendent, Native Refugee Department, ORC to G. F. de Lotbinière (3 February 1902), FAB, CSO 54, no. 326/02.
93. Superintendent, Native Refugee Department, ORC to de Lotbinière (3 February 1902), FAB, CSO 54, no. 326/02.
94. "Final Report Native Refugee Department Transvaal," NAP, TKP 135, p. 3.
95. Haccius, *Lichtbilder*, 13–16.
96. "Report on Refugee Camps Established for the Benefit of ORC Refugees," NAL, WO 32/8010.
97. General Superintendent, "Cir. 38" (30 April 1901), NAP, GOV 259.

98. "Cir. 16" (19 March 1901), NAL, WO 32/8008.
99. See, for example, Goodwin to the Military Governor, NAL, WO 32/8008.
100. "Report on Kroonstad, Vredefort Rd & Brandfort Camps," FAB, SRC 5, no. 1304; and "Report for month of May, Burgher Camp Middelburg" (7 June 1901), NAL, WO 32/8009, pp. 67–70.
101. John G. Maxwell to the Commander in Chief (5 July 1901), NAL, WO 32/8009.
102. Chief Superintendent Trollope to the Secretary to the ORC Administration, urgent (12 April 1901), FAB, SRC 2, no. 363.
103. Ibid. See also the letter from C W Champion "re requiring more trucks," FAB, SRC 5, no. 1301.
104. Maxwell to Milner (13 November 1901), NAP, MGP 133, pp. 54–70.
105. See, for example, Martin, *The Concentration Camps*, 21.
106. Telegram from the Quartermaster General to the Deputy Administrator (14 February 1901), FAB, SRC 2, no. 363.
107. See the correspondence in "Civil Supplies, extra truck accommodation required owing to heavy requirements S.A.C. & refugee camps" (15 April 1901), FAB, CSO 12, no. 896/01.
108. Kessler, "South African War," 138–43.
109. G. F. de Lotbinière to the Chief Supply Officer, "Lines of Communications" (2 August 1901), FAB, CSO 29, no. 2758, quoted in Kessler, "South African War," 143.
110. As Isabel Hull depicts, the needs of the colonial forces in South-West Africa always prevailed over those of internees. In this respect, German military culture broadly resembled that of other European armies. Hull, *Absolute Destruction*, 84 and 98–103.
111. See, for example, "Report on Education in ORC," NAL, CO 224/6, pp. 239–41; and "Monthly Report September, Burgher Camp Pietersburg" (30 September 1901), NAL, CO 417/335, pp. 484–90.
112. Cd. 893, *Report on the Concentration Camps*, 20.
113. See, for example, "Nativ [sic] RC Bloemfontein. Natives brought in without notice," FAB, SRC 4, no. 1107.
114. "Report Edenburg," FAB, SRC 5, no. 1206.
115. Commandant to Chief Superintendent Trollope (9 June 1901), FAB, SRC 8, no. 2613.
116. Wilson Fox to Hamilton Goold-Adams (27 February 1902), FAB, CSO 57, no. 586/02.
117. "Final Report Native Refugee Department Transvaal," NAP, TKP 135, pp. 3–4; and "Native Refugee Camps. Return for the month of July 1901" (15 August 1901), NAP, SNA 59, pp. 103–4.
118. General Superintendent Tucker to John G. Maxwell (22 February 1902), NAL, CO 417/349, pp. 904–26, here p. 924.
119. Spies, *Methods of Barbarism*, 215.
120. Tucker to Maxwell (22 February 1902), NAL, CO 417/349, p. 909.
121. "Feeding of Indigent Boers" (1 December 1900), NAL, WO 32/8008.
122. Early ration lists for the Orange River Colony can be found in Hobhouse, *The Brunt of the War*, 117.
123. Hobhouse, *Report*, 35.
124. Copy of telegram to all superintendents (27 February 1901), NAL, WO 32/8008.
125. "Cir. Nr. 7" (8 March 1901), FAB, SRC 2, no. 487A.
126. Walter Hely-Hutchinson to Alfred Milner (29 December 1900), BLO, MP 172, pp. 147–50.
127. *Westminster Gazette*, 4 December 1901, quoted in Hobhouse, *The Brunt of the War*, 158–59.
128. The Fawcett Commission believed that treating women and children according to standards for soldiers was the source of various problems. Cd. 893, *Report on the Concentration Camps*, 17–18.

129. *Westminster Gazette*, 4 December 1901, quoted in Hobhouse, *The Brunt of the War*, 158–59.
130. Cd. 893, *Report on the Concentration Camps*, 15. See also the report by the district surgeon in Johannesburg, reprinted in *Daily News*, 10 April 1901.
131. "Hospital Report compiled by Medical Officer Kroonstad RC" (16 February 1901), FAB, SRC 1, no. 69.
132. "Kroonstad Refugee Camp and Hospital. Medical Report for February 1901," FAB, SRC 2, no. 375. There were another fourteen deaths in the hospital, mostly caused by typhoid. On cases of diarrhea in other camps, see, for example: "Report Refugee Camp Brandfort," FAB, SRC 1, no. 126; "Report on Deaths at Heilbron RC," FAB, SRC 2, no. 411; and "Medical Report for May 1901, Burgher Camp Middelburg" (6 June 1901), NAL, WO 32/8009, pp. 71–76.
133. Hobhouse, *Report*, 9; Superintendent Refugee Camp Heilbron to Chief Superintendent (14 March 1901), FAB, SRC 3, no. 653; "Coal for RC's," FAB, SRC 6, no. 1618; and "Infantile Mortality in Concentration Camps: reasons suggested therefore," (12 November 1901), FAB, CSO 44, no. 4103/01.
134. Cd. 893, *Report on the Concentration Camps*, 10, 12, 44, 76, and 79.
135. See, for example, Superintendent to the General Superintendent, Burgher Camp Standerton (4 January 1902), NAL, CO 417/348, pp. 975–79; and Chief Superintendent to the High Commissioner (June 1902), NAL, CO 224/7, pp. 669–86.
136. See, for example, "Shortage of Meat at B[loemfon]tein RC" (8 March 1901), FAB, SRC 2, no. 493; "Report RC Norvals Pont," ibid., no. 381; and Lückhoff, *Woman's Endurance*, 21.
137. Kendal Franks, "Report on Irene Camp" (11 July 1901), NAP, GOV 260; Cd. 893, *Report on the Concentration Camps*, 18; Lückhoff, *Woman's Endurance*, 12 and 43; and Brandt, *The War Diary*, 203.
138. Strictly speaking, Vitamin C is not found in meat, only in some internal organs, especially the liver.
139. See, for example, Medical Officer to the Superintendent, Burgher Camp Johannesburg (31 October 1901), NAL, CO 417/327, pp. 184–86; "Statistical Return for Burgher Camp Nylstroom month ending 30th Nov. 1901," NAL, CO 417/348, p. 205; "Report by Medical Officer, Burgher Camp Potchefstroom" (22 November 1901), ibid., pp. 233–34; "Monthly Report November, 1901, Burgher Camp Vereeniging" (1 December 1901), ibid., pp. 249–52; and "Report by Medical Officer, Burgher Camp Volksrust" (22 November 1901), ibid., pp. 262–65.
140. General Superintendent to the Military Governor (19 December 1901), NAL, CO 417/348, pp. 31–37. See also Heyningen, *The Concentration Camps*, 127–32.
141. Hobhouse, *The Brunt of the War*, 117–18.
142. Heyningen, "British doctors," 179–81.
143. As in "Report by Medical Officer, Burgher Camp Heidelburg" (21 November 1901), NAL, CO 417/348, pp. 116–17. See also Turner to the Military Governor (6 March 1901), NAL, WO 32/8008.
144. The commission's suggestions for the rations can be found in Cd. 893, *Report on the Concentration Camps*, 10–12 and 23–24.
145. Whiteside Hime and Pratt Yule to Hamilton Goold-Adams (12 December 1901), FAB, SRC 17, no. 6705. At nearly the same time, Dr. Martin criticized the Transvaal rations. See Cd. 902, *Further Papers*, 133; and the correspondence in "Concentration Camps Ration Scale" (15 January 1902), NAL, CO 417/348, pp. 471–86.
146. For the Transvaal, see "Cir. Nr. 107. New Ration Scale" (13 January 1902), NAL, CO 417/349, pp. 525–27. For the Orange River Colony, see "Scale of Rations in the ORC RC's" (16 January 1902), FAB, SRC 18, no. 7191.

147. "Scale of Rations for Indigent Refugees at P.M.burg and Howick," NAL, WO 32/8010. The ration list is undated but must have gone into effect, at the latest, in March 1901 because it was included with a letter from 21 March.
148. "Memorandum from Commandant Edenburg, Re Rations," FAB, SRC 1, no. 33. See also Kessler, "Shifting the Paradigm," 130.
149. Kessler, "South African War," 68 and 132. See also Heyningen, *The Concentration Camps*, 67–70 on the "ideology of imperial relief."
150. De Lotbinière to Goold-Adams (18 January 1902), NAP, SNA 20, p. 114.
151. "Scale for Rations Native RC" (15 February 1901), FAB, SRC 2, no. 291 and "Cir. Nr. 7" (8 March 1901), ibid., no. 487A. Children under twelve received reduced adult rations.
152. "Scale of Rations for the month of June 1901" (5 August 1901), NAL, CO 224/4, p. 90; and "Monthly Return—July 1901" (5 August 1901), ibid., p. 91. See also Warwick, *Black People*, 152–53.
153. Significantly, this was the first goal to be dropped during the peace negotiations. Pakenham, *The Boer War*, 563–65; and Nasson, *The War for South Africa*, 256.
154. "Report Native RC," FAB, SRC 2, no. 486.
155. Telegram from General Officer Commanding Kroonstad to Hamilton Goold-Adams (23 May 1901), FAB, SRC 7, no. 2121.
156. "Native Refugee Camp at Doorn Kop near Rhenoster," FAB, SRC 8, no. 2613.
157. Telegram from Superintendent Native Refugee Camp Edenburg to the Chief Superintendent (28 February 1901), FAB, SRC 1, no. 182.
158. See, for example, "Report NRC Bloemfontein," FAB, SRC 1, no. 157; and "Health Report Aliwal North," FAB, SRC 5, no. 1163.
159. Health Report of Boer Refugee Camp from 1 February 1901 to 1 March 1901, FAB, SRC 2, no. 479.
160. "Monthly Report, Native Refugee Camp Kaffirfontein" (1 March 1901), FAB, SRC 2, no. 372.
161. See the reports from the Native Refugee Camp Bloemfontein from 9 and 23 March: FAB, SRC 3, nos. 500 and 770.
162. "Report Edenburg Native RC," FAB, SRC 2, no. 486.
163. Officer Commanding Native Refugee Camp Edenburg to Superintendent Refugee Camps (21 February 1901), FAB, SRC 1, no. 182.
164. "Report of the Native Refugee Camp Edenburg for the month of March 1901" (3 April 1901), FAB, SRC 4, no. 1064.
165. De Lotbinière to Milner (30 September 1901), NAP, SNA 59, pp. 93–94.
166. Ibid., pp. 94–95.
167. Ibid., p. 93. See also "Final Report Native Refugee Department Transvaal," NAP, TKP 135, pp. 1 and 4; and de Lotbinière to Goold-Adams (18 January 1902), NAP, SNA 20, p. 113.
168. De Lotbinière to Milner (30 September 1901), NAP, SNA 59, pp. 95–96.
169. "Final Report Native Refugee Department Transvaal," NAP, TKP 135, p. 4.
170. "Repatriation of Native Refugees" (6 June 1902), NAP, SNA 31, p. 116.
171. The Taaibosch Camp, for example, was raided twice. See G. F. de Lotbinière to John G. Maxwell (31 December 1901), NAP, MGP 144, p. 27; "Recent Boer Attack on Native Refugee Camp Taaibosch: report on" (6 January 1902), FAB, CSO 52, no. 71/02; and "Boer Attack on Taaibosch Native Refugee Camp: report of Supt." (10 February 1902), FAB, CSO 55, no. 401/02. On an attack on Thaba 'Nchu, see ibid., no. 390/02. See also Mongalo and Pisani, "Victims of a White Man's War," 161.
172. "Final Report Native Refugee Department Transvaal," NAP, TKP 135, p. 4.
173. Ibid., p. 3.

174. De Lotbinière to Goold-Adams (18 January 1902), NAP, SNA 20, p. 118.
175. Resident Magistrate to Secretary to the ORC Administration (26 November 1901), FAB, CSO 48, no. 4353/01. See also "Scarcity of food at Native Refugee Camp, Honigspruit," FAB, CSO 46, no. 4282/01.
176. On this assessment, see also Warwick, *Black People*, 152–53; and Mongalo and Pisani, "Victims of a White Man's War," 164–65.
177. De Lotbinière to Goold-Adams (18 January 1902), NAP, SNA 20, pp. 118 and 121.
178. "Final Report Native Refugee Department Transvaal," NAP, TKP 135, p. 3.
179. Superintendent, Native Refugee Department, ORC to de Lotbinière (3 February 1902), FAB, CSO 54, no. 326/02.
180. On the dispute over the dairy cows, see NAP, MGP 146, pp. 40–47.
181. Chief Superintendent Trollope to Hamilton Goold-Adams (12 July 1901), FAB, CSO 26, no. 2436.
182. Medical Officer to Superintendent, Refugee Camp Bloemfontein (1 June 1901), FAB, CSO 25, no. 2266. For similar problems, see also Kendal Franks, "Report on Irene Camp" (11 July 1901), NAP, GOV 260; as well as the reports on Klerksdorp (3 August 1901) and Potchefstroom (1 and 2 August 1901), NAP, GOV 261.
183. Hamilton Goold-Adams to Alfred Milner (4 May 1901), NAL, CO 224/6, pp. 215–38, here p. 224.
184. Telegram from Hamilton Goold-Adams to Alfred Milner (6 February 1901), NAL, CO 224/3, p. 138; "Precis," ibid., p. 141; and "Refugee Camps. Nurses" (20 February 1901), ibid., pp. 189–94. There were similar problems in the Transvaal. See the correspondence in "Refugee Camps in T[rans]vaal" (13 February 1901), NAL, CO 291/27, pp. 397–402.
185. Heyningen, "A Tool for Modernisation?," 4.
186. See, for example, Brandt, *The War Diary*, 210–11.
187. Hobhouse, *Report*, 10.
188. Heyningen, "A Tool for Modernisation?," 4–5.
189. Telegram from Hamilton Goold-Adams to Joseph Chamberlain (15 May 1901), NAL, CO 224/3, p. 376.
190. Telegram from Alfred Milner to Joseph Chamberlain (23 September 1901), NAL, CO 224/4, p. 253; and telegram from Alfred Milner to Joseph Chamberlain (24 October 1901), NAL, CO 291/29, p. 607.
191. These figures are from Heyningen, "A Tool for Modernisation?," 5.
192. General Superintendent to the Governor of Natal (6 May 1902), NAL, CO 179, pp. 138–43.
193. Medical Assistant to Superintendent, Burgher Camp Mafeking (6 October 1901), NAL, CO 417/335, pp. 470–76.
194. Henry McCallum to Joseph Chamberlain (21 February 1902), NAL, CO 179/222, pp. 316–23, here p. 316.
195. Heyningen, "British Doctors."
196. Ibid., 183–84.
197. Ibid., 187–91.
198. Cd. 893, *Report on the Concentration Camps*, 16–17.
199. Ibid., 16.
200. Kendal Franks, "Report on Irene Camp" (11 July 1901), NAP, GOV 260; and Cd. 893, *Report on the Concentration Camps*, 15–16. On the importance of cleanliness in Victorian society, see Heyningen, "British Doctors," 183.
201. Cd. 893, *Report on the Concentration Camps*, 17; and Kendal Franks, "Report on Irene Camp" (11 July 1901), NAP, GOV 260.
202. Neethling, *Fünfzehn Monate*, 65 and 70–71.

203. Brandt, *The War Diary*, 246–47. See also Kendal Franks, "Report on Irene Camp" (11 July 1901), NAP, GOV 260; and Cd. 893, *Report on the Concentration Camps*, 17.
204. "Report by Medical Officer, Burgher Camp Klerksdorp," NAL, CO 417/348, pp. 166–69.
205. Cd. 893, *Report on the Concentration Camps*, 16.
206. See, for example, Chief Superintendent to Secretary ORC Administration (12 June 1901), NAL, CO 417/325, pp. 333–47; and Kendal Franks, "Report on the Burgher Camp at Middelburg" (23 August 1901), NAP, GOV 262.
207. "Report by Medical Officer, Burgher Camp Klerksdorp," NAL, CO 417/348, pp. 166–69; General Superintendent to the Military Governor (23 May 1901), NAP, GOV 259; and Kendal Franks, "Report on the Burgher Camp at Middelburg" (23 August 1901), NAP, GOV 262.
208. Heyningen, "British Doctors," 195. See also Brandt, *The War Diary*, 249–50, 253, 268, and especially the passages on the Boer doctor "Dandy" Neethling, 230–31. In Bethulie, Reverend Lückhoff emphasized the importance of cleanliness and encouraged internees to go to the infirmaries. See Lückhoff, *Woman's Endurance*, 6, 9, and 42.
209. Otto, *Die Konsentrasiekampe*, 121.
210. "Report for February 1901 Brandfort RC," FAB, SRC 2, no. 402; Superintendent Refugee Camp Brandfort to Chief Superintendent Trollope (9 March 1901), FAB, SRC 3, no. 543.
211. "Application from Dr. Watson Aliwal North RC for an assistant," FAB, SRC 4, no. 962; "Health Report Aliwal North," FAB, SRC 5, no. 1163; "Monthly Report, Refugee Camp Aliwal North" (5 April 1901), ibid., no. 1335; and Chief Superintendent Trollope to Superintendent Refugee Camp Aliwal North (18 June 1901), SRC 8, no. 2746.
212. Chief Superintendent Trollope to Superintendent Refugee Camp Heilbron (1 June 1901), FAB, SRC 8, no. 2306.
213. "Appointment of Dr. Friedman at Native RC Bloemfontein," FAB, SRC 2, no. 262; and "Report Native Refugee Camp Bloemfontein," FAB, SRC 6, no. 1739.
214. The superintendent wrote: "I have no building in my camp to be used as hospital. Would you kindly (with an eye on Bubonic Plague) authorize me to have one constructed." Superintendent to Chief Superintendent Trollope (30 March 1901), FAB, SRC 4, no. 930. On the previous arrangements, see "Monthly Statement of expenses Edenburg Native RC," FAB, SRC 2, no. 355.
215. Kessler, "The Black and Coloured Concentration Camps," 149.
216. "Medical treatment for Native Refugees," FAB, SRC 6, no. 1619.
217. De Lotbinière to Goold-Adams (18 January 1902), NAP, SNA 20, p. 121; and "Final Report Native Refugee Department Transvaal," NAP, TKP 135, 3.
218. Resident Magistrate to the Secretary to the ORC Administration (26 November 1901), FAB, CSO 48, no. 4353/01.
219. "Tour of inspection through the Native Refugee Camps—ORC" (4 February 1902), FAB, CSO 54, no. 326/02.
220. "Native Refugee Camp Returns for October 1901," NAP, SNA 59, pp. 111–12; and "Native Refugee Camp Returns for November 1901," FAB, CSO 52, no. 29/02. Later reports no longer itemize labor expenses, so any subsequent changes cannot be determined.
221. Alternatively, doctors could also be hired for £2 per day, which would not have significantly lowered the costs per visit. See de Lotbinière to Goold-Adams (18 January 1901), NAP, SNA 20, p. 117.
222. In July 1901, there were six doctors for eleven camps. In October, nine doctors were responsible for thirteen camps, and in April 1902 there were thirty-four doctors for thirty-six camps. These medical personnel were presumably military doctors who

were paid per visit. If we assume the level of wages was similar to that in the Orange River Colony, we arrive at an average of 7.36 visits per camp for the month of July 1901, 11.92 visits for October 1901, and 12.44 visits for April 1902. See "Native Refugee Camps Return for the month of July 1901, October 1901 and April 1902," NAP, SNA 59, pp. 103 and 108–9 and SNA 30, pp. 136–37.
223. Kessler, "South African War," 160–201.
224. See Elira Wessels's depiction of daily life in the Bloemfontein camp. Wessels, "'A Cage Without Bars,'" as well as the report by Mrs G. in Hobhouse, *The Brunt of the War*, 264.
225. General Superintendent to the Military Governor (22 March 1901), NAL, WO 32/8008, including the following attachments: "A: Cir. General Superintendent to the Superintendents" and "B: Cir. Letter A. Burgher Camps Regulations."
226. Smith, "The Concentration Camps in South Africa."
227. Cd. 893, *Report on the Concentration Camps*, 4.
228. Ibid., 42, 45, and 114.
229. Ibid., 9 and 13.
230. See the Fawcett Commission's different reports from the individual camps, ibid.
231. General Superintendent to all Superintendents (15 February 1901), NAL, WO 32/8008.
232. Cd. 893, *Report on the Concentration Camps*, 172.
233. Paula Krebs also draws this connection in "'The Last of the Gentlemen's Wars,'" 48.
234. Kitchener to Brodrick (21 June 1901), quoted in Spies, *Methods of Barbarism*, 256.
235. Quoted in Kessler, "South African War," 175.
236. Kessler, "South African War," 174–75.
237. See the entry on "going native" in Bill Ashcroft, Gareth Griffiths, and Helen Tiffin, *Key Concepts in Post-Colonial Studies* (London, 1998), 115. See also Sebastian Conrad, *Deutsche Kolonialgeschichte* (Munich, 2008), 75–79.
238. Cd. 893, *Report on the Concentration Camps*, 16.
239. Cd. 819, *Working of the Refugee Camps*, 216. On the interpretation of the camps as "poor relief," see also Heyningen, "A Tool for Modernisation?," 1; Krebs, "'The Last of the Gentlemen's Wars,'" 48–49; and especially Forth, *Barbed-Wire Imperialism*, 130–31.
240. M. Anne Crowther, *The Workhouse System 1834–1929* (London, 1981), especially 196–201.
241. For the German colonial discourse, see Katharina Walgenbach, *"Die weiße Frau als Trägerin deutscher Kultur": Koloniale Diskurse über Geschlecht, "Rasse" und Klasse im Kaiserreich* (Frankfurt, 2005); and Conrad, "'Eingeborenenpolitik,'" 117–19. On the interdependence between the categories of race and class in other contexts, see (for example) Annalee Newitz and Matt Wray, eds., *White Trash: Race and Class in America* (London, 1997).
242. Stoler and Cooper, "Between Metropole and Colony," 7. Julian Go has further emphasized the heterogeneity of racial difference. Julian Go, "'Racism' and Colonialism: Meaning of Difference and Ruling Practices in America's Pacific Empire," *Qualitative Sociology* 27, no. 1 (2004): 35–58.
243. Partha Chatterjee, *The Nation and Its Fragments: Colonial and Postcolonial Histories* (Princeton, 1993), especially 16–34.
244. Helen Fein, "Definition and Discontent," 20.
245. Sargant to Maxwell (24 July 1901), NAL, CO 291/29, pp. 390–98; "Report on the Schools Established in the Refugee Camps of the Orange River Colony" (13 June 1901), NAL, CO 417/325, pp. 348–56; and Hamilton Goold-Adams to Alfred Milner (27 May 1902), NAL, CO 224/7, pp. 527–34. See also Zietsman, "The Concentration Camp Schools."

246. Goold-Adams to Milner (27 May 1902), NAL, CO 224/7, pp. 527–34 and 554; "Education Report 1901/02," NAL, CO 224/8, pp. 145–55; and Zietsman, "The Concentration Camp Schools," 89.
247. Sargant to Maxwell (24 July 1901), NAL, CO 291/29, pp. 397–98; and Zietsman, "The Concentration Camp Schools," 89.
248. See, for example, Sargant to Maxwell (24 July 1901), NAL, CO 291/29, p. 394; and "Education Report 1901/02," NAL, CO 224/8, p. 150. See also Riedi, "Teaching Empire."
249. Goold-Adams to Milner (27 May 1902), NAL, CO 224/7, p. 528.
250. Cd. 893, *Report on the Concentration Camps*, 10. See also "Report upon the Burgher Camp Schools at Heidelburg, Standerton, Volksrust and upon the Government Schools at Marthinus Wesselstroom and the Nigel," NAL, CO 291/29, pp. 399–405, here pp. 404–5.
251. Zietsman, "The Concentration Camp Schools," 89–90; and Goold-Adams to Milner (27 May 1902), NAL, CO 224/7, pp. 529–30.
252. Zietsman, "The Concentration Camp Schools," 90. See also Sargant to Maxwell (24 July 1901), NAL, CO 291/29, p. 394.
253. Zietsman, "The Concentration Camp Schools," 97–102 and 107; and Riedi, "Teaching Empire," especially 1319–21 and 1343.
254. Zietsman, "The Concentration Camp Schools," 106.
255. "Natal. Monthly Report June 1902" (7 July 1902), NAL, CO 291/40, pp. 346–52, here p. 350.
256. See, for example, Johanna Rousseau, "My Experiences During the South African War," in Hobhouse, *War without Glamour*, 88–100, here 98; Lückhoff, *Woman's Endurance*, 54 and 65; and Mrs. Dickenson's report on her visit to the Merebank camp (12 October 1901), in Hobhouse, *The Brunt of the War*, 204–8, here 207–8.
257. Hobhouse, *Report*, 14.
258. "Report on Refugee Camps Established for the Benefit of ORC Refugees," NAL, WO 32/8010.
259. Wessels, "'A Cage Without Bars,'" 78–79.
260. Ibid. See also Trollope to the Secretary Orange River Colony Administration (10 January 1902), NAL, CO 417/348, p. 637.
261. "Cricket team for match between two RC's," FAB, SRC 21, no. 7815.
262. "Monthly Report December 1901, Burgher Camp Irene" (5 January 1902), NAL, CO 417/348, pp. 891–97; and "Monthly Report December 1901, Burgher Camp Krugersdorp" (5 January 1902), ibid., pp. 925–28.
263. "Natal. Monthly Report December 1901" (9 January 1902), NAL, CO 179/222, pp. 94–102, here p. 98.
264. Cd. 893, *Report on the Concentration Camps*, 114.
265. Martin, *The Concentration Camps*, 59.
266. "Appointment of ministers for Refugee Camps, Port Elizabeth and Norval's Pont" (5 March 1901), FAB, CSO 4, no. 282/01. See also Wessels, "'A Cage Without Bars,'" 74–76.
267. "Ministers for Potchefstroom (Transvaal) Refugee Camp: question of Ministers for Transvaal Camps," FAB, CSO 27, no. 2525/01. See also the comments under "Minister of Religion" in the individual camp reports, Cd. 893, *Report on the Concentration Camps*.
268. Wessels, "'A Cage Without Bars,'" 76.
269. Mongalo and Pisani, "Victims of a White Man's War," 162.
270. Ibid., 164.
271. Ibid., 163; and Stanley, *Mourning Becomes*, 179.
272. Kessler, "The Black and Coloured Concentration Camps," 139–43.

273. "Final Report Native Refugee Department Transvaal," NAP, TKP 135, pp. 1–3; and Warwick, *Black People*, 149–50.
274. De Lotbinière to Goold-Adams (18 January 1902), NAP, SNA 20, pp. 112 and 125.
275. Warwick, *Black People*, 155.
276. Resident Magistrate to the Secretary to the ORC Administration (26 November 1901), FAB, CSO 48, no. 4353; and "Reports on Kronstad, Vredefort Rd. and Brandfort Camps" (15 April 1901), FAB, SRC 5, no. 1304.
277. De Lotbinière to Goold-Adams (18 January 1902), NAP, SNA 20, p. 112.
278. A letter of complaint from two internees in the Honingspruit black camp stated: "We have to work hard all day long." Gert Olifant and Daniel Marome to Goold-Adams (23 November 1901), FAB, CSO 46, no. 4282/01.
279. District Inspector Gresson to Commandant Honingspruit (26 December 1901), ibid.
280. "Reports on Kronstad, Vredefort Rd. and Brandfort Camps" (15 April 1901), FAB, SRC 5, no. 1304.
281. G. F. de Lotbinière to Godfrey Lagden, Commissioner for Native Affairs (17 May 1902), NAP, SNA 28, p. 144. Lagden agreed with this assessment. See Godfrey Lagden to G. F. de Lotbinière (20 May 1902), ibid., p. 147.
282. Revd. J. Pels to G. F. de Lotbinière [undated, probably March 1902, J. K.], NAP, SNA 21, pp. 153–55.
283. District Inspector Gresson to Commandant Honingspruit (26 December 1901), FAB, CSO 46, no. 4282/01.
284. Haccius, *Lichtbilder*, 13–16.
285. Letter to a Friend in Cape Colony (6 June 1901), in Hobhouse, *The Brunt of the War*, 267–68.
286. General Superintendent to the Military Governor (22 March 1901), NAL, WO 32/8008.
287. Brandt, *The War Diary*, 238–42.
288. Ibid., 239.
289. Hobhouse, *The Brunt of the War*, 315; and Wessels, "'A Cage Without Bars,'" 62.
290. Letter from H. Dahms, in Hobhouse, *War without Glamour*, 146–51. Albert Grundlingh discusses *hendsoppers* who served as scouts for the British forces, participating in the deportation of Boer families and preventing them from taking along important possessions. Grundlingh, *The Dynamics of Treason*, 247.
291. Grundlingh, *The Dynamics of Treason*, 199–200.
292. Letter from Mrs. Klazinga, Mafeking Camp in August 1901, in Hobhouse, *War without Glamour*, 274–79. See also ibid., 280–81; and Brandt, *The War Diary*, 239–40.
293. Wessels, "'A Cage Without Bars,'" 62.
294. Cd. 893, *Report on the Concentration Camps*, 8.
295. Ibid., 5.
296. Kendal Franks, "Report on Burgher Camp Aliwal North, 3.–4. January 1902," NAL, CO 417/349, pp. 106–28, here p. 124. See also "Medical Report for the month of June, 1901, Burgher Camp Irene," NAP, GOV 260.
297. Heyningen, "British Doctors," 181.
298. Ibid.; and Pretorius, "A Debate Without End," 43.
299. See, for example, "Journal of the War, Beginning October 12, 1900, Written by me, A. M. van den Berg," in Hobhouse, *War without Glamour*, 23–40, here 36; and the excerpt from the diary of Mrs. Liebenberg in Hobhouse, *War without Glamour*, 68–72, here 71.
300. Haccius, *Drangsalszeit*, 9–10.
301. See, for example, Neethling, *Fünfzehn Monate*, 33; and the report from Mrs. Ellie De Kock in Hobhouse, *War without Glamour*, 101–4.

302. Grundlingh, *The Dynamics of Treason*, 195–96, 279–81; and "Statistical Return for Burgher Camp Meintjeskop Pretoria, month ending 31. 1. 1902," NAL, CO 417/349, p. 797. On the separation in one camp, see W. M. Brown, "Report Burgher Camp Vereeniging" (12 September 1901), NAP, GOV 262.
303. Henry McCallum to Joseph Chamberlain (8 January 1902), NAP, CO 179/222, pp. 88–89.
304. See, for example, "Experiences of Gezina Willemina Joubert, 1899 to 1902," in Hobhouse, *War without Glamour*, 73–86, here 84–85.
305. Cd. 819, *Working of the Refugee Camps*, 9.
306. Grundlingh, *The Dynamics of Treason*, 193.
307. Following Ronald Robinson, I use the term "collaboration" in a morally neutral sense and disregard the term's negative connotations, particularly within the context of National Socialism, insofar as this is possible. The term "collaboration" is useful because it does not suggest an even relationship between "cooperating" partners. Rather, there was a tremendous imbalance of power in the camps, and collaboration was often the only means for internees to improve their living conditions, or simply to increase their chances of survival. See Ronald Robinson, "Non-European Foundations of European Imperialism: Sketch for a Theory of Collaboration," in *Studies in the Theory of Imperialism*, ed. Roger Owen and Bob Sutcliffe (London, 1972), 120–21.
308. Spies, *Methods of Barbarism*, 224–25; and Grundlingh, *The Dynamics of Treason*, 196.
309. Three petitions are reprinted in Hobhouse, *The Brunt of the War*, 217–22. See also "Petition for Removal of S[enior] M[edical] O[fficer] at Orange River RC," FAB, SRC 22, no. 8270; and "Petition Re moving RC at Vredefort Rd to Kroonstad," FAB, SRC 24, no. 8523. For confrontation with a superintendent, see Lückhoff, *Woman's Endurance*, 12.
310. See, for example, the anonymous letter from the Potchefstroom camp (22 May 1901), in Hobhouse, *The Brunt of the War*, 256–57.
311. Spies, *Methods of Barbarism*, 236.
312. Reverend Lückhoff reported that a Bethulie camp doctor was attacked by a furious internee. Lückhoff, *Woman's Endurance*, 58 and 60.
313. "Mrs. Grobler—From My Diary" (4 February 1903), in Hobhouse, *War without Glamour*, 7–10, here 9.
314. Brandt, *The War Diary*, 227; see also 229.
315. Heyningen, "A Tool For Modernisation?," 7.
316. Cd. 893, *Report on the Concentration Camps*, 8.
317. Brandt, *The War Diary*, 263–64. She wrote: "They [the patients] have such funny ideas about us and look upon us as supernatural beings."
318. Ibid., 230. On Neethling, who joined the Red Cross in the Transvaal at the beginning of the war and was captured by English forces in Pietersburg in April 1901, see ibid., 210, especially note 26; and Kendal Franks, "Report on Irene Camp (11 July 1901), NAP, GOV 260.
319. "Mrs. Grobler—From My Diary" (4 February 1903), in Hobhouse, *War without Glamour*, 9; and Lückhoff, *Woman's Endurance*, 27.
320. Hobhouse, *The Brunt of the War*, 179.
321. "Refugee Camps to be put out of bounds to all soldiers," FAB, SRC 3, no. 520. Beginning 1 August 1901, there seems to have been a general rule barring soldiers from entering the camps. See also "Report on immoral activities at Bloemfontein RC," FAB, SRC 30, no. 10092; and Cd. 893, *Report on the Concentration Camps*, 8.
322. In the Vredefort Road camp, for example, there was a shortage of pots, pans, clothing, and blankets; and soldiers sold these furnishings to internees. "Report on Kroon-

stad, Vredefort Rd & Brandfort Camps," FAB, SRC 5, no. 1304. On prostitution in the camps, see Stanley, *Mourning Becomes*, 130, especially note 20.
323. See, for example, Neethling, *Fünfzehn Monate*, 51; and the story of Miss Cameron in Hobhouse, *The Brunt of the War*, 238–45.
324. General Superintendent to the Military Governor (22 March 1901), NAL, WO 32/8008; "Report on Refugee Camps Established for the Benefit of ORC Refugees," NAL, WO 32/8010. In some (but not all) camps, internees needed passes to visit the next town. On the different local arrangements, see the reports in Cd. 893, *Report on the Concentration Camps*.
325. Attachment A: Cir. General Superintendent to the Superintendents, NAL, WO 32/8008.
326. Cd. 893, *Report on the Concentration Camps*, 120.
327. Heyningen. "A Tool For Modernisation?," 5.
328. During the height of the epidemic, a doctor in Mafeking wrote: "I am sorry that I am so overworked and exhausted, that I must stop my work except giving all over to Dr. Morrow." "Medical Report September, Burgher Camp Mafeking," NAL, CO 417/335, pp. 467–69. The Fawcett Commission reported that the superintendents had thirteen- to sixteen-hour workdays. Cd. 893, *Report on the Concentration Camps*, 7.
329. In his January report, Chief Superintendent Trollope pointed to the improved health of camp internees, but many employees were exhausted, ill, or had died as a result of their "arduous duties." Trollope to Secretary Orange River Colony Administrator (10 February 1902), NAL, CO 417/349, pp. 452–62, here p. 457. On the difficulties of hiring new staff, see Cd. 893, *Report on the Concentration Camps*, 6.
330. Resident Magistrate to the Secretary to the ORC Administration (26 November 1901), FAB, CSO 48, no. 4353/01.
331. Ibid. A special "Basuto camp" is also mentioned. Another inspection report refers to a separate "Bushmen and Hottentot location" in the Smaldeel camp. See "Tour of inspection through the Native Refugee Camps—ORC" (4 February 1902), FAB, CSO 54, no. 326/02.
332. De Lotbinière to Goold-Adams (18 January 1902), NAP, SNA 20, pp. 127–28.
333. See, for example, "Report on visit of NRCs" (26 November 1901), FAB, CSO 48, no. 4353/01.
334. Olifant and Marome to Goold-Adams (23 November 1901), FAB, CSO 46, no. 4282/01.
335. Peter Warwick counts 149 "desertions" for the Transvaal camps through the end of 1901. During the same time period, there were 136 desertions in the neighboring colony, and another 117 in the months that followed. Warwick, *Black People*, 157.
336. Kendal Franks, "Report on the Irene Burgher Camp" (11 July 1901), NAP, GOV 260.
337. See, for example, ibid. and "Report by Medical Officer, Burgher Camp Irene" (23 November 1901), NAL, CO 417/348, pp. 133–35.
338. Devitt, *Concentration Camps*, 38; and Heyningen, "'Fools Rush in,'" 20.
339. On the connection between measles and mortality in the camps, see Fetter and Kessler, "Scars from a Childhood Disease"; and Low-Beer, Smallman-Raynor, and Cliff, "Disease and Death."
340. "Sterblichkeit in den Kriegsgefangenenlagern," BAL, R 1001/2140, pp. 161–62.
341. Ortschronik Omaruru, ELCRN, V.23.1, p. 312.
342. Chronik Windhuk, ELCRN, V.37, p. 27.
343. Missionary Eisenberg to the Rhenish Missionary Society, Berseba, AVEM, C/h 5a, p. 409, quoted in Bühler, *Der Namaaufstand*, 340.
344. Heinrich Vedder to the Imperial District Office Swakopmund (27 May 1905), ELCRN, I.1.40. Folio 5, pp. 62–69, here 67–68.
345. Eich to Spiecker (7 March 1905), AVEM, RMG 1.609d, pp. 13–18; and Wilhelm Eich to Johannes Spiecker (23 March 1905), ibid., pp. 20–26.

346. Cai Dame, "Verfügung betr. Abtransport der gefangenen und freiwillig gestellten Hottentotten" (13 January 1906), NAN, ZBU 2369 VIII.G, pp. 52–55; Cai Dame to the Great General Staff (6 February 1906), BAL, R 1001/2138, pp. 41–42; and Friedrich von Lindequist to the Foreign Office (19 February 1906), ibid., p. 56.
347. Missionary August Kuhlmann to Friedrich von Lindequist (8 February 1906), AVEM, RMG 1.644a, pp. 8–9; and Missionary Johannes Olpp to Friedrich von Lindequist (14 August 1906), BAL, R 1001/2119, pp. 77–78.
348. See, for example, Diehl, "Konferenzbericht über Okahandja von Januar 1904 bis September 1906" (September 1906), ELCRN, I.1.22, p. 166.
349. See, for example, Georg Maercker to the Colonial Governor (14 December 1905), BAL, R 151 F 82097, D.IV.L.3 vol. 1, pp. 121–22; and telegram from Schlüpmann to the Colonial Governor (3 February 1906), NAN, ZBU 2292 L.V.1.E, p. 49.
350. Kommando der Schutztruppen im Reichs-Kolonialamt, *Sanitäts-Bericht über die Kaiserliche Schutztruppe für Südwestafrika während des Herero- und Hottentottenaufstandes für die Zeit vom 1. Januar 1904 bis 31. März 1907* (Berlin, 1909), vol. 1, 139–41.
351. A kraal was a cage for animals. Use of the term *Gefangenenkraal* for sites of internment reflected the attitude of many colonizers that the imprisoned Herero and Nama were animal-like creatures and not fully human. The description of the concentration camps in the mission chronicle for Swakopmund is striking: "Like cattle, hundreds were driven to their deaths, and like cattle, they were buried." Ortschronik Swakopmund, ELCRN, V.31, p. 7.
352. On the conflict between the police and military over access to the Swakopmund camp, see Local Command to the District Office (6 July 1907), NAN, Bezirksamt Swakopmund (BSW) 48, XVII.d.
353. Philipp Diehl to Johannes Spiecker (end of May 1905), AVEM, RMG 1.606c, pp. 119–20.
354. Heinrich Vedder to Johannes Spiecker (3 March 1905), AVEM, RMG 1.660a, pp. 50–57.
355. "Bericht über eine Reise nach Lüderitzbucht" (10 August 1905), AVEM, RMG 1.644a, pp. 35–36.
356. Samuel Kariko to Eich (3 March 1907), ELCRN, II.1.9. The letter is written in Otjiherero. I am grateful to the archive staff for the English translation.
357. Heinrich Vedder to Johannes Spiecker (26 May 1905), AVEM, RMG 1.660a, pp. 64–67.
358. Vedder to Spiecker (3 March 1905), ibid., pp. 50–57; Heinrich Vedder to District Office Swakopmund (27 May 1905), ibid., pp. 60–63; and Ortschronik Swakopmund, ELCRN, V.31, p. 7.
359. "Protokoll einer brüderlichen Besprechung abgehalten in Okahandja vom 11.–13. October [sic] 1905," ELCRN, I.1.3, p. 473.
360. Ibid., pp. 472–73.
361. Ibid., p. 473.
362. Dame to the Rhenish Missionary Society, ELCRN, VII.11.3, p. 144. This proposal seems to have been implemented. See Johannes Spiecker, "Visitationsbericht Okahandja," AVEM, RMG 2.510a.
363. Krüger, *Kriegsbewältigung*, 178–79.
364. Karl Laaf to Johannes Spiecker (3 September 1906), AVEM, RMG 1.656a, pp. 50–53.
365. Heinrich Vedder to Johannes Spiecker (27 November 1905), AVEM, RMG 1.660a, pp. 30–32; and Vedder to the District Office Swakopmund (27 May 1905), ibid., pp. 60–63.
366. Wilhelm Eich to Johannes Spiecker (15 December 1905), AVEM, RMG 1.609d, pp. 132–36.
367. Kommando der Schutztruppen, *Sanitäts-Bericht*, vol. 1, 141.

368. Diehl, "Konferenzbericht über Okahandja von Januar 1904 bis September 1906" (September 1906), ELCRN, I.1.22.
369. Spiecker, "Visitationsbericht Okahandja," AVEM, RMG 2.510a.
370. Kuß, *Deutsches Militär auf kolonialen Kriegsschauplätzen*, 302–4; and also more thoroughly in Kuß, "Sonderzone Eingeborenenlazarett: Geschlechtskranke Frauen im Kriegsgefangenenlager Windhuk in Deutsch-Südwestafrika 1906," in Jahr and Thiel, *Lager vor Auschwitz*, 84–98.
371. "Visitationsbericht des Herrn Inspektor Spiecker über die Station Windhuk vom 29. III.–6. IV. 1906," AVEM, RMG 2.533a, pp. 208–25.
372. See the sketch in Karl Laaf to Johannes Spiecker (5 October 1906), AVEM, RMG 1.656a, pp. 48–49; and also Erichsen, *"The Angel of Death,"* 110–11.
373. Eich to Spiecker (2 December 1905), AVEM, RMG 1.609d, pp. 122–28.
374. Lothar von Trotha to District Office Windhuk (16 January 1905), NAN, BWI 403 E.V.2 spec. vol. 2, pp. 106–7.
375. Eduard Dannert to Deputation (7 January 1907), AVEM, RMG 2.514a, pp. 147–51; Johannes Spiecker, "Zweiter Visitationsbericht der Gemeinde Swakopmund, 8. und 12. 9. 1906," AVEM, RMG 2.528a, pp. 305–11; and Kommando der Schutztruppen, *Sanitäts-Bericht*, vol. 1, 141.
376. Ortschronik Omaruru, ELCRN, V.23.1, p. 312.
377. Karl Laaf, "Jahresbericht 1906" (22 November 1906), AVEM, RMG 2.509a, pp. 354–59.
378. Heinrich Vedder to Johannes Spiecker (1 March 1905), AVEM, RMG 1.660a, pp. 46–47.
379. "Bericht über die Arbeit des Missionars Elger am Eingeborenenlazarett in Karibib, April 1904 bis Juni 1906" (16 September 1906), AVEM, RMG 2.505a, pp. 313–14.
380. Vedder to the District Office Swakopmund (27 May 1905), AVEM, RMG 1.660a, p. 62.
381. Eich to Spiecker (15 December 1905), AVEM, RMG 1.609d, pp. 132–36; and "Verordnung des Bezirksamtmann Boesel" (30 December 1905), NAN, BWI 134 G.7.r vol. 1. There was already a "native lazaretto" in Windhuk, but not close to the concentration camp, and its supplies were wholly inadequate. See Kommando der Schutztruppen, *Sanitäts-Bericht*, vol. 1, 141.
382. Trotha to the Etappenkommando (14 March 1905), BAL, R 151 F 82097, D.IV.L.3 vol. 1, p. 40.
383. Omaruru was not included in the statistics, and Karibib, only in part. The highest mortality in Windhuk was recorded in September 1906. See "Sterblichkeit in den Kriegsgefangenenlagern," BAL, R 1001/2140, pp. 161–62.
384. Missionary Philipp Diehl discussed the unexpectedly large number of Herero who surrendered. Diehl to Spiecker (end of May 1905), AVEM, RMG 1.606c, pp. 119–20.
385. Epp's diary, in Eckl, *"S'ist ein übles Land hier,"* 264.
386. Trotha to Bülow (14 January 1905), BAL, R 1001/2089, p. 120.
387. Lothar von Trotha to Bernhard von Bülow (16 January 1905), ibid., pp. 122–23.
388. Diehl, "Konferenzbericht über Okahandja von Januar 1904 bis September 1906" (September 1906), ELCRN, I.1.22.
389. Kuhlmann, "Bericht über eine Reise nach Lüderitzbucht" (10 August 1905), AVEM, RMG 1.644a, pp. 33–41.
390. See, for example, the circular order from Georg Maercker (1 December 1905), NAN, BWI 406 E.V.8 spec. vol. 3, p. 58.
391. Oberstleutnant Mühlenfels to the Feldintendantur (15 February 1906), NAN, ZBU 2338 L.VI.1.E, pp. 25–26. Unfortunately, the files do not reveal how many uniforms were ordered, or if and where these were distributed.
392. Six thousand shirts, three thousand skirts, two thousand headscarves, four thousand old blankets, and two thousand old convalescent gowns. See Deputy Command to the

Colonial Government (30 November 1906), BAL, R 151 F 82098, D.IV.L.3 vol. 2, pp. 63–64.
393. Maercker to the Governor (14 December 1905), BAL, R 151 F 82097, D.IV.L.3 vol. 1, pp. 121–22.
394. Hull, *Absolute Destruction*, 153–54.
395. Report from the medical office (23 December 1905), NAN, ZBU 839 H.II.C.7, pp. 11–14; circular order from the deputy command (25 April 1906), BAL, R 151 F 82098, D.IV.L.3 vol. 2, p. 149; "Feeding of Indigent Boers" (1 December 1900), NAL, WO 32/8008; "Cir. Nr. 7" (8 March 1901), FAB, SRC 2, no. 487A; "Scale of Rations in the ORC RC's" (16 January 1902), FAB, SRC 18, no. 7191; "Scale of Rations for Indigent Refugees at P.M.burg and Howick," NAL, WO 32/8010]; and "Scale for Rations Native RC" (15 February 1901), FAB, SRC 2, no. 291. GSWA stands for German South-West Africa, and ORC for Orange River Colony. "Or" in the table indicates that internees either received flour or rice or corn.
396. On the "native lazarettos," see Kommando der Schutztruppen, *Sanitäts-Bericht*, vol. 1, 139–44.
397. Johannes Spiecker to Wilhelm Eich (1 May 1905), ELCRN, II.5.2.
398. Vedder to the District Office Swakopmund (27 May 1905), ELCRN, I.1.40, pp. 62–69.
399. Nyhof to Deputation (22 April 1907), AVEM, RMG 2.509a, pp. 347–52; Vedder to Spiecker (1 March 1905), AVEM, RMG 1.660a, pp. 46–47; and Heinrich Vedder to Johannes Spiecker (26 June 1905), ibid., pp. 64–67; ELCRN, VII.12., p. 28.
400. Wilhelm Eich, "Konferenzbericht, Okahandja den 4. 9. 1906," ELCRN, I.1.22; and Spiecker, "Visitationsbericht Okahandja," AVEM, RMG 2.510a.
401. Friedrich Meier. "1. Quartalsbericht" (end of May 1905), AVEM, RMG 2.533a, pp. 237–45.
402. "Bericht über die Arbeit des Missionars Elger am Eingeborenenlazarett in Karibib" (16 September 1906), AVEM, RMG 2.505a, pp. 313–14.
403. Trotha to the Etappenkommando (14 March 1905), BAL, R 151 F 82097, D.IV.L.3 vol. 1, p. 40.
404. "Protokoll einer brüderlichen Besprechung abgehalten in Okahandja vom 11.–13. October 1905," ELCRN, I 1.3, pp. 470–86; and Laaf to Spiecker (25 January 1907), AVEM, RMG 1.656a, pp. 38–41.
405. Order from Lothar von Trotha (6 September 1905), NAN, BWI 406 E.V.8, p. 7.
406. On Lüderitzbucht, see Peter Bernsmann to the Rhenish Missionary Society (28 October 1905), AVEM, RMG 1.613d, pp. 82–85. On Swakopmund, see Vedder, "Jahresbericht 1905" (15 January 1906), ELCRN, VII.31.5, pp. 239–40. On the overall situation, see Rheinische Missionsgesellschaft, *Sechsundsiebzigster Jahresbericht der Rheinischen-Missionsgesellschaft vom Jahre 1905* (Barmen, 1906), 14.
407. This was Mission Inspector Spiecker's assessment of detainee provisions in Swakopmund in September 1906. See Spiecker, "Zweiter Visitationsbericht der Gemeinde Swakopmund," AVEM, RMG 2.528a, pp. 305–11.
408. Hugo Bofinger, "Einige Mitteilungen über Skorbut," *Deutsche Militärärztliche Zeitschrift* 39, no. 15 (1910): 569.
409. Nachlass Sanitätsoffizier Julius Ohlemann, BA-MA, Militärgeschichtliche Sammlung (MSg. 2), 2576, pp. 82 and 91.
410. See, for example, Oberarzt Müller to District Office Karibib (4 December 1905), NAN, ZBU 839 H.II.C.7, pp. 5–6.
411. Bofinger, "Einige Mitteilungen über Skorbut," 578.
412. On the term *Feldkost*, see Kommando der Schutztruppen im Reichs-Kolonialamt, *Sanitäts-Bericht über die Kaiserliche Schutztruppe für Südwestafrika während des Herero- und Hottentottenaufstandes für die Zeit vom 1. Januar 1904 bis 31. März 1907* (Berlin, 1920), vol. 2, 420.

413. "Gutachten des Sanitätsamtes" (23 December 1905), NAN, ZBU 839 H.II.C.7, pp. 11–14; and Lindequist to the Kommando (30 December 1905), ibid., p. 3.
414. Tecklenburg to the Colonial Department (3 July 1905), BAL, R 1001/2118, pp. 154–55.
415. Hull, *Absolute Destruction*, 84–85. The mission chronicle stated that "the Herero had to be treated in such a way that they remained aware that they were prisoners." Ortschronik Omaruru, ELCRN, V.23.1, p. 309.
416. Vedder to District Office Swakopmund (27 May 1905), AVEM, RMG 1.660a, pp. 60–63.
417. "Bericht über Sanitätsdienst und Gesundheitsverhältnisse im Berichtsjahr 1907/08," NAN, ZBU 833 H.I.I.5 vol. 2, pp. 241–48.
418. Johannes Spiecker, "Visitationsprotokoll der Station Lüderitzbucht, 31. 8.–2. 9. 1906," AVEM, RMG 2.509a, pp. 361–68.
419. "Sterblichkeit in den Kriegsgefangenenlagern in Südwestafrika," BAL, R 1001/2140, pp. 161–62.
420. Letter from Hermann Nyhof (early 1907), AVEM, RMG 1.650a.
421. Average mortality for the Herero on the island was around 2.5 percent, but for the Nama, it was 10.1 percent. The maximum mortality for the Herero in a single month was 7.19 percent (November 1906). For the Nama, it reached 18.85 percent (December 1906). See "Sterblichkeit in den Kriegsgefangenenlagern in Südwestafrika," BAL, R 1001/2140, pp. 161–62.
422. Bofinger, "Einige Mitteilungen über Skorbut," 576–77. See also Hermann Nyhof to Johannes Spiecker (22 April 1907), AVEM, RMG 2.509a, pp. 347–52.
423. Laaf to Spiecker (21 October 1906), AVEM, RMG 1.656a, pp. 46–47.
424. Bofinger, "Einige Mitteilungen über Skorbut," 577.
425. "Bericht über Sanitätsdienst und Gesundheitsverhältnisse im Berichtsjahr 1907/08" (5 July 1908), NAN, ZBU 833 H.I.I.5 vol. 2, p. 247.
426. Bofinger, "Einige Mitteilungen über Skorbut," 574–75.
427. Kommando der Schutztruppen, *Sanitäts-Bericht*, vol. 1, 144.
428. Ortschronik Lüderitzbucht, ELCRN, V.16, p. 24.
429. Heinrich Vedder to Johannes Spiecker (7 November 1906), AVEM, RMG 1.660a, pp. 93–98.
430. See, for example, Erichsen, *"The Angel of Death,"* 63; and Steinmetz, *The Devil's Handwriting*, 211–12.
431. Laaf to Spiecker (3 September 1906), AVEM, RMG 1.656a, pp. 50–53.
432. Ortschronik Omaruru, ELCRN, V.23.1, p. 309.
433. Vedder to Spiecker (1 August 1905), AVEM, RMG 1.660a, pp. 68–76.
434. Spiecker, "Zweiter Visitationsbericht der Gemeinde Swakopmund," AVEM, RMG 2.528a, pp. 305–11. It is impossible to determine from the available sources whether these working hours were representative for the entire colony, or for the entire period of internment. However, numerous sources confirm a longer midday break. It seems plausible that a regular workday ended in the late afternoon because the sun sets in the winter around 5:00 pm, and in the summer around 7:00 p.m.
435. Vedder to Spiecker (1 March 1905), AVEM, RMG 1.660a, pp. 46–47; and Vedder to Spiecker (3 March 1905), ibid., pp. 50–57.
436. Vedder to Spiecker (1 August 1905), AVEM, RMG 1.660a, pp. 68–76.
437. Vedder to Spiecker (7 November 1906), ibid., pp. 93–98.
438. On the variety of sites where prisoners of war were employed, see "Übersicht über die im Etappenbereich befindlichen Gefangenen pp. mit dem Bestande vom 25. 1. 1905," NAN, BWI 406 E.V.8 spec. vol. 1, pp. 75–76. Of the 16,420 prisoners at the end of December 1906, 1,060 worked for the government or state railroad, 5,170 for private employers such as the Otavi and southern railroads, 5,700 for the military

forces, 750 for the mission, and 1,340 on Shark Island; 2,400 were unable to work. See telegram from Berthold von Deimling to the Colonial Government (9 December 1906), BAL, R 151 F 82098, D.IV.L.3 vol. 4, p. 36.
439. "Kopfsteuer für Kriegsgefangene," NAN, ZBU 2338 L.VI.1.E, pp. 43–48; and "Gefangenen-Nachweisung der 1. Eisenbahn-Baukompagnie über die Gefangenen der Firma Lenz & Co," NAN, BLU 32 E.6.i vol. 1, pp. 89–90.
440. Etappenkommando (21 February 1906), NAN, ZBU 2292 L.V.1.E, p. 74.
441. Spiecker, "Visitationsprotokoll der Station Lüderitzbucht, 31. 8.–2. 9. 1906," AVEM, RMG 2.509a, pp. 361–68; and Eduard Dannert to the Deputation of the Rhenish Missionary Society (8 October 1905), AVEM, RMG 1.615c, pp. 106–9.
442. Copy of an ordinance from the Etappenkommando (29 March 1905), NAN, BWI 406 E.V.8 Generalia, pp. 3–4.
443. Ibid.
444. Circular order from the colonial governor (5 September 1905), ibid., p. 8.
445. Circular order from Friedrich von Lindequist (25 June 1906), ibid., p. 12.
446. See Lindequist's circular orders from 14 December 1905, 2 January 1906, and 14 March 1906, ibid., pp. 7–10.
447. See the wage lists in NAN, Bauverwaltung (BAU) 74 H 13.
448. NAN, ZBU 2338 L.VI.1.E, pp. 71–72.
449. NAN, BSW 119 UA.21/1, p. 20.
450. Missionary Vedder drew this connection. Vedder to Spiecker (27 November 1905), AVEM, RMG 1.660a, pp. 30–32. See also Colonial Government to Etappenkommando (5 September 1905), BAL, R 151 F 82097, D.IV.L.3 vol. 1, p. 105.
451. Building Administration to the management of the Military Native Lazaretto (12 December 1906), NAN, BAU 74 H 13, p. 36; "Nachweisung über die im Monat November an eingeborene Kriegsgefangene gezahlten Löhne," ibid., pp. 32–33.
452. Division head Strahler to District Office Windhuk (13 July 1906), NAN, DOK 27 E.2.E vol. 1, pp. 10–12.
453. Circular order from Friedrich von Lindequist (7 February 1906), NAN, BLU 200 V.2.B vol. 1. See also Strahler to the Colonial Government und District Office Windhuk (18 May 1906), NAN, BWI 407 E.V.8 spec. vol. 6.
454. "Betreffend Eingeborenenverhältnisse" (1 March 1908), NAN, BLU 101 S. 14.M vol. 1, pp. 18–19.
455. A farmer named Wiehager, for example, regularly abused his workers and had to answer in court for three of their deaths. See Heinrich Vedder, "Erster Quartalsbericht 1907" (25 February 1907), ELCRN, VII.31.5, pp. 202–10.
456. Vedder to District Office Swakopmund (27 May 1905), AVEM, RMG 1.660a, pp. 60–63.
457. Ortschronik Omaruru, ELCRN, V.23.1, p. 311.
458. August Kuhlmann, "Erster Bericht über meine Arbeit in Karibib u. an den Kriegsgefangenen an der Otavi-Bahn" (14 August 1905), AVEM, RMG 1.644a, pp. 42–43.
459. In June 1906, 156 of approximately 1,400 total prisoners died on the southern railway. See the summary of "native" deaths in the period between 1 April 1906 and 31 March 1907, NAN, BLU 98 S. 14.D, p. 139. See also "Zusammenstellung der Todesfälle unter den Kriegsgefangenen der Bahnbaufirma," BAL, R 151 F 82099, D.IV.L.3 vol. 5, p. 170. The maximum monthly mortality in Windhuk and Karibib was around 5 percent. See "Sterblichkeit in den Kriegsgefangenenlagern in Südwestafrika," BAL, R 1001/2140, pp. 161–62.
460. Mission Inspector Spiecker came to this conclusion after visiting Lüderitzbucht. See Spiecker, "Visitationsprotokoll der Station Lüderitzbucht, 31. 8.–2. 9. 1906," AVEM, RMG 2.509a, pp. 361–68.
461. "Zusammenstellung der Todesfälle unter den Kriegsgefangenen der Bahnbaufirma," BAL, R 151 F 82099, 82099, D.IV.L.3 vol. 5, p. 170. The summary of native deaths in

the period between 1 April 1906 to 31 March 1907 indicates a mortality of around 2 percent in May.
462. Karl Laaf to Johannes Spiecker (4 June 1906), AVEM, RMG 1.656a, pp. 62–63.
463. Laaf to Spiecker (25 January 1907), ibid., pp. 38–41.
464. Karl Laaf to Johannes Spiecker (12 January 1906), ibid., pp. 69–70; and Spiecker, "Visitationsprotokoll der Station Lüderitzbucht, 31. 8.–2. 9. 1906," AVEM, RMG 2.509a, pp. 361–68.
465. Laaf to Spiecker (25 January 1907), AVEM, RMG 1.656a, pp. 38–41.
466. See the correspondence between the District Office Windhuk and the Division Office Okahandja in Oktober and November 1906, NAN, BWI 407 E.V.8.spec. vol. 4.
467. See, for example, Müller to the Port Office (21 November 1906), NAN, HBS 52 4/1.
468. Cläre Rohrbach to her parents and sister (28 June 1905), Bundesarchiv Koblenz (BAK), N 1408, vol. 68.
469. Friedrich Meier to Deputation (4 April 1907), AVEM, RMG 2.533a, pp. 183–87.
470. Kuhlmann, "Bericht über eine Reise nach Lüderitzbucht" (10 August 1905), AVEM, RMG 1.644a, pp. 33–41.
471. "Jahresbericht Laaf 1906" (22 November 1906), AVEM, RMG 2.509a, pp. 354–59.
472. Report from missionary F. Meier (end of May 1905), AVEM, RMG 2.533a, pp. 237–45.
473. Ortschronik Swakopmund, ELCRN, V.31, p. 8; Philipp Diehl, "Konferenzbericht über die Station Okahandja von Oktober 1906 bis Oktober 1907" (1 October 1907), ELCRN, I.1.23, pp. 250–57.
474. Friedrich Meier, "Vierter Quartalsbericht" (9 January 1907), AVEM, RMG 2.533a, pp. 188–90; "Visitationsbericht über die Station Karibib durch Herrn Inspektor Spiecker vom 22.–26. März 1906," AVEM, RMG 2.505a, pp. 319–26; Eich to Spiecker (15 December 1905), AVEM, RMG 1.609d, pp. 132–36; and Gewald, *Herero Heroes*, 196–97.
475. Friedrich Meier (21 and 22 December 1905), AVEM, RMG 2.533a, pp. 230–31; circular letter from August Elger (1 June 1906), ELCRN, VII.12.4, pp. 128–37; and Heinrich Vedder to Johannes Spiecker (18 December 1906), AVEM, RMG 1.660a, pp. 100–2.
476. See, for example, "Konferenzbericht des Missionars F. Lang z.Z. in Karibib" (10 September 1906), AVEM, RMG 2.505a, pp. 315–16; and Ortschronik Omaruru, ELCRN, V.23.1, pp. 335 and 338.
477. Ortschronik Karibib, ELCRN, V.12, p. 46. See also Diehl, "Konferenzbericht über die Station Okahandja von Oktober 1906 bis Oktober 1907," ELCRN, I.1.23, pp. 250–57.
478. Ortschronik Omaruru, ELCRN, V.23.1, pp. 328–29. See also Gewald, *Herero Heroes*, 202–3.
479. Kuhlmann, "Erster Bericht über meine Arbeit in Karibib u. an den Kriegsgefangenen an der Otavi-Bahn" (14 August 1905), AVEM, RMG 1.644a, pp. 42–43. On the role of evangelists, see also Hans-Martin Milk, *Der Stimme der Gnade Gehör schenken: Zur Rolle der Rheinischen Missionsgesellschaft bei der Errichtung von Konzentrationslagern in Namibia—1905 bis 1907* (Berlin, 2016).
480. Gewald, *Herero Heroes*, 197–204.
481. Zimmerer, *Deutsche Herrschaft über Afrikaner*, 243.
482. Vedder to Spiecker (7 November 1906), AVEM, RMG 1.660a, pp. 93–98; Eduard Dannert to Johannes Spiecker (11 March 1905), AVEM, RMG 1.615c, pp. 114–17; and "Vierter Quartalsbericht Okahandja" (end of December 1906), AVEM, RMG 2.510a, pp. 259–60.
483. Heinrich Vedder, "Konferenz-Jahresbericht 1907," AVEM, RMG 2.528a, pp. 286–87.
484. Spiecker, "Visitationsbericht Okahandja," AVEM, RMG 2.510a.
485. Entry from 14 April 1906, diary of Captain Franke, BAK, N 1030, vol. 6a, p. 462.
486. Kommando der Schutztruppen, *Sanitäts-Bericht*, vol. 1, 142–43.

487. Spiecker, "Zweiter Visitationsbericht der Gemeinde Swakopmund," AVEM, RMG 2.528a, pp. 305–11.
488. Ortschronik Lüderitzbucht, ELCRN, V.16 p. 24.
489. "Mitteilungen von der Vermittelungsarbeit" (23 April 1906), AVEM, RMG 1.644a, pp. 18–20; and Spiecker, "Zweiter Visitationsbericht der Gemeinde Swakopmund," AVEM, RMG 2.528a, pp. 305–11.
490. Vedder to Spiecker (3 March 1905), AVEM, RMG 1.660a, Bl. 50–57. See also Ortschronik Windhuk, ELCRN, V.37, p. 27.
491. August Elger to Oberleutnant Kuhn (11 August 1905), ELCRN, VII.12.4, p. 16.
492. Kuhlmann, "Bericht über eine Reise nach Lüderitzbucht" (10 August 1905), AVEM, RMG 1.644a, pp. 33–41.
493. Circular order from Dame (27 August 1905), ELCRN, VII.11.3, pp. 157–59.
494. Circular order from Georg Maercker (4 March 1906), ibid., pp. 127–29; and Wilhelm Diehl to Wilhelm Eich (12 February 1906), ELCRN, II.1.7b.
495. Kuhlmann, "Bericht über eine Reise nach Lüderitzbucht," AVEM, RMG 1.644a, pp. 33–41. The consequences were not particularly far-reaching. Benkesser was still on Shark Island when missionary Bernsmann visited in September 1905. He had, however, grown milder, according to the local evangelist Samuel Kariko. See Bernsmann to Deputation (28 October 1905), AVEM, RMG 1.613d, pp. 82–85.
496. Hull, *Absolute Destruction*, 78–79.
497. See, for example, Spiecker, "Zweiter Visitationsbericht der Gemeinde Swakopmund," AVEM, RMG 2.528a, pp. 305–11.
498. See, for example, John Ludwig to the District Office Windhuk (30 January 1907), NAL, BWI 407 E.V.8 spec. vol. 6; and Walter Fischer to the District Office Windhuk (4 July 1906), BWI 407 E.V.8.spec. vol. 4.
499. See, for example, Albert Voigt to the District Office Windhuk (24 February 1906), NAN, ZBU 2338 L.VI.1.E, p. 1; and Lieutenant Colonel Mühlenfels to District Office Windhuk (14 March 1906), ibid., pp. 1–2.
500. Spiecker, "Zweiter Visitationsbericht der Gemeinde Swakopmund," AVEM, RMG 2.528a, pp. 305–311. See also Gewald, *Herero Heroes*, 201.
501. August Kuhlmann, "Mitteilungen für die Gesellschaft" (15 May 1906), AVEM, RMG 1.644a, pp. 36–37.
502. Johannes Spiecker, "Sitzung mit den 3 Ältesten und einigen älteren Gliedern der Gemeinde Karibib" (23 March 1906), AVEM, RMG 2.505a, pp. 327–28. On the stigmatizing of black women, see Walgenbach, *"Die weiße Frau als Trägerin deutscher Kultur,"* 47.
503. Heinrich Vedder to Johannes Spiecker (23 February 1905), AVEM, RMG 2.528a, pp. 313–16.
504. Wandres also expressed doubts about the voluntary nature of this prostitution. See Wolfram Hartmann, "Sexual Encounters and Their Implications on an Open and Closing Frontier: Central Namibia From the 1840s to 1905," (PhD diss., Columbia University, 2002), 195.
505. Spiecker, "Zweiter Visitationsbericht der Gemeinde Swakopmund," AVEM, RMG 2.528a, pp. 305–11; and August Kuhlmann to Friedrich von Lindequist (28 February 1906), AVEM, RMG 1.644a, pp. 28–29.
506. So, for example, with Deputy Governor Tecklenburg, see "Visitationsbericht des Herrn Inspektor Spiecker über die Station Windhuk vom 29. III.-6. IV. 1906," AVEM, RMG 2.533a, pp. 208–25.
507. Kommando der Schutztruppen, *Sanitäts-Bericht*, vol. 1, 140.
508. Kommando der Schutztruppen, *Sanitäts-Bericht*, vol. 2, 339–44.
509. It can be presumed that a smaller number of soldiers also had sexual relations with interned men, although this is not documented in any sources.

510. Quoted in Kommando der Schutztruppen, *Sanitäts-Bericht*, vol. 2, 343.
511. "Bericht über eine vertrauliche Besprechung des Inspektor Spiecker mit dem Gouverneur von Lindequist am 10. Mai 1906" (10 May 1906), AVEM, RMG 2.697f, pp. 205–8.
512. Ortschronik Karibib, ELCRN, V.12, p. 36.
513. Laaf to Spiecker (25 January 1907), AVEM, RMG 1.656a, pp. 38–41.
514. In May 1907, for example, 21 percent of sick prisoners recuperated and left the lazarettos of the colony, while 7 percent died. See "Bericht über Sanitätsdienst und Gesundheitsverhältnisse im Berichtsjahr 1907/08," NAN, ZBU 833 H.I.I.5 vol. 2, p. 19.
515. "Bericht über die Besprechung des Inspektor Spiecker mit Sr. Exzellenz Herrn Gouverneur Dr. von Lindequist am Donnerstag den 4. Oktober 1906" (6 October 1906), ELCRN, II.5.2.
516. Bofinger, "Einige Mitteilungen über Skorbut."
517. Ibid.; and Wolfgang U. Eckart, "Medizin und kolonialer Krieg: Die Niederschlagung der Herero-Nama-Erhebung im Schutzgebiet Deutsch-Südwestafrika, 1904–1907," in *Studien zur Geschichte des deutschen Kolonialismus in Afrika: Festschrift zum 60. Geburtstag von Peter Sebald*, ed. Peter Heine and Ulrich van der Heyden (Pfaffenweiler, 1995), 230.
518. Zeller, "'Ombepera i koza,'" 77. The Charité hospital in Berlin returned some of these skulls to a Namibian delegation in September 2011. Other German research institutions followed suit, among them the universities of Freiburg, Jena, and Greifswald. Human remains from South-West Africa, formerly a part of the anthropologist Felix von Luschan's collection, even made their way to the American Museum of Natural History in New York, where they are still kept today.
519. Holger Stoecker, "Knochen im Depot: Namibische Schädel in anthropologischen Sammlungen aus der Kolonialzeit," in *Kein Platz an der Sonne: Erinnerungsorte der deutschen Kolonialgeschichte*, ed. Jürgen Zimmerer and Marianne Bechhaus-Gerst (Monmouth, 2008), 448.
520. "Bericht über Sanitätsdienst und Gesundheitsverhältnisse im Berichtsjahr 1907/08," NAN, ZBU 833 H.I.I.5 vol. 2, p. 163.
521. Bofinger, "Einige Mitteilungen über Skorbut," 575–76.
522. Johannes Spiecker to Wilhelm Eich (27 September 1905), ELCRN, II.5.2.
523. Friedrich Meier to Etappenkommandantur, ELCRN, II.11.11, pp. 160–61.
524. Evidence of this trusting relationship can also be found in the few sources that were written by prisoners. A letter from Sem Kauimo asks the Windhuk missionary Meier to come right away, to visit a deathly ill internee one last time. Sem Kauimo to Friedrich Meier, from the camp, ELCRN, box XI.3.14, letter no. 1.
525. Gewald, *Herero Heroes*, 195.
526. Johannes Lucas de Vries was among the first to emphasize the conflicting nature of the Rhenish mission's actions during the war. Johannes Lucas de Vries, *Namibia: Mission und Politik (1880–1918): Der Einfluß des deutschen Kolonialismus auf die Missionsarbeit der Rheinischen Missionsgesellschaft im früheren Deutsch-Südwestafrika* (Neukirchen-Vluyn, 1980), 168–197.
527. August Kuhlmann to Johannes Spiecker (20 June 1905), AVEM, RMG 1.644a, pp. 29–32.
528. Quoted in Kurd Schwabe, *Krieg in Deutsch-Südwestafrika 1904–1906* (Berlin, 1907), 412–13.
529. "Allgemeine Gesichtspunkte über Unterbringung und Behandlung der Kriegsgefangenen Hottentotten," NAN, ZBU 2369 VIII.G, p. 56.
530. Kommando der Nordtruppen (10 March 1907), BAL, R 151 F 82097, D.IV.L.2. vol. 5, pp. 280–84; and Spiecker, "Sitzung mit den 3 Ältesten und einigen älteren Gliedern der Gemeinde Karibib" (23 March 1906), AVEM, RMG 2.505a, pp. 327–28.

531. Meier to Deputation (4 April 1907), AVEM, RMG 2.533a, pp. 183–87.
532. Ortschronik Karibib, ELCRN, V.12, p. 32.
533. Wilhelm Diehl to the Fathers of the Mission (1 May 1906), AVEM, RMG 1.664, pp. 90–97. See also Wilhelm Diehl to Wilhelm Eich (20 October 1906), ELCRN, II.1.7b.
534. Johannes Olpp to Johannes Spiecker (3 September 1906), AVEM, RMG 1.636b, pp. 78–79.
535. See, for example, NAN, BWI 406 E.V.8 spec. vol. 1, pp. 47–49, 76–77.
536. On the role ascribed to the Herero in many histories of South-West Africa, Gewald writes: "Effectively these studies have done what the German colonial state so anxiously hoped for but failed to do: rob the Herero completely of independent action and thought." Gewald, *Herero Heroes*, 5. Beginning in the 1980s, the Subaltern Studies Group formulated a call to restore the voice and agency of the colonized. See the brief summary in Ulrike Lindner, "Neuere Kolonialgeschichte und Postcolonial Studies, Version 1.0," *Docupedia-Zeitgeschichte*, 15 April 2011.
537. See, for example, the files of the criminal proceedings against the Herero women Anna and Johanna for attacking a white person. NAN, BLU 220 SPS Strafprozess-Sachen 49 and 81. See also August Kuhlmann to the Colonial Government (28 February 1906), BAL, R 151 F 82097, D.IV.L.3 vol. 1, pp. 197–98; and Gewald, *Herero Heroes*, 190.
538. By comparison, only 188 of the prisoners died. "Verzeichnis der überwiesenen Eingeborenen," NAN, BWI 407 E.V.8 spec. vol. 6; and Colonial Governor (by proxy) to the District Office Windhuk (1 August 1907), ibid. Some of the files suggest that the period of time in question included only 1906 and 1907, but some entries in the list extend back to early 1905.
539. Vedder to Spiecker (26 June 1905), AVEM, RMG 1.660a, pp. 64–67.
540. Telegram from Cai Dame (10 August 1906), BAL, R 151 F 82098, D.IV.L.3 vol. 3, p. 53; and Vedder to Spiecker (26 June 1905), AVEM, RMG 1.660a, pp. 64–67.
541. On the impossibility of sustaining a larger number of prisoners in the south, see the telegram from Otto Gelshorn to the Colonial Government (28 November 1905), BAL, R 151 F 82105 D.IV.M.3. vol. 1, pp. 33–34; and District Office Gibeon to the Colonial Government (11 December 1905), ibid., pp. 37–38. Even along the railroad in Okahandja, prisoners had to be moved because they could not be fed. See Wilhelm Eich to Heinrich Vedder (24 June 1905), ELCRN, VII.31.1, pp. 389–90.
542. Ortschronik Omaruru, ELCRN, V.23.1, p. 314.
543. "Protokoll einer brüderlichen Besprechung abgehalten in Okahandja vom 11.–13. October 1905," ELCRN, I 1.3, p. 472. Numerous transfers of sick internees are documented in NAN, BSW 39 XI. vol. 1, 1904–9.
544. Erichsen, *"The Angel of Death,"* 109; and Nuhn, *Feind überall*, 266–67.
545. Nachlass Deimling, MA-BA, N 559, vol. 3, pp. 15–16.

## Chapter 4

# Deadly Learning?
## Observation and Knowledge Transfer

To this point, I have sought to explain why concentration camps were built in South Africa and South-West Africa by identifying the goals that Great Britain and Imperial Germany associated with the camps. But the question "Why?" can also be understood differently. Why concentration camps? Why did the two powers not seek to resolve the difficulties of colonial warfare another way? Were these camps the obvious solution to the structural problems of colonial guerrilla warfare? Or did the British and Germans borrow the concept of concentrating populations from earlier wars? Did the German colonial military "copy" the concept of the concentration camp from South Africa, where camps established by Roberts and Kitchener had themselves been inspired by Weyler's reconcentration measures in Cuba?

Contemporaries already saw a connection between concentration measures in Cuba and South Africa. Their choice of words made this clear, as when they spoke of Boer *concentrados*[1] or "reconcentration camps"[2] in South Africa. Emily Hobhouse was certain that "England, by the hands of Lord Roberts and Lord Kitchener, adopted the policy of Spain, while improving upon her methods."[3] Valeriano Weyler reiterated this conviction in his autobiography of 1910–11, in which he asserted that the British military—like the Americans in the Philippines—had adopted "his" method in slightly altered form.[4] Particularly during the early phase of the South African concentration camps at the end of 1900, various newspaper articles and letters from readers associated the new concentration policies with Weyler's methods in Cuba. The *Pall Mall Gazette*, for example, asserted that Kitchener's assumption of the high command meant that it was time for "stern 'reconcentration' into the towns, minus the Weylerian barbarity of the starvation of the *reconcentrados*."[5] In response, one reader emphasized the importance of timely measures to feed the "reconcentration towns," and pointed to the danger of typhoid outbreaks in the camps.[6] Various members of the House of Commons likewise saw a close relationship to Weyler's reconcentration policy.[7]

In general, the era's policymakers looked beyond national boundaries and oriented themselves toward the practices of earlier wars. The Colonial Office looked especially to the Franco-Prussian War of 1870–71 and the US Civil War to determine what measures were permissible in counter-guerrilla combat. The United States' contemporaneous actions in the Philippines were considered as well.[8] British leaders noted the US military's establishment of "concentration camps," although long after the camp system in South Africa was already in place.[9] Furthermore, the standard work on colonial warfare in this era, Charles Callwell's *Small Wars*, was international in scope. Callwell looked not only to British small wars but also drew conclusions from other colonial conflicts.[10]

There was clearly interest in "learning" from the wars of others, although the archives offer no concrete proof that the concentration of civilians was learned from Cuba. One indication does appear in the press. On 20 August 1900—one month before Lord Roberts agreed to build the first concentration camps—the *St. James Gazette* discussed the most recent proclamation of the commander-in-chief. The announcement that all burghers who did not swear an oath of neutrality (or who broke this oath) would be taken into custody as prisoners of war, the *Gazette* believed, was an unconscious imitation of the Spanish captain general Weyler's measures in Cuba. But the British attempt was only a "half measure" because all other persons were left on their farms. The *Gazette* recommended "copying" Weyler properly: "If the burghers are not to be trusted, it would be far better to adopt the policy of thorough at once, and 'reconcentrate' the whole Dutch population of the Transvaal at St. Helena or in Ceylon."[11]

It is impossible to say whether Roberts or Kitchener were influenced by this article, or if they even knew about it. However, they probably knew about Weyler's reconcentration policy in Cuba because of reports in British and even some South African newspapers.[12] But it is questionable whether they initiated the construction of concentration camps in South Africa based on the Cuban "model." The linguistic proximity of "concentration camp" and *reconcentratión* suggests a causal relationship. On the other hand, the camps in South Africa first operated under other names: refugee camps, refugee *laager*, or burgher camps. The term "concentration camp" appeared only in 1901, but it was increasingly accepted.[13]

It is also possible that the British military arrived independently at the strategy of concentration. Like the Spanish in Cuba, the British faced the military and strategic problem of how to deal with elusive guerrilla fighters who enjoyed the support of much of the civilian population. Depriving the guerrillas of sustenance by concentrating and controlling the civilian population was a natural course of action. In this view, concentration policy in South Africa—and earlier, in Cuba—would be the logical outcome of a certain structural constellation.[14]

In the end, the degree to which the British concentration camps were inspired by the Cuban model, or rather occurred independently, cannot be determined. Internally, however, the camp management clearly drew from past experience—the experience of British colonialism. The most important points of reference were the Indian plague camps and famine camps.[15] Particularly at the end of 1901, as mortality in the Boer camps was peaking and panic gripped the Colonial Office, there was an attempt to apply lessons previously learned in India. Camp authorities studied reports on the Indian "famine operations" of 1896–97.[16] The Indian Office facilitated contacts with doctors who had worked in the Indian camps so they could offer suggestions for properly managing the camps in South Africa. In a memorandum for the Colonial Office, Surgeon General James Cleghorn summarized the lessons learned from his time with the Indian plague camps: strict discipline had to be upheld. If necessary, internees should be compelled to keep clean and follow the rules of sanitation. Doctors' assistants should search internee residences daily for sick persons, so they could be sent to the hospital immediately—by force if necessary. He further recommended the use of huts, not tents, and dramatically reducing the size of the camps. No more than five hundred to one thousand persons should be entrusted to one doctor.[17]

Interestingly enough, most of these suggestions had already been implemented in the Boer camps by the end of 1901. Emphasis on personal hygiene, rules of sanitation, daily tent visits to identify the sick, and compulsory hospital transfers had been firmly established in most camps.[18] These practices seem to have been anchored in the Empire's medical culture and were implemented promptly, independent of one another in different contexts. Reducing camp size and replacing tents with huts were the only new suggestions. Thomas Holderness from the Indian Office further emphasized the importance of clean water.[19]

The suggestions were immediately forwarded to South Africa. Colonial secretary Chamberlain wired Milner on 16 November 1901:

> Indian experience in famine camps indicates that question of a pure water supply is paramount and that as soon as a camp becomes unhealthy and the water supply affected it must be evacuated; also that camps ought not to be too large—not over, say, 5,000. Camps of that size might be subdivided into smaller sections, with a person in subordinate charge for reporting sickness and for sanitary arrangements.[20]

A few days later, after speaking with Cleghorn, Chamberlain added:

> The compulsory removal of those suffering from infectious disease and of those seriously ill is essential, and for the detection of disease it would seem that great assistance would be given to the medical staff by utilizing Boer women of the right stamp as probationers in uniform, who would readily obtain access to the tents at any time of the day. As regards the observance of cleanly habits and sanitary rules some suitable and efficacious form of punishment appears to be necessary.[21]

Some of these recommendations—as mentioned—already corresponded to existing practice. In other cases, they provided a basis for reform, if not always implemented consistently. The new camps in Natal and the Cape Colony helped to reduce the size of some older camps. However, the five-thousand-person limit was not always upheld. Merebank in Natal, with eight thousand persons, became the largest concentration camp.[22] Milner did not believe that the size of the camps necessarily affected mortality: "A camp of 500 would have developed epidemics as much as a camp of 5,000."[23] However, the new camps were distinguished by better accommodations. Based on experiences in India, the South African authorities shifted from tents to huts.[24] And in the old camps, too, superintendents increasingly replaced tents with sturdier dwellings.[25]

Chamberlain ended his telegram with the suggestions for improvement with the following offer: "If you are in any need of trained men, I am sure that I shall be able to obtain through the India Office the services of officers who have had very analogous experience in the famine camps, and you must not fail to ask for such assistance if you require it."[26] Milner accepted the assistance, and in early March 1902 Lieutenant Colonel Samuel John Thomson took control of the camp system in the Transvaal, and Colonel James Wilkins, in the Orange River Colony. The "new geniuses from India"[27] were accompanied by other officers with experience in the Indian plague camps and famine camps, who became superintendents of individual Boer camps.[28] Thus, expertise from India came to the South African camps through two different channels—suggestions from the Colonial Office in London (based on its evaluation of experiences in India), and the employment of camp experts who had served in India themselves.

Experience from India affected not only the white camps. De Lotbinière, head of the Department of Native Refugees, explained in his final report on the black camps: "Having had experience in Indian Famine Camps and the advisability of keeping natives employed, a system was introduced by which the natives could earn a good wage and purchase all their requirements at very reasonable prices."[29] This system eventually developed into the agricultural program, which made sure not only that younger men worked but also that women and older men could farm in order to support themselves. This system resembled the *zonas de cultivo*, the agricultural zones in Cuba that were farmed by *reconcentrados* to provide a secure source of food. This does not necessarily mean, however, that the idea was borrowed from Cuba. British newspaper reports hardly mentioned the agricultural zones, so it is questionable whether authorities in South Africa even knew about this Cuban practice.[30]

The conviction that work had to be the basis for all forms of aid, because a policy of handouts would necessarily contribute to pauperizing the needy, was firmly anchored within the British Empire.[31] Stowell Kessler writes that British policy:

> forbade any assistance to the indigenous population except in the most dire circumstances, such as levels of starvation that would lead to death or endanger the British settler populations or the military. This was everywhere evident in the Empire from the black locations in the Cape Colony during famine from poor rainfall and crop destruction by locusts, to the famine and plague camps in the largest colony of the Empire, India.[32]

During the war in German South-West Africa, when numerous Herero fled to the British enclave Walvis Bay, women and children who could not immediately be sent to work in South Africa were expected to load coal and complete other tasks for food.[33] Thus, it seems plausible that the agricultural zones in the black camps where "natives" had to work for food were not the result of transfer processes from India or Cuba. Rather, they can be understood as the product of a "basic assumption" of British colonial policy.[34] Indeed, the agricultural zones appear to reflect a general principle of colonial policy, since propagating a Western work ethic was on the agenda of all European colonial powers.[35] There were strong parallels to British doctrine in the German colonizers' emphasis on compulsory labor and "educating" the Herero and Nama to work, so the Africans did not lapse into poverty and indolence.[36] Likewise, one might ask whether the establishment of agricultural zones in Cuba can be understood not only as a means to reduce the cost of feeding internees but also to prevent the *reconcentrados*' permanent pauperization.

There were additional parallels between welfare policy in the large European cities and the practice in colonial concentration camps. The workhouses that were first established in early modern Europe likewise promoted "educating to work." As Sebastian Conrad has shown, colonial and metropolitan work-education programs shared numerous common ties.[37] The compulsory enforcement of hygiene rules in these houses became a model for many colonial administrators. Lord Onslow, undersecretary of state in the British Colonial Office, commented on the general guidelines for the camps in Natal:

> I still think there seems to be too much inclination to "hope" that people in the camps will be clean, decent, + sanitary, instead of making it obligatory under pain of some punishment that they should be so. When a tramp comes into an English workhouse he has to take a bath. He hates it, but it is a condition of getting a meal[.] Why not the same in a concentration camp[?][38]

With this background in mind, we can better understand Andreas Gestrich's depiction of the workhouses as one of the origins of modern concentration camps. Apparently, this connection was also meaningful for colonial camps.[39]

British administrators sought to learn not only from the experiences of other parts of the Empire: there was also exchange between the different camp administrations in the Transvaal, the Orange River Colony, and Natal. In February 1901, the general superintendent of Boer camps in the Transvaal sought the advice of his colleagues in the neighboring colony by inquiring how they handled the distribution of clothing to internees.[40] In November of that same year, an employee in the Colonial Office subtitled a memorandum about the concentration camps: "Points Where the Camp Administration seems to have been Successful and Deserving of Imitation."[41] And soon thereafter, the Colonial Office recommended that camp superintendents read the monthly reports on the Natal camps: "I think the Natal camps may provide some useful lessons to those in charge of the T[rans]V[aal] and O[range] R[iver] C[olony] camps."[42]

The organizers of the black camps also drew from local experience, explicitly orienting these camps toward the compound system of the South African mines.[43] The closed compounds, which had been introduced in the diamond mines near Kimberley in the Cape Colony in 1885, shared significant similarities with the black camps. Thousands of African workers were effectively cut off from the outside world in completely fenced-in compounds for the duration of their contracts. The mine managers had originally hoped to maintain better control over the workers and to improve their living conditions. In practice, however, neglect, inadequate provisions, and overcrowding led to higher death rates within the closed compounds.[44]

Whatever influence Cuban reconcentration may have had on British authorities, German decision makers were clearly aware of the British concentration camps when they opted to build their own camps in South-West Africa in 1904–05. The South African War was a media event in Germany, too, with daily reports in the German press. A prominent theme was the internment of Boer women and children.[45] Books on the war sold briskly. A recent bibliography has counted 358 German publications on the war in South Africa from 1910 and earlier,[46] including excerpts from the official British blue books on the camps, the report by Emily Hobhouse, and Elizabeth Neethling's portrait of the suffering of Boer camp internees.[47] So it is hardly surprising that Paul Leutwein, son of the former colonial governor, associated Trotha's style of warfare with the South African War: "He could also refer to the example of Kitchener, who had established concentration camps for Boer women and children just a few years before, in order to force these people who were struggling for independence into submission."[48]

But knowledge about the British camps came not solely through the media. Some German officials who later assumed a prominent role in establishing and shaping the concentration camps in South-West Africa had a direct personal connection to the camps in South Africa. Ludwig von Estorff, who evacuated the camp on Shark Island soon after becoming commander-in-chief of the German forces in Southwest-Africa in April 1907, spent time in South Africa in 1901. He had accompanied the troops of Walter Kitchener (brother of the South African commander-in-chief) during the guerrilla war for several weeks, even visiting one of the concentration camps.

Friedrich von Lindequist, Germany's consul general in Cape Town and later the colonial governor of German South-West Africa, also participated in this visit.[49] Lindequist visited concentration camps on multiple occasions during the South African War—whether intervening on behalf of German citizens who had been detained, or overseeing the distribution of donations from Germany for Boer families.[50] Decades later he recalled: "During my visits to the largest women's and children's camps in Bloemfontein and Johannesburg, I could confirm the proper arrival and quality of the gifts that went through the hands of our local German pastors."[51] He reported thoroughly on these visits to Imperial Chancellor Bülow and described his "not very favorable" impression of the camps; with respect to personal freedom, conditions in the "refugee camps" differed "very little" from the conditions for prisoners of war. He continued:

> Naturally, accommodations are tight for the mostly very large families. Corrugated iron barracks or small tents do not offer sufficient protection against the harsh cold for poorly clothed refugees. At first, food provisions in Johannesburg were very bad and much too meager. But the change in superintendents brought significant improvement. Mortality was already very high but increased even further with the measles epidemics that broke out in the camps, climbing to 100 or more cases per week among 3,000 to 4,000 persons.[52]

In an earlier report to Berlin he had depicted the camps as part of the British counter-guerrilla strategy, which involved "ridding the land of everything that could possibly be a source of assistance to the Boers, especially cattle and food."[53]

Finally, there was Oskar Hintrager, deputy governor under Lindequist and Estorff's antagonist in the dispute over the evacuation of Shark Island. He had volunteered to fight on the side of the Boers in the South African War, but he never set eyes on a concentration camp himself because he returned home to Germany as early as September 1900.[54] Nevertheless, he remained interested in the fate of the Boers and became an active member of a pro-Boer association in Munich that collected donations for interned women and children, so he was certainly well-informed about the camps.[55]

Archival evidence suggests that the proposal for building concentration camps in the German colony first came from the Rhenish mission—and not from Count Georg von Stillfried und Rattonitz, as is sometimes asserted.[56] Mission Inspector Haussleiter wrote to the imperial chancellor on 25 November 1904, repeating the mission's offer to help with peace negotiations in the colony and adding a new suggestion:

> Finally, we would like to recommend the prompt designation of sites of refuge (*Freistätten*) where those Herero who participated in the war, but not in treacherous acts of murder (*Meuchelmord*), could find protection after laying down their weapons ... Individual watering holes could initially be designated as sites of refuge, and concentration camps built nearby.[57]

The imperial chancellor was familiar with the concept of concentration camps at this time, and not merely because of intensive coverage in the press. He had received detailed reports from Lindequist and other diplomats during the South African War.[58] He also had access to the exhaustive British blue books, which presented a detailed portrait of the concentration camps and how they functioned.[59] Bülow promptly took up the mission's suggestion, and on 11 December he directed Trotha to build concentration camps after the extermination order was lifted.[60] Bülow reiterated this order soon thereafter, adding that the Herero in the camps should be put to work while under supervision. The margin of this document contains a handwritten note indicating Consul General Lindequist's "full approval."[61] Thus, Lindequist, who had firsthand knowledge of the South African camps, was directly involved in the decision.

The Rhenish mission, too, had a special connection to South Africa. The territory of its mission in southern Africa stretched all the way to the Cape Colony, so the Rhenish missionaries were directly affected by the South African War, even if they—unlike many of their colleagues from the Hermannsburg and Berlin missions—were not interned themselves.[62] Archival holdings nevertheless indicate that the Rhenish mission was closely observing the South African camps.[63]

Of course, even Lindequist's participation in the decision does not prove that the concept of the concentration camp was transferred from the neighboring British colony. But some additional considerations support this thesis. To begin, it was not unusual for the experienced British colonial power to be seen as a role model. Ulrike Lindner asserts in her recent study that Great Britain invariably served as a "point of reference for colonial considerations," as "the role model that the Germans worked toward, imitating and distancing."[64] In this spirit, one contemporary author wrote: "As a foremost requirement, I would like that every civil servant in our colony who has been called to assume a position of authority first be sent to South Africa, to study conditions there and to see how things ought to be done and not done."[65] And specialized military journals specifically inquired about the lessons that Imperial Germany might learn from the South African War.[66]

Above all, it is noteworthy that the term "concentration camp" (*Konzentrationslager*) entered the German language with the South African War. The term did not yet appear in German encyclopedias around the turn of the century, but first showed up in the 1920s, usually in conjunction with the Boer camps.[67] At first, German newspapers tended to identify the South African camps as "women's camps" or "refugee camps." As in the British press, the term "concentration camp" only gradually took hold.[68] By 1904, the term "concentration camp" in Germany was unambiguously associated with the camps of the South African War. The fact that, from the start, German officials and others used this term for the internment camps of South-West Africa strongly suggests an orientation toward the British concentration camps. Thus, the British secretary of state for war St. John Brodrick was correct in his assertion that "the foreign troops realized they had much to learn from the English army" in the South African War.[69]

If we consider the broad differences in how the camps in South Africa and South-West Africa functioned, we can see that knowledge transfer is necessarily a "creative" process—"rarely linear, always fragmentary, quite idiosyncratic, and full of imagination," as Birthe Kundrus describes.[70] The system of the Boer camps could not be established in the German colony in exactly the same way; the contexts were too different. The primary function of the Boer camps—to remove guerrilla fighters' base of support by concentrating the civilian population—was not transferrable to South-West Africa. The Herero did not act as guerrilla fighters, and the Nama, who did use guerrilla tactics, did not depend on the civilian population for support. Preventive separation of civilians and combatants did not make sense in this situation—nor did the policy of anglicization, the second important function of the Boer camps. Reception of the concentration camp concept in South-West Africa meant extracting fragments of the "foreign" import, reworking them, then combining with existing traditions in order to arrive at a usable concept, as Christiane Eisenberg describes in her reflections on cultural transfer.[71] All that could be transferred was a vague idea of detaining a population that was identified as hostile—women and children, too—in a fenced location or camp. This is what was implemented in South-West Africa, and this, too, was the dominant image of the Boer camps—insofar as they were not immediately depicted as sites of annihilation—among the German public.[72] By emphasizing parallels between the internment camps and the detention of prisoners of war, Lindequist conveyed a similar impression in his internal report to the imperial chancellor about his visit to the camps in Johannesburg and Bloemfontein.[73] Although Boer women and children were officially "refugees," not prisoners, and some British camps were not even fenced, such details were hardly noticed in Imperial Germany and played no role in the adaptation process.

A rough idea of the concentration camp concept was imported, and then mixed on site with local influences. Captured Herero and Nama were expected to build their own dwellings; these *pontoks* were assembled on site with available materials in the traditional manner. Some camps were "fenced" with thorn branches, typical practice in the colony for enclosing cattle. Likewise, the compulsory labor performed by internees was a familiar punishment in South-West Africa for "rebellious" colonized peoples. The Swartboois, a Nama group in the north of the colony, were compelled to work as punishment for their 1898 "uprising."[74]

There was a closer resemblance between the Herero and Nama camps and the South African black camps, particularly with respect to accommodations and the exploitation of internee labor. But the camps for Africans during the South African War were hardly noticed within Germany.[75] In this situation, a transfer of knowledge was unlikely.

Parallels between the camps—like the similarities in administering the Indian famine camps and the South African camps—can be more plausibly understood as products of a common "colonial culture."[76] These shared principles included educating the "natives" for work, permitting them to work as wage earners only in service to Europeans, and coming to their aid only in crisis situations where the well-being of the white population was also endangered. These doctrines proved highly potent in the South-West African prisoner of war camps and the South African black camps. They did not, however, arise in a vacuum, but rather combined with various structural factors on site. One factor was the labor shortage in both South Africa and South-West Africa, which compelled the British and German militaries to employ internees. And transport problems exacerbated the inadequate provisions for interned "natives" and Boers alike.[77]

In conclusion, we can establish that the construction and operation of concentration camps in South Africa and South-West Africa was a product of different influences. International models certainly played a role. The structural conditions of each wartime situation affected how the imported concept of the camp was received, as this concept mixed with local traditions and was shaped by broader colonial cultures. Older historiographical approaches once explained concentration policies in Cuba, the Philippines, South Africa, and South-West Africa solely in terms of colonial powers "copying" one another, or through the structural similarities of colonial wars. However, such approaches are too simple and cannot sufficiently explain all of the differences and similarities between individual cases.

## Notes

1. Rose Innes to Lord Monk Betton (25 July 1901), CRLB, JC 13/1/164.
2. Jean Veber, *Das Blutbuch von Transvaal* (Berlin, 1901).
3. Hobhouse, *The Brunt of the War*, 317.
4. Stucki, "Streitpunkt Lager," 85.
5. "An Old Man Obstinate," *Pall Mall Gazette*, 24 November 1900.

6. "Reconcentration," *Pall Mall Gazette*, 28 November 1900. Additional articles referencing Cuba include "Lord Roberts Decree," *Northern Echo*, 30 August 1900; and "Farm Burning in the Transvaal and Orange River Colonies," *The Times*, 26 November 1900.
7. Stucki, "Streitpunkt Lager," 84–85.
8. "Memorandum on certain points connected with the conduct of hostilities" (24 October 1901), NAL, CO 417/335, pp. 8–31.
9. Joseph Chamberlain to Arthur Balfour (13 November 1901), CRLB, JC 11/5/1.
10. Callwell, *Small Wars*.
11. *St. James Gazette*, 20 August 1900, quoted in NAP, Jan Ploeger Papers (A 2030), vol. 29.
12. See, for example, "The Situation in Cuba," *The Times*, 30 November 1896; "The Cuban Atrocities," *Daily News*, 13 April 1898; and "The Cuban War," *Manchester Guardian*, 30 April 1898. In South Africa, the *Cape Argus* carried a report on events in Cuba on 26 March 1897. See A. M. Davey, "The Reconcentrados of Cuba," *Historia* 5, no. 3 (1960): 194.
13. See also Annette Wieviorka, "L'expression 'camp de concentration' au 20e siècle," *Vingtième Siècle* 54, no. 2 (1997).
14. Ian Beckett supports this view while Andreas Stucki prefers a hybrid explanation for the emergence of concentration policies around 1900. Beckett, *Modern Insurgencies*, 36; and Andreas Stucki, "Aufbruch ins Zeitalter der Lager? Zwangsumsiedlung und Deportation in der spanischen Antiguerilla auf Kuba, 1895–1898," (PhD diss., University of Bern, 2009), 339.
15. Plague camps were established during the epidemic of 1896–97 to keep residents away from unhygienic neighborhoods that were considered dangerous to public health. During the famines of the 1870s and 1880s, famine camps served as makeshift workhouses; internees were fed but also expected to work, and they had to agree to live in camps. On the plague camps and famine camps, see Forth, *Barbed-Wire Imperialism*, 43–99.
16. J. W. Holderness to H. W. Just (13 November 1901), NAL, CO 417/335, pp. 201–2.
17. Memorandum (18 November 1901), NAL, CO 417/335, pp. 218–20.
18. See, for example, camp inspector Dr. Kendal Franks's reports from August 1901. He found that these principles had already been implemented in the camps in Barberton and Balmoral. In Middelburg, where there was no system of daily tent visitation, he found the camp administration too lax and recommended changes. All reports are in NAP, GOV 262.
19. Holderness to Just (13 November 1901), NAL, CO 417/335, pp. 201–2.
20. Telegram from Joseph Chamberlain to Alfred Milner (16 November 1901), CRLB, JC 14/4/2/201.
21. Telegram from Joseph Chamberlain to Alfred Milner (20 November 1901), CRLB, JC 14/4/2/203.
22. "Monthly Report on Natal camps for February 1902" (12 March 1902), NAL, CO 179/222, p. 453. On the camp in Merebank, see Annette U. Wohlberg, "The Merebank Concentration Camp in Durban, 1901–1902," (unpublished thesis, University of the Orange Free State, 2000).
23. Telegram from Alfred Milner to Joseph Chamberlain (1 December 1901), CRLB, JC 14/4/2/212.
24. Ibid.
25. Ibid.; and Alfred Milner to Hamilton Goold-Adams (14 January 1902), BLO, MP 173, pp. 253–57.
26. Telegram from Chamberlain to Milner (20 November 1901), CRLB, JC 14/4/2/203.

27. Milner to Goold-Adams (14 January 1902), BLO, MP 173, pp. 253–57.
28. Thomson brought along three officers from the subcontinent. See "General Report on Transvaal Burgher Camps for February 1902" (17 March 1902), NAL, CO 417/350, p. 193. Wilkins mentioned three officers from India who were doing especially good work as superintendents, or serving in the headquarters of the Orange River Colony's refugee department. James Wilkins to the Colonial Secretary, ORC (9 March 1903), FAB, CSO 149, 1633/03.
29. "Final Report Native Refugee Department Transvaal," NAP, TKP 135, p. 1.
30. This article, which briefly mentions "zones of cultivation," was an exception: "Spain's Great Offence in Cuba: 'Concentration,'" *Manchester Times*, 29 April 1898.
31. For an example of this way of thinking, see Beak, *The Aftermath of War*, 25, 29, and 149.
32. Kessler, "South African War," 132.
33. Ulrike Lindner, *Koloniale Begegnungen: Deutschland und Großbritannien als Imperialmächte in Afrika 1880–1914* (Frankfurt, 2011), 257.
34. Hull, *Absolute Destruction*, 96–97 and 275 (note 10).
35. Dirk van Laak, "Kolonien als 'Laboratorien der Moderne?,'" in Conrad and Osterhammel, *Das Kaiserreich transnational*, 261–62. See also Jürgen Osterhammel, *Kolonialismus: Geschichte—Formen—Folgen* (Munich, 2004), 115–16; and Andreas Eckert, *Kolonialismus* (Frankfurt, 2006), 103 and 107–8.
36. German Colonial Government for South-West Africa to the Colonial Department (17 April 1906), BAL, R 1001/2119, pp. 42–44.
37. Conrad, "'Eingeborenenpolitik.'" See also John L. Comaroff and Jean Comaroff, "Hausgemachte Hegemonie," in *Jenseits des Eurozentrismus: Postkoloniale Perspektiven in den Geschichts- und Kulturwissenschaften*, ed. Sebastian Conrad and Shalini Randeria (Frankfurt, 2002), 247–82.
38. Note from William Onslow (23 November 1901), NAL, CO 179/220, p. 98.
39. Gestrich, "Voraussetzungen und Vorläufer." See also Caplan, "Political Detention."
40. Telegram from General Superintendent Refugee Camps to Lieutenant Governor Bloemfontein (26 February 1901), FAB, SRC 2, no. 284.
41. "Memorandum on the Concentration Camps" (18 November 1901), NAL, CO 417/335, pp. 178–80.
42. Note from William Onslow (3 December 1901), NAL, CO 179/220, p. 212.
43. De Lotbinière to Goold-Adams (18 January 1902), NAL, CO 224/7, p. 563. See also Heyningen, *The Concentration Camps*, 162.
44. Rob Turrell, "Kimberley's Model Compounds," *Journal of African History* 25, no. 1 (1984): 59–75. Focusing primarily on the camps in German South-West Africa, Tilman Dedering also emphasizes the connection between "camps" and "compounds." Tilman Dedering, "Camps, Compounds, Colonialism," *Journal of Namibian Studies* 12 (2012): 29–46.
45. Bender, *Der Burenkrieg und die deutschsprachige Presse*, 13–23.
46. Nicol Stassen and Ulrich van der Heyden, *German Publications on the Anglo-Boer War* (Pretoria, 2007).
47. *Die Concentrationslager im Transvaal und Orange River Colonie* (London, 1902); Hobhouse, *Die Zustände in den südafrikanischen Konzentrationslagern: Bericht von Miss E. Hobhouse* (Berlin, 1902); and Neethling, *Fünfzehn Monate*.
48. BAK, N 1145, vol. 4.
49. Estorff, *Wanderungen und Kämpfe*, 93–94.
50. On Lindequist's role in the distribution of donations, see Politisches Archiv des Auswärtigen Amtes (PA AA), Kapstadt 54. On the collection of donations in Germany, see Ulrich Kröll, *Die internationale Buren-Agitation 1899–1902: Haltung der Öffent-*

*lichkeit und Agitation zu Gunsten der Buren in Deutschland, Frankreich und den Niederlanden während des Burenkrieges* (Münster, 1973).

51. "Generalkonsul des Deutschen Reiches für Britisch-Südafrika in Kapstadt," BAK, N 1669. See also NAL, CO 417/348, pp. 1021–24. Bloemfontein and Johannesburg were by no means the largest camps.
52. Friedrich von Lindequist to Bernhard von Bülow (23 June 1901), PA AA, Kapstadt 34, no. 2563.
53. Friedrich von Lindequist to Bernhard von Bülow (16 June 1901), ibid., no. 2464. See also G. to Bernhard von Bülow (29 April 1901), ibid., no. 1763.
54. See the biographical information on Hintrager, BAK, N 1037.
55. J. J. Oberholster, "Inleiding," *Christiaan deWet-Annale* 2 (1973): 6; and Oskar Hintrager, *Steijn, de Wet und die Oranje-Freistaater: Tagebuchblätter aus dem südafrikanischen Kriege* (Tübingen, 1902).
56. Olusoga and Erichsen, *The Kaiser's Holocaust*, 159f. Stillfried's report to the Kaiser mentioned "confined areas" (*geschlossene Niederlassungen*) near worksites where the "natives" might be housed in the future. However, we can only speculate whether Stillfried meant concentration camps and not the villages or "locations" that had already existed in southern Africa before the war. Of particular significance, Stillfried's report is dated 12 December 1904—one day after the first order for building the concentration camps. Thus, it cannot be the origin of concentration policy. "Bericht des Oberleutnants Graf von Stillfried und Rattonitz betreffend Eingeborenenfrage und militärische Verhältnisse in SWA i. d. letzten zwei Jahren" (12 December 1904), BAL, R 1001/2117, pp. 59–60. Claudia Siebrecht has recently suggested that a parliamentary debate over reservations was the origin of the decision to build the camps, providing the background for Bülow's instructions at the end of 1904. But "concentration camps" were not specifically mentioned anywhere in this debate, so the association remains unclear. Claudia Siebrecht, "Formen von Unfreiheit und Extreme der Gewalt: Die Konzentrationslager in Deutsch-Südwestafrika, 1904–1908," in Greiner and Kramer, *Welt der Lager*, 87–109.
57. Inspector Haussleiter to Bernhard von Bülow (25 November 1904), ELCRN, II.5.14.
58. See, for example, Lindequist to Bülow (23 June 1901), PA AA, Kapstadt 34, no. 2563; G. to Bülow (29 April 1901), ibid., no. 1763; Consul Pretoria to Bernhard von Bülow (5 December 1901), PA AA, AI Afrika, R 14757, no. 13912.
59. Copies of the important blue books Cd. 819, Cd. 853, and Cd. 902 can be found in the files of the Foreign Office, which was subordinate to Bülow. See PA AA, AI Afrika, R 14758–14760.
60. Bülow to Trotha (11 December 1904), BAL, R 1001/2089, p. 54.
61. Bülow to Trotha (13 January 1905), ibid., pp. 116–17.
62. See BRMG 59 (1902); Haccius, *Drangsalszeit*; and Ulrich van der Heyden, "Der 'Burenkrieg' von 1899 bis 1902 und die deutschen Missionsgesellschaften," in *Mission und Gewalt: Der Umgang christlicher Missionen mit Gewalt und die Ausbreitung des Christentums in Afrika und Asien in der Zeit von 1792 bis 1918/19*, ed. Ulrich van der Heyden and Jürgen Becher (Stuttgart, 2000), 214.
63. Hanns Lessing has pointed to the corresponding holdings in the mission archive in Wuppertal. Hanns Lessing, "'In der Nähe dieser Wasserstelle sollen Konzentrationslager errichtet werden': Eine theologische Rekonstruktion der Rolle der Rheinischen Missionsgesellschaft während des Kolonialkrieges in Namibia (1904–1908)," in *Deutsche evangelische Kirche im kolonialen südlichen Afrika: Die Rolle der Auslandsarbeit von den Anfängen bis in die 1920er Jahre*, ed. Hanns Lessing et al. (Wiesbaden, 2011), 493.
64. Lindner, *Koloniale Begegnungen*, 8, and also 40–41, 52–59, and 84–100.

65. Georg Hartmann, *Deutsch-Südwestafrika im Zusammenhang mit Südafrika* (Berlin, 1899), 12.
66. See, for example, "Was lehrt uns der Burenkrieg?," *Militär-Wochenblatt* 42 (1902): 1146–47; and "Die Nutzbarmachung der Erfahrungen des Südafrikanischen Krieges," *Militär-Wochenblatt* 85 (1902): 2273–74. However, these articles were primarily concerned with infantry tactics, not counter-guerrilla measures such as the concentration camps.
67. See, for example, "Konzentrationslager," in *Meyers Lexikon*, vol. 6 (Leipzig, 1927), column 1723.
68. These quotes come from the *Neue Preußische Zeitung* (also known as the *Kreuzzeitung*), which first used the term *Konzentrations-Lager* on 24 July 1901. *Neue Preußische Zeitung*, 21 June 1901, 22 June 1901, 24 July 1901, and 13 September 1901.
69. "Der Krieg zwischen England und den Buren," *Neue Preußische Zeitung*, 6 June 1901.
70. Birthe Kundrus, "Kontinuitäten, Parallelen, Rezeptionen: Überlegungen zur 'Kolonialisierung' des Nationalsozialismus," *WerkstattGeschichte* 43 (2006): 61.
71. Eisenberg, "Kulturtransfer als historischer Prozess."
72. Bender, *Der Burenkrieg und die deutschsprachige Presse*, 118–19.
73. Lindequist to Bülow (23 June 1901), PA AA, Kapstadt 34, no. 2563.
74. Zimmerer, *Deutsche Herrschaft über Afrikaner*, 182.
75. The concentration of Africans was rarely mentioned. For a rare exception, see "Der Krieg zwischen England und den Buren," *Neue Preußische Zeitung*, 5 August 1901.
76. Elsewhere I have argued that this culture was part of a shared repository of imperial knowledge, or an "imperial cloud." See *Journal of Modern European History* 14, no. 2 (2016), especially Aidan Forth and Jonas Kreienbaum, "A Shared Malady: Concentration Camps in the British, Spanish, American and German Empires," 245–67.
77. This explanatory model can be understood as a synthesis of Isabel Hull's concept of military culture, which emphasizes the influence of unquestioned assumptions, and Susanne Kuß's concept of the "theater of war" (*Kriegsschauplatz*) which emphasizes how local circumstances shaped the development of colonial wars. Hull does, however, certainly take local circumstances into consideration. Hull, *Absolute Destruction*; and Kuß, *Deutsches Militär auf kolonialen Kriegsschauplätzen*, 29–37.

CHAPTER 5

# COMPARATIVE REFLECTIONS ON COLONIAL AND NATIONAL SOCIALIST CAMPS

The term "concentration camp" emerged around the turn of the century in a colonial context, but today it is primarily associated with camps that were established between 1933 and 1945 in National Socialist Germany. Intense debate over the possible continuities between colonial violence and National Socialist crimes consistently returns to the comparability of colonial and National Socialist camps. Joachim Zeller has suggested that the camps in German South-West Africa can be compared, "with some justification," to later National Socialist concentration camps such as Buchenwald or Dachau.[1] Jürgen Zimmerer argues that "the beginnings of a bureaucratic form of extermination"—a "form of mass murder" that "is seen as characteristic of the Holocaust"—were already present in the colony.[2] According to Joël Kotek and Pierre Rigoulot, Wilhelmine Germany created "a model for the National Socialist camps or even the Holocaust"[3] in South-West Africa by ridding itself of imprisoned men, women, and children "in a form of annihilation through labor."[4] Benjamin Madley even sees the camp on Shark Island "as a rough model for later Nazi *Vernichtungslager* . . . like Treblinka and Auschwitz, whose primary purpose was murder," while the other work camps "provided a rough template" for camps such as Buchenwald and Dachau.[5] Casper Erichsen and David Olusoga share this view, asserting that "the death camp was invented" on Shark Island.[6]

These comparative efforts are problematic to varying degrees, on a number of different levels. To begin, they proceed from a false understanding of the colonial camps, and they are further based on an image of National Socialist camps that in no way does justice to their complexity.

We should most sharply reject the comparison to National Socialist extermination camps (*Vernichtungslager*). The three camps associated with Operation Reinhard—Belzec, Sobibor, and Treblinka—and also Chelmno, Majdanek, and Auschwitz, are typically identified as extermination camps. At the first four sites (which were not technically concentration camps), deportees were killed within hours in gas chambers or vans, while the last two sites can be considered hybrid institutions. On one hand, Majdanek and Auschwitz were concentration camps; they admitted and registered newcomers who remained alive for at least a short period. But they were simultaneously extermination camps, where certain groups of deportees were killed in gas chambers upon arrival (as at the Operation Reinhard sites), without being sent to the actual concentration camp. The sole function of extermination camps was the immediate murder of all who were sent there.[7]

All colonial concentration camps and centers around the turn of the century admitted and—at least in South Africa and South-West Africa—registered new arrivals. The murder of internees did occur from time to time—as in the case of the sick Herero woman who was shot by the overseer Benkesser on Shark Island—but this played a comparatively small role in the overall mortality in the camps. In none of the cases discussed in this book—not even Shark Island—did the colonizers systematically seek to murder internees. This was not the camps' purpose. It is misleading to speak of extermination camps in the colonial context. If anything, the term "death camp" (*Sterbelager*) is more appropriate, as used by Karin Orth for Bergen-Belsen and special satellite camps like the Boelcke barracks outside the Mittelbau-Dora camp. In the final phase of the war, the Camp SS sent prisoners who were too sick to work to death camps—or to separate death zones in some larger camps—where they succumbed to "systematic malnourishment."[8] But because the intent here, too, was to kill internees, a crucial difference exists between these sites and the colonial camps. Many internees in the colonial camps also died of malnourishment, but not as the result of an intentional plan. Malnourishment was the result of logistical problems, insufficient resources, (racist) indifference, and setting priorities elsewhere—but it was not the expression of a desire to annihilate.

Thus, in the context of the colonial camps it is incorrect to speak of a "bureaucratic form of extermination," or "annihilation through labor," because these terms, which scholars subsequently coined for the National Socialist concentration camps, imply planned extermination. In German South-West Africa, the Herero and Nama were "annihilated" by compulsory labor to the extent that the prisoners' extreme workload often led to death. But here, work was not intended as a means of murder; rather, Herero and Nama were supposed to provide a source of labor for postwar society. By contrast, Jewish camp internees who were not immediately murdered in the final years of World War II so that the last bit of labor could be extracted from them, were generally not expected to survive. Their deaths were being delayed for only a few weeks. They were killed, not by gas or bullets, but by the systematic and excessive exploitation of their labor.[9]

Comparison with the Buchenwald and Dachau concentration camps is likewise problematic because it disregards these camps' radical transformation over time. This was especially true for Dachau, which was established in March 1933 and liberated at the end of April 1945, thereby undergoing all of the changes of the National Socialist concentration camp system. Dachau—like all of the "early camps"[10]—first served as a means of suppressing political opponents and securing the National Socialists' seizure of power. After 1934, the camp became part of the program of "general racial prevention," which involved imprisoning "asocials," habitual criminals, and others who deviated from the norm of the "people's community (*Volksgemeinschaft*)." After the annexation of Austria and the partial occupation of Czechoslovakia in 1938, Dachau admitted numerous political prisoners from the new territories and again served as an instrument for fighting political opponents. After the November pogrom (Kristallnacht), the Gestapo temporarily sent more than ten thousand Jews to Dachau, seeking to terrorize them into emigration. Exploiting prisoner labor, a motive that had been present since 1934, simultaneously gained new significance in the immediate run-up to the war.[11] The function and architecture of the Dachau camp changed radically. Initially housed within an old munitions factory from World War I, from 1937 to 1938 the camp was thoroughly renovated as a "small city of terror,"[12] becoming (in the words of Heinrich Himmler) a "modern,"[13] genuine "National Socialist concentration camp"[14] with barracks, watchtowers, workshops, and SS quarters.[15]

With the outbreak of war, the overall camp system—and Dachau, too—transformed once again. Masses of incoming prisoners from the occupied territories fed the camps' rapid growth. Until 1937, Dachau usually housed between 2,000 and 2,500 persons. In 1938, the number of internees temporarily rose to 14,232, and after April 1939 it hovered between 3,300 and 3,900. Internee numbers rose quickly once the war started, reaching around 10,000 persons in the winter of 1940–41. The concentration camp system simultaneously expanded as a whole; the total number of internees climbed from 21,400 on 1 September 1939 (the beginning of the war in Europe) to 53,000 at the end of 1940. The internee population became more international, conditions within the camps deteriorated, and mortality increased significantly. Until 1937, the annual number of deaths in Dachau consistently remained in the low double digits. This figure rose to 276 in 1938, and then multiplied during the war. In the six-month period between December 1940 and May 1941 alone, 2,347 prisoners died.

Defeat at Stalingrad, and the realization that the war would not be ending soon, ushered in the camp system's next fundamental transformation. The arms industry began to systematically employ camp internees as forced labor. In 1942, the Business and Administration Main Office (WVHA, or Wirtschaftsverwaltungshauptamt) succeeded the Inspectorate of Concentration Camps as the chief SS authority responsible for overseeing the camps, establishing numerous satellite camps near arms factories. Other satellite camps provided labor for huge projects that resettled factories in bomb-resistant cave systems or bunkers. Main camps such as Dachau soon served merely as "hubs"[16] that distributed rapidly incoming prisoners to different satellite camps. Mortality in the camps initially decreased, as the WVHA made some improvements to the living conditions of prisoners who were forced to work in weapons production, but it ultimately exploded in the final year of the war. The concentration camp system kept expanding, so there were 524,286 interned prisoners in August 1944, and 714,211 in January 1945. The overcrowding, violence, inadequate provisions, and grueling workloads grew worse after the spring of 1944, when the easternmost camps were evacuated in advance of the encroaching Red Army, and prisoners transferred to the remaining camps in the core German territories. In April 1945, 65,613 internees were housed in the Dachau camp network, including 27,649 internees in the main camp. A total of 14,511 internees died between December 1944 and the camps' liberation on 29 April 1945.[17]

In light of the rapid, fundamental changes that Dachau underwent in the twelve years of its existence, a broad comparison between the colonial concentration camps and Dachau says very little. A much more useful question is whether similarities existed between specific colonial and National Socialist concentration camps (or concentration camp systems) at certain points in time. To begin, we can direct this question to the purpose of the camps. The colonial concentration camps primarily served as a military tool for ending colonial wars. The military usually sought to isolate opposing combatants and civilians, interning the latter and depriving the former of all support. In the Third Reich, concentration camps were initially an instrument of domestic politics, used to destroy political opposition and, increasingly, to implement "general racial prevention." After the start of the war, the camps also became an instrument of occupation—as with the internment of Polish elites.[18]

In the context of the war, there was a functional parallel to colonial practice—the concentration of population groups as a counter-guerrilla measure. German occupation forces fighting partisans encountered typical problems of guerrilla warfare, as Christian Gerlach has determined in his work on Belarus. Partisans hid among the civilians who supported them—sometimes voluntarily, sometimes under coercion. The occupiers established "dead zones" in some areas to enforce a clear separation between partisans and civilians. All persons, potential hiding places, and food reserves were removed from these areas. The National Socialists' scorched earth strategy differed from its colonial predecessors, above all, in its radical implementation. At first, the civilian population in the zones was murdered outright—unlike in the colonies, where civilians were typically deported to camps or secure settlements. Persons who could work, especially men, were kept alive only after the demand for labor rose in the second half of the war. The establishment of dead zones was no longer driven solely by military goals such as isolating partisans, but also by the need to procure compulsory laborers and food for the German troops. Those who were fit to work were sent to secure areas and resettled in forced labor camps.[19] Some civilians from the dead zones were transported to the Auschwitz and Majdanek concentration camps in 1943. In Auschwitz, most landed in the "Vitebsk Russian family camp." Any prisoners who did not die from conditions in the camps or forced labor were murdered in gas chambers in the fall of 1944.[20]

It would be wrong to see this as a key similarity between the colonial and National Socialist camps. The internment of civilians from partisan areas played only a negligible role in the Nazi camp system; this never determined how the camps functioned. In the colonial context, by contrast, the military function of ending colonial warfare always assumed central—or even sole—importance.

Nevertheless, a common tie does unite the Nazi camps (especially in the second half of the war), the camps in German South-West Africa, and—to a lesser degree—the black camps in South Africa. In all of these circumstances, exploiting internee labor became a central function of the camps. The wars led to an extreme shortage of workers, and the camps were one of the last reservoirs of labor. Whereas the British hired internees from the black camps as wage earners on a comparatively voluntary basis, the Germans turned to compulsory labor. The high demand for forced labor at least partially explains the Germans' attempt to drive up internee numbers in South-West Africa, and also in the Nazi camps in the second half of World War II. It is noteworthy that both the German colony and the National Socialist universe of the camps developed comparable systems of renting out camp internees and "satellite camps" close to workplaces.

In South-West Africa, private individuals and companies could apply to the closest district or division office to be assigned prisoners of war as forced laborers. In return, they paid a small daily or monthly fee. Larger companies such as the Woermann line or the Lenz and Koppel railroad companies were even allowed to set up their own camps near their worksites for captive workers. In key points, this system resembled the cooperation that developed between the SS and arms industry after 1942. At the end of September 1942, Hitler, Himmler, and armaments minister Albert Speer made the formative decision that concentration camp prisoners could be rented out to the arms industry in the future. By the war's end, a far-reaching network of more than one thousand satellite camps had emerged, each belonging to one of the existing main camps. These satellite camps were usually located near sites of industrial production. They were guarded by the SS but established by the individual companies for whom the internees were forced to work. There was a daily rental fee for every prisoner who was fit to work—four Reichsmarks for every unskilled worker, and six Reichsmarks for every skilled worker. Payments flowed to the state treasury via the WVHA.[21]

Of course, there were differences between the colonial and National Socialist systems of renting out workers—especially from a quantitative perspective. In the last year of the war, nearly a half-million concentration camp prisoners were forced to work in the arms industry, or in the moving of production facilities to sites that could not be bombed. In South-West Africa, however, there were never more than twenty thousand prisoners of war, not all of whom were fit to work.[22] Organizationally, the company camps in the colony did not belong to the military concentration camps, so their relationship to one another differed from the Nazis' main and satellite camps. However, the military camps did function as a kind of hub, similar to the main Nazi camps. Prisoners of war were brought to the military camps from the field or from missionary collection sites, and then were sent on to different employers or company camps. Sick prisoners, or those who were needed elsewhere, were sent back to the military camps for redistribution. Thus, on a functional level there were similarities between the systems of forced labor.

Another purpose of the colonial concentration sites was "educating" internees—to become "modern" English subjects (South Africa), "civilized" persons (the Philippines), or a compliant working class (South-West Africa). Here, too, the National Socialist concentration camps most closely resembled the camps in South-West Africa, where educating the internees "through work" (*Erziehung durch Arbeit*) was understood as a step toward the broader goal of educating them "to work" (*Erziehung zur Arbeit*). In other words, forcing inmates to work was how to make them into willing laborers in the future. These phrases echo the official explanation that Nazi concentration camps, particularly in their early phase, were "education" camps (*Erziehungslager*). The Camp SS sought to "educate" prisoners primarily through work. Labor in the camps often had no economic utility, but it was intended to reintegrate those who had been "seduced" by Marxism back into the "people's community." In the early Nazi camps, work was primarily an instrument of terror, humiliation, and punishment, and education appears to have been mostly a strategy of justification.[23] In South-West Africa, too, there was always a dimension of punishment to compulsory labor, for "rebellion" and killing German settlers. But economics had also figured prominently from the very beginning; the German colonial power used forced labor to ease the shortage of workers that arose during the war.[24]

The differing functions of the colonial and National Socialist concentration sites resulted in numerous differences in the camps' physical appearance. The colonial concentration camps and zones arose primarily as a means to end their respective colonial wars. They lost their reason to exist once these wars ended, and they dissolved soon thereafter. The "genuine" National Socialist concentration camps, by contrast, were conceived as permanent institutions. Planned as "small cities of terror," their infrastructure included barracks, stone buildings, kitchens, and lavatories. The difference between these facilities and the tent camps and improvised huts of the camps for Africans in South Africa and South-West Africa was visibly apparent. Internment in existing towns in Cuba and the Philippines represents yet another model of concentration that was likewise characterized by a high degree of improvisation. Only the British Boer camps in their final phase gradually approached the infrastructure of the Nazi camps, once the British administration recognized that better structural and sanitary facilities were essential for reducing mortality.

The differing functions of the camps also affected the number of internees. In contrast to the colonial camps, the prewar Nazi camp system was quite small. The colonial powers sought to depopulate entire regions, which meant that internee numbers grew rapidly. Within just a few months, concentration sites in Cuba held 400,000 people; in South Africa, more than 200,000; in the Philippines, 300,000 in Batangas province alone; and in South-West Africa, just under 20,000. By contrast, after the first wave of internment that followed the Reichstag fire in early 1933, the number of prisoners in the National Socialist concentration camps had already dropped significantly by the year's end. The Nazi camp population did not approach the prisoner numbers of the camps in German South-West Africa until mid-1938. In the summer of 1935, the camp population was still about 4,000. On 1 November 1936, it was 4,761, and it was 7,750 at the end of 1937. The clear majority of internees were men—in contrast to the colonial context, where male combatants were usually difficult to apprehend, and so most internees were women and children.[25] The National Socialist camp system did not reach dimensions comparable to South Africa until the second half of the war; there were 224,000 internees in August 1943. In the last year of fighting, the concentration camp system expanded to accommodate as many as 714,211 internees, finally exceeding all quantitative dimensions from the colonial context.[26]

The lower internee numbers in the prewar Nazi camps point toward another finding that may seem surprising. Mortality in the prewar camps was usually far lower than in the colonial concentration sites. Annual mortality in Dachau between 1933 and 1937 ranged between 0.5 and 2 percent.[27] In Mauthausen, which was one of the deadliest camps, monthly mortality before the war was 1.1 percent.[28] The camps in Swakopmund and Okahandja experienced a comparable death rate only in their "best" periods. In "bad" months, 5, 10, or (in extreme cases) more than 18 percent of internees perished in the colonial camps. The Nazi camps attained—and eventually outstripped—such dimensions only during the war, particularly during its chaotic final year. Between September 1939 and March 1940, the monthly death rate in Mauthausen was 8.6 percent; between July 1941 and April 1943, it reached 9.7 percent; and between January and April 1945, 12.5 percent.[29]

The initially low mortality in the Nazi concentration camps can be largely attributed to fewer internees and to the construction of the camps as permanent institutions. Prisoners in the prewar era did not suffer as much from malnourishment or overcrowding. Every prisoner usually had his or her own bed in one of the camp barracks. There were sanitary facilities, and food rations did not necessarily lead to starvation. In this respect, initial conditions were better than in the colonial context, where logistical problems in hastily improvised camps resulted in catastrophic conditions for masses of internees. A large proportion of deaths in the prewar Nazi camps did not come from sickness or starvation, but rather torture, violence, and murder. The role of terror of the Nazi camps was always more significant than in the colonial concentration sites.[30] Mass death in the Nazi camps did not reach its height until after the internee population exploded during World War II (and especially during the logistical breakdown that occurred in the war's final months), as overcrowding, malnourishment, and disease proliferated, akin to the colonial context. Of the more than seven hundred thousand prisoners in the concentration camp system in mid-January 1945, one-third to one-half are thought to have died by the end of the war. In all, around two million people lost their lives in Nazi concentration camps, more than half in the extermination sections of the "hybrid" Auschwitz-Birkenau and Majdanek camps, which had no parallel in the colonial context.[31]

Overall, the differences between the colonial and National Socialist concentration systems outweigh their similarities. The systems emerged in distinct historical contexts and mostly fulfilled different tasks. But there were some significant similarities, particularly with respect to South-West Africa—the exploitation of internees as forced laborers, and the supposed "education" of internees through work.[32] Do these parallels indicate a connection between the colonial and National Socialist camps? Directing our attention to the respective regimes of compulsory labor, is it possible to speak of a continuity from Windhuk to Auschwitz-Monowitz (where IG Farben "rented" concentration camp prisoners for its Buna factory early on)?[33] The current state of research does not provide a definitive answer. A comprehensive, empirically sound investigation of the colonial influences on National Socialism's crimes, plans, and techniques of dominance has yet to be written.

Above all, it is unclear how the corresponding knowledge from Africa might have reached the levers of power in the National Socialist camp system. This does not appear to have occurred through personal continuities, as is sometimes proposed. Benjamin Madley, for example, points to Franz Xaver Ritter von Epp, who participated in the Herero campaign and subsequently served as governor (*Reichsstatthalter*) of Bavaria after 1933. There is no evidence, however, that Epp presided over the construction of Dachau. Madley further suggests that Hermann Göring was responsible for building the Nazis' first concentration camp as Prussian interior minister in 1933.[34] Hermann Göring's father Ernst was the first Reichskommissar of German South-West Africa, but he left the colony in 1890, after only five years—before Hermann's birth, and more than one decade before the colony's concentration camps were established in

1904–05. But there is also no evidence that Hermann Göring was closely informed about the Herero and Nama camps. In any event, initiative for building the first concentration camps did not come from Göring, but rather from local authorities, and in 1933–34 Göring—like Epp—opposed the expansion of the concentration camp system, which was controlled by Himmler.[35]

Overall, the war in South-West Africa—and with it, the concentration camps for the Herero and Nama—seem to have faded from Germany's historical memory in the 1930s and 1940s. The war hardly played a role even in colonialist propaganda, as Andreas Eckl shows.[36] Christian Goeschel and Nikolaus Wachsmann conclude that "there is no evidence that the Nazis borrowed organizational or other features from the German colonial camps, nor was there any continuity of personnel."[37]

When Nazi leaders cited colonial precedents for their own camps, they invariably pointed to South Africa. In 1938, for example, Göring responded to the British ambassador's criticism of the concentration camps by explaining that these were a British invention from the Boer War.[38] Numerous publications from the late 1930s depicted atrocities in the Boer camps and described the camps as sites where women and children were intentionally starved to death. The best known of these concoctions was the 1941 film *Ohm Krüger*.[39] On 30 January 1940, Hitler explained to an audience in the Berlin Sportpalast that "it was then [in the war against the Boers, J. K.] that concentration camps were invented. The English brain gave birth to this idea. We only read about it in the encyclopedias and later copied it—with one crucial difference: England locked up women and children in these camps. Over twenty thousand Boer women died wretchedly at the time."[40]

But such statements do not tell us whether the South African camps actually served as a model for the later Nazi camps. Hitler's speech was first and foremost anti-English propaganda, akin to a growing number of German media productions from the late 1930s and early 1940s. With an eye to the bombing campaigns that lay ahead, Hitler used the example of the South African War to illustrate that England had never refrained from harming women and children.[41] In fact, the Boer camps were an imperfect role model because their goals did not align with those of the early National Socialist camps, which were instruments of domestic politics.

It makes more sense, as Jane Caplan observes, to seek the roots of the National Socialist camps in the Prussian tradition of "protective custody" (*Schutzhaft*) and in institutions that enforced social discipline through work, such as workhouses or the work camps of the Voluntary Labor Service (*Freiwilllige Arbeitsdienst*), which were often repurposed as concentration camps in 1933.[42] The connection to workhouses may best explain why the idea of "educating through work" appears in both South-West African and National Socialist concentration camps. The approach was borrowed from the same source. Nor should we neglect the so-called "concentration camps" that were established between 1908 and 1933.[43] During World War I, camps for interning the citizens of enemy nations sprang up in Germany and elsewhere around the globe. The authorities who presided over these camps did not identify them as "concentration camps" (because of the term's negative connotations), but the governments whose citizens were interned in them certainly did.[44] German president Friedrich Ebert invoked emergency powers numerous times between 1920 and 1923, and the military placed thousands of people—primarily communists—in protective custody to suppress uprisings all over Germany. Detainees were often held in former prisoner-of-war or military camps, which contemporary critics called "concentration camps."[45] In this period there were two officially designated "concentration camps" for "undesired foreigners"—mostly Jews from eastern Europe—in the Prussian jurisdictions of Cottbus-Sielow and Stargard.[46] These camps from the years 1914 to 1923 were domestic political instruments, closer typologically to the later Nazi camps than to the colonial concentration sites. In light of these considerations, Hitler's assertion that the National Socialist camps merely "copied" a colonial invention seems unlikely.

## Notes

1. Zeller, "'Ombepera i koza,'" 76. The English quotation is from Zimmerer and Zeller, *Genocide in German South-West Africa*, 78.
2. Zimmerer, "Krieg, KZ und Völkermord," 63. The English quotation is from Zimmerer and Zeller, *Genocide in German South-West Africa*, 60.
3. Kotek and Rigoulot, *Das Jahrhundert der Lager*, 84.
4. Ibid., 80.
5. Madley, "From Africa to Auschwitz," 446.
6. Olusoga and Erichsen, *The Kaiser's Holocaust*, 10.
7. On the individual extermination camps, see the corresponding articles in Wolfgang Benz and Barbara Distel, eds., *Der Ort des Terrors: Geschichte der nationalsozialistischen Konzentrationslager*, vols. 5, 7, and 8 (Munich, 2005–2009); and Sarah Berger, *Experten der Vernichtung: Das T4-Reinhardt-Netzwerk in den Lagern Belzec, Sobibor und Treblinka* (Hamburg, 2013).
8. Karin Orth, *Das System der nationalsozialistischen Konzentrationslager: Eine politische Organisationsgeschichte* (Hamburg, 1999), 260–69. On the Boelcke barracks, see Jens-Christian Wagner, "Gesteuertes Sterben: Die Boelcke-Kaserne als zentrales Siechenlager des KZ Mittelbau," *Dachauer Hefte* 20 (2004): 127–38, and "Nordhausen (Boelcke-Kaserne)," in Benz and Distel, *Der Ort des Terrors*, vol. 7, 320–22.

9. It should be emphasized, however, that "annihilation through labor" was not consistently practiced in the National Socialist camps and did not involve all internee groups. Jens-Christian Wagner rightly underscores that the practice affected only those prisoner groups who were considered "unredeemable," especially Jews. The majority of non-Jewish German internees, by contrast, were not killed as a matter of principle. Jens-Christian Wagner, "Das Außenlagersystem des KL Mittelbau-Dora," in *Die nationalsozialistischen Konzentrationslager: Entwicklung und Struktur*, ed. Ulrich Herbert, Karin Orth, and Christoph Dieckmann (Göttingen, 1998), vol. 2, 707–29; and Buggeln, *Arbeit und Gewalt*, 53–54.
10. Karin Orth distinguishes between the "early camps" of 1933–34 and the later, genuine "National Socialist concentration camps," which were built after 1936. Orth, *System*, 23–66. Other authors use the term "early concentration camps," which does not distinguish as sharply between the early and later camps. See Johannes Tuchel, "Organisationsgeschichte der 'frühen' Konzentrationslager," in Benz and Diestel, *Der Ort des Terrors*, vol. 1, 43–57.
11. On the changing functions and periodization of the prewar concentration camps, see Orth, *System*, 23–66; Wachsmann, "The Dynamics of Destruction"; and Ulrich Herbert, Karin Orth, and Christoph Dieckmann, "Die nationalsozialistischen Konzentrationslager: Geschichte, Erinnerung, Forschung," in Herbert, Orth, and Dieckmann, *Die nationalsozialistischen Konzentrationslager*, vol. 1, 17–40. On Dachau in particular, see Stanislav Zámečník, "Dachau-Stammlager," in Benz and Diestel, *Der Ort des Terrors*, vol. 2, 233–74, and *Das war Dachau* (Luxemburg, 2002). On "general racial prevention," see Ulrich Herbert, "Von der Gegnerbekämpfung zur 'rassischen Generalprävention': 'Schutzhaft' und Konzentrationslager in der Konzeption der Gestapo-Führung 1933–1939," in Herbert, Orth, and Dieckmann, *Die nationalsozialistischen Konzentrationslager*, vol. 1, 60–86; and Johannes Tuchel, "Planung und Realität des Systems der Konzentrationslager 1934–1938," in Herbert, Orth, and Dieckmann, *Die nationalsozialistischen Konzentrationslager*, vol. 1, 43–59.
12. Wachsmann, "The Dynamics of Destruction," 22.
13. Heinrich Himmler, quoted in Orth, *System*, 36.
14. Orth, *System*, 36.
15. On the camp architecture, see Stefanie Endlich, "Die äußere Gestalt des Terrors: Zu Städtebau und Architektur der Konzentrationslager," in Benz and Diestel, *Der Ort des Terrors*, vol. 1, 210–29. On Dachau in particular, see Zámečník, "Dachau-Stammlager."
16. Angelika Königseder uses this term, for example, in "Die Entwicklung des KZ-Systems," in Benz and Diestel, *Der Ort des Terrors*, vol. 1, 39.
17. On the wartime development of the concentration camp system, see Orth, *System*, 67–336; Wachsmann, "The Dynamics of Destruction," and *KL: A History of the Nazi Concentration Camps* (New York, 2015), 190–594; and Herbert, Orth, and Dieckmann, "Die nationalsozialistischen Konzentrationslager." On Dachau during the war, see Zámečník, "Dachau-Stammlager," and "Das war Dachau." On the number of prisoners in Dachau, see also Martin Weimann, ed., *Das nationalsozialistische Lagersystem* (Frankfurt, 2001), 554.
18. On the SS leaders' changing expectations for the concentration camp system, see Orth, *System*, 339.
19. On the different forms of National Socialist forced labor camps, see Wolfgang Benz, "Nationalsozialistische Zwangslager: Ein Überblick," in Benz and Diestel, *Der Ort des Terrors*, vol. 1, 11–29.
20. Christian Gerlach, *Kalkulierte Morde: Die deutsche Wirtschafts- und Vernichtungspolitik in Weißrußland 1941 bis 1944* (Hamburg, 1999), 859–1055. Alexander Hill also mentions that civilians who were suspected of supporting partisans in north-

western Russia were deported to concentration camps. Alexander Hill, *The War Behind the Eastern Front: The Soviet Partisan Movement in North-West Russia 1941–44* (London, 2005), 115 and 153.
21. On the Nazi system of renting out prisoners and the satellite camps, see Hermann Kaienburg, "Zwangsarbeit: KZ und Wirtschaft im Zweiten Weltkrieg" in Benz and Diestel, *Der Ort des Terrors*, vol. 1, 179–94; Orth, *System*, 162–98 and 237–55; and Wachsmann, *KL*, 392–427.
22. On the quantitative dimension of prisoner labor in the Nazi concentration camps, see Kaienburg, "Zwangsarbeit"; and Orth, *System*, 255.
23. Paul Moore, "'Man hat es sich viel schlimmer vorgestellt': German Concentration Camps in Nazi Propaganda, 1933–1939: Representation and Reception," in *Kontinuitäten und Brüche: Neue Perspektiven auf die Geschichte der NS-Konzentrationslager*, ed. Christiane Heß et al. (Berlin 2011), especially 102–3; and Caplan, "Political Detention," 36.
24. An economic function has sometimes been attributed to prisoner labor already in the early Nazi concentration camps. See, for example, Zámečník, "Dachau-Stammlager," 240; and Carina Baganz, *Erziehung zur "Volksgemeinschaft"? Die frühen Konzentrationslager in Sachsen 1933–34/37* (Berlin, 2005), 188. In the early 1930s, however, the exploitation of prisoner labor was not nearly as significant as in South-West Africa.
25. The proportion of female prisoners in the Nazi camps rose over time, but even near the war's end they made up less than one-third of all internees. See Wachsmann, "The Dynamics of Destruction," 36. In contrast to colonial precedent, the SS usually housed men and women in different camps, or at least in different camp sections. On the significance of gender in the Nazi camps, see Caplan, "Gender and the Concentration Camps," in Caplan and Wachsmann, *Concentration Camps in Nazi Germany*.
26. These prisoner numbers come from Wachsmann, "The Dynamics of Destruction," 33.
27. Zámečník counts twenty-two deaths in 1933, thirty-four in 1934, thirteen in 1935, eleven in 1936, and thirty-eight in 1937, with an average camp population that ranged between 2,000 and 2,500 prisoners. See Zámečník, "Dachau-Stammlager," 234 and 265.
28. Michel Fabréguet, "Entwicklung und Veränderung der Funktion des Konzentrationslagers Mauthausen 1938–1945," in Herbert, Orth, and Dieckmann, *Die nationalsozialistischen Konzentrationslager*, vol. 1, 202.
29. In the periods between these dates, monthly mortality sank to levels between 1.9 and 3.5 percent. On the number of deaths in Mauthausen, see Fabréguet, "Mauthausen." In the second half of 1942, monthly mortality for the entire concentration camp system was 9.89 percent. See Zámečník, *Das war Dachau*, 239. For comprehensive figures on wartime mortality in the different camp complexes, see Buggeln, *Das System der KZ-Außenlager*, 68–75.
30. In German South-West Africa (insofar as we can draw conclusions from the fragmentary documentation), violence against prisoners seems to have been frequent. But this violence was usually due to disinterest in the prisoners' well-being and to military commanders' lax supervision of camp personnel, which allowed the latter to live out their fantasies of power. Such violence must be distinguished from the systematic terror of the Nazi concentration camps, which was codified in the camp rules (*Lagerordnung*) of Theodor Eicke. The difference is particularly apparent with respect to the Boer camps, as illustrated by the role of prisoner functionaries. In the Nazi camps, prisoner functionaries (or *Kapos*) were a part of the terror apparatus, and the Camp SS involved them directly in murder. Boers who accepted positions within the camps did not participate in the system in a comparable way. On prisoner functionaries' participation in terror, see Karin Orth, *Die Konzentrationslager-SS:*

*Sozialstrukturelle Analysen und biographische Studien* (Göttingen, 2000), 139–41. On Eicke's *Lagerordnung*, see Orth, *System*, 28–30.

31. On the number of deaths in the entire system, see Orth, *System*, 345–50. This figure does not include deaths in the Operation Reinhard camps.
32. Another common detail was that internees in both sets of camps had to wear around their necks metal tags that were stamped with their prisoner numbers. On the tags in South-West Africa, see Gordon McGregor, *Die Kriegsgefangenenmarken von Deutsch-Südwestafrika* (Windhoek, 2003). On the tags in the Nazi camps, see Orth, *System*, 54.
33. Jürgen Zimmerer's well-known essay collection on the relationship between colonialism and the Holocaust is titled *Von Windhuk nach Auschwitz?* On Auschwitz-Monowitz, see Piotr Setkiewicz, "Häftlingsarbeit im KZ Auschwitz III-Monowitz: Die Frage nach der Wirtschaftlichkeit der Arbeit," in Herbert, Orth, and Dieckmann, *Die nationalsozialistischen Konzentrationslager*, vol. 2, 584–605; and Jens-Christian Wagner, "Work and Extermination in the Concentration Camps," in Caplan and Wachsmann, *Concentration Camps in Nazi Germany*, 133–34.
34. Madley, "From Africa to Auschwitz," 450–53.
35. Christian Goeschel and Nikolaus Wachsmann, "Before Auschwitz: The Formation of the Nazi Concentration Camps, 1933–9," *Journal of Contemporary History* 45, no. 3 (2010): 527.
36. Andreas Eckl, "'Zu leben, nur um da zu sein, hat niemand ein Recht': Der Kolonialkrieg mit dem Volk der Herero 1904 im Spiegel kolonialpropagandistischer Literatur der NS-Zeit," in *Afrika—Kultur und Gewalt: Hintergründe und Aktualität des Kolonialkriegs in Deutsch-Südwestafrika: Seine Rezeption in Literatur, Wissenschaft und Populärkultur (1904–2004)*, ed. Christof Hamann (Iserlohn, 2005), 166–67.
37. Goeschel and Wachsmann, "Before Auschwitz," 527–28.
38. Spies, *Methods of Barbarism*, 327.
39. Moore, "'And What Concentration Camps Those Were!,'" 668–73.
40. The speech is reprinted in Max Domarus, ed., *Hitler: Speeches and Proclamations, 1932–1945: The Chronicle of a Dictatorship* (Wauconda, 1990), vol. 3, 1930.
41. Ibid. See also Moore, "'And What Concentration Camps Those Were!,'" 672.
42. Caplan, "Political Detention"; and Goeschel and Wachsmann, "Before Auschwitz." On protective custody, see also Klaus Drobisch and Günther Wieland, *System der Konzentrationslager: 1933–1939* (Berlin, 1993), 16–21.
43. Robert Gerwarth and Stephan Malinowski have rightly warned that interest in the continuities between colonialism and National Socialism ought not distract from the central importance of World War I for the events that followed. Robert Gerwarth and Stephan Malinowski, "Der Holocaust als 'kolonialer Genozid'? Europäische Kolonialgewalt und nationalsozialistischer Vernichtungskrieg," *Geschichte und Gesellschaft* 33, no. 3 (2007): 453–54.
44. Matthew Stibbe, "Ein globales Phänomen: Zivilinternierung im Ersten Weltkrieg in transnationaler und internationaler Dimension," in Jahr and Thiel, *Lager vor Auschwitz*, 158–76.
45. Caplan, "Political Detention," 27; and Drobisch and Wieland, *System der Konzentrationslager*, 18–19.
46. Wippermann, *Konzentrationslager*, 24–28; and Drobisch and Wieland, *System der Konzentrationslager*, 20.

# Final Observations
## "A Sad Fiasco"

From the perspective of camp internees, the concentration policies discussed in this study were certainly a "sad fiasco"—a devastating catastrophe that resulted in mass death.[1] More than two hundred thousand people lost their lives in the concentration camps and centers in Cuba, South Africa, the Philippines, and German South-West Africa. Some internees lost their entire family within a few weeks. Many were traumatized by the experiences of deportation, scarcity, disease, violence, and death.

For the colonizers, the concentration policies were likewise a sad fiasco—in the sense of "utter failure"[2]—as Lord Milner himself conceded in the letter that is quoted at the beginning of this book. The mass death of internees was not intentional in any of the case studies presented here. The colonial concentration sites were not designed to murder internees and were therefore not "extermination camps," as has sometimes been argued.

This brings us to one of the first questions that was posed in this study: Was the purpose of the colonial concentration camps to civilize, or to annihilate, internees? At first, the primary purpose of colonial concentration efforts was military—to end colonial war. The underlying calculus of concentration policy in Cuba, the Philippines, and South Africa was essentially the same; the goal was to separate civilians from guerrilla fighters, depriving the latter of their basis for resistance and compelling their surrender. The situation was somewhat different in

German South-West Africa, where combatants in the field were accompanied by their families, so that interning a settled civilian population was not possible. In this case, the camps were for men, women, and children who were captured or voluntarily surrendered. But here, too, the goal was to end the war, so internees could no longer participate in the fight against the colonial power.

In addition, the concentration centers served as sites of education and social engineering. The interned Boers were to become "modern" English subjects, and the Herero and Nama, wage earners who willingly served the German colonizers. The Americans sought to "civilize" concentrated Filipinos by introducing them to the "American way of life." Social engineering in the South African black camps involved the conservation of existing structures; the goal was that interned Africans would resume their work as farmhands for whites. Only Cuban concentration policy was apparently not accompanied by a program of education.

Alongside education and military control, procurement of labor was an important motive in South-West Africa and in the South African camps for blacks. While the German colony clearly supported compulsory labor, the system in the British colony was more subtle. Africans who were fit to work received no food rations, so those without means had little choice but to work for the military or in the camps' cultivation zones. Punishment for "rebellion" played a role, especially in the camps in South-West Africa, and the British camps also served as repatriation centers after the end of the South African War.

The multifunctionality of the camps and concentration zones underscores that colonial history—or "colonialism"—cannot be reduced to a single theme, such as "civilization" or "annihilation." The colonial project was a polyvalent phenomenon that can be explained only by the interplay of various motives. The concentration sites' intended functions reflect three of the colonizers' central concerns: first, the desire for complete control over the colonized population and effective state penetration of the colony, which usually existed only on paper; second, the education, or "civilization," of the colonized people, which (according to Sebastian Conrad) represents the "ideological core of the colonial project";[3] and third, a resolution to the "worker question," which Conrad considers "the most important objective of all colonial policy." The significance of the worker question had grown tremendously with the abolition of slavery, a cause that all colonial powers rallied behind in the late nineteenth century.[4] In fact, the unusually high degree of control that colonial authorities enjoyed in the camps created a unique opportunity for them to resolve the worker question and focus effectively on the "civilizing mission." The hope that concentration would further the main goals of the colonial project must have enhanced the appeal of camp policy, leading to the proliferation of concentration policies around 1900. The concentration efforts analyzed here did not seek the total physical annihilation of internees, but mass murder was nevertheless a part of colonial rule. Trotha's policy before the establishment of concentration camps is only one example.[5]

The concentration camps successfully fulfilled the functions of repatriation (in South Africa) and punishment (of the Herero and Nama in South-West Africa), but their other goals were mostly unmet. In South Africa, the internment of women and children initially had a negative military effect; the commandos became much more mobile and more effective once they were involuntarily "freed" from their family responsibilities. Over time, however, Kitchener's scorched earth policy prevailed, and the Boer guerrilla units were forced to surrender. The anglicization campaign in the camps did not achieve its desired effects. Before long, it was apparent that the Boers, not the British, would dominate the Union of South Africa that was founded in 1910. The memory of Boer suffering in the concentration camps became an effective political weapon for mobilizing Afrikaners, particularly after the 1930s.[6] In the long run, the concentration camps hindered exactly what they were supposed to have helped—binding South Africa to the British Empire.

The situation in Cuba can be described in a similar way. Weyler's concentration policy was effective in military terms, but the suffering of the *reconcentrados* was one of the reasons for the intervention of the United States. Here, too, concentration policy ultimately resulted in the opposite of what the colonial power had sought; Spain lost Cuba instead of keeping it.

In South-West Africa, concentration policy likewise failed in one important point. Mass death in the camps became a serious problem for the colonial economy, creating a shortage of labor in both the short- and long-term. Some building projects that were to have been completed with the help of interned workers had to be stopped or interrupted. And hundreds of workers had to be recruited from other countries at a high cost. For the military officer Ludwig von Estorff, this "foolish" policy even contributed to the eventual loss of the colony in World War I. In retrospect, he wrote:

> The Herero people were nearly obliterated by the war, the pursuit in the sandveld, and this last irrationality [the concentration camps, J. K.]. The people were proud, talented, and full of promise. Our duty was to educate them, not to annihilate. The latter [choice] was bad and foolish. Later on there were not enough workers in the land, and the penalty was losing the colony in the world war.[7]

Measured according to its own goals, concentration policy failed in Cuba, South Africa, and South-West Africa. Only in the Philippines does concentration appear not to have ended in catastrophe, although limited research in this field hardly supports a definitive conclusion.

Alongside the similarities in concentration policies, there were also numerous differences in how the camps functioned, how they were organized, and how they were experienced by internees. Were these differences due to specific national features or national traditions of colonization?

Isabel Hull suggests that national particularities can explain the "striking difference" between the camp systems in South Africa and South-West Africa;[8] she maintains that provisioning in the German camps was much worse, and that German political culture—in contrast to the British example—did not succeed in ending the mass death that military culture had caused.[9] In fact, there seems to have been a more fundamental reason for the different reactions to mortality in the camps, which becomes clearer if we broaden our view to include the concentration camps for Africans in South Africa—a perspective that Hull does not fully consider. Provisioning in the black camps was just as miserable as in the German-run camps, and the British colonial power was similarly reluctant to introduce reform. The political culture in Great Britain, as in Germany, was hardly interested in the suffering of Africans, and so the British, too, did not intervene. Emily Hobhouse mentioned the black camps in passing, but neither she nor the Fawcett Commission visited them.[10] The death of blacks played no role in the intensive discussion about the miserable conditions in the South African concentration camps that gripped the United Kingdom in mid-1901. Within this context, Elizabeth Neethling's reflections following her experiences in a burgher camp are particularly insightful: "And if we Boers, of European heritage, able to speak and write for ourselves, have been treated this barbarically by a civilized power, what would be the lot of a savage people who is oppressed by a European state? Surely no one would be willing to lift a finger for them!"[11] Neethling's prognosis was correct, as demonstrated by the experience of the Herero and Nama in German South-West Africa (among others). But even as her fellow Boers were suffering in the camps, she did not seem to realize that "a savage people" was already experiencing a similar fate, and that no one had expressed concern.

National tradition may explain a further difference in the two colonial powers' treatment of African internees. The German colony's compulsory labor regime appears to be rooted in the authoritarian traditions of Imperial Germany, while the South African black camps' system of wage labor—although not entirely free of coercion—seems to reflect a more liberal British approach. This interpretation is complicated, however, by a lesser-known example of internment policy in South Africa. During the South African War, the port of Durban hosted a kind of camp for Africans who were suspected of supporting Boer commandos. These suspects were forced to perform heavy labor,[12] and they were viewed as enemies, not neutrals, unlike other black internees. The combination of "enemy" and "black"—which defined the experience of South-West African camp internees—evidently legitimated compulsory labor in the British context, too. Thus, the different forms of exploiting labor in South Africa and South-West Africa were not necessarily a product of liberal or authoritarian tradition but may simply have reflected that the interned Herero and Nama were not being treated merely as "natives," but also as enemies.

Other differences between the camps in the individual colonies can be explained by specific local conditions. Internment in South-West Africa did not involve separating civilians and guerrilla fighters, but not because of a special German approach to waging colonial war. Rather, the style of internment had much more to do with the strategies and ways of life of the Herero and the Nama. Likewise, the fact that the Germans and British concentrated prisoners in special camps, while the Spanish and Americans used existing localities, does not appear to be an expression of distinctive styles of colonization.

The one important exception in this respect is the US colonizers' handling of colonized Filipinos, who were to be "Americanized" and "lifted up" to Western living standards. Similar initiatives existed in South Africa—but only for white Boers. The "natives" were excluded from all assimilation efforts. Indeed, the US colonizers seemed to take the "civilizing mission" more seriously than their European contemporaries. At least in this point, we can speak of an exceptional style of American colonialism, as scholars and other observers have often postulated.[13]

Overall, analysis of the different concentration policies suggests more similarities than differences between the colonial powers. The comparison of colonial concentration policies and centers around 1900 confirms the thesis that colonialism in the decades around the turn of the century was, in many respects, a shared Western project.[14]

Closely related to the question of similarities and differences is the question of transimperial or transcolonial exchange, and the transnational history of the camps. Although knowledge about the concentration practices of other colonial powers was widespread in an increasingly globalized world, the concentration camps in South Africa and South-West Africa cannot be understood solely as an adaptation of foreign practice. Particularly in the German case, there was surely a transfer of knowledge from neighboring South Africa, but the imported concept of the concentration camp underwent enormous transformation in response to local circumstances and demands. For the British camps, transcolonial exchange within the Empire—with India, but also between South Africa's individual colonies—seems to have been more important than transimperial exchange, particularly with respect to administrative issues.

Similarities in concentration policies were not always the result of knowledge transfer, but frequently arose from a shared "colonial culture," a common repository of colonial knowledge. A shared conviction that interned "natives" ought to be "educated to work," combined with drastic labor shortages in both South Africa and South-West Africa, seems to have led to the exploitation of African internees' labor. The same was true for many of the sanitary and medical rules that existed in the South African camps, as well as in the Indian plague camps and famine camps.

The colonial concentration camps investigated here should not be described solely as flashpoints of transnational history. When the idea of the "concentration camp" was imported to a new situation, it adapted to the given structural conditions of colonial warfare. The idea of the camp was mixed with local traditions and was shaped by colonial and other cultures (medical, military, etc.). Older historiographical approaches have explained concentration policies in Cuba, the Philippines, South Africa, and South-West Africa solely in terms of colonial powers "copying" one another, or through the structural similarities of colonial wars. However, such approaches are too simple and cannot sufficiently explain all of the differences and similarities between individual cases. The transnational perspective is important but should not obscure the significance of local and national factors.

While Wilhelmine Germany did in fact orient its South-West African concentration camps toward other colonial models, the supposed colonial origins of the National Socialist concentration camp system are less plausible. Scholarly comparisons between the camps in South-West Africa and National Socialist Germany misconstrue not only the character of the colonial camps, but also the rapidly changing character of the Nazi camp system. With respect to how the camps looked and functioned, differences between the two systems clearly prevail—despite a few significant similarities, such as renting out prisoners as forced laborers. The camps in South-West Africa were not, as Benjamin Madley asserts, "more akin to Nazi death camps than to Spanish and British concentration camps."[15] Precisely the opposite was true.

Above all, there is no empirical evidence that the relevant National Socialist actors took inspiration from the colonial example. Hitler's few documented references about the South African Boer camps were pure propaganda, and German South-West Africa played no role in Nazi discourse. Advocates of the continuity thesis should not rely on the standard argument—here, in the words of Jeremy Sarkin—that "it is indisputable that many of the practices of the Nazi era, such as concentration camps and experimentations, originated in the colonies."[16] This was simply not the case. Terminology alone suggests that the National Socialist concentration camps had colonial origins.

A different diachronic comparative perspective is empirically much more interesting and should be studied more closely in the future: colonial concentration policies in the interwar era and the era of decolonization. Of particular interest are the concentration camps that were introduced by the Italian colonial power in Libyan Cyrenaica in the 1930s, the "new villages" built by the British military during the Emergencies in Malaya and Kenya, the *camps de regroupement* and *nouveaux villages* of the Algerian War, and finally, the "strategic hamlets" of the Vietnam War. All of these cases, like the concentration efforts around the turn of the century, primarily involved the effective separation of guerrilla units and a supportive civilian population. At the same time, the colonial powers in these decolonization conflicts used their leverage over resettled populations to "educate" or "modernize" colonized peoples who were perceived as backward. Thus, the colonial powers continued to develop a functional thread that had already existed in the early colonial concentration camps and centers. Living conditions in the "new villages" were often miserable, and the mortality was alarming.[17] Future scholars will have to evaluate whether these concentration efforts also ended in a "sad fiasco."

## Notes

1. "Fiasco," in *The New Oxford Thesaurus of English*, ed. Patrick Hanks (Oxford, 2000), 279; and "Fiasko," in *Wörterbuch der Synonyme und Antonyme*, ed. Erich and Hildegard Bulitta (Frankfurt, 1990), 279.
2. "Fiasko," in *Duden: Fremdwörterbuch*, vol. 5 (Mannheim, 2001).
3. Conrad, *Deutsche Kolonialgeschichte*, 70. On the effective control of the colonized population and domination of the colonial territory, see ibid., 43–47. On the centrality of "civilization," see Osterhammel, "'The Great Work of Uplifting Mankind.'"
4. Conrad, *Deutsche Kolonialgeschichte*, 57, and "'Eingeborenenpolitik,'" 109–11. See also Eckert, "Der langsame Tod der Sklaverei."
5. See, for example, Alison Palmer, *Colonial Genocide* (Adelaide, 2000); and Jonas Kreienbaum, "Koloniale Gewaltexzesse – Kolonialkriege um 1900," in *Koloniale Politik und Praktiken Deutschlands und Frankreichs 1880–1962*, ed. Alain Chatriot and Dieter Gosewinkel (Stuttgart, 2010), 155–72.

6. Nasson, *The War for South Africa*, 284–303; and Grundlingh, "Afrikaner Consciousness."
7. Estorff, *Wanderungen und Kämpfe*, 134.
8. Hull, *Absolute Destruction*, 153. In Chapter 1, I show that German political culture did, in fact, succeed in enabling the repeal of Trotha's extermination order. The concentration camps were a direct result of this intervention.
9. Ibid., 149–57 and 182–93.
10. Elizabeth van Heyningen has recently noted that at least one member of the Ladies Commission, Jane Waterston—if not the group itself—visited the black camps when she could. Heyningen, *The Concentration Camps*, 193.
11. Neethling, *Fünfzehn Monate*, 81–82.
12. Johan M. Wassermann, "'The Suspects Are Not to Be Treated as Prisoners or Convicts'—A Labour Camp for Africans Associated with the Boer Commandoes During the Anglo-Boer War," *Journal for Contemporary History* 36, no. 2 (2011): 25–47.
13. See, for example, Julian Go, *Patterns of Empire: The British and American Empires, 1688 to the Present* (New York, 2011), 14–19; and May, *Social Engineering*, 179.
14. Lindner, *Koloniale Begegnungen*, 8; Conrad, *Deutsche Kolonialgeschichte*, 16; and Steinmetz, *The Devil's Handwriting*, 19 and 69–70. On colonial powers' shared traditions of violence, see Gerwarth and Malinowski, "Der Holocaust als 'kolonialer Genozid'?"
15. Madley, "From Africa to Auschwitz," 447.
16. Jeremy Sarkin, *Germany's Genocide of the Herero: Kaiser Wilhelm II, His General, His Settlers, His Soldiers* (Cape Town, 2011), 26–27.
17. On Libya, see Aram Mattioli, "Die vergessenen Kolonialverbrechen des faschistischen Italien in Libyen 1923–1933," in *Völkermord und Kriegsverbrechen in der ersten Hälfte des 20. Jahrhunderts*, ed. Irmtrud Wojak and Susanne Meinl (Frankfurt, 2004), 203–27. On concentration attempts during the wars of decolonization, see Beckett, *Modern Insurgencies*, 86–216; Fabian Klose, *Menschenrechte im Schatten kolonialer Gewalt: Die Dekolonisierungskriege in Kenia und Algerien 1945–1962* (Munich, 2009), 190–214; Moritz Feichtinger, "'Détruire et construire'—Die französische Umsiedlungspolitik in Algerien 1954–1962 zwischen Repression und Reform," in Chatriot and Gosewinkel, *Koloniale Politik und Praktiken*, 173–94, and "Villagization—A People's History of Strategic Resettlement and Violent Transformation, Kenya & Algeria, 1952–1962," (PhD diss., University of Bern, 2017); and Dierk Walter, "Kolonialkrieg, Globalstrategie und Kalter Krieg: Die Emergencies in Malaya und Kenia 1948–1960," in *Heiße Kriege im Kalten Krieg*, ed. Bernd Greiner et al. (Hamburg, 2006), 109–40.

# Bibliography

## Abbreviations

| | |
|---|---|
| AACRLS | Archives on Anti-Colonial Resistance and Liberation Struggle in Namibia |
| AVEM | Archiv der Vereinten Evangelischen Mission (Archive of the United Evangelical Mission) |
| BAL | Bundesarchiv Berlin-Lichterfelde (Federal Archive Berlin-Lichterfelde) |
| BAK | Bundesarchiv Koblenz (Federal Archive Koblenz) |
| BA-MA | Bundesarchiv-Militärarchiv (Federal Military Archive) |
| BAU | Bauverwaltung (Building Administration) |
| BLO | Bodleian Library Oxford |
| BLU | Bezirksamt Lüderitzbucht (District Office Lüderitzbucht) |
| BRMG | *Berichte der Rheinischen Missions-Gesellschaft* |
| BSW | Bezirksamt Swakopmund (District Office Swakopmund) |
| BWI | Bezirksamt Windhuk (District Office Windhuk) |
| C-in-C | Commander-in-Chief |
| CO | Colonial Office |
| CRLB | Cadbury Research Library Birmingham |
| CSO | Secretary to the Orange River Colony Administration |
| DOK | Distriktsamt Okahandja (Division Office Okahandja) |
| GSWA | German South-West Africa |
| ELCRN | Archives of the Evangelical Lutheran Church in the Republic of Namibia |
| FAB | Free State Archives Bloemfontein |
| GOV | Private Secretary of the Governor of the Transvaal |
| HBS | Hafenbauamt Swakopmund (Port Construction Office Swakopmund) |
| JC | Joseph Chamberlain Papers |
| MGB | Military Governor, Bloemfontein |
| MGP | Military Governor, Pretoria |
| MP | Milner Papers |
| MSg. 2 | Militärgeschichtliche Sammlung (Military History Collection) |
| N | Nachlass (Papers) |
| NAL | National Archives London |

NAN        National Archives of Namibia
NAP        National Archives Pretoria
ORC        Orange River Colony
PA AA      Politisches Archiv des Auswärtigen Amtes (Political Archive of the Foreign Office)
PMO        Provost Marshal's Office, Army Headquarters, South Africa
PRO        Public Records Office
RM         Reichs-Marine-Amt (Imperial Naval Office)
RMG        Rheinische Missionsgesellschaft (Rhenish Missionary Society)
SNA        Secretary for Native Affairs
SRC        Superintendent of the Department of Refugees, Orange River Colony
TKP        Transvaal Administrative Reports
WO         War Office
WVHA       Wirtschaftsverwaltungshauptamt (Business and Administration Main Office)
ZBU        Zentralbureau des Gouvernements (Central Office of the Colonial Government)

## Archival Sources

### AVEM – Archiv der Vereinten Evangelischen Mission
RMG – Rheinische Missionsgesellschaft
- 1.606 Philipp Diehl
  - Vol. 3, 1900–1918 (c)
- 1.609 Wilhelm Eich
  - Vol. 4, 1905 (d)
  - Vol. 5, 1906 (e)
- 1.613 Peter Friedrich Bernsmann
  - Vol. 4, 1900–1920 (d)
- 1.615 Eduard Dannert
  - Vol. 3, 1900–1915, 1927 (c)
- 1.636 Johannes Olpp jun.
  - Vol. 2, 1900–1910 (b)
- 1.644 August Kuhlmann
  - Vol. 1, 1892–1907 (a)
- 1.650 Hermann Nyhof
  - Vol. 1, 1893, 1900–1915 (a)
- 1.656 Karl Emil Laaf
  - Vol. 1, 1894–1909 (a)
- 1.660 Heinrich Vedder
  - Vol. 1, 1894–1906 (a)
- 1.664 Wilhelm Emil Jakob Diehl
- 2.505 Karibib
  - Vol. 1, 1902–1945 (a)
- 2.509 Lüderitzbucht
  - Vol. 1, 1904–1945 (a)
- 2.510 Okahandja
  - Vol. 1, 1899–1936 (a)
- 2.514 Omaruru (mit Kalkfeld und Omatjette)
  - Vol. 1, 1899–1913 (a)
- 2.528 Swakopmund (mit Walfischbay)
  - Vol. 1, 1905–1939 (a)

2.533   Windhoek (mit Klein-Windhoek)
        Vol. 1 1900–1913 (a)
2.697   Afrikareisen von Inspektor J. Spiecker (1902–03 and 1905–06)
        Vol. 6, 1906–07 (f)

**BAK – Bundesarchiv Koblenz**
N – Nachlässe
   1030   Nachlass Viktor Franke (1866–1936)
          Vol. 6a, Tagebuch, 1906
   1037   Nachlass Oskar Hintrager
   1145   Nachlass Paul Leutwein (1882–1946)
          Vol. 4, Manuskript: "Im Banne Afrikas. Romantisches Geschichtsbild des alten Wild-Südwestafrikas"
   1408   Nachlass Paul Rohrbach (1869–1956)
          Bd. 68, Briefe an die Frau aus Südwestafrika, Mai bis Dez. 1905
   1669   Nachlass Friedrich von Lindequist (1895–1903)
          Manuskript: "Generalkonsul des Deutschen Reiches für Britisch-Südafrika in Kapstadt"

**BAL – Bundesarchiv Berlin-Lichterfelde**
R 1001 – Reichskolonialamt
   2089   Differenzen zwischen Generalleutnant Lothar v. Trotha und Gouverneur Theodor Gotthilf Leutwein über das Verhältnis von militärischen und politischen Maßnahmen zur Beendigung des Krieges
   2090   Deportation der Kriegsgefangenen aus Südwestafrika in andere Kolonien
   2117–2119 Aufstand der Hereros 1904–1909
   2136–2140 Aufstand im Namaland (Namaqualand) und seine Bekämpfung, 1905–1909
R 151 F – Kaiserliches Gouvernement in Deutsch-Südwestafrika, 1884–1915
   Feldzüge-Expedit. Niederwerfung v. Aufständen
   D.IV.L.2 Vol. 5 (Film 82097)
   D.IV.L.3 Vol. 1 (Film 82097)
   D.IV.L.3 Vol. 2 (Film 82098)
   D.IV.L.3 Vol. 3 (Film 82098)
   D.IV.L.3 Vol. 4 (Film 82098)
   D.IV.L.3 Vol. 5 (Film 82099)
   D.IV.M.3 Vol. 1 (Film 82105)

**BA-MA – Bundesarchiv-Militärarchiv**
RM – Reichs-Marine-Amt
   3     Nachrichtenbüro, Allgemeines Marinedepartement
         4287–4292 Expeditionskorps nach Südwestafrika. 6 vols. (1905–1907)
   5     Admiralstab der Marine
         6055 Aufstand in Deutsch-Südwestafrika, (1904) Okt. 1905–März 1906
   121   Landstreitkräfte der Kaiserlichen Marine
   435   Kriegstagebuch: 3. Kompanie, Marine-Inf.-Bataillon, vol. 2, 23. Nov. 1904–5. März 1905
N – Nachlässe
   559   Nachlass Berthold von Deimling
         "Von der alten in die neue Welt," Lebenserinnerungen des Generals der Infanterie Berthold von Deimling, vol. 3
MSg. 2 – Militärgeschichtliche Sammlung
   2576  Nachlass Sanitätsoffizier Julius Ohlemann

**BLO – Bodleian Library Oxford**
MP – Milner Papers
D.1.2 Private correspondence of Lord Milner with Joseph Chamberlain 1900–1903, and Alfred Lyttleton 1904
    171   1901–1904
D.1.3 Correspondence with Governors
    173   Correspondence with the Governor of the Orange River Colony, Major General Pretyman, and other officials, 1900–1904
D.2.1 General Correspondence, with some related papers, 1897–1925
    185   1901

**CRLB – Cadbury Research Library Birmingham**
JC – Joseph Chamberlain Papers
11    General correspondence, A–Z: 1900–1902
13    South Africa: 1900–1902
14    Colonial affairs (other than South Africa): 1900–1902

**ELCRN – Archives of the Evangelical Lutheran Church in the Republic of Namibia**
I. Konferenzprotokolle und Beilagen
  1.3    Hererokonferenzen, 1873–1905
  1.22   Konferenz Protokoll, 1906–07
  1.23   Konferenzprotokoll Omaruru und Beilagen, 1907
  1.40   Beilage zum Konferenzprotokoll 1901, 1902, 1903, 1905. Folio 5. Verschiedene Berichte 1904–1905

II. Innere Verwaltung
  1.7b   Briefe A–Z, 1906
  1.9    Briefe, 1907, E.–M.
  5.2    Schreiben von Inspektor Haussleiter, Sekretär Th. Olpp, Inspektor Spiecker, 1904–1907
  5.14   Deputation. Verschiedenes, 1904–1907
  11.11  Behörden Diverse, 1905–1926

V. Chroniken
  2      Ortschronik Karibib
  16     Chronik Lüderitzbucht
  23.1   Ortschronik Omaruru
  31     Ortschronik Swakopmund
  37     Chronik Windhuk: Herero/Ovambo 1904–1949

VII. Einzelne Stationen
  11. Windhuk
    3    Korrespondenz Etappe: Kommando, Kommandantur, Militärbeamte, 1905–1910
  12. Karibib
    3    Extract from the Autobiography of Missionary Elger. Karibib 1902–1914
    4    Copierbuch, 1905–1907
  31. Swakopmund
    1    Letters to Heinrich Vedder by Eich, Olpp, Spiecker, Warneck, 1904–1909
    5    Quartals- und Jahresberichte. Conferenz-Berichte. Jahresabrechnungen, 1906–1930

XI. 3.14 Tagesbriefe in Herero

## FAB – Free State Archives Bloemfontein
CSO – Secretary to the Orange River Colony Administration
    Box 4, 12, 25–27, 29, 44, 46, 48, 52, 54, 55, 57, 149
MGB – Military Governor, Bloemfontein
    Box 2, 3, 4, 7
SRC – Superintendent of the Department of Refugees, Orange River Colony
| | |
|---|---|
| 1–8 | Correspondence Files General, Feb.–June 1901 |
| 15 | Correspondence Files General, Oct. 1901 |
| 17 | Correspondence Files General, Nov.–Dec. 1901 |
| 19 | Correspondence Files General, Jan. 1902 |
| 21f. | Correspondence Files General, Feb.–Apr. 1902 |
| 24 | Correspondence Files General, May–June 1902 |
| 30 | Correspondence Files General, Sept.–Nov. 1902 |
| 70–73 | Camp Register Bloemfontein |
| 132 | Statistics. Refugee Camps, June 1901–Jan. 1902 |

## NAL – National Archives London
CO – Colonial Office
    CO 179 Natal
| | |
|---|---|
| 220 | Vol. IV. Despatches, Oct.–Dec. 1901 |
| 222 | Vol. I. Despatches, Jan.–Apr. 1902 |
| 223 | Vol. II. Despatches, 1. May–15. Aug. 1902 |

    CO 224 Orange River Colony
| | |
|---|---|
| 3 | Vol. I. Despatches, Jan.–July 1901 |
| 4 | Vol. II. Despatches, Aug.–Oct. 1901 |
| 5 | Vol. III. Despatches, Nov. & Dec. 1901/Public Offices |
| 6 | Vol. IV. Miscel. Offices & Individuals, 1901 |
| 7 | Bd. I. Despatches, Jan.–July 1902 |
| 8 | Vol. II. Despatches, Aug.–Dec. 1902 |
| 11 | Vol. I. Governor, Jan.–Apr. 1903 |

    CO 291 Transvaal
| | |
|---|---|
| 27 | Vol. I. Despatches, Jan.–Apr. 1901 |
| 29 | Vol. III. Despatches, 1. Sept.–15 Nov. 1901 |
| 39 | Vol. III. Despatches, 1 May–8 July 1902 |
| 40 | Vol. IV. Despatches, 9 July–3 Aug. 1902 |

    CO 417 South Africa
| | |
|---|---|
| 323 | Vol. V. Miscellaneous. Despatches, 8 Feb.–26 Mar. 1901 |
| 325 | Vol. VII. Miscellaneous. Despatches, June–Aug. 1901 |
| 327 | Vol. IX. Miscellaneous. Despatches, 23 Nov.–31 Dec. 1901 |
| 334 | Vol. XVI. War Office, 2 July–19 Oct. 1901 |
| 335 | Vol. XVI. War Office, 28 Oct.–30 Dec. 1901 |
| 348 | Vol. VI. Miscellaneous. Despatches, January 1902 |
| 349 | Vol. VII. Miscellaneous. Despatches, 1 Feb.–7 Mar. 1902 |
| 350 | Vol. VIII. Miscellaneous. Despatches, 8 Mar.–18 Apr. 1902 |

PRO – Public Records Office
| | |
|---|---|
| 30/57 | Papers of General Lord Kitchener |
| 22 | Correspondence Kitchener-Brodrick |

WO – War Office
| | |
|---|---|
| 32 | Registered Files (General Series) |

8008 Report on Refugee Camps in the Transvaal
8009 Lord Kitchener. General Report on working of Refugee Camps in the Transvaal
8010 Burgher Refugee Camps ORColony & Natal
8061 Concentration Camps Committee. General Report
8063 The Concentration Camps in S. Africa
8064 Refugee Camps

**NAN – National Archives of Namibia**
AACRLS – Archives on Anti-Colonial Resistance and Liberation Struggle in Namibia
    70    Nachlass Kurt von Frankenberg und Proschlitz, 1904–1907

BAU – Bauverwaltung
    74    H 13 Kriegsgefangene, 1905–1908

BLU – Bezirksamt Lüderitzbucht
    32    E.6.i Vol. 1 Bahnbau Lüderitzbucht–Kubub, 1905–1909
    98    S. 14.D Statistik und Jahresbericht. Zählung der eingeborenen Bevölkerung
    101    S. 14.M Eingeborenenverhältnisse Vierteljahresberichte. Vol. 1, 1907–1912
    165    O.6 Lazarettaufnahme und Sterbefälle von Farbigen, 1906–1907
    166    O.7 Krankheiten und Sterbefälle von Farbigen, 1907–1910
    200    V.2.B Vol. 1 Rundverfügungen. Verordnungen, 1901–1907
    220    SPS Strafprozess-Sachen

BSW – Bezirksamt Swakopmund
    39    XI. Gesundheitswesen Vol. 1, 1904–1909
    48    XVII.d Kriegsgefangene
    119    UA.21/1 Jahresbericht, 1906

BWI – Bezirksamt Windhuk
    134    G.7.r Vol. 1 Gesundheitswesen. Regierungskrankenhaus für Eingeborene, 1900–1912
    403    E.V.2 spec. Vol. 2, Kriege mit Eingeborenen. Hereroaufstand, 1904–1907
    406    E.V.8 spec. Vol. 1 Kriegsgefangene, 1905–1906
            E.V.8 spec. Vol. 2 Kriegsgefangene. Anträge auf Überweisung, 1905–1906
            E.V.8 spec. Vol. 3 Kriegsgefangene, 1906
            E.V.8 Kriegsgefangene Eingeborene, Generalia, 1905–1909
    407    E.V.8 spec. Vol. 4 Kriegsgefangene, 1906
            E.V.8 spec. Vol. 6 Kriegsgefangene, 1906–1907

DOK – Distriktsamt Okahandja
    27    E.2.E Vol. 1 Eingeborene Arbeiter. Anträge auf Zuweisung, 1906–1914
    117    S. 14.Q Bd. 1 Statistik und Jahresberichte. Jahresberichte, 1901–1913

HBS – Hafenbauamt Swakopmund
    4/1 Haifischinsel. Arbeiter auf der Haifischinsel, 1906–1907

Private Accessions
    A 109    Nachlass Stuhlmann

ZBU – Zentralbureau des Gouvernements
    833    H.I.I.5 Bd. 2 Jahresmedizinalberichte 1907/1910, 1908–1910
    839    H.II.C.7 Bekämpfung von Skorbut, Beriberi, Pellagra pp. Generalia, 1902–1912
    2292    L.V.1.E Lüderitzbucht – Eisenbahnbau. Arbeiterbeschaffung, 1906–1908
    2338    L.VI.1.E Otavibahn. Bahnbau (Arbeiterbeschaffung), 1906–1909
    2369    VIII.G Geheimakten der Witboi-Hottentotten, 1905–1908

**NAP – National Archives Pretoria**
PMO – Provost Marshal's Office, Army Headquarters, South Africa
    70      Information Files, 1900–1902
MGP – Military Governor, Pretoria
    73      Incoming Correspondence, Feb.–March 1901
    101    Incoming Correspondence, June–July 1901
    109    Incoming Correspondence, July–Sept. 1901
    133    Incoming Correspondence, 1901
    144    Incoming Correspondence, 1901–02
    146    Incoming Correspondence, 1902
    207    Incoming Correspondence, Confidential, Jan.–March 1901
    258    Chief of Staff Circular Memoranda, Confidential, Nos. 1–60: Jan. 1900–Jan. 1902; No. 1–Jan. 1902
GOV – Private Secretary of the Governor of the Transvaal
    259–262 P.S. Correspondence Files 20, vols. 11–14, 1901
    270    P.S. Correspondence Files 20, vol. 22, 1902
    276    P.S. Correspondence Files 20, vol. 28, 1902–03
SNA – Secretary for Native Affairs
    Vols. 15, 20, 21, 28, 30, 31, 44, 45, 59, 98
TKP – Transvaal Administrative Reports
    135    Transvaal Administration Reports for 1902. Part I. Administration, Pretoria 1903
A 2030 – Jan Ploeger Papers
    29      Konsentrasiekampe, 1899–1900

**PA AA – Politisches Archiv des Auswärtigen Amtes**
AI Afrika
    R 14757–14760 Den Krieg Englands gegen Transvaal und den Oranjefreistaat, 23.8.1901 bis 7.2.1902, Bd. 41–44.
Kapstadt
    34      Politische Angelegenheiten B1, März 1901 bis Juli 1901.
    54      Bi. Liebesgaben für die Konzentrationslager, 1899–1904.

# Published Sources
## Newspapers and Journals

*Atlanta Constitution*, 1901
*Berichte der Rheinischen Missions-Gesellschaft* (BRMG), 1902 and 1906
*Berliner Lokalanzeiger*, 1904
*Berliner Tageblatt*, 1908
*Boston Daily Globe*, 1902
*Daily News*, 1898 and 1901
*Manchester Guardian*, 1898
*Manchester Times*, 1898
*Militär-Wochenblatt*, 1902 and 1904
*Neue Preußische Zeitung*, 1901
*Northern Echo*, 1900
*Pall Mall Gazette*, 1900
*The Times*, 1896, 1900–01

## Primary Sources

Amery, Leo, ed. *The Times History of the War in South Africa 1899–1902*. Vol. 6. London: Low, Marston, 1909.
Auer, G. *In Südwestafrika gegen die Hereros: Nach den Kriegstagebüchern des Obermatrosen G. Auer*. Berlin: Ernst Hofmann, 1911.
Bayer, Maximilian. *Mit dem Hauptquartier in Südwestafrika*. Leipzig: Spamer, 1909.
Beak, George Bailey. *The Aftermath of War: An Account of the Repatriation of Boers and Natives in the Orange River Colony 1902–1904*. London: Edward Arnold, 1906.
Bofinger, Hugo. "Einige Mitteilungen über Skorbut." *Deutsche Militärärztliche Zeitschrift* 39, no. 15 (1910): 569–82.
Brandt, Johanna. *The War Diary of Johanna Brandt*. Pretoria: Protea, 2007.
Bülow, Bernhard Wilhelm von. *Denkwürdigkeiten*. Vol. 2: Von der Marokkokrise bis zum Abschied. Berlin: Ullstein, 1930.
Callwell, Charles E. *Small Wars: Their Principles and Practice*. London: Harrison and Sons, 1906.
Cd. 819. *Reports, &c., on the Working of the Refugee Camps in the Transvaal, Orange River Colony, Cape Colony, and Natal*. London: HMSO, 1901.
Cd. 853. *Further Papers Relating to the Working of the Refugee Camps in the Transvaal, Orange River Colony, Cape Colony, and Natal*. London: HMSO, 1901.
Cd. 893. *Report on the Concentration Camps in South Africa by the Committee of Ladies Appointed by the Secretary of State for War*. London: HMSO, 1902.
Cd. 902. *Further Papers Relating to the Working of the Refugee Camps in South Africa*. London: HMSO, 1902.
Deimling, Berthold von. *Südwestafrika: Land und Leute—unsere Kämpfe—Wert der Kolonie: Vortrag, gehalten in einer Anzahl deutscher Städte*. Berlin: R. Eisenschmidt, 1906.
*Die Concentrationslager im Transvaal und Orange River Colonie*. London: Siegle, 1902.
Domarus, Max, ed. *Hitler: Speeches and Proclamations, 1932–1945*. Vol. 3. Wauconda, IL: Bolchazy-Carducci, 1990.
Doyle, Arthur Conan. *The War in South Africa: Its Causes and Conduct*. London: Smith, Elder & Co., 1902.
———. *The War in South Africa: Its Causes and Conduct*. Leipzig: Tauchnitz, 1902.
Erichsen, Casper W., ed. *"What the Elders Used to Say": Namibian Perspectives on the Last Decade of German Colonial Rule*. Windhoek: Namibian Institute for Democracy, 2008.
Estorff, Ludwig von. *Wanderungen und Kämpfe in Südwestafrika, Ostafrika und Südafrika 1894–1910*. Wiesbaden: Kutscher, 1968.
Großer Generalstab. *Die Kämpfe der deutschen Truppen in Südwestafrika*. Vol. 1: Der Feldzug gegen die Hereros. Berlin: Mittler, 1906.
———. *Die Kämpfe der deutschen Truppen in Südwestafrika*. Vol. 2: Der Hottentottenkrieg. Berlin: Mittler, 1907.
Haccius, Georg. *Aus der Drangsalszeit des südafrikanischen Lüneburg*. Kleine Hermannsburger Missionsschriften 41. Hermannsburg, [1904?].
———. *Die Hermannsburger Mission in Südafrika in und nach dem Burenkriege*. Kleine Hermannsburger Missionsschriften 36. Hermannsburg, [1904?].
———. *Lichtbilder aus dunkler Kriegszeit in Transvaal*. Kleine Hermannsburger Missionsschriften 35. Hermannsburg, [1904?].
Hartmann, Georg. *Deutsch-Südwestafrika im Zusammenhang mit Südafrika*. Berlin: Süsserott, 1899.
Heywood, Annemarie, Brigitte Lau, and Raimund Ohly, eds. *Warriors, Leaders, Sages, and Outcasts in the Namibian Past: Narratives Collected from Herero Sources for the Michael Scott Oral Records Project (MSORP) 1985–6*. Windhoek: MSORP, 1992.

Hintrager, Oskar. *Steijn, de Wet und die Oranje-Freistaater: Tagebuchblätter aus dem südafrikanischen Kriege.* Tübingen: Laupp, 1902.
Hobhouse, Emily. *The Brunt of the War and Where It Fell.* London: Methuen, 1902.
———. *Report of a Visit to the Camps of Women and Children in the Cape and Orange River Colonies.* London: Friars Printing Association, 1901.
———. *War without Glamour: or, Women's War Experiences Written by Themselves 1899–1902.* Hill Cliffe: Portrayer Publishers, 2007. First published in 1927.
———. *Die Zustände in den südafrikanischen Konzentrationslagern: Bericht von Miss E. Hobhouse.* Berlin: Deutscher Burenhilfsbund, 1902.
Kommando der Schutztruppen im Reichs-Kolonialamt. *Sanitäts-Bericht über die Kaiserliche Schutztruppe für Südwestafrika während des Herero- und Hottentottenaufstandes für die Zeit vom 1. Januar 1904 bis 31. März 1907.* Vol. 1: Administrativer Teil. Berlin: Mittler, 1909.
———. *Sanitäts-Bericht über die Kaiserliche Schutztruppe für Südwestafrika während des Herero- und Hottentottenaufstandes für die Zeit vom 1. Januar 1904 bis 31. März 1907.* Vol. 2: Statistischer Teil. Berlin: Mittler, 1920.
"Konzentrationslager." In *Meyers Lexikon.* Vol. 6: Hornberg–Korrektiv. Leipzig: Bibliographisches Institut, 1927.
Kukuri, Andreas. *Herero-Texte.* Berlin: Reimer, 1983.
Leutwein, Paul. *Afrikanerschicksal: Gouverneur Leutwein und seine Zeit.* Stuttgart: Union, 1929.
Leutwein, Theodor. *Elf Jahre Gouverneur in Deutsch-Südwestafrika.* Windhoek: Namibia Wissenschaftliche Gesellschaft, 1997. First published in 1906.
Lückhoff, August Daniel. *Woman's Endurance.* Cape Town: S.A. News, 1904.
Neethling, Elizabeth. *Fünfzehn Monate in den Konzentrationslagern. Erinnerungen einer Burenfrau aus ihrer Gefangenschaft.* Bern: Berner Tagblatt, 1903.
———. *Should We Forget?* Cape Town: HAUM, 1902.
Phillips, Lisle March. *A Tiger on Horseback: The Experiences of a Trooper & Officer of Rimington's Guides—the Tigers—During the Anglo-Boer War 1899–1902.* London: Leonaur, 2006. First published as *With Rimington* in 1902.
Rheinische Missionsgesellschaft. *Sechsundsiebzigster Jahresbericht der Rheinischen-Missionsgesellschaft vom Jahre 1905.* Barmen: Westdeutsche Druckerei, 1906.
Rohrbach, Paul. *Aus Südwest-Afrikas schweren Tagen: Blätter von Arbeit und Abschied.* Berlin: Weicher, 1909.
Schwabe, Kurd. *Krieg in Deutsch-Südwestafrika 1904–1906.* Berlin: Weller, 1907.
Silvester, Jeremy, and Jan-Bart Gewald, eds. *Words Cannot be Found: German Colonial Rule in Namibia: An Annotated Reprint of the 1918 Blue Book.* Leiden: Brill, 2003.
*Stenographische Berichte über die Verhandlungen des Reichstags.* Berlin: 1903–1906. Retrieved 17 July 2018 from http://reichstagsprotokolle.de.
Thomson, Samuel John. *The Transvaal Burgher Camps.* Allahabad: Pioneer Press, 1904.
Union of South Africa. *Report on the Natives of South-West Africa and Their Treatment by Germany.* London: HMSO, 1918.
United Nations. "Convention on the Prevention and Punishment of the Crime of Genocide." 9 December 1948. Retrieved 3 December 2018 from https://treaties.un.org/doc/publication/unts/volume%2078/volume-78-i-1021-english.pdf.
Veber, Jean. *Das Blutbuch von Transvaal.* Berlin: Verlag der "Lustigen Blätter" Dr. Eysler & Co., 1901.

## Secondary Sources

Adas, Michael. *Dominance by Design: Technological Imperatives and America's Civilizing Mission.* Cambridge: Belknap Press, 2006.

Arendt, Hannah. *The Origins of Totalitarianism.* New York: Harcourt, Brace and Co., 1951.
Ashcroft, Bill, Gareth Griffiths, and Helen Tiffin. *Key Concepts in Post-Colonial Studies.* London: Routledge, 1998.
Baganz, Carina. *Erziehung zur "Volksgemeinschaft"? Die frühen Konzentrationslager in Sachsen 1933–34/37.* Berlin: Metropol, 2005.
Balfour, Sebastian. *The End of the Spanish Empire: 1898–1923.* Oxford: Clarendon Press, 1997.
Barth, Boris. *Genozid: Völkermord im 20. Jahrhundert: Geschichte—Theorien—Kontroversen.* Munich: C. H. Beck, 2006.
Barth, Boris, and Jürgen Osterhammel, eds. *Zivilisierungsmissionen: Imperiale Weltverbesserung seit dem 18. Jahrhundert.* Konstanz: UVK, 2005.
Beckett, Ian F. W. *Modern Insurgencies and Counter-Insurgencies: Guerrillas and Their Opponents since 1750.* London: Routledge, 2001.
Bender, Steffen. *Der Burenkrieg und die deutschsprachige Presse: Wahrnehmungen und Deutungen zwischen Bureneuphorie und Anglophobie 1899–1902.* Paderborn: Schöningh, 2009.
Benz, Wolfgang. "Nationalsozialistische Zwangslager: Ein Überblick." In Benz and Diestel, *Der Ort des Terrors*, vol. 1, 11–29.
Benz, Wolfgang, and Barbara Diestel, eds. *Der Ort des Terrors: Geschichte der nationalsozialistischen Konzentrationslager.* 9 vols. Munich: C. H. Beck, 2005–2009.
Berger, Sara. *Experten der Vernichtung: Das T4-Reinhardt-Netzwerk in den Lagern Belzec, Sobibor und Treblinka.* Hamburg: Hamburger Edition, 2013.
Birtle, Andrew J. *U.S. Army Counterinsurgency and Contingency Operations Doctrine, 1860–1941.* Washington DC: Center of Military History, 1998.
———. "The US Army's Pacification of Marinduque, Philippine Islands, April 1900–April 1901." *The Journal of Military History* 61, no. 2 (1997): 255–82.
Bley, Helmut. *Kolonialherrschaft und Sozialstruktur in Deutsch-Südwestafrika 1894–1914.* Hamburg: Leibniz, 1968.
———. *South-West Africa under German Rule, 1894–1914.* Translated by Hugh Ridely. Evanston: Northwestern University Press, 1971.
Bloxham, Donald. "The Armenian Genocide of 1915–1916: Cumulative Radicalization and the Development of a Destruction Policy." *Past and Present* 181, no. 1 (2003): 141–91.
Boemeke, Manfred F., Roger Chickering, and Stig Förster, eds. *Anticipating Total War: The German and American Experiences, 1871–1914.* Cambridge: Cambridge University Press, 1999.
Bossenbroek, Martin. *The Boer War.* Translated by Yvette Rosenberg. New York: Seven Stories, Press, 2018.
Bridgman, Jon M. *The Revolt of the Hereros.* Berkeley: University of California Press, 1981.
Buggeln, Marc. *Arbeit und Gewalt: Das Außenlagersystem des KZ Neuengamme.* Göttingen: Wallstein, 2009.
———. *Slave Labor in Nazi Concentration Camps.* Translated by Paul Cohen. Oxford: Oxford University Press, 2014.
———. *Das System der KZ-Außenlager: Krieg, Sklavenarbeit und Massengewalt.* Bonn: Archiv der Sozialen Demokratie, 2012.
Bühler, Andreas Heinrich. *Der Namaaufstand gegen die deutsche Kolonialherrschaft in Namibia von 1904–1913.* Frankfurt: IKO-Verlag für Interkulturelle Kommunikation, 2003.
Bührer, Tanja, et al., eds. *Imperialkriege von 1500 bis heute: Strukturen—Akteure—Lernprozesse.* Paderborn: Schöningh, 2011.
"Camp." In *Encyclopædia Britannica.* Vol. 5, 120f. London: Encyclopædia Britannica, 1926.

Caplan, Jane. "Gender and the Concentration Camps." In Caplan and Wachsmann, *Concentration Camps in Nazi Germany*, 82–107.

———. "Political Detention and the Origin of the Concentration Camps in Nazi Germany, 1933–1935/6." In Gregor, *Nazism, War and Genocide*, 22–41.

Caplan, Jane, and Nikolaus Wachsmann, eds. *Concentration Camps in Nazi Germany: The New Histories*. London: Routledge, 2010.

Chakrabarty, Dipesh. *Provincializing Europe: Postcolonial Thought and Historical Difference*. Princeton: Princeton University Press, 2000.

Chalk, Frank, and Kurt Jonassohn. "Genozid—ein historischer Überblick." In Dabag and Platt, *Genozid und Moderne*, 294–308.

Changuin, Louis, Frik Jacobs, and Paul Alberts. *Suffering of War: A Photographic Portrayal of the Suffering in the Anglo-Boer War Emphasising the Universal Elements of All Wars*. Bloemfontein: Kraal, 2003.

Chatriot, Alain, and Dieter Gosewinkel, eds. *Koloniale Politik und Praktiken Deutschlands und Frankreichs 1880–1962*. Stuttgart: Franz Steiner, 2010.

Chatterjee, Partha. *The Nation and Its Fragments: Colonial and Postcolonial Histories*. Princeton: Princeton University Press, 1993.

Comaroff, John L., and Jean Comaroff. "Hausgemachte Hegemonie." In Conrad and Randeria, *Jenseits des Eurozentrismus*, 247–82.

Conklin, Alice L. *A Mission to Civilize: The Republican Idea of Empire in France and West Africa, 1895–1930*. Stanford: Stanford University Press, 1997.

Conrad, Sebastian. *Deutsche Kolonialgeschichte*. Munich: C. H. Beck, 2008.

———. "'Eingeborenenpolitik' in Kolonie und Metropole: 'Erziehung zur Arbeit' in Ostafrika und Ostwestfalen." In Conrad and Osterhammel, *Das Kaiserreich transnational*, 107–28.

———. *What Is Global History?* Princeton: Princeton University Press, 2016.

Conrad, Sebastian, and Andreas Eckert, "Globalgeschichte, Globalisierung, multiple Modernen: Zur Geschichtsschreibung der modernen Welt." In Conrad, Eckert, and Freitag, *Globalgeschichte*, 7–49.

Conrad, Sebastian, Andreas Eckert, and Ulrike Freitag, eds. *Globalgeschichte: Theorien, Ansätze, Themen*. Frankfurt: Campus, 2007.

Conrad, Sebastian, and Jürgen Osterhammel, eds. *Das Kaiserreich transnational: Deutschland und die Welt 1871–1914*. Göttingen: Vandenhoeck und Ruprecht, 2004.

Conrad, Sebastian, and Shalini Randeria, eds. *Jenseits des Eurozentrismus: Postkoloniale Perspektiven in den Geschichts- und Kulturwissenschaften*. Frankfurt: Campus, 2002.

Cooper, Frederick. *Colonialism in Question: Theory, Knowledge, History*. Berkeley: University of California Press, 2005.

———. *From Slaves to Squatters: Plantation Labor and Agriculture in Zanzibar and Coastal Kenya, 1890–1925*. New Haven: Yale University Press, 1980.

Crowther, M. Anne. *The Workhouse System 1834–1929*. London: Batsford Academic and Educational, 1981.

Cuthbertson, Greg, Albert Grundlingh, and Mary-Lynn Suttie, eds. *Writing a Wider War: Rethinking Gender, Race, and Identity in the South African War, 1899–1902*. Athens: Ohio University Press, 2002.

Dabag, Mihran, Horst Gründer, and Uwe-K. Ketelsen. "Einleitung." In Dabag, Gründer, and Ketelsen, *Kolonialismus: Kolonialdiskurs und Genozid*, 7–18.

———, eds. *Kolonialismus: Kolonialdiskurs und Genozid*. Munich: Fink, 2004.

Dabag, Mihran, and Kristin Platt, eds. *Genozid und Moderne*. Vol. 1. Opladen: Leske und Budrich, 1998.

Dampier, Helen. "Women's Testimonies of the Concentration Camps of the South African War: 1899–1902 and After." PhD diss., University of Newcastle, 2005.

Davenport, Thomas, Rodney Hope, and Christopher Saunders. *South Africa: A Modern History*. New York: St. Martin's Press, 2000.
Davey, A. M. "The Reconcentrados of Cuba." *Historia* 5, no. 3 (1960): 193–95.
Dedering, Tilman. "Camps, Compounds, Colonialism." *Journal of Namibian Studies* 12 (2012): 29–46.
Denoon, Donald. *A Grand Illusion: The Failure of Imperial Policy in the Transvaal Colony during the Period of Reconstruction 1900–1905*. London: Longman, 1973.
Deocampo, Nick. "Imperialist Fictions: The Filipino in the Imperialist Imaginary." In Shaw and Francia, *Vestiges of War*, 225–36.
Devitt, Napier. *The Concentration Camps in South Africa*. Pietermaritzburg: Shuter & Shooter, 1941.
Drechsler, Horst. *Let Us Die Fighting: The Struggle of the Herero and Nama against German Imperialism, 1884–1915*. Translated by Bernd Zöllner. London: Zed Press, 1980.
―――. *Südwestafrika unter deutscher Kolonialherrschaft: Der Kampf der Herero und Nama gegen den deutschen Imperialismus (1884–1915)*. 2nd ed. Berlin: Akademie, 1984.
Drobisch, Klaus, and Günther Wieland. *System der Konzentrationslager: 1933–1939*. Berlin: Akademie, 1993.
Eberspächer, Cord. "'Albion zal hier dietmaal zijn Moskou vinden!': Der Burenkrieg (1899–1902)." In Klein and Schumacher, *Kolonialkriege*, 182–207.
Eckart, Wolfgang U. "Medizin und kolonialer Krieg: Die Niederschlagung der Herero-Nama-Erhebung im Schutzgebiet Deutsch-Südwestafrika, 1904–1907." In Heine and van der Heyden, *Studien zur Geschichte des deutschen Kolonialismus in Afrika*, 220–35.
Eckert, Andreas. "Europa, Sklavenhandel und koloniale Zwangsarbeit: Einleitende Bemerkungen." *Journal of Modern European History* 7, no. 1 (2009): 26–35.
―――. *Kolonialismus*. Frankfurt: Fischer, 2006.
―――. "Der langsame Tod der Sklaverei: Unfreie Arbeit und Kolonialismus in Afrika im späten 19. und im 20. Jahrhundert." In Hermann-Otto, *Sklaverei und Zwangsarbeit zwischen Akzeptanz und Widerstand*, 309–22.
―――. "Namibia—ein deutscher Sonderweg in Afrika? Anmerkungen zur internationalen Diskussion." In Zimmerer and Zeller, *Völkermord in Deutsch-Südwestafrika*, 226–36.
Eckl, Andreas. *"S'ist ein übles Land hier": Zur Historiographie eines umstrittenen Kolonialkrieges: Tagebuchaufzeichnungen aus dem Herero-Krieg in Deutsch-Südwestafrika 1904 von Georg Hillebrecht und Franz Ritter von Epp*. Cologne: Köppe, 2005.
―――. "'Zu leben, nur um da zu sein, hat niemand ein Recht': Der Kolonialkrieg mit dem Volk der Herero 1904 im Spiegel kolonialpropagandistischer Literatur der NS-Zeit." In Hamann, *Afrika—Kultur und Gewalt*, 159–89.
Eisenberg, Christiane. "Kulturtransfer als historischer Prozess: Ein Beitrag zur Komparatistik." In Kaelble and Schriewer, *Vergleich und Transfer*, 399–417.
Endlich, Stefanie. "Die äußere Gestalt des Terrors: Zu Städtebau und Architektur der Konzentrationslager." In Benz and Diestel, *Der Ort des Terrors*, vol. 1, 210–29.
Erichsen, Casper W. *"The Angel of Death Has Descended Violently Among Them": Concentration Camps and Prisoners-of-War in Namibia, 1904–1908*. Leiden: African Studies Centre, 2005.
―――. "Zwangsarbeit im Konzentrationslager auf der Haifischinsel." In Zimmerer and Zeller, *Völkermord in Deutsch-Südwestafrika*, 80–85.
Etzemüller, Thomas, ed. *Die Ordnung der Moderne: Social Engineering im 20. Jahrhundert*. Bielefeld: Transcript, 2009.
―――. "Social engineering als Verhaltenslehre des kühlen Kopfes: Eine einleitende Skizze." In Etzemüller, *Die Ordnung der Moderne*, 11–39.

Fabréguet, Michel. "Entwicklung und Veränderung der Funktion des Konzentrationslagers Mauthausen 1938–1945." In Herbert, Orth, and Dieckmann, *Die nationalsozialistischen Konzentrationslager*, vol. 1, 193–214.
Featherstone, Donald. *Victorian Colonial Warfare, Africa: From the Campaigns against the Kaffirs to the South African War*. London: Cassell, 1993.
Feichtinger, Moritz. "'Détruire et construire'—Die französische Umsiedlungspolitik in Algerien 1954–1962 zwischen Repression und Reform." In Chatriot and Gosewinkel, *Koloniale Politik und Praktiken*, 173–94.
———. "Villagization—A People's History of Strategic Resettlement and Violent Transformation, Kenya & Algeria, 1952–1962." PhD diss., University of Bern, 2017.
Fein, Helen. "Definition and Discontent: Labelling, Detecting, and Explaining Genocide in the Twentieth Century." In Förster and Hirschfeld, *Genozid in der modernen Geschichte*, 11–21.
Fetter, Bruce, and Stowell Kessler. "Scars From a Childhood Disease: Measles in the Concentration Camps During the Boer War." *Social Science History* 20, no. 4 (1996): 593–611.
"Fiasco." In *The New Oxford Thesaurus of English*, edited by Patrick Hanks, 358. Oxford: Oxford University Press, 2000.
"Fiasko." In *Duden: Fremdwörterbuch*. Vol. 5. Mannheim: Duden, 2001.
"Fiasko." In *Wörterbuch der Synonyme und Antonyme*, edited by Erich and Hildegard Bulitta, 279. Frankfurt: Fischer Taschenbuch, 1990.
Förster, Stig, and Gerhard Hirschfeld, eds. *Genozid in der modernen Geschichte*. Münster: Lit, 1999.
Forth, Aidan. *Barbed-Wire Imperialism. Britain's Empire of Camps, 1876–1903*. Berkeley: University of California Press, 2017.
———. "Britain's Archipelago of Camps: Labor and Detention in a Liberal Empire, 1871–1903." *Kritika* 16, no. 3 (2015): 651–680.
Forth, Aidan, and Jonas Kreienbaum. "A Shared Malady: Concentration Camps in the British, Spanish, American and German Empires." *Journal of Modern European History* 14, no. 2 (2016): 245–67.
Gates, John M. *Schoolbooks and Krags: The United States Army in the Philippines, 1898–1902*. Westport: Greenwood Press, 1973.
Gerlach, Christian. *Kalkulierte Morde: Die deutsche Wirtschafts- und Vernichtungspolitik in Weißrußland 1941 bis 1944*. Hamburg: Hamburger Edition, 1999.
Gerwarth, Robert, and Stephan Malinowski. "Hannah Arendt's Ghosts: Reflections on the Disputable Path from Windhoek to Auschwitz." *Central European History* 42, no. 2 (2009): 279–300.
———. "Der Holocaust als 'kolonialer Genozid'? Europäische Kolonialgewalt und nationalsozialistischer Vernichtungskrieg." *Geschichte und Gesellschaft* 33, no. 3 (2007): 439–66.
Gestrich, Andreas. "Konzentrationslager: Voraussetzungen und Vorläufer vor der Moderne." In Greiner and Kramer, *Welt der Lager*, 43–61.
Gewald, Jan-Bart. *Herero Heroes: A Socio-Political History of the Herero of Namibia 1890–1923*. Oxford: James Currey, 1999.
Go, Julian. *Patterns of Empire: The British and American Empires, 1688 to the Present*. New York: Cambridge University Press, 2011.
———. "'Racism' and Colonialism: Meaning of Difference and Ruling Practices in America's Pacific Empire." *Qualitative Sociology* 27 no. 1 (2004): 35–58.
Goeschel, Christian, and Nikolaus Wachsmann. "Before Auschwitz: The Formation of the Nazi Concentration Camps, 1933–9." *Journal of Contemporary History* 45, no. 3 (2010): 515–34.
Grant, Kevin. *A Civilised Savagery: Britain and the New Slaveries in Africa, 1884–1926*. New York: Routledge, 2005.

Gregor, Neil, ed. *Nazism, War and Genocide: Essays in Honour of Jeremy Noakes*. Exeter: University of Exeter Press, 2005.
Greiner, Bernd, et al., eds. *Heiße Kriege im Kalten Krieg*. Hamburg: Hamburger Edition, 2006.
Greiner, Bettina, and Alan Kramer, eds. *Welt der Lager: Zur "Erfolgsgeschichte" einer Institution*. Hamburg: Hamburger Edition, 2013.
Grosser, Alfred. *Ermordung der Menschheit: Der Genozid im Gedächtnis der Völker*. Translated by Ulrike Bokelmann. Munich: Hanser, 1990.
Gründer, Horst. "Genozid oder Zwangsmodernisierung?—Der moderne Kolonialismus in universalgeschichtlicher Perspektive." In Dabag and Platt, *Genozid und Moderne*, 135–151.
———. *Geschichte der deutschen Kolonien*. 5th ed. Paderborn: UTB, 2004.
Grundlingh, Albert. "The Anglo-Boer War in 20th-Century Afrikaner Consciousness." In Pretorius, *Scorched Earth*, 242–65.
———. *The Dynamics of Treason: Boer Collaboration in the South African War of 1899–1902*. Translated by Bridget Theron. Pretoria: Protea, 2006.
Hall, Darrell. *The Hall Handbook of the Anglo Boer War*. Pietermaritzburg: University of Natal Press, 1999.
Hamann, Christof, ed. *Afrika—Kultur und Gewalt: Hintergründe und Aktualität des Kolonialkriegs in Deutsch-Südwestafrika: Seine Rezeption in Literatur, Wissenschaft und Populärkultur (1904–2004)*. Iserlohn: Institut für Kirche und Gesellschaft, 2005.
Hartesveldt, Fred R. van. *The Boer War: Historiography and Annotated Bibliography*. Westport: Greenwood Press, 2000.
Hartmann, Wolfram. "Sexual Encounters and Their Implications on an Open and Closing Frontier: Central Namibia from the 1840s to 1905." PhD diss., Columbia University, 2002.
Hasian, Marouf, Jr. *Restorative Justice, Humanitarian Rhetorics, and Public Memories of Colonial Camp Cultures*. Basingstoke: Palgrave Macmillan, 2014.
Hattingh, Johan. "The British Blockhouse System." In Pretorius, *Scorched Earth*, 226–41.
Häußler, Matthias. "From Destruction to Extermination: Genocidal Escalation in Germany's War against the Herero, 1904." *Journal of Namibian Studies* 10 (2011): 55–81.
———. *Der Genozid an den Herero: Krieg, Emotion und extreme Gewalt in Deutsch-Südwestafrika*. Weilerswist: Velbrück Wissenschaft, 2018.
———. "Zwischen Vernichtung und Pardon: Die Konzentrationslager in 'Deutsch-Südwestafrika' (1904–1908)." *Zeitschrift für Geschichtswissenschaft* 61, no. 7/8 (2013): 601–20.
Häußler, Matthias, and Trutz von Trotha. "Brutalisierung 'von unten': Kleiner Krieg, Entgrenzung der Gewalt und Genozid im kolonialen Deutsch-Südwestafrika." *Mittelweg 36* 21, no. 3 (2012): 57–89.
Heine, Peter, and Ulrich van der Heyden, eds. *Studien zur Geschichte des deutschen Kolonialismus in Afrika: Festschrift zum 60. Geburtstag von Peter Sebald*. Pfaffenweiler: Centaurus, 1995.
Herbert, Ulrich. "Von der Gegnerbekämpfung zur 'rassischen Generalprävention': 'Schutzhaft' und Konzentrationslager in der Konzeption der Gestapo-Führung 1933–1939." In Herbert, Orth, and Dieckmann, *Die nationalsozialistischen Konzentrationslager*, vol. 1, 60–86.
Herbert, Ulrich, Karin Orth, and Christoph Dieckmann. "Die nationalsozialistischen Konzentrationslager: Geschichte, Erinnerung, Forschung." In Herbert, Orth, and Dieckmann, *Die nationalsozialistischen Konzentrationslager*, vol. 1, 17–40.
———, eds. *Die nationalsozialistischen Konzentrationslager: Entwicklung und Struktur*. 2 vols. Göttingen: Wallstein, 1998.

Herbst, Ludolf. *Komplexität und Chaos: Grundrisse einer Theorie der Geschichte*. Munich: C. H. Beck, 2004.
Hermann-Otto, Elisabeth, ed. *Sklaverei und Zwangsarbeit zwischen Akzeptanz und Widerstand*. Hildesheim: Olms, 2011.
Heß, Christiane, et al., eds. *Kontinuitäten und Brüche: Neue Perspektiven auf die Geschichte der NS-Konzentrationslager*. Berlin: Metropol, 2011.
Heyden, Ulrich van der. "Der 'Burenkrieg' von 1899 bis 1902 und die deutschen Missionsgesellschaften." In Heyden and Becher, *Mission und Gewalt*, 207–23.
———. "Die 'Hottentottenwahlen' von 1907." In Zimmerer and Zeller, *Völkermord in Deutsch-Südwestafrika*, 97–102.
Heyden, Ulrich van der, and Jürgen Becher, eds. *Mission und Gewalt: Der Umgang christlicher Missionen mit Gewalt und die Ausbreitung des Christentums in Afrika und Asien in der Zeit von 1792 bis 1918/19*. Stuttgart: Franz Steiner, 2000.
Heyningen, Elizabeth van. "British Doctors versus Boer Women: The Clash of Medical Cultures." In Pretorius, *Scorched Earth*, 178–97.
———. *The Concentration Camps of the Anglo-Boer War: A Social History*. Johannesburg: Jacana, 2013.
———. "The Concentration Camps of the South African (Anglo-Boer) War, 1900–1902," *History Compass* 7, no. 1 (2009): 22–43.
———. "Costly Mythologies: The Concentration Camps of the South African War in Afrikaner Historiography." *Journal of Southern African Studies* 34, no. 2 (2008): 494–513.
———. "'Fools Rush in': Writing a History of the Concentration Camps of the South African War." *Historia* 55, no. 2 (2010): 12–33.
———. "Pietermaritzburg Concentration Camp." *Natalia* 40 (2010): 62–76.
———. "A Tool for Modernisation? The Boer Concentration Camps of the South African War, 1900–1902." *South African Journal of Science* 106, no. 5/6 (2010): 58–67.
———. "Women and Disease: The Clash of Medical Cultures in the Concentration Camps of the South African War." In Cuthbertson, Grundlingh, and Suttie, *Writing a Wider War*, 186–212.
Heywood, Annemarie, ed. *History and Historiography: 4 Essays in Reprint*. Windhoek: MSORP, 1995.
Hill, Alexander. *The War behind the Eastern Front: The Soviet Partisan Movement in North-West Russia 1941–44*. London: Frank Cass, 2005.
Hull, Isabel V. *Absolute Destruction: Military Culture and the Practices of War in Imperial Germany*. Ithaca: Cornell University Press, 2005.
Hyslop, Jonathan. "The Invention of the Concentration Camp: Cuba, Southern Africa and the Philippines, 1896–1907." *South African Historical Journal* 63, no. 2 (2011): 251–76.
Ileto, Reynaldo C. "The Philippine-American War: Friendship and Forgetting." In Shaw and Francia, *Vestiges of War*, 3–21.
Jahr, Christoph. "'Diese Concentrationen sollten die Pflanzstätten für den militärischen Geist des Heeres bilden...': Fragmente einer Begriffsgeschichte des Lagers." In Jahr and Thiel, *Lager vor Auschwitz*, 20–37.
Jahr, Christoph, and Jens Thiel, eds. *Lager vor Auschwitz: Gewalt und Integration im 20. Jahrhundert*. Berlin: Metropol, 2013.
Jones, Adam. "Editor's Preface: The Present and Future of Genocide Studies." In Jones, *New Directions in Genocide Research*, xix–xxvii.
———, ed. *New Directions in Genocide Research*. London: Routledge, 2012.
Kaelble, Hartmut. *Der historische Vergleich: Eine Einführung zum 19. und 20. Jahrhundert*. Frankfurt: Campus, 1999.

Kaelble, Hartmut, and Jürgen Schriewer, eds. *Vergleich und Transfer: Komparatistik in den Sozial-, Geschichts- und Kulturwissenschaften*. Frankfurt: Campus, 2003.

Kaienburg, Hermann. "Zwangsarbeit: KZ und Wirtschaft im Zweiten Weltkrieg." In Benz and Diestel, *Der Ort des Terrors*, vol. 1, 179–94.

Kaminski, Andrzej J. *Konzentrationslager 1896 bis heute: Geschichte, Funktion, Typologie*. Munich: Piper, 1990.

Kamissek, Christoph. "Lernorte des Völkermordes? Die Kolonialerfahrung des Generals Lothar von Trotha in Ostafrika, China und Südwestafrika (1894–1907)." Unpublished thesis, Humboldt University of Berlin, 2007.

Kessler, Stowell V. "The Black and Coloured Concentration Camps." In Pretorius, *Scorched Earth*, 132–53.

———. *The Black Concentration Camps of the Anglo-Boer War 1899–1902*. Bloemfontein: War Museum of the Boer Republics, 2012.

———. "The Black Concentration Camps of the Anglo-Boer War 1899–1902: Shifting the Paradigm from Sole Martyrdom to Mutual Suffering." *Historia* 44, no. 1 (1999): 110–47.

———. "The Black Concentration Camps of the South African War." PhD diss., University of Cape Town, 2003.

Killingray, David. "Guardians of Empire." In Kilingray and David Omissi, *Guardians of Empire*, 1–24.

Killingray, David, and David Omissi, eds. *Guardians of Empire: The Armed Forces of the Colonial Powers c. 1700–1964*. Manchester: Manchester University Press, 1999.

Klein, Thoralf, and Frank Schumacher, eds. *Kolonialkriege: Militärische Gewalt im Zeichen des Imperialismus*. Hamburg: Hamburger Edition, 2006.

Klose, Fabian. *Menschenrechte im Schatten kolonialer Gewalt: Die Dekolonisierungskriege in Kenia und Algerien 1945–1962*. Munich: Oldenbourg, 2009.

Königseder, Angelika. "Die Entwicklung des KZ-Systems." In Benz and Diestel, *Der Ort des Terrors*, vol. 1, 30–42.

Kotek, Joël, and Pierre Rigoulot. *Das Jahrhundert der Lager: Gefangenschaft, Zwangsarbeit, Vernichtung*. Berlin: Propyläen, 2001.

Kraft, Claudia, Alf Lüdtke, and Jürgen Martschukat, eds. *Kolonialgeschichten: Regionale Perspektiven auf ein globales Phänomen*. Frankfurt: Campus, 2010.

Kramer, Alan. "Einleitung." In Greiner and Kramer, *Welt der Lager*, 7–42.

Krebs, Paula M. "'The Last of the Gentlemen's Wars': Women in the Boer War Concentration Camp Controversy." *History Workshop Journal* 33 (1992): 38–56.

Kreienbaum, Jonas. "Guerrilla Wars and Colonial Concentration Camps: The Exceptional Case of German South West Africa (1904–1908)." *Journal of Namibian Studies* 11 (2012): 85–103.

———. "Koloniale Gewaltexzesse—Kolonialkriege um 1900." In Chatriot and Gosewinkel, *Koloniale Politik und Praktiken*, 155–72.

———. "'Vernichtungslager' in Deutsch-Südwestafrika? Zur Funktion der Konzentrationslager im Herero- und Namakrieg (1904–1908)." *Zeitschrift für Geschichtswissenschaft* 58, no. 12 (2010): 1014–26.

Kröll, Ulrich. *Die internationale Buren-Agitation 1899–1902: Haltung der Öffentlichkeit und Agitation zu Gunsten der Buren in Deutschland, Frankreich und den Niederlanden während des Burenkrieges*. Münster: Regensberg, 1973.

Krüger, Gesine. *Kriegsbewältigung und Geschichtsbewusstsein: Realität, Deutung und Verarbeitung des deutschen Kolonialkriegs in Namibia 1904 bis 1907*. Göttingen: Vandenhoeck und Ruprecht, 1999.

Kruger, Rayne. *Goodbye Dolly Gray: The Story of the Boer War*. Alberton: Galago Books, 2008. First published in 1957.

Kundrus, Birthe. "Grenzen der Gleichsetzung: Kolonialverbrechen und Vernichtungspolitik." *iz3w* 275 (2004): 30–33.

———. "Kontinuitäten, Parallelen, Rezeptionen: Überlegungen zur 'Kolonialisierung' des Nationalsozialismus." *WerkstattGeschichte* 43 (2006): 45–62.

———. "Von den Herero zum Holocaust? Einige Bemerkungen zur aktuellen Debatte." *Mittelweg 36* 14, no. 4 (2005): 82–92.

Kundrus, Birthe, and Henning Strotbek. "'Genozid': Grenzen und Möglichkeiten eines Forschungsbegriffs—ein Literaturbericht." *Neue Politische Literatur* 51, no. 2/3 (2006): 397–423.

Kuß, Susanne. *Deutsches Militär auf kolonialen Kriegsschauplätzen: Eskalation und Gewalt zu Beginn des 20. Jahrhunderts*. Berlin: Links, 2010.

———. "Kriegführung ohne hemmende Kulturschranke: Die deutschen Kolonialkriege in Südwestafrika (1904–1907) und Ostafrika (1905–1908)." In Klein and Schumacher, *Kolonialkriege*, 208–47.

———. "Sonderzone Eingeborenenlazarett: Geschlechtskranke Frauen im Kriegsgefangenenlager Windhuk in Deutsch-Südwestafrika 1906." In Jahr and Thiel, *Lager vor Auschwitz*, 84–98.

Laak, Dirk van. "Kolonien als 'Laboratorien der Moderne?'" In Conrad and Osterhammel, *Das Kaiserreich transnational*, 257–79.

"Lager." In *Brockhaus Wahrig: Deutsches Wörterbuch in sechs Bänden*. Vol. 4: K–OZ, 381. Wiesbaden: Brockhaus, 1982.

Langbehn, Volker, and Mohammad Salama, eds. *German Colonialism: Race, the Holocaust, and Postwar Germany*. New York: Columbia University Press, 2011.

Lau, Brigitte. "Uncertain Certainties." In Heywood, *History and Historiography*, 39–52.

Lehmkuhl, Ursula, and Gustav Schmidt, eds. *From Enmity to Friendship: Anglo-American Relations in the 19th and 20th Century*. Augsburg: Wissner, 2005.

Lessing, Hanns. "'In der Nähe dieser Wasserstelle sollen Konzentrationslager errichtet werden': Eine theologische Rekonstruktion der Rolle der Rheinischen Missionsgesellschaft während des Kolonialkrieges in Namibia (1904–1908)." In Lessing et al., *Deutsche evangelische Kirche im kolonialen südlichen Afrika*, 471–95.

Lessing, Hanns, et al., eds. *Deutsche evangelische Kirche im kolonialen südlichen Afrika: Die Rolle der Auslandsarbeit von den Anfängen bis in die 1920er Jahre*. Wiesbaden: Harrassowitz, 2011.

Lindner, Ulrike. "German Colonialism and the British Neighbor in Africa Before 1914: Self-Definitions, Lines of Demarcation, and Cooperation." In Langbehn and Salama, *German Colonialism*, 254–72.

———. *Koloniale Begegnungen: Deutschland und Großbritannien als Imperialmächte in Afrika 1880–1914*. Frankfurt: Campus, 2011.

———. "Neuere Kolonialgeschichte und Postcolonial Studies, Version 1.0." *Docupedia-Zeitgeschichte*, 15 April 2011. Retrieved 3 November 2018 from http://docupedia.de/zg/lindner_neuere_kolonialgeschichte_v1_de_2011.

Linn, Brian M. *The Philippine War, 1899–1902*. Lawrence: University Press of Kansas, 2000.

———. *The US Army and Counterinsurgency in the Philippine War, 1899–1902*. Chapel Hill: University of North Carolina Press, 1989.

Low-Beer, Daniel, Matthew Smallman-Raynor, and Andrew Cliff. "Disease and Death in the South African War: Changing Disease Patterns from Soldiers to Refugees." *Social History of Medicine* 17, no. 2 (2004): 223–45.

Madley, Benjamin. "From Africa to Auschwitz: How German South West Africa Incubated Ideas and Methods Adopted and Developed by Nazis in Eastern Europe." *European History Quarterly* 35, no. 3 (2005): 429–64.

Mann, Michael. "Die Mär von der freien Lohnarbeit: Menschenhandel und erzwungene Arbeit in der Neuzeit: Ein einleitender Essay." *Comparativ* 13, no. 4 (2003): 7–22.

Martin, Arthur C. *The Concentration Camps, 1900–1902: Facts, Figures and Fables*. Cape Town: Howard Timmins, 1957.

Marx, Christoph. *Südafrika: Geschichte und Gegenwart*. Stuttgart: Kohlhammer, 2012.

Mattioli, Aram. "Die vergessenen Kolonialverbrechen des faschistischen Italien in Libyen 1923–1933." In Wojak and Meinl, *Völkermord und Kriegsverbrechen*, 203–27.

May, Glenn A. *The Battle for Batangas: A Philippine Province at War*. New Haven: Yale University Press, 1991.

———. *Social Engineering in the Philippines: The Aims, Execution and Impact of American Colonial Policy, 1900–1913*. Westport: Greenwood Press, 1980.

———. "Was the Philippine-American War a 'Total War'?" In Boemeke, Chickering, and Förster, *Anticipating Total War*, 437–57.

———. "The 'Zones' of Batangas." *Philippine Studies* 29, no. 1 (1981): 89–103.

McGregor, Gordon. *Die Kriegsgefangenenmarken von Deutsch-Südwestafrika*. Windhoek: Namibia Wissenschaftliche Gesellschaft, 2003.

McLeod, Andrew J. "Emily Hobhouse: Her Feet Firmly on the Ground." In Pretorius, *Scorched Earth*, 198–225.

Melber, Henning. "Ein deutscher Sonderweg? Einleitende Bemerkungen zum Umgang mit dem Völkermord in Deutsch-Südwestafrika." In Melber, *Genozid und Gedenken*, 13–21.

———, ed. *Genozid und Gedenken: Namibisch-deutsche Geschichte und Gegenwart*. Frankfurt: Brandes und Apsel, 2005.

Milk, Hans-Martin. *Der Stimme der Gnade Gehör schenken: Zur Rolle der Rheinischen Missionsgesellschaft bei der Errichtung von Konzentrationslagern in Namibia—1905 bis 1907*. Berlin: Wichern, 2016.

Miller, Stuart Creighton. *"Benevolent Assimilation": The American Conquest of the Philippines, 1899–1903*. New Haven: Yale University Press, 1984.

Mink, Charles R. "General Orders, No. 11: The Forced Evacuation of Civilians during the Civil War." *Military Affairs* 34, no. 4 (1970): 132–37.

Mohlamme, Jacob Saul. "African Refugee Camps in the Boer Republics." In Pretorius, *Scorched Earth*, 110–31.

Mommsen, Hans. "Forschungskontroversen zum Nationalsozialismus." *Aus Politik und Zeitgeschichte* 14–15 (2007): 14–21.

Mongalo, B. E., and Kobus du Pisani. "Victims of a White Man's War: Blacks in Concentration Camps during the South African War (1899–1902)." *Historia* 44, no. 1 (1999): 148–82.

Moor, Johannes A. de, and Henk L. Wesseling, eds. *Imperialism and War: Essays on Colonial Wars in Asia and Africa*. Leiden: Brill, 1989.

Moore, Paul. "'And What Concentration Camps Those Were!': Foreign Concentration Camps in Nazi Propaganda, 1933–9." *Journal of Contemporary History* 45, no. 3 (2010): 649–74.

———. "'Man hat es sich viel schlimmer vorgestellt': German Concentration Camps in Nazi Propaganda, 1933–1939: Representation and Reception." In Heß et al., *Kontinuitäten und Brüche*, 99–114.

Morlang, Thomas. *Askari und Fitafita: "Farbige" Söldner in den deutschen Kolonien*. Berlin: Links, 2008.

Moses, A. Dirk. "Empire, Colony, Genocide: Keywords and the Philosophy of History." In A. Dirk Moses, *Empire, Colony, Genocide*, 3–54.

———, ed. *Empire, Colony, Genocide: Conquest, Occupation, and Subaltern Resistance in World History*. New York: Berghahn Books, 2008.

Nasson, Bill. *Abraham Esau's War: A Black South African War in the Cape, 1899–1902*. Cambridge: Cambridge University Press, 1991.

——. *The South African War 1899–1902*. London: Arnold, 1999.
——. *The War for South Africa: The Anglo-Boer War 1899–1902*. Cape Town: Tafelberg, 2010.
Newitz, Annalee, and Matt Wray, eds. *White Trash: Race and Class in America*. London: Routledge, 1997.
Nuhn, Walter. *Feind überall: Der Große Nama-Aufstand (Hottentottenaufstand) 1904–1908 in Deutsch-Südwestafrika (Namibia): Der erste Partisanenkrieg in der Geschichte der deutschen Armee*. Bonn: Bernard und Graefe, 2000.
——. *Sturm über Südwest: Der Hereroaufstand von 1904—Ein düsteres Kapitel der deutschen kolonialen Vergangenheit Namibias*. Koblenz: Bernard und Graefe, 1989.
Oberholster, J. J. "Inleiding." *Christiaan deWet-Annale* 2 (1973): 5–10.
Olusoga, David, and Casper W. Erichsen. *The Kaiser's Holocaust: Germany's Forgotten Genocide and the Colonial Roots of Nazism*. London: Faber and Faber, 2010.
Orth, Karin. *Die Konzentrationslager-SS: Sozialstrukturelle Analysen und biographische Studien*. Göttingen: Wallstein, 2000.
——. *Das System der nationalsozialistischen Konzentrationslager: Eine politische Organisationsgeschichte*. Hamburg: Hamburger Edition, 1999.
Osterhammel, Jürgen. "'The Great Work of Uplifting Mankind': Zivilisierungsmission und Moderne." In Barth and Osterhammel, *Zivilisierungsmissionen*, 363–425.
——. *Kolonialismus: Geschichte—Formen—Folgen*. Munich: C. H. Beck, 2004.
——. *Die Verwandlung der Welt: Eine Geschichte des 19. Jahrhunderts*. 4th ed. Munich: C. H. Beck, 2009.
Otto, Johannes C. *Die Konsentrasiekampe*. Pretoria: Protea Boekhuis, 2005. First published in 1954.
Overmans, Rüdiger, ed. *In der Hand des Feindes: Kriegsgefangenschaft von der Antike bis zum Zweiten Weltkrieg*. Cologne: Böhlau, 1999.
Owen, Roger, and Bob Sutcliffe, eds. *Studies in the Theory of Imperialism*. London: Longman, 1972.
Pakenham, Thomas. *The Boer War*. London: MacDonald, 1982.
Palmer, Alison. *Colonial Genocide*. Adelaide: Crawford House, 2000.
Patel, Kiran Klaus. "Transnationale Geschichte: Ein neues Paradigma?" *Connections*, 2 February 2005. Retrieved 8 May 2019 from https://www.connections.clio-online.net/article/id/artikel-573.
Pitzer, Andrea. *One Long Night: A Global History of Concentration Camps*. New York: Little, Brown and Company, 2017.
Pretorius, Fransjohan. "The Fate of the Boer Women and Children." In Pretorius, *Scorched Earth*, 36–59.
——. "The White Concentration Camps of the Anglo-Boer War: A Debate Without End." *Historia* 55, no. 2 (2010): 34–49.
——, ed. *Scorched Earth*. Cape Town: Human & Rousseau, 2001.
Riedi, Eliza. "Teaching Empire: British and Dominions Women Teachers in the South African War Concentration Camps." *English Historical Review* 120, no. 489 (2005): 1316–47.
Roberts, Brian. *Those Bloody Women: Three Heroines of the Boer War*. London: J. Murray, 1991.
Robinson, Ronald. "Non-European Foundations of European Imperialism: Sketch for a Theory of Collaboration." In Owen and Sutcliffe, *Studies in the Theory of Imperialism*, 117–42.
Rodogno, Davide. *Against Massacre: Humanitarian Interventions in the Ottoman Empire, 1815–1914*. Princeton: Princeton University Press, 2012.
Sarkin, Jeremy. *Germany's Genocide of the Herero: Kaiser Wilhelm II, His General, His Settlers, His Soldiers*. Cape Town: UCT Press, 2011.

Saunders, Christopher C. *Historical Dictionary of South Africa*. 2nd ed. London: Scarecrow Press, 2000.
Schaller, Dominik J. "Genozidforschung: Begriffe und Debatten: Einleitung." In Schaller et al., *Enteignet—Vertrieben—Ermordet*, 9–26.
———. "Kolonialkrieg, Völkermord und Zwangsarbeit in 'Deutsch-Südwestafrika.'" In Schaller et al., *Enteignet—Vertrieben—Ermordet*, 147–230.
Schaller, Dominik, et al., eds. *Enteignet—Vertrieben—Ermordet: Beiträge zur Genozidforschung*. Zurich: Chronos, 2004.
Scharnagl, Hermann. *Kurze Geschichte der Konzentrationslager*. Wiesbaden: Marix, 2004.
Scheipers, Sybille. "The Use of Camps in Colonial Warfare," *The Journal of Imperial and Commonwealth History* 43, no. 4 (2015): 678–98.
Schmidl, Erwin A. "Der Zweite Anglo-Burenkrieg 1899–1902: Ein Rückblick nach 100 Jahren." *Österreichische Militärische Zeitschrift* 38, no. 2 (2000): 179–89.
Schumacher, Frank. "Kulturtransfer und *Empire*: Britisches Vorbild und US- amerikanische Kolonialherrschaft auf den Philippinen im frühen 20. Jahrhundert." In Kraft, Lüdtke, and Martschukat, *Kolonialgeschichten*, 306–27.
———. "Lessons of Empire: The United States, the Quest for Colonial Expertise and the British Example, 1898–1917." In Lehmkuhl and Schmidt, *From Enmity to Friendship*, 71–98.
———. "'Niederbrennen, plündern und töten sollt ihr': Der Kolonialkrieg der USA auf den Philippinen (1899–1913)." In Klein and Schumacher, *Kolonialkriege*, 109–44.
Setkiewicz, Piotr. "Häftlingsarbeit im KZ Auschwitz III-Monowitz: Die Frage nach der Wirtschaftlichkeit der Arbeit." In Herbert, Orth, and Dieckmann, *Die nationalsozialistischen Konzentrationslager*, vol. 2, 584–605.
Shaw, Angel Velasco, and Francia, Luis H., eds. *Vestiges of War: The Philippine-American War and the Aftermath of an Imperial Dream 1899–1999*. New York: New York University Press, 2002.
Siebrecht, Claudia. "Formen von Unfreiheit und Extreme der Gewalt: Die Konzentrationslager in Deutsch-Südwestafrika, 1904–1908." In Greiner and Kramer, *Welt der Lager*, 87–109.
Smith, Iain R. "The Concentration Camps in South Africa, 1900–1902." Paper presented at International History of Concentration Camps workshop, Dublin, 10 October 2008.
———. *The Origins of the South African War, 1899–1902*. London: Longman, 1996.
Smith, Iain R., and Andreas Stucki. "The Colonial Development of Concentration Camps (1868–1902)." *The Journal of Imperial and Commonwealth History* 39, no. 3 (2011): 417–37.
Sofsky, Wolfgang. *Die Ordnung des Terrors: Das Konzentrationslager*. Frankfurt: Fischer, 2004.
Spies, Stephanus Burridge. "The Hague Convention of 1899 and the Boer Republics." In Pretorius, *Scorched Earth*, 168–77.
———. *Methods of Barbarism? Roberts and Kitchener and Civilians in the Boer Republics, January 1900–May 1902*. Johannesburg: Jonathan Ball Publishers, 2001.
Spraul, Gunter. "Der 'Völkermord' an den Herero: Untersuchung zu einer neuen Kontinuitätsthese." *Geschichte in Wissenschaft und Unterricht* 12 (1988): 713–39.
Stanley, Liz. *Mourning Becomes . . . : Post/Memory and Commemoration of the Concentration Camps of the South African War 1899–1902*. Manchester: Manchester University Press, 2006.
Stanley, Liz, and Helen Dampier. "The Number of the South African War (1899–1902) Concentration Camp Dead: Standard Stories, Superior Stories and a Forgotten Proto-Nationalist Research Investigation." *Sociological Research Online* 14, no. 5 (2009). Retrieved 30 August 2018 from http://www.socresonline.org.uk/14/5/13.html.

Stassen, Nicol, and Ulrich van der Heyden. *German Publications on the Anglo-Boer War.* Pretoria: Protea, 2007.

Steenkamp, Ewald. *Helkampe.* Johannesburg: Voortrekkerpers, 1941.

Steinmetz, George. *The Devil's Handwriting: Precoloniality and the German Colonial State in Qingdao, Samoa, and Southwest Africa.* Chicago: University of Chicago Press, 2007.

Stibbe, Matthew. "Ein globales Phänomen: Zivilinternierung im Ersten Weltkrieg in transnationaler und internationaler Dimension." In Jahr and Thiel, *Lager vor Auschwitz,* 158–76.

Stoecker, Holger. "Knochen im Depot: Namibische Schädel in anthropologischen Sammlungen aus der Kolonialzeit." In Zimmerer and Bechhaus-Gerst, *Kein Platz an der Sonne,* 442–57.

Stoler, Ann Laura, and Frederick Cooper. "Between Metropole and Colony: Rethinking a Research Agenda." In Stoler and Cooper, *Tensions of Empire,* 1–56.

———. *Tensions of Empire: Colonial Cultures in a Bourgeois World.* Berkeley: University of California Press, 1997.

Stone, Dan. *Concentration Camps: A Short History.* Oxford: Oxford University Press, 2017.

Strandmann, Hartmut Pogge von. "The Purpose of German Colonialism, or the Long Shadow of Bismarck's Colonial Policy." In Langbehn and Salama, *German Colonialism,* 193–214.

Stucki, Andreas. "Aufbruch ins Zeitalter der Lager? Zwangsumsiedlung und Deportation in der spanischen Antiguerilla auf Kuba, 1868–98." *Mittelweg 36* 20, no. 4 (2011): 20–34.

———. "Aufbruch ins Zeitalter der Lager? Zwangsumsiedlung und Deportation in der spanischen Antiguerilla auf Kuba, 1895–1898." PhD diss., University of Bern, 2009.

———. *Aufstand und Zwangsumsiedlung: Die kubanischen Unabhängigkeitskriege 1868–1898.* Hamburg: Hamburger Edition, 2012.

———. "Die spanische Antiguerilla-Kriegführung auf Kuba 1868–1898: Radikalisierung—Entgrenzung—Genozid?" *Zeitschrift für Geschichtswissenschaft* 56, no. 2 (2008): 123–38.

———. "Streitpunkt Lager: Zwangsumsiedlung an der imperialen Peripherie." In Greiner and Kramer, *Welt der Lager,* 62–86.

Surridge, Keith. "The Politics of War: Lord Kitchener and the Settlement of the South African War, 1901–1902." In Cuthbertson, Grundlingh, and Suttie, *Writing a Wider War,* 213–32.

Tone, John Lawrence. *War and Genocide in Cuba, 1895–1898.* Chapel Hill: University of North Carolina Press, 2006.

"Transvaal." In *Encyclopædia Britannica.* Vol. 27, 187–210. London: Encyclopædia Britannica, 1926.

Tuchel, Johannes. "Organisationsgeschichte der 'frühen' Konzentrationslager." In Benz and Diestel, *Ort des Terrors,* vol. 1, 43–57.

———. "Planung und Realität des Systems der Konzentrationslager 1934–1938." In Herbert, Orth, and Dieckmann, *Die nationalsozialistischen Konzentrationslager,* vol. 1, 43–59.

Turrell, Rob. "Kimberley's Model Compounds." *Journal of African History* 25, no. 1 (1984): 59–75.

Vries, Johannes Lucas de. *Namibia: Mission und Politik (1880–1918): Der Einfluß des deutschen Kolonialismus auf die Missionsarbeit der Rheinischen Missionsgesellschaft im früheren Deutsch-Südwestafrika.* Neukirchen-Vluyn: Neukirchener, 1980.

Waag, Ian van der. "Boer Generalship and the Politics of Command." *War in History* 12, no. 1 (2005): 15–43.

Wachsmann, Nikolaus. "The Dynamics of Destruction: The Development of the Concentration Camps, 1933–1945." In Caplan and Wachsmann, *Concentration Camps in Nazi Germany*, 17–43.

———. *KL: A History of the Nazi Concentration Camps*. New York: Farrar, Straus and Giroux, 2015.

Wagner, Jens-Christian. "Das Außenlagersystem des KL Mittelbau-Dora." In Herbert, Orth, and Dieckmann, *Die nationalsozialistischen Konzentrationslager*, vol. 2, 707–29.

———. "Gesteuertes Sterben: Die Boelcke-Kaserne als zentrales Siechenlager des KZ Mittelbau." *Dachauer Hefte* 20 (2004): 127–38.

———. "Nordhausen (Boelcke-Kaserne)." In Benz and Diestel, *Ort des Terrors*, vol. 7, 320–22.

———. "Work and Extermination in the Concentration Camps." In Caplan and Wachsmann, *Concentration Camps in Nazi Germany*, 127–48.

Walgenbach, Katharina. *"Die weiße Frau als Trägerin deutscher Kultur": Koloniale Diskurse über Geschlecht, "Rasse" und Klasse im Kaiserrreich*. Frankfurt: Campus, 2005.

Walter, Dierk. "Imperialkriege: Begriff, Erkenntnisinteresse, Aktualität (Einleitung)." In Bührer et al., *Imperialkriege*, 1–29.

———. "Kolonialkrieg, Globalstrategie und Kalter Krieg: Die Emergencies in Malaya und Kenia 1948–1960." In Greiner et al., *Heiße Kriege im Kalten Krieg*, 109–40.

———. "Warum Kolonialkrieg?" In Klein and Schumacher, *Kolonialkriege*, 14–43.

Warwick, Peter. *Black People in the South African War 1899–1902*. Cambridge: Cambridge University Press, 1983.

Wassermann, Johan M. *The Eshowe Concentration and Surrendered Burghers Camp during the Anglo-Boer War*. Congella: Waterman, 1999.

———. "'The Suspects Are Not to Be Treated as Prisoners or Convicts'—A Labour Camp for Africans Associated with the Boer Commandoes During the Anglo-Boer War." *Journal for Contemporary History* 36, no. 2 (2011): 25–47.

Weimann, Martin, ed. *Das nationalsozialistische Lagersystem*. Frankfurt: Zweitausendeins, 2001.

Weitz, Eric D. *A Century of Genocide: Utopias of Race and Nation*. Princeton: Princeton University Press, 2003.

Werner, Michael, and Bénédicte Zimmermann. "Vergleich, Transfer, Verflechtung: Der Ansatz der Histoire croisée und die Herausforderung des Transnationalen." *Geschichte und Gesellschaft* 28, no. 4 (2002): 607–36.

Wesseling, Henk L. "Colonial Wars: An Introduction." In de Moor and Wesseling, *Imperialism and War*, 1–11.

Wessels, Elira. "'A Cage without Bars'—The Concentration Camp in Bloemfontein." In Pretorius, *Scorched Earth*, 60–85.

Wieviorka, Annette. "L'expression 'camp de concentration' au 20e siècle." *Vingtième Siècle* 54, no. 2 (1997): 4–12.

Wippermann, Wolfgang. *Konzentrationslager: Geschichte, Nachgeschichte, Gedenken*. Berlin: Elefanten Press, 1999.

Wirz, Albert. "Für eine transnationale Geschichte." *Geschichte und Gesellschaft* 27, no. 3 (2001): 489–98.

Wisan, Joseph E. *The Cuban Crisis as Reflected in the New York Press (1895–1898)*. New York: Columbia University Press, 1934.

Wohlberg, Annette U. "The Merebank Concentration Camp in Durban, 1901–1902." Unpublished thesis, University of the Orange Free State, 2000.

Wojak, Irmtrud, and Susanne Meinl, eds. *Völkermord und Kriegsverbrechen in der ersten Hälfte des 20. Jahrhunderts*. Frankfurt: Campus, 2004.

Záměčník, Stanislav. "Dachau-Stammlager." In Benz and Diestel, *Der Ort des Terrors*, vol. 2, 233–74.
———. *Das war Dachau*. Luxemburg: Dr. Stanislav Záměčník, 2002.
Zeller, Joachim. "'Ombepera i koza—Die Kälte tötet mich': Zur Geschichte des Konzentrationslagers in Swakopmund (1904–1908)." In Zimmerer and Zeller, *Völkermord in Deutsch-Südwestafrika*, 64–79.
———. "'Wie Vieh wurden hunderte zu Tode getrieben und wie Vieh begraben.' Fotodokumente aus dem deutschen Konzentrationslager in Swakopmund/Namibia 1904–1908." *Zeitschrift für Geschichtswissenschaft* 49, no. 3 (2001): 226–43.
Zietsman, Paul. "The Concentration Camp Schools—Beacons of Light in the Darkness." In Pretorius, *Scorched Earth*, 86–109.
Zimmerer, Jürgen. "Annihilation in Africa: The 'Race War' in German Southwest Africa (1904–1908) and its Significance for a Global History of Genocide." *Bulletin of the German Historical Institute* 37 (2005): 51–57.
———. *Deutsche Herrschaft über Afrikaner: Staatlicher Machtanspruch und Wirklichkeit im kolonialen Namibia*. Hamburg: Lit, 2001.
———. "Krieg, KZ und Völkermord in Südwestafrika: Der erste deutsche Genozid." In Zimmerer and Zeller, *Völkermord in Deutsch-Südwestafrika*, 45–63.
———. "Kriegsgefangene im Kolonialkrieg: Der Krieg gegen die Herero und Nama in Deutsch-Südwestafrika, 1904–1907." In Overmans, *In der Hand des Feindes*, 277–94.
———. "Lager und Genozid: Die Konzentrationslager in Südwestafrika zwischen Windhuk und Auschwitz." In Jahr and Thiel, *Lager vor Auschwitz*, 54–67.
———. *Von Windhuk nach Auschwitz? Beiträge zum Verhältnis von Kolonialismus und Holocaust*. Berlin: Lit, 2011.
Zimmerer, Jürgen, and Marianne Bechhaus-Gerst, eds. *Kein Platz an der Sonne: Erinnerungsorte der deutschen Kolonialgeschichte*. Frankfurt: Campus, 2013.
Zimmerer, Jürgen, and Joachim Zeller, eds. *Genocide in German South-West Africa: The Colonial War (1904–1908) in Namibia and its Aftermath*. Translated by Edward Neather. Monmouth: Merlin Press, 2008.
———. *Völkermord in Deutsch-Südwestafrika: Der Kolonialkrieg (1904–1908) in Namibia und seine Folgen*. Berlin: Links, 2003.

# Index

Abercrombie, H. R., 76, 104n6
Afrikaners, 28, 37, 74, 80, 81, 146, 243
agency (of the colonized), 184–185, 211n536
Allison, A. A., 75
Amery, Leo, 29
apartheid, 38
Arendt, Hannah, 3
Armstrong, O., 72
Auob, 53
Australia, 74, 147
Austria, 229

Barmen, 169, 183
Barth, Boris, 45
Bauer, Major, 174
Bayer, Maximilian, 59n104
Bebel, August, 47
Bechuanaland, 29, 45, 52
Beckett, Ian, 223n14
Bell, J. Franklin, 26n112
Benkesser, overseer, 179–180, 183, 209n495, 228
Berlin, 10, 42, 43, 46, 47, 48, 49, 87, 91–92, 96, 97, 166, 183, 210n518, 219, 236
Bermuda, 109n123
Bernsmann, Peter Friedrich, 209n495
Berseba, 158
Bethanie, 98
Beyers, Christiaan, 33
Bley, Helmut, 9

Bloemfontein, 8, 9, 31, 32, 37, 64, 65
Boer republics, 1, 29, 30, 31, 33, 37, 38, 39, 74, 75, 123, 156, 157
Boer War. *See* South African War
Bofinger, Hugo, 170, 172–173, 182
Bosman, reverend, 131
Botha, Louis, 32, 35, 68
Boxer War, 43
Brabant, Edward, 104n6
Brandt, Johanna. *See* Warmelo-Brandt, Johanna van
Brockdorff, Count von, 89, 96
Brodrick, William St. John, 73, 121, 221
Bühler, Andreas Heinrich, 10
Buller, Redvers, 30, 31, 57n17
Bülow, Bernhard von, 47–49, 62n142, 91, 96, 99, 111n165, 219, 220, 225n59
Burger, Schalk, 71
Burgsdorff, Henning von, 103

Callwell, Charles E., 213
Canada, 74
Cape Colony, 27, 29, 30, 33, 35, 38, 42, 51, 52, 65, 72, 84, 119, 123, 124, 137, 140, 143, 215, 216, 218, 220
Cape Town, 29, 31, 42, 55, 218
Caplan, Jane, 236
Ceylon, 109n123, 213
Chamberlain, Joseph, 1, 9, 29, 30, 36, 69, 73, 80, 82, 86, 215
Chatterjee, Partha, 146
China, 43

Christian, Johannes, 55
civilizing mission, 3, 15, 74–75, 106n65, 216–217, 233, 241, 242, 245, 247
Cleghorn, James, 214, 215
Clement, Richard, 33
Colenso, 30
colonialism, 2, 3, 4, 9, 146, 214, 216–217, 240n33, 240n43, 242, 245
  settler, 5, 28, 47, 74, 80, 216
colonial war, 2, 6, 12, 27, 39, 58n73, 212, 213, 222, 226n77, 231, 233, 241–242, 245, 246
concentration camps, 2, 3, 4–5, 7, 13, 16, 17, 217
  daily life in, 6
  during wars of decolonization, 247
  epidemics and disease in, 2
  functions of, 3, 5, 6, 217, 228, 231, 233, 241–243
  internees, 6, 233–234, 239n30, 240n32, 241
  Italian camps in Libya, 247
  malnourishment, 2, 228, 234–235
  mortality, 234–235, 241, 247
  personnel, 6
  term, 11–12, 214, 220–221, 227, 247
  *See also* German South-West African concentration camps; South African concentration camps; National Socialism
Cooper, Simon, 56
Cottbus-Sielow, 237
Cromer, Evelyn Baring, 1st Earl of, 29
Cronjé, Piet, 31
Cuba, 2, 4, 5, 7, 11, 12, 13–15, 16–17, 25n93, 27, 69, 137–138, 212–214, 216–217, 218, 222, 233, 234, 241–247
  reconcentration or concentration centers, 2, 4, 7, 11–12, 13–15, 16–17, 25n101, 27, 137–138, 212–214, 216, 218, 222, 233, 234, 241–247
Czechoslovakia, 229

Damara, 41, 184
Dame, Cai Friedrich Theodor, 55, 95, 100–101, 110n144, 179
Dannert, Eduard, 89
Deare, Russell, 154
Deimling, Berthold von, 53, 55, 93–95, 97, 186

De La Rey, Koos, 32, 33
Dernburg, Bernhard von, 95
De Wet, Christian, 32, 37, 38
Diehl, Philipp, 92, 166, 204n384
Diehl, Wilhelm Emil Jakob, 89, 179
Doyle, Arthur Conan, 69
Drechsler, Horst, 9, 41, 49, 51, 53
dum-dum bullets, 39
Durban, 245

Ebert, Friedrich, 237
Eckl, Andreas, 236
Egypt, 29
Eich, Wilhelm, 89, 158–159, 168, 169
Eicke, Theodor, 239n30
Eisenberg, Christiane, 221
Eisenberg, Friedrich Gustav, 158
Elger, August, 47, 165, 169, 179
Epp, Franz Xaver (Ritter von), 166, 235, 236
Epukiro, 158–159
Erichsen, Casper W., 10, 91, 92, 111n172, 228
Erzberger, Matthias, 61n136
Esselin (or Esselen), G. F., 155
Estorff, Ludwig von, 95, 218, 219, 243
ethnic cleansing, 45, 60n116
Ewing, Thomas, 17

Fashoda, 31
Fawcett, Millicent Garrett, 121
Fein, Helen, 146–147
Fenchel, Tobias, 93, 94, 186
Fiji, 36, 82
Flint, E. M., 72, 73
Foraker, Joseph Benson, 15–16
Fox, Wilson, 127, 139, 143
Franco-Prussian War, 44, 213
Franke, Victor, 42, 178
Franks, Kendal, 146, 152, 190n47, 223n18
Frederiks, Cornelius, 53, 54, 55, 90, 97, 98, 113n210
Frederiks, Paul, 98
Frey, staff doctor, 173

genocide, 3, 9, 12–13, 44–50, 54, 59–60n104–105, 60n117, 61n124, 61n126, 80–83, 87–95, 242–243. *See also* mass death
German South-West Africa, 2, 3, 5, 6, 9, 28, 39, 40–56, 87–103, 124, 146,

157–187, 216, 218–222, 227, 229, 231, 234, 235, 236, 239n30, 241–247
  colonial government, 10, 95, 100, 101, 167, 174
  district and division office, 10, 50, 54, 100, 161, 173, 174, 179, 185, 232
  *Etappenkommando*, 93, 100, 101, 103, 162, 164, 166, 169, 171, 173, 174, 179, 180, 183
  literature on, 9–10
  military dictatorship, 43, 55
  Native Ordinances, 101–102
  "old Africans," 47
  "protection force" (*Schutztruppe*) or colonial force, 2, 18n6, 40, 41, 42–43, 46, 48, 52, 53, 87, 89, 96, 98, 101, 165, 166, 174, 176, 181, 185, 186, 193n110, 212, 218
  railways, 40, 41, 51–52, 89, 99, 100, 159–160, 171, 174, 175, 176, 178, 180, 186, 206–207n438, 207n459, 211n541, 232
  rinderpest (cattle plague), 40, 52
  settlers, 40, 41, 47, 50, 102, 103, 171, 186, 233
German South-West African concentration camps, 2, 4, 5, 6, 7, 9, 11, 41, 50, 54, 55, 56, 78, 87–103, 115, 146, 157–187, 212, 218–222, 227–237, 241–247
  administration of, 91–92, 100, 158, 180
  architecture and infrastructure of, 160–165
  daily life in, 157, 173–178, 185
  epidemics and disease in, 100, 160, 161, 164, 166, 169, 170, 171–173, 175–176, 178, 181, 182, 184, 185–186
  extermination in, 87–95, 103, 115, 157, 186, 227–229
  functions of, 87–103, 157, 221, 228
  internees, 87–91, 99–103, 110n144, 111n153, 166, 170, 171, 175, 180, 182, 183, 184, 185, 239n30
  journey to and between, 157–160, 177
  Karibib, 90, 91, 97, 165, 169, 179, 181, 204n383
  lazarettos, 160, 162–164, 165, 167, 169, 171, 172, 174, 176, 178, 179, 180, 181–182, 185, 210n514
  literature on, 9–10
  mortality in, 87–95, 146, 157–8, 160, 161, 162 164–165, 165–173, 175–176, 179, 181, 183, 185–187, 204n383, 206n421, 207n459, 207–208n461, 210n514, 228, 229, 234, 243, 244
  nourishment, 165, 166–168, 169, 170–173, 174, 175–176, 179, 180, 183
  Okahandja, 45, 90, 92, 94, 159, 161, 164, 166, 169, 176–177, 211n541, 234
  Omaruru, 90, 159, 164, 173, 178, 180, 204n383
  physical violence in, 178, 179–180, 185, 239n30
  primary sources on, 10–11
  schools, 177, 178, 184
  sexual relations and violence, 180–181, 184, 185, 209n504, 209n509
  Shark Island or Lüderitzbucht, 9, 10, 90, 91, 92, 93–95, 97, 100, 111n153, 158, 159, 160, 161, 162, 163, 164, 165, 166, 169, 170, 171, 172–173, 176, 179, 182, 183, 185, 186–187, 206n421, 206–207n438, 209n495, 218, 219, 227, 228
  social relations in, 178–185
  supplying the, 165–173
  Swakopmund, 9, 90, 92, 102, 158, 159, 160, 161, 162–164, 165–166, 169, 171, 173, 176, 177, 179, 183, 185, 186, 203n351–352, 234
  Windhuk, 90, 94, 97, 158, 159, 160, 162, 163, 164, 165, 167, 169, 177, 179, 181, 183, 184, 186, 204n381, 204n383, 207n459, 235
German South-West African War (1904–08), 2, 5, 6, 9, 27, 39, 40–56, 95–96, 97, 102, 171, 216, 219, 235, 236
  Battle of the Waterberg (Ohamakari), 43–44, 45, 46, 50, 51, 59n104, 60n105, 96
  deportation of Nama, 92–93, 97, 111n172
  genocidal quality of the, 44–50
  Herero style of fighting, 42, 98, 221
  Herero War, 2, 40–50, 51, 102, 235
  horror stories about Herero atrocities, 41–42, 102
  mortality, 56

Nama style of fighting, 51, 53, 98, 221
Nama War, 2, 50–56, 102
  origins of, 40–41 (Herero), 51 (Nama)
  peace negotiations, 55–56, 96
  Proclamation to the Herero (*Vernichtungsbefehl*), 44–49, 54, 61n126, 87, 89, 91, 92, 110n147, 158, 220, 248n8
  Proclamation to the Nama, 54
  structuralist (functionalist) and intentionalist interpretations, 46, 60–61n120
Germany, 4, 5, 17, 28, 41, 47, 48, 49, 52, 53, 55, 56, 115, 166, 169, 181, 182, 212, 218, 219, 220, 221, 222, 227, 236, 237, 244, 246
  Foreign Office (*Auswärtiges Amt*), 225n59
  General Staff, 41, 43, 45, 48, 51
  Imperial Colonial Office (*Reichskolonialamt*) and Colonial Department, 10, 43, 47, 48, 92, 95, 183
  Imperial Naval Office (*Reichsmarineamt*), 48
  Palatinate region, 17
  Reichstag (German parliament), 47, 49, 52, 63n168, 96, 234
Gerwarth, Robert, 240n43
Gestrich, Andreas, 17, 217
Gewald, Jan-Bart, 10, 41, 178, 183, 211n536
Gibeon, 50, 51, 52, 54, 96, 97, 159
Glasenapp, Franz Georg von, 43
Go, Julian, 198n242
Goeschel, Christian, 236
Goldman, P. L. A., 81
Gómez, Máximo, 14
Goodwin, George, 72, 121, 145, 188n6
Goold-Adams, Hamilton, 72, 73, 74, 122, 129, 130, 140, 190n54
Göring, Ernst, 235
Göring, Hermann, 235–236
Great Britain, British Empire and England, 1, 5, 27, 28, 29, 30, 38, 39, 52, 74–75, 80, 81 82, 85, 87, 94, 115, 121, 124, 140, 141, 147, 148, 153, 187, 212, 216, 217, 220, 222, 236, 243, 244, 246
  Colonial Office, 73, 85, 213, 214, 216, 217
  House of Commons or parliament, 69, 70, 73, 132, 213
  India Office, 214–215
  War Office, 9, 31, 73
Great Karas Mountains, 50, 53, 55
Great Nabas (Battle of), 53, 55
Great Trek, 28, 29
Grundlingh, Albert, 200n290
Gudewill, Hans, 42, 102
guerrilla war, 1, 2, 17, 52–53, 54, 56, 96, 98, 212, 213, 214, 221, 231, 241, 245, 247
  counter-guerrilla warfare or "scorched earth policy," 17, 52–53, 55, 98, 213, 214, 219, 221, 226n66, 231, 241, 245, 247
  *See also* Cuba; Philippines; South African War
Gulag, 19n17

Hague Convention, 39
Haldane, Richard, 1
Haldane, T. S., 132–133
Hamilton, Ian, 37
Hartebeestmund, 55
Hartesveldt, Fred R. van, 7
Haussleiter, D. Gottlob, 219
Häußler, Matthias, 59–60n104, 60n119, 61n124, 61n126
Hely-Hutchinson, Walter, 132
Hendrik, Hans, 184
Hertzog, J. B. M., 32
Herero, 2, 9, 10, 11, 27, 40–50, 51, 53, 54, 56, 60n105, 61n126, 62n142, 87–92, 93, 95–96, 97–103, 110n144, 110n146, 112n181, 112n201, 113n218, 157–187, 204n384, 206n421, 211n536, 216, 217, 219, 220, 221, 222, 228, 229, 235, 236, 242, 243, 244, 245
  Ovaherero, 184
  Ovambanderu, 184
Heyningen, Elizabeth van, 8, 75, 81, 141, 154, 182, 248n10
Hill, Alexander, 238n20
Hime, Whiteside, 134, 140–141
Himmler, Heinrich, 229, 232, 236
Hintrager, Oskar, 94–95, 97, 219
Hitler, Adolf, 23n74, 60n120, 232, 236, 237, 246–247
Hobhouse, Emily, 8, 65, 71, 77, 80, 82, 86, 108n104, 116, 117, 118, 121, 123, 125, 128, 134, 140, 148, 149, 154, 157, 212, 218, 244

Hobson, John A., 29
Holderness, Thomas, 215
Hottentot elections, 52, 63n168
Hull, Isabel V., 4, 11, 42, 46, 49, 95, 167, 180, 193n110, 226n77, 244
Hülsen-Haeseler, Dietrich Graf von, 59n102
human remains, 182, 210n518
Hume, Superintendent, 188n7
Hunter, Archibald, 34

imperial cloud, 226n76
India, 30, 31, 32, 36, 109n123, 124, 170, 214–216, 224n28, 246
    plague and famine camps, 214–216, 222, 223n15, 246
Isaak, Samuel, 96, 184

Jameson, Leander Starr, 29
Java, 36
Johannesburg, 31, 37, 77, 78, 105n41
Jonas, P. C., 153
Jordt, Hans Peter, 150

Kaminski, Andrzej, 7
Kamissek, Christoph, 59n102
Karibib, 165, 172, 181, 184
Kariko, Samuel, 161, 209n495
Kauimo, Sem, 210n524
Keetmanshoop, 50, 52, 96, 97, 99, 159
Kelly-Kenny, Thomas, 34, 65
Kessler, Stowell, 8, 77, 78, 81, 108n112–113, 130, 143, 216
Kimberley, 30, 31, 218
Kipling, Rudyard, 58n73
Kitchener, Horatio Herbert, 9, 16, 31–32, 33, 34–35, 36, 37, 38, 39, 65, 68, 69, 70, 71, 72, 73, 74, 76, 77, 78, 79, 82, 85, 95, 104n18, 118, 122, 123, 124, 130, 137, 146, 153, 156, 212, 213, 218, 243
Kitchener, Walter, 218
Komane, Matthäus, 150
Koppel company, 174, 180, 232
Kotek, Joël, 7, 227
Kritzinger, Piet, 32
Kromspruit, 32
Krüger, Gesine, 10, 162
Kruger, Paul, 29, 31
Kubub, 52, 113n210
Kuhlmann, August, 111n153, 161, 176, 179, 183
Kuhn, District Commissioner, 179

Kundrus, Birthe, 12, 221
Kuß, Susanne, 164, 226n77

Laaf, Karl Emil, 93, 169
labor or work, 3, 10, 13, 17, 35, 37, 47, 54, 76, 77–80, 83, 84, 85, 86, 92, 97, 99–102, 103, 109n135, 135, 143, 144–145, 146, 149–150, 151, 155, 158, 159, 162, 172, 173–177, 178, 179, 180, 183, 185–186, 187, 206–207n438, 216–217, 220, 221–222, 223n15, 227, 228, 229, 231–233, 235, 236, 237, 238n24, 242, 243, 244–245, 246
    annihilation through, 10, 227, 229, 238n9
    forced or compulsary, 10, 13, 99–102, 103, 159, 172, 173–177, 180, 217, 221–222, 229, 230, 231–233, 235, 242, 244–245, 246
    slave, 13, 24n89–90, 101, 242
Ladysmith, 30, 31
Lansdowne, Henry Petty-Fitzmaurice, 5th Marquess of, 31
Lau, Brigitte, 44
Ledebour, Georg, 47, 61n136
Lemkin, Raphael, 12, 24n84
Lenz & Co., 100, 174, 176, 181, 232
Lessing, Hanns, 225n63
Leutwein, Paul, 63n180, 218
Leutwein, Theodor Gotthilf, 18n12, 40, 41, 42, 43, 44, 45, 47, 49
Lindequist, Friedrich von, 55, 89, 92, 95, 96–97, 100, 101, 103, 170, 174, 175, 184, 186, 218–219, 220, 221
Lindner, Ulrike, 220
Lloyd George, David, 81
London, 9, 17, 28, 29, 30, 31, 33, 35, 36, 37, 38, 68, 73, 82, 216
Lotbinière, G. F. de, 76, 78, 79, 80, 85, 86, 108n113, 127, 130, 135, 137, 138, 139, 150, 155, 216
Lückhoff, August Daniel, 197n208, 201n312
Lüderitzbucht, 52, 55, 93, 99, 172, 176, 179, 183, 186
Luschan, Felix von, 210n518

Madagascar, 36, 82
Madley, Benjamin, 10, 227, 235, 246
Maercker, Georg, 166, 179
Mafeking, 30, 31
Magersfontein, 30

*Index* 277

Maharero, Samuel, 41
Malinowski, Stephan, 240n43
Martin, Arthur C., 148
mass death, 1, 2, 3, 9, 12–13, 15, 44–50, 54, 56, 60–61n120, 61n126, 72, 75, 80–83, 87–95, 102, 115, 121, 139, 140, 142, 146, 153, 156, 157, 158, 159, 160, 165, 167, 172, 182, 185–187, 227, 235, 241, 242–243, 244
    intentionality, 3, 12–13, 44–50, 59–60n104, 80–83, 91, 92–95, 115, 130, 156, 167, 185–187, 228, 236, 241, 242–243
Maxwell, John G., 72, 73, 128, 129, 132, 139, 149
McCallum, Henry, 140–141, 152–153
Meier, Friedrich, 158, 169, 177, 183, 210n524
Middelburg, 35, 36, 38
military doctrine, 43, 46, 95, 130, 193n110
Milner, Alfred, 1, 2, 9, 29, 30, 33, 35, 37, 38, 72, 73, 74, 75, 82, 85, 86, 95, 104n6, 122, 132, 140, 189n37, 215, 241
missionaries or mission, 6, 9, 10, 11, 41, 46–47, 62n142, 62n159, 89, 91, 92, 93, 96, 98, 100, 101, 103, 113n222, 117, 127, 150, 156, 158, 159, 160, 161, 165, 166, 167–170, 171, 172, 173, 174 176, 177–178, 179–180, 181, 182–183, 184, 185, 206–207n438, 219–220, 232
    Berlin Missionary Society, 220
    collection camps, 89, 90, 96, 100, 103, 110n151, 159, 160, 169, 179, 184, 185, 232
    evangelists, 150, 161, 177–178, 183, 184
    Hermannsburg Mission, 188n8, 220
    "native" patrols or messengers, 89, 96, 159, 184
    Oblates of Mary Immaculate, 169, 177
    Rhenish Missionary Society, 10, 47, 89, 91, 92, 93, 96, 159, 161–162, 167–169, 171, 177–178, 183, 186, 187, 210n526, 219–220
modernization, 3, 75, 106n60
Mongalo, B. E., 149
Morenga, Jacob, 50, 53, 54, 55, 56, 62n154
Morlang, Thomas, 112n200
Mozambique, 31, 32

Mühlenfels, Karl Ludwig von, 166
Munich, 219

Nama, 2, 27, 41, 50–56, 62n153–154, 62n158, 87–103, 110n144, 112n201, 157–187, 203n351, 206n421, 217, 221–222, 229, 236, 242, 243, 244, 245
    Berseba, 50
    Bethanie, 50, 53, 90, 97, 98
    Bondelswarts, 41, 42, 50, 54, 55, 56, 62n154, 95
    Fransman, 50
    Red Nation, 50
    Swartboois, 50, 222
    Topnaar, 50
    Veldschoendragers, 50, 97
    Witbooi, 50, 51, 53, 54, 95, 96, 97, 103
Namib Desert, 52, 186
Napoleonic Wars, 27, 30
Nasson, Bill, 71
Natal, 27, 28, 30, 31, 35, 65, 72, 84, 119, 120, 123, 124, 132, 135, 140, 145, 188n20, 215, 217
national paths, 4, 244–245
National Socialism, 3, 4, 5, 7, 9, 11, 12, 64, 201n307, 227–237, 240n43, 246, 247
    Auschwitz, 4, 9, 10, 227, 228, 231, 235
    Belzec, 228
    Bergen-Belsen, 228
    Buchenwald, 227, 229
    Chelmno, 228
    concentration camps, 3–4, 5, 6, 7, 9, 10, 11–12, 24n89, 26n121, 64, 227–237, 238n9–11, 239n24–25, 239n30, 246, 247
    Dachau, 227, 228, 229–230, 234, 235, 239n27
    extermination camps (*Vernichtungslager*), 10, 227, 228, 246
    Holocaust, 60–61n120, 227, 240n33
    Majdanek, 228, 231, 235
    Mauthausen, 234, 239n29
    Mittelbau-Dora, 228
    Sobibor, 228
    Treblinka, 10, 227, 228
Neethling, Andries Christoffel, 154, 197n208, 201n318
Neethling, Elizabeth, 81, 116, 141, 218, 244
New Zealand, 74, 147

Nooitgedacht, 33
Nuhn, Walter, 10, 23n71, 51
Nyhof, Hermann, 93, 169

Ohlemann, Julius, 170
Okahandja, 41, 43, 45, 89, 94, 97, 112n201
Okawayo, 159, 172
Okomitombe, 90, 110n151, 160
Olpp, Johannes, 184
Olusoga, David, 10, 91, 228
Omaheke Desert, 44, 45, 46, 50, 60n116, 61n126, 87, 92, 96, 165
Omaruru, 89, 96, 158, 165, 173, 176, 178, 180
Omburo, 90, 110n151
Omdurman (Battle of), 31
Onganjira, 43
Onslow, William, 217
Orange Free State, 27, 28, 29, 31, 32, 33, 38, 147
Orange River Colony, 31, 32, 33, 65, 69, 72, 73, 76, 77, 78, 79, 82, 83, 84, 85, 86, 104n3, 108n113, 109n135, 111n160, 117, 119–150, 192n92, 197–198n222, 215, 217
Orth, Karin, 228, 238n10
Osona, 97
Otavi, 40, 89, 99, 159, 174, 175, 176, 206n438
Otjihaenena, 90, 110n151, 160, 179, 181, 184
Otjimbingwe, 169
Otjombinde, 159
Otjozongombe, 90, 110n151
Otto, Johannes Cornelius, 8, 142
Oviumbu, 43

Paardeberg, 31
Pakenham, Thomas, 37, 38, 39, 56n12, 71, 104n18
Papenfus, H. B., 72
Pedi, 28
Philippines, 2, 5, 7, 11–12, 14, 15–16, 17, 212–213, 222, 233, 234, 241–247
    Batangas, 25n108, 26n112, 234
    Batangas City, 16
    Cebu, 16, 25n108
    concentration centers or zones, 2, 7, 11–12, 13, 15–16, 26n112, 213, 222, 233, 234, 241–247
Phillips, L. March, 115

Pisani, Kobus Du, 149
Pitzer, Andrea, 7
Pretoria, 9, 31, 37, 65, 139, 152, 154
prison, 17, 122, 132
prisoners of war, 17, 33, 39, 56, 65, 70–71, 83, 84, 87–103, 109n123, 110n144, 112n201, 113n218, 122, 148, 151, 154, 157–187, 206n415, 206n438, 207n459, 210n514, 211n541, 213, 219, 221 222, 229, 232, 237, 245

race and racism, 18n6, 39, 40, 42, 45, 47, 126, 135, 146–147, 157, 180, 181, 187, 203n351, 228
    going native, 146
Rehobother Basters, 41
Rhodes, Cecil, 28–29
Rigoulot, Pierre, 7, 227
Roberts, Frederick Sleigh, 1st Earl, 30–31, 32, 33, 34, 35, 65, 69, 70, 71, 85, 104n18, 212, 213
Robinson, Ronald, 201n307
Rohrbach, Paul, 47
Russia, 17, 238–239n20
    Caucasus, 17

Salisbury, Robert Gascoyne-Cecil, 3rd Marquess of, 30
San, 184
Sargant, Edmund, 74, 147, 150
Sarkin, Jeremy, 247
Schlieffen, Alfred von, 43, 45, 47–49, 59n102, 60n116, 62n142
Scholtz, N. J., 154
Sem, Evangelist (possibly Sem Kauimo), 184
Siebrecht, Claudia, 225n56
Smuts, Jan, 32, 38
social engineering, 3, 25n110, 72–76, 79–80, 85, 87, 101–102, 106n65, 216–217, 222, 233, 242
South Africa, 1–2, 4, 5, 6, 7, 8, 9, 11, 14, 16, 27–39, 52, 64–87, 91, 94, 98, 99, 101, 102, 103, 113n218, 115–157, 160, 164, 165, 167, 170, 178, 182, 185, 187, 214–222, 223n12, 228, 231, 233, 234, 236, 241–247
    high commissioner, 1, 9, 29, 35, 72, 73, 74, 82, 95, 140
    Jameson Raid, 28–29
    relief works, 83
    Transvaal War (1880/81), 28, 30

*Index* 279

South African concentration camps, 1–2, 4, 5, 6, 7–8, 9, 10, 11, 14, 15, 16, 27, 32, 35, 36, 37, 64–87, 91, 97, 99, 101, 103, 115–157, 160, 164–165, 167–168, 170, 175, 178, 182, 187, 214–222, 228, 231, 233, 234, 236, 241–247
   administration and responsibility, 8, 72–74, 75, 76–78, 81, 83, 84, 85, 107n80, 108n113, 121, 122, 124–125, 128, 131, 135, 139, 142, 143, 148, 154, 155, 156, 167, 246
   agricultural program, 119, 125, 127, 137–138, 143, 149, 157, 216
   Aliwal North, 120, 121, 139, 142, 152
   architecture and infrastructure of, 119–128, 164
   Balmoral, 190n47, 223n18
   Barberton, 188n17, 190n47, 223n18
   Belfast, 150
   Bethulie, 8, 64, 139, 140, 151, 154, 197n208, 201n312
   black camps, 8, 9, 11, 37, 76–80, 81–82, 84–85, 86–87, 91, 101, 102, 107n78, 107n80, 108n112–113, 111n160, 119, 125–128, 130, 131, 135–139, 142–144, 149–150, 155–156, 157, 164–165, 167–168, 192n88, 200n278, 216, 217–218, 222, 231, 232, 242, 244, 248n10
   Bloemfontein, 65, 70, 116, 127, 136, 140, 143, 145, 149, 218, 221, 225n51
   Brandfort, 82, 84, 108n113, 142, 192n84
   Burgher Camps Department (Transvaal), 73, 77, 131, 188n20
   daily life in, 144–157
   Department of Refugees (Orange River Colony), 77, 224n28
   Department of Native Refugees, 78, 79, 80, 86, 108n113, 125, 127, 131, 136–137, 138, 139, 143, 144, 156, 216
   doctors and medical staff, 75, 106n63, 123, 125, 136, 138, 139–144, 153, 155, 156, 197–198n221–222, 202n328
   Doorn Kop (near Rhenoster), 131, 136
   Edenburg, 126, 127, 131, 136, 143, 191n72
   epidemics and disease in, 82, 85, 119, 122, 123, 130, 131, 133–134, 136, 138, 140, 141–142, 147, 148, 155, 156, 157, 202n328, 213, 215, 219
   Eshowe, 188n24
   extermination in, 80–83, 84, 115, 221, 236
   Fawcett or Ladies Commission, 8, 121–122, 123, 130, 133, 134, 140, 145, 146, 147, 148, 149, 151–152, 154, 155, 193n128, 202n328, 244, 248n10
   functions of, 64–87, 97–98, 221
   Harrismith, 139, 143, 155, 191n72
   Heidelburg or Heidelberg, 65, 75, 77
   Heilbron, 65, 126, 143, 188n23
   Honingspruit, 150, 191n72, 200n278
   hospitals, 83, 122, 123, 127, 133, 136, 139–144, 146, 167, 192n88, 194n132, 197n214, 214
   Houtenbek, 191n72
   Howick, 65, 104n10, 151
   internees, 8, 65–72, 76–77, 82, 84, 85, 108n114, 109n135, 115, 120, 123–124, 125, 127, 130, 131, 137, 139, 141, 145–156, 217, 218
   Irene, 65, 117, 122, 151, 154, 155, 190n47
   Johannesburg, 65, 120, 145, 148, 218, 219, 221, 225n51
   journey to and between, 115–119
   Kimberley, 122, 137, 140, 218
   Klerksdorp, 65
   Kroonstad, 65, 71, 108n113, 122, 133, 136, 188n23
   Krugersdorp, 65, 120, 122, 188n17
   literature on, 7–8
   Mafeking, 65, 82, 140, 145, 202n328
   Meintjeskop, 152
   Merebank, 148, 188n24, 215
   Middelburg, 129, 223n18
   mortality, 72, 75, 80, 81–82, 85–87, 91, 108nn112–114, 111n160, 117–118, 121–122, 123, 126, 127, 131, 133–134, 138–144, 146, 153, 154, 155, 156–157, 164–165, 167, 187, 214, 219, 233, 244
   Nigel, 77
   Norvals Pont, 64, 65, 74, 120, 145
   nourishment in, 70, 125, 131–139, 144, 152, 153, 157, 167–168, 242
   Orange River, 137

periodization of the history of the, 85–87
personnel, 8, 72, 75, 122, 125, 139, 140, 141, 142, 153–156, 202n329
Pietermaritzburg, 65, 120, 152
Pietersburg, 119
Port Elizabeth, 65
Potchefstroom, 65, 77
primary sources on, 8–9
Rietfontein, 127, 150
Roodevaal, 143
schools, 74–75, 122, 127, 130, 144, 147–148, 150, 156
Smaldeel, 202n331
social relations in, 150–156
Standerton, 65, 77, 153, 190n47
superintendents, 9, 72, 73, 75, 77, 85, 86, 107n80, 108n113, 117, 121, 122, 124, 125, 126, 128, 131, 132, 136, 139, 140, 143, 144, 145, 148, 150, 152, 153, 154, 155, 188nn6–7, 202n328, 215, 216, 217, 219, 224n28
supplying the, 119, 124, 128–144, 187
Taaibosch, 195n171
Thaba 'Nchu, 143
Vereeniging, 65
Volksrust, 81
Vredefort Road, 65, 104n10, 126, 150, 201n322
Wentworth, 188n24
Winburg, 116
South African Republic (Transvaal), 27–29, 31, 33, 38, 68, 147, 213
South African War, 1, 2, 5, 6, 7, 8, 11, 21n39, 23n75, 27–39, 52, 66, 81, 84, 87, 91, 95, 98, 149, 218–222, 236, 242, 245
*bittereinders*, 37, 118, 150–155
Black Week, 30
blockhouses, 33, 35, 36–37, 122, 190n47
counter-guerrilla measures, 33–35, 36–37, 68–72, 76–77, 78–79, 83, 84, 85, 86, 87, 214, 219, 221, 243
farm burning and "scorched earth policy," 27, 33–34, 39, 68–69, 71, 86, 98, 108n113, 115–116, 119, 137, 152, 243
drives or sweeps, 35, 36, 122
guerrilla war, 1, 13, 27, 32–35, 38, 39, 64, 68–72, 74, 76, 79, 83, 84, 85, 121, 214, 218

*hendsoppers*, 118, 119, 150–155, 200n290
involvement of Africans, 35, 37
joiners, 37, 152, 154
origins of, 29–30
peace talks, 35–36, 37–38, 95
Treaty of Vereeniging, 38–39, 71–72, 153
South Seas Islands, 92
Spain, 5, 13–15, 212, 243
Speer, Albert, 232
Spiecker, Johannes, 98, 168–169, 172, 181, 182, 207n460
Spies, Stephanus Burridge, 8, 33, 39, 70, 73, 77, 104n18
Spraul, Gunter, 49
Stalingrad, 230
Stargard, 237
St. Helena, 109n123, 213
Stillfried und Rattonitz, Georg von, 219, 225n56
Stormberg, 30
Strahler, Division Head, 112n201
Strotbek, Henning, 12
Stucki, Andreas, 14, 223n14
Stuhlmann, Eugen, 113n218
Stürman, Skipper, 51
Swakopmund, 40, 41, 42, 52, 99, 113n218, 180, 186, 203n351

Tecklenburg, Hans, 92, 102, 171
Thomson, Samuel John, 8, 215, 224n28
Thomson, W. A., 124
Tone, John Lawrence, 15, 25n101
transfer of knowledge, 4, 6, 20n26, 212–222, 245–246
transimperial connections, 4–5, 212–222, 245
transnational history, 4–5, 7, 245–246
Transvaal Colony, 31, 32, 33, 65, 72, 73, 76, 77, 78, 80, 82, 83, 84, 85, 86, 105n41, 107n80, 108n113, 109n135, 119–139, 143, 144, 147, 148, 149, 151, 167, 188n17, 188n20, 194n145, 201n318, 202n335, 213, 215, 217.
independent republic (*see* South African Republic)
Trollope, Arthur Grant, 72, 125, 128, 129, 136, 140, 142, 148, 202n329
Trotha, Lothar von, 23n74, 42, 43–50, 52, 53, 54–55, 59n102, 60n105, 60n110, 60n119, 61n124, 61n126, 61n136,

*Index*

87, 89, 91, 92, 96, 99, 103, 110n144, 110n146, 164, 166, 169, 171, 218, 220, 243, 248n8
Trotha, Trutz von, 61n124
Tucker, W. K., 72, 132

Umub, 113n210
United States, 2, 5, 14, 15–17, 212–213, 242, 243, 245
    Civil War, 17, 213
    Lawrence, Kansas, 17
    Missouri, 17
    war against Native Americans, 17
Upper Silesia, 49

Vaalgras, 54
Vedder, Heinrich, 160–161, 162–164, 165, 169, 173–174, 176, 180
Vries, Johannes Lucas de, 210n526

Wachsmann, Nikolaus, 236
Wagner, Jens-Christian, 238n9
Walvis Bay, 113n218, 185, 216
Wandres, Karl Friedrich, 180, 209n504
Warmbad, 50, 54
Warmelo-Brandt, Johanna van, 8, 117, 151, 153–154, 190n47
Warwick, Peter, 8, 81, 202n335
Waterston, Jane, 248n10

Wessels, Elira, 149
Weyler y Nicolau, Valeriano, 2, 13–15, 16–17, 25n93, 69, 212–213, 243
Wiehager, Paul, 207n455
Wilhelm II, Kaiser, 43, 47, 48, 49, 54, 59n102, 63n168, 91, 225n56
Wilkins, James, 215, 224n28
Windhuk, 4, 9, 40, 41, 52, 94, 96, 158–159, 177, 180, 183, 185, 186
Witbooi, Hendrik, 50, 51, 53, 54, 96
Woermann shipping line, 158, 159, 174, 176, 232
Wolseley, Garnet, 31
workhouse, 17, 26n121, 146, 217, 223n15, 236–237
World War I, 5, 11, 30, 229, 237, 240n43, 243
World War II, 5, 10, 48, 229, 230, 231, 232, 234, 235

Yule, Pratt, 126, 134

Zeller, Joachim, 227
Zimmerer, Jürgen, 3, 5, 9, 60n105, 93, 101, 227, 240n33
Zoutpansberg, 118
Zülow, Captain von, 93
Zulu, 28, 155, 188n24
Zürn, Rolf, 41

CPSIA information can be obtained
at www.ICGtesting.com
Printed in the USA
LVHW080308140919
631033LV00003B/42/P

9 781789 203264